AI-Driven Security and Intelligence in Cloud and Internet of Things Systems

Mohd Sakib
UPES University, Dehradun, India

Muneer Khan
https://orcid.org/0000-0002-6586-4286
Cadre Tech Labs, USA

Shantanu Awasthi
Missouri Southern State University, USA

Mohd Vaseem Khan
https://orcid.org/0000-0002-7222-6864
Bansal Institute of Engineering and Technology, India

IGI Global
Scientific Publishing
Publishing Tomorrow's Research Today

Vice President of Editorial Melissa Wagner
Director of Acquisitions Mikaela Felty
Director of Book Development Jocelynn Hessler
Production Manager Mike Brehm
Cover Design Jose Rosado

Published in the United States of America by
IGI Global Scientific Publishing
701 East Chocolate Avenue
Hershey, PA, 17033, USA
Tel: 717-533-8845 | Fax: 717-533-7115
Website: https://www.igi-global.com E-mail: cust@igi-global.com

Library of Congress Cataloging-in-Publication Data

CIP Data Pending
ISBN13: 9798337375038
Isbn13Softcover: 9798337375045
EISBN13: 9798337375052

British Cataloguing in Publication Data
A Cataloguing in Publication record for this book is available from the British Library.

Dedicated with heartfelt gratitude to the beloved teaching and research community, whose tireless pursuit of knowledge continues to inspire generations.

Table of Contents

Detailed Table of Contents

The escalating use of anonymization networks creates a considerable hurdle in differentiating between users seeking privacy and those engaged in malicious conduct within encrypted data streams. To address this, a novel multi-modal deep learning architecture is presented for the intricate analysis and categorization of darknet traffic. This framework integrates sophisticated feature engineering with a hybrid Convolutional Neural Network-Recurrent Neural Network (CNN-RNN) design, enabling the effective capture of both spatial and temporal patterns within network flows. The model demonstrates a pronounced ability to analyze varied traffic, such as that from Virtual Private Networks (VPNs) and The Onion Router (Tor), achieving a high degree of accuracy in detection and classification.Its performance was assessed using a robust dataset that combines established benchmarks (ISCXVPN2016, ISCXTor2017) with newly captured real-time traffic.The evaluation yielded an overall accuracy of 91.5%, with exceptional performance in the categorization of challenging traffic

The rapid growth of Internet of Things (IoT) devices has changed modern digital ecosystems by allowing smooth connectivity, automation and real-time data sharing. However, this massive increase has also widened the attack surface, making IoT devices more vulnerable to numerous cyber threats.Traditional intrusion detection methods often find it hard to manage the dynamic, diverse and large-scale nature of IoT data. Therefore, there is a need for smart and scalable security solutions.In this chapter, we discuss how feature selection techniques effect the performance of different ML classifiers for IoT attack detection on the UNSW-NB15 dataset. This experiment is conducted in two scenarios, firstly without any feature selection and without any class balancing technique. Secondly using SMOTE to address class imbalance and Boruta for optimal feature selection. The experimental results demonstrate the effectiveness of combining data balancing and feature selection

blockchain capabilities, we propose a hybrid cryptographic architecture utilizing edge computing, blockchain smart contracts, and lattice-based cryptography. Our hypothesis demonstrated that the system performed very well within controlled testing, achieving 94% storage success, 65ms latency and 99% security. In decentralized environments, the hybrid cryptographic architecture performed with minimal usage of resources while maintaining high efficiency, and ensured the secure transfer and integrity of data with scalability. In addition, it also furthers a flexible and secure foundation for future IoT applications that experience quantum threats. The next chapters in the research will investigate ways to amalgamate an even greater privacy and performance, for evolving IoT and cloud ecosystems, by looking at merging AI-infused security methods with advanced quantum cybersecurity.

This paper illustrates an AI-based system that revolutionizes software testing for distributed cloud-native environments. The system leverages machine learning, deep learning, natural language processing, and reinforcement learning to improve and automate defect identification, dynamic test scheduling, and test case generation. By using models such as Convolutional Neural Networks (CNN), Recurrent Neural Networks (RNN), Random Forests, and Decision Trees, the models boost entity coverage and anomaly detection. Reinforcement learning reduces the mean test run time from 120 seconds to 80 seconds. By using serverless computing, testing costs dropped from $5,000 to $1,500 per cycle, and feedback lag time went from 60 minutes to 20 minutes. The AI-based defect finding accuracy was 90% compared to only 65% for traditional methods. Heatmaps can be used to discover defect-prone modules. In addition, the deep learning models were faster and outperformed XGBoost and Logistic Regression in defect prediction performance with AUC values of 0.9934.

This chapter explores how Oracle APEX serves as a low-code development platform for creating sophisticated IoT data management and visualization applications. We examine APEX's capabilities in handling real-time data streams from connected devices, creating interactive dashboards for monitoring sensor networks, and building responsive web applications that can scale with growing IoT deployments. The chapter includes practical implementation strategies for integrating APEX with IoT data pipelines, REST APIs for device communication, and techniques for creating intuitive user interfaces that enable non-technical stakeholders to interact with complex IoT ecosystems. Through analysis of real-world implementations and comparative evaluation with other low-code platforms, we demonstrate both the capabilities and limitations of using APEX for IoT application development.

In response to the growing limitations of traditional encryption techniques within the cloud, this chapter presents a new framework named BioCrypt. Biocrypt applies bioinformatics and molecular biology concepts to the development of cryptography. BioCrypt tackles such issues through advanced DNA encoding and biologically inspired approaches to deliver a highly resistant, high-entropy encryption solution that is difficult to breach. The BioCrypt framework consists of a multi-tiered architecture with a security layer, DNA engine, and data storage module. Here, the plain text is converted to binary, and then following pre-determined rituals to bind them into DNA spells, they are permuted with a key and undergo simulated DNA hybridization and Watson and Crick complementing. The development also employs biologically based control over keys and multi-factor authentication, which greatly complicates access to the system without proper authorization. The BioCrypt system exhibits strong resistance against brute force, replay, and chosen-plaintext attacks.

Foreword

The last decade has witnessed an extraordinary transformation in the way intelligence, connectivity, and automation converge to define the modern digital ecosystem. The rapid proliferation of cloud computing and the Internet of Things (IoT) has accelerated the creation of intelligent environments that sense, learn, and act in real time. Yet, with this exponential growth comes an equally profound escalation in security vulnerabilities, data breaches, and trust deficits. The line between intelligence and insecurity has never been thinner. In this context, the integration of artificial intelligence (AI) into cloud and IoT systems emerges not just as an advantage but as an imperative for the future of safe and sustainable computing.

The edited volume, *"AI-Driven Security and Intelligence in Cloud and Internet of Things Systems,"* arrives at a critical juncture in this technological evolution. It presents an impressive collection of contributions that weave together the threads of AI, cybersecurity, cryptography, and distributed systems into a coherent tapestry of next-generation solutions. Each chapter reveals the remarkable potential of AI—not merely as a computational tool, but as an adaptive and cognitive ally capable of learning from, and responding to, the dynamic threat landscape that characterizes our connected world.

The strength of this book lies in its multidisciplinary integration. From intelligent scheduling of scientific workflows and resilient IoT architectures, to NLP-based adversarial defense, hybrid deep learning for darknet intrusion detection, quantum-resistant cryptography, and bio-inspired encryption models—this volume traverses the entire spectrum of intelligence-enabled security innovation. It speaks equally to researchers in algorithm design, practitioners in cybersecurity engineering, and policymakers shaping the digital future. The meticulous experimentation, robust benchmarking, and clear articulation of practical relevance make this work both scholarly and actionable.

What makes this book particularly timely is its forward-thinking orientation. As we move toward an era of autonomous systems, edge computing, and quantum-resilient infrastructure, our ability to safeguard privacy and integrity will depend on how seamlessly AI can be embedded into every layer of the digital stack. The frameworks, models, and architectures discussed in this volume not only respond to today's security challenges but also anticipate the emerging paradigms of cognitive defense, decentralized trust, and biologically inspired computation that will define the coming decade.

I commend the editors and contributing authors for curating a work that bridges academic rigor and industrial relevance with exceptional clarity. This volume is a valuable addition to the growing body of research in AI-driven cybersecurity and intelligent cloud systems. It will undoubtedly serve as an essential reference for students, researchers, engineers, and innovators striving to build safer, smarter, and more sustainable digital ecosystems.

It is my firm belief that the book will inspire future inquiry, inform policy decisions, and help shape a new era of trust and intelligence in interconnected technologies.

Durgesh Pant

Uttarakhand Council of Science and Technology (U-COST), Department of Science and Technology, Govt of Uttarakhand, India

Preface

The rapid expansion of cloud computing and the Internet of Things (IoT) has revolutionized digital ecosystems by enabling unprecedented levels of data exchange, connectivity, and automation. However, these advancements have also introduced complex security and privacy challenges that traditional methods can no longer adequately address. Artificial intelligence (AI), with its adaptive and intelligent capabilities, has become a central force in reimagining the security architectures of the future. This book, *AI-Driven Security and Intelligence in Cloud and Internet of Things Systems*, explores this convergence by examining cutting-edge research, practical implementations, and emerging technologies that are shaping resilient, scalable, and trustworthy digital environments.

The chapters in this volume address a wide range of challenges and opportunities at the intersection of AI, cloud computing, IoT, and cybersecurity. Together, they provide a roadmap for researchers, practitioners, and policymakers to navigate the complexities of safeguarding intelligent systems.

Chapter 1 introduces an AI-enhanced hybrid scheduling framework designed for scientific workflows in intelligent cloud-connected devices. By combining cost models, task duplication strategies, and adaptive heuristic selectors, this approach significantly improves efficiency and reduces costs, demonstrating its scalability through bioinformatics workflow evaluations.

Chapter 2 explores the integration of AI and blockchain to create a resilient IoT security framework. This dual-layered approach leverages AI for anomaly detection and proactive defense while employing blockchain's decentralized integrity to ensure transparency and trust in connected systems.

Chapter 3 examines the growing threat of adversarial attacks in e-commerce platforms, where malicious actors exploit machine learning vulnerabilities. Through the use of natural language processing strategies such as adversarial training, anomaly detection, and behavior-based analytics, this chapter highlights emerging defenses to strengthen industrial cybersecurity and preserve user trust.

Chapter 4 presents a multi-modal deep learning model for intrusion detection in encrypted darknet traffic. By combining convolutional and recurrent neural networks to capture both spatial and temporal features, the system achieves high accuracy in distinguishing between benign privacy-seeking users and malicious actors, offering critical insights for privacy-aware threat detection.

Chapter 5 focuses on intrusion detection for IoT environments through feature selection and data balancing techniques. Using approaches such as SMOTE and Boruta, the study demonstrates how carefully optimized data preparation improves detection accuracy, reduces false negatives, and enhances scalability across diverse IoT attack scenarios.

Chapter 6 introduces an ensemble approach for phishing detection that combines Gradient Boosting and recurrent neural networks. This hybrid framework analyzes both structured URL features and sequential character-level data, delivering high detection accuracy and adaptability against evolving phishing tactics while minimizing false positives.

Chapter 7 addresses quantum-era security risks by proposing a hybrid cryptographic architecture that combines lattice-based cryptography, blockchain, and edge computing. Tested in decentralized environments, this system demonstrates strong resilience against quantum threats while maintaining efficiency and scalability for cloud and IoT ecosystems.

Chapter 8 examines the role of AI in automating software testing and validation for cloud computing. Leveraging machine learning, deep learning, and reinforcement learning, the framework enhances defect detection, reduces costs, and accelerates testing cycles, offering a blueprint for quality assurance in intelligent and distributed systems.

Chapter 9 explores the use of Oracle APEX as a rapid development platform for IoT data visualization and management. By enabling real-time dashboards, scalable applications, and intuitive interfaces, APEX demonstrates its value in bridging technical and non-technical user needs for IoT system oversight.

Chapter 10 introduces *BioCrypt*, a bioinformatics-driven cryptography framework that applies molecular biology principles such as DNA encoding and hybridization for secure cloud computing. By employing biologically inspired encryption methods and multi-factor authentication, the system achieves strong resistance against advanced cyberattacks, opening new horizons for unconventional cryptographic innovation.

Together, these chapters underscore the transformative potential of AI in securing next-generation digital infrastructures. By bringing together perspectives from multiple disciplines—including bioinformatics, blockchain, intrusion detection, and quantum-resistant cryptography—this book provides a comprehensive understanding of both the theoretical foundations and practical applications of AI-driven security. It is our hope that this collection will inspire further exploration, foster collaboration across domains, and guide the development of innovative, ethical, and robust solutions to safeguard the cloud- and IoT-enabled future.

This book is designed for graduate students, researchers, practitioners, and policymakers seeking to understand the intersection of artificial intelligence and the Internet of Things. While each chapter addresses distinct challenges and solutions, together they present a cohesive vision of digital ecosystems that are intelligent, secure, and sustainable.

We extend our sincere gratitude to all the contributing authors for their commitment and scholarly insight, which have been instrumental in shaping this book into a comprehensive and impactful resource. We are equally thankful to the reviewers and the editorial team at IGI Global for their invaluable support and guidance throughout the publication process. It is our hope that this volume will spark new research, encourage meaningful collaboration, and provide a strong foundation for innovation within the rapidly evolving fields of AI and IoT.

Acknowledgement

I would like to express my heartfelt gratitude to all those who have supported me throughout the process of writing this book, *AI Advancements in Internet of Things and Intelligent Devices*, to be published by IGI Global, Hershey, Pennsylvania, USA.

First and foremost, I dedicate this work to my beloved parents, whose love, guidance, and unwavering encouragement have been the foundation of my journey. Their constant belief in me has been my greatest strength.

I am deeply thankful to my supervisors, Prof. Tamanna Siddiqui and Prof. Suhel Mustajab, for their invaluable mentorship, insightful guidance, and continuous support. Their encouragement and wisdom have been instrumental in shaping both this book and my academic path.

I would also like to acknowledge the contributions of all those who reviewed this work, offering their valuable time, constructive feedback, and thoughtful suggestions to enhance its quality.

To everyone who stood by me, inspired me, and believed in my vision, I extend my deepest gratitude. This book is as much yours as it is mine.

Chapter 1

AI-Enhanced Hybrid Scheduling Framework for Scientific Workflows in Intelligent Cloud-Connected Devices

N. Raghu
https://orcid.org/0000-0002-2091-8922
Jain University, India

Anil Kumar D. B.
https://orcid.org/0000-0001-9803-7466
REVA University, India

Ganesh Srinivasa Shetty
https://orcid.org/0009-0007-5165-3326
Shri Madhwa Vadiraja Institute of Technology and Management, India

Ranjith Bhat
https://orcid.org/0009-0000-6149-1243
NMAM Institute of Technology, India

P. Rajashree Nambiar
https://orcid.org/0000-0001-9209-4451
NMAM Institute of Technology, India

DOI: 10.4018/979-8-3373-7503-8.ch001

ABSTRACT

Scheduling scientific workflows in the cloud is a big challenge due to varying resource availability, different virtual machine (VM) configurations, resource intensive tasks and the trade-offs between time and cost. This paper presents a new approach combining Optimistic Cost Table (OCTd and OCTu) called LJINES along with a cost model that covers pre-, during- and post-scheduling phases. To further optimize the performance, a task duplication strategy is used based on communication overhead and critical path analysis. A Dynamic Heuristic Selector (DHS) is also integrated to adaptively choose the best scheduling algorithm (GA or PSO) based on the workflow. The framework is evaluated using the SIPHT bioinformatics workflow in WorkflowSim. Compared with standard algorithms (HEFT, PEFT, RHEFT, GA, PSO) the proposed method reduces makespan and overall cost, with better speedup, efficiency and near optimal Schedule Length Ratio (SLR) making it scalable and effective for complex cloud based scientific workflows.

1. INTRODUCTION

In the last few years, cloud computing has emerged as an infrastructure which is being used to host cluster-based scientific applications. These applications usually require lots of computing capabilities, high levels of scalability and freedom in allocating resources all which cloud platforms are capable of doing in an exclusive manner (Kadhim et al., 2018). The cloud is the perfect environment to run complex workflows in the form of on-demand delivery of resources and support for distributed computing. Scientific Workflow Scheduling (SWFS) is a core element of controlling of such workflows (Ahmad et al., 2021). It entails coordination and management of the execution of many related tasks that are required to run on an extended network of cloud-based resources. Scientific workflows often described as Directed Acyclic Graphs (DAGs) involve series of tasks such that the output of one task can be used as input of the next (Liu et al., 2020). The mentioned dependencies require strategic schedules of best performance which is more so difficult in the context of complexity and size of such processes. Performing tasks management efficiently within a cloud environment is not easy. Cloud environments bring a number of challenges: the resources have diverse capabilities and costs, transferring data between jobs and tasks may add delays, and constraints have to be met frequently. In this way, SWFS turns into a very complex and computationally challenging task (Sadeeq et al., 2021).

One of the main challenges of managing scientific workflows effectively in the cloud is due to the nature of the heterogeneity of cloud infrastructure. Cloud environments are made up of a wide variety of virtual machines (VMs) unlike a traditional computing system that has a homogeneous computing consistency over resources. These VMs can be considerably different in processing power, memory size, band width capacity and the cost of using them. Consequently, the process of allocating computations to the suitable VMs will become a tricky decision analysis (Singh & Walia, 2023). An application that works fine on one VM may be very slow or unnecessarily expensive on a different type of VM, which will waste resources. This variability should thus be addressed by effective scheduling strategies. Makespan is one of the most common measures of performance in the workflow of this nature, as it is the amount of time it takes to accomplish every action within a sequence of actions. The other is total computational cost which involves costs of using cloud resources. It is a daunting task to design a scheduling algorithm to minimize both these metrics taking into account the disparate nature of available VMs.

The other challenge is task dependencies. Scientific workflows do not normally involve standalone tasks; rather, the tasks are closely integrated by means of intricate dependencies. An implication of this is that one task can only start running when all the tasks it relies on are completed (Ludäscher et al., 2018). This kind of structure minimizes the extent of concurrency and also limits the concurrency of parallel processing. Unless such dependencies are handled in an intelligent way, they may impose a bottleneck-and workflows involving long, sequential chains of tasks are especially prone to such a situation-causing too many delays and poor performance.

1.1. Heuristic and Metaheuristic Approaches

Researchers have proposed a variety of heuristic and metaheuristic scheduling algorithms in an attempt to deal with the complexity of scheduling workloads in cloud environments, especially in the case of scientific workload scheduling (Al-Arasi & Saif, 2020; Gawali & Shinde, 2018). All these methods are structured to locate relatively acceptable, not necessarily optimum, answers within a feasible time span of computation considering the complexity of the problem to be computed. A group of strategies often deployed is one that comes under the priority-based list scheduling algorithms. Examples that are well known are Heterogeneous Earliest Finish Time (HEFT) and Critical Path on a Processor (CPOP) (Samadi et al., 2018; Doostali et al., 2021). These are the ways in which every particular task is given a priority upon its consideration in terms of factors such as anticipated time of its execution and the level of importance of the task. The algorithms crawl the DAG structure of the workflow both forward and backward, in order to compute these priorities and how to execute the tasks in order. Ranking results in tasks which are then allocated to the best resource at hand.

Such heuristics usually work well in minimizing makespan (particularly in cases of simple or moderately complex systems), but they suffer in larger, more dynamic or heterogeneous cloud systems. This is especially so in workflows where the communication overheads among work elements or variable user availability are high, and the wound-up nature of the prioritization of tasks becomes needlessly redundant. To address the inflexibility of the static heuristics, more dynamic and flexible modes have been tried in shape of metaheuristic algorithms.

1.2. Advancements Through Hybrid and Hyper-Heuristic Models

As a way of overcoming limitations of single-strategy heuristics and metaheuristics, there has been a growing interest in hybrid approaches as well as hyper-heuristic methods. The objectives of these state-of-the-art scheduling methods are to synthesize the relative merits of several algorithms and diminish their respective shortcomings, especially regarding the stability of performance, solution quality, and cross-workflow adaptivity and cross-cloud scalability. They combine two or more heuristic or metaheuristic techniques into hybrid models and exploit their complementary strengths. An example shows that a Genetic Algorithms (GA) and Particle Swarm Optimization (PSO) can offer a potent synergy: GA offers excellent global search capabilities through genetic diversity and a wide search around the solution space, and PSO can speed convergence and focus on promising regions using swarm behavior. These hybrids also are likely to provide superior performance on solution accuracy and rate of convergence as compared to those using one algorithm or the other.

Hyper-heuristics, on the other hand, work at the higher level of abstraction. Hyper-heuristics, as an alternative to solving the scheduling problem directly, manages a and controls a pool of low-level heuristics (Dokeroglu et al., 2023). The scheduling process proceeds by means of a hyper-heuristic choosing, mixing, or generating suitable low-level strategies in a dynamically way on the basis of the characteristics of the present problem instance. Hyper-heuristics provide such a level of flexibility that it can be effectively utilized addressing such variances and changes of real-world scientific workflows. Such advanced methods tend to perform better where there is a high level of complexity or ambiguity. As an example, they can better respond to changes in the structure of work flow, in the availability of resources, genetic expression, or pattern of communication. Nevertheless, there is a price to pay to the benefits of hybrid and hyper-heuristic models. Use of such systems is normally implemented with high level of computational overhead particularly in handling several layers of algorithms. Moreover, these models are sensitive to their parameters and they should be tuned carefully to achieve best performance; otherwise, their performance can also be seriously affected by improper parameter choices.

1.3. Limitations in Existing Models and Emerging Needs

Although the concept of heuristic, noise, metaheuristic, hybrid, that of hyper-heuristic help improve the overall effectiveness, some of the key limitations still apply to the overall effectiveness of the existing SWFS methods. These gaps presuppose the necessity to introduce more flexible and detailed scheduling models, especially in the cloud environment where variations and sensitivity to the constraints are highly apparent. The first weakness is that most of the current algorithms minimize one objective, whether it is makespan or cost. Infrequently do they combine the two together into a single model of optimization, which is necessary in the realistic scientific practice where one wants to do something that is efficient and yet is within his budget (Khan et al., 2023). Lack of bona fide multi-objective view may result in trade-offs in which gains on time-measures involve trade-offs with expenditure cuts or the other way around.

The other significant gap is the lack of utilisation in communication-aware methods of task duplication. Information exchange among the dependent operations in scientific workflows can cause large delays in data transfer, particularly where they are scheduled on different virtual machines (Almutairi & Aslam, 2023). Duplicating of essential predecessor tasks on several machines is one way of preventing this problem. This, because of selective treatment, has the potential of removing latency in communications and idleness in tasks that follow it. Nonetheless, scientists cannot mindlessly copy the material, as it can lead to excessive expenses on resources and excess in financial overheads. Thus, the strategy of intelligent duplication where it is selective and depends on such factors as the criticality of the task, conversational cost, and the available resources is required. Moreover, the existing cost models applied in planning schedules do not usually have detail. Most people consider cost as one, lump sum kind of measure instead of disaggregating cost by phases of implementation.

These limitations are reflected in a broad scope of matters, i.e., the necessity of flexible, multi-dimensional scheduling models which support various complex features such as cost-awareness, dependency management, duplication strategies, and dynamic resource assignments. These frameworks should be capable of functioning with different types of workflows and with different cloud environments, and preferably with little to no manual tuning or action by the user.

1.4. Proposed Hybrid Scheduling Framework and Its Innovations

In response to the identified challenges and limitations discussed in previous section, this paper proposes a new system of hybrid scheduling framework to efficiently deal with scientific workflows in heterogeneous cloud systems. The solution proposed in this paper incorporates several strategies; cost-aware prioritization of specific tasks, communication-efficient construction of redundant tasks, and the heuristic adaptivity in the context of task prioritization built around creation of a single, flexible architecture. The center of this model is the employment of optimistic cost tables. These tables provide the foundation of determining priorities to be given to activities based on estimating the actual earliest start time and complete time in perfect conditions. Such ranking system can assist in making sure that the most important tasks in terms of overall workflow advancement can be scheduled earlier, taking into account both the urgency of the execution as well as the overhead that there may be on communication. Direct incorporation of cost sensitivity into the prioritization mechanism allows the model to foster a more-balanced trade-off between the speed of execution and resource-efficiency of each action.

One of the most interesting novelties in the strategy is its dynamic, selective duplication. Rather than performing a hodgepodge of tasks blindly, which is how resorting to replication of tasks can be a waste of resources, the framework has thoughtful ways of picking tasks that are ready on the critical path or tend to be bottlenecks because of delays in communication (He et al., 2018). The tasks are then repeated purposefully on many virtual machines so that the successors tasks can get started earlier and therefore waste less idle time. This method is especially useful where computation workflows have a high inter-task communication requirement where the data transfer may cause latency. The other feature or signature feature of the proposed framework is adaptive scheduling engine; this engine can change between the various heuristics approach according to the current workload in real time (Yao et al., 2021). As an illustration, the engine can engage GA in work flows requiring wide exploration search, PSO in faster convergence tasks with well-structured task graphs or even hyper-heuristics in uncertain or dynamic resource contexts. Such dynamic flexibility guarantees that the scheduling algorithm can respond well irrespective of the kind or make-up of the flow of the work.

The rest of the paper is structured as follows. Section 2 summarises existing research on workflow scheduling and cloud resource optimisation. In section 3, the proposed methodology will be described with the discussion of algorithm design and heuristic integration. Section 4 covers a discussion of the results and Section 5 of the paper concludes the paper on a note of the directions of the future research.

2. LITERATURE SURVEY

Efficient scheduling of scientific workflows in distributed and heterogeneous cloud environments remains a challenging research problem. The complexity arises due to factors such as inter-task dependencies, non-uniform computational resources, and communication delays. To mitigate these challenges, numerous approaches have been developed, focusing particularly on task duplication, heuristic algorithms, and intelligent scheduling techniques.

Shi et al. address the complexity of scheduling multiple jobs in cloud environments by introducing a multijob-associated task scheduling algorithm that combines task duplication with insertion techniques. In contrast to single-job workflow models, this approach focuses on optimizing resources when multiple independent workflows run concurrently—a common real-world scenario. The authors integrate task duplication to shorten execution paths for critical tasks and task insertion to efficiently utilize idle time slots within virtual machines. This dual-strategy model ensures better VM utilization, reduced execution time, and improved throughput. Their scheduling framework dynamically assesses inter-task dependencies and uses a graph-theoretic approach to optimize the mapping of tasks to cloud resources. One of the most impactful elements of this research is its flexibility: it can adapt to various types of workloads and resource heterogeneity. Evaluation against existing models shows significant gains in performance, particularly in high-concurrency settings where resource contention is a challenge. For cloud service providers or research labs dealing with multiple workflows simultaneously, this method offers a realistic and effective solution. By combining duplication and insertion techniques, the study balances the trade-offs between speed, efficiency, and resource optimization—contributing to more resilient and adaptable workflow scheduling strategies in dynamic cloud systems (Shi et al., 2021).

Shirvani et all., introduce a hybrid heuristic-based list scheduling algorithm that targets makespan minimization in heterogeneous cloud environments. Recognizing the inherent complexity of cloud platforms—where virtual machines vary in performance and cost—they combine elements of traditional list scheduling with intelligent heuristics to better manage task-resource allocation. Their hybrid model incorporates factors like task execution time, communication delay, and resource capabilities into the scheduling priority function. A major feature is its ability to dynamically adapt task priorities based on system load and task interdependencies. The authors design the algorithm to be both scalable and computationally efficient, ensuring that it performs well even for large-scale workflows. Experimental comparisons with benchmark algorithms show clear reductions in makespan, especially under conditions of high task heterogeneity. This research is particularly valuable for applications in scientific computing, where timely completion of complex workflows is essential. By blending heuristic methods with list scheduling's structured task ordering, the study provides a well-rounded solution that performs reliably under various cloud constraints. The paper contributes meaningfully to ongoing efforts in workflow optimization, especially for users requiring predictable execution timelines without excessive overhead in real-time or near real-time cloud scheduling environments (Shirvani & Talouki, 2021).

Chen et al. take a modern approach to workflow scheduling by leveraging deep reinforcement learning (DRL) for handling heterogeneous workflows in cloud environments. Their collaborative scheduling framework utilizes DRL agents that learn from interaction with the environment, improving task-resource mapping through experience. This model is designed to deal with the non-deterministic nature of cloud resources—where availability, performance, and costs can fluctuate unpredictably. The DRL model continuously refines its policy based on feedback, enabling it to balance competing objectives like task completion time, energy consumption, and cost. A novel aspect of the work is its collaborative strategy: multiple agents work together to schedule different parts of a workflow, ensuring global optimization rather than isolated local decisions. Simulation results show that the DRL-based scheduler outperforms traditional heuristics and static planning models, particularly in heterogeneous and resource-constrained settings. The adaptive nature of the system allows it to respond effectively to changing workload patterns, VM availability, and user constraints. This makes the framework especially relevant for scientific and enterprise-scale cloud workflows where adaptability, scalability, and cost-efficiency are crucial. Overall, the study exemplifies how machine learning—specifically DRL—can transform workflow scheduling into a more intelligent, autonomous process (Chen et al., 2022).

Ahmad et al., propose an enhanced list scheduling algorithm that incorporates task duplication techniques for scientific big data workflows operating in heterogeneous computing environments. Their method builds on the traditional list scheduling structure, where tasks are ordered based on priority and mapped to available resources, by adding a duplication mechanism for critical path tasks. This prevents bottlenecks caused by waiting on predecessor task completion and significantly reduces idle time across computational resources. Designed specifically for scientific workflows involving big data (e.g., genomics, climate modeling), the algorithm targets high-throughput environments where even minor delays can compound into substantial inefficiencies. The authors validate their approach using simulated workflows and real-world datasets, demonstrating consistent improvements in makespan and resource utilization. A strength of this research is its focus on heterogeneity—acknowledging that not all virtual machines or nodes in a cloud setup offer the same capabilities or reliability. The algorithm dynamically adjusts to VM availability and performance variance, ensuring robust execution in unpredictable settings. By integrating duplication into an otherwise efficient list scheduling model, this study bridges performance gaps without adding excessive computational overhead, offering a scalable and cost-efficient solution for large-scale scientific data processing in cloud ecosystems (Ahmad & Alam, 2020).

Li et al., explore a refined task scheduling method based on heterogeneous priority assessment and critical task duplication. Their model recognizes that not all tasks in a workflow hold equal importance when it comes to execution time and impact on the overall makespan. By assigning higher priority to critical tasks and allowing their duplication across multiple nodes, the algorithm seeks to reduce workflow latency and improve efficiency. Unlike standard duplication strategies, their approach incorporates heterogeneous resource performance in its priority calculations—ensuring that high-performance VMs handle critical tasks more frequently. The model also leverages insertion strategies for non-critical tasks, filling idle resource gaps and maximizing utilization. A key highlight is its flexible, two-tiered decision-making process: one layer optimizes task prioritization while the other refines the actual task-to-resource mapping in real time. Results from the International Conference on Computer Engineering and Intelligent Control demonstrate that this dual-layered strategy leads to reduced execution time and cost across various workflow scenarios. This study is particularly relevant for hybrid and cloud-native systems that aim to improve execution predictability under budget and resource constraints. It contributes to the growing field of fine-grained, QoS-aware workflow scheduling that prioritizes adaptability and efficiency in heterogeneous cloud environments (Li et al., 2023).

Gupta et al. present an enhancement of the HEFT (Heterogeneous Earliest Finish Time) algorithm by introducing advanced prioritization and processor selection strategies aimed at minimizing makespan in cloud environments. The study refines the ranking phase by incorporating a dynamic weight adjustment technique that considers task dependencies and communication overhead. In the processor selection phase, the authors implement a cost-aware mapping that ensures efficient resource utilization without increasing scheduling complexity. Experimental evaluations using standard workflow datasets show significant performance gains over traditional HEFT and its variants, particularly in terms of reduced execution time. What makes this approach notable is its focus on adaptiveness; rather than relying on fixed rules, the improved HEFT dynamically adjusts to workload characteristics. The study emphasizes practical applicability in real-world cloud platforms, especially where task heterogeneity and resource variability are significant. Overall, the improved prioritization and mapping scheme makes HEFT more responsive to changing conditions, which is valuable for scientific workflows requiring deadline-sensitive task scheduling in distributed cloud infrastructures (Gupta et al., 2022).

Guo, Zhou, et al., develop a limited duplication-based list scheduling algorithm tailored for heterogeneous computing systems. Unlike full duplication models, which replicate critical tasks extensively and may consume excess resources, this approach introduces a constraint on duplication levels to optimize trade-offs between execution time and resource usage. The algorithm targets communication delays between dependent tasks, a common bottleneck in distributed systems. By duplicating only the most critical tasks, the method effectively minimizes idle time across processors while avoiding unnecessary overhead. It integrates traditional list scheduling with a duplication policy governed by execution and communication cost thresholds. The results show that this limited duplication strategy outperforms basic list scheduling in makespan and processor efficiency, particularly in scenarios involving tightly coupled tasks. The algorithm is lightweight, making it ideal for embedded or low-resource cloud environments. The paper stands out for its balance between efficiency and practicality, demonstrating that even modest levels of duplication can yield substantial performance improvements without compromising scalability or incurring excessive costs (Guo et al., 2022).

Kelefouras et al., focus on enhancing workflow simulation and task scheduling by making their algorithm multi-threading aware in heterogeneous cloud environments. The research acknowledges a gap in many workflow scheduling methods that overlook multi-core and multi-threaded processor capabilities. To address this, the authors develop a scheduling technique that simulates workflows with full awareness of core-level parallelism. By optimizing task placement not just across different machines but also within multi-threaded architectures, their solution significantly improves CPU utilization and execution time. They also propose a cost model that reflects execution and communication trade-offs at both the thread and processor levels. The evaluation, performed on both synthetic and real-world workflows, confirms notable improvements in makespan and scheduling efficiency. This study is especially relevant in an era where cloud providers offer increasingly powerful multi-core virtual machines. The paper's strength lies in its practical, simulation-based approach that enables better mapping of parallelizable tasks to available cores, making it highly applicable to complex scientific workflows and performance-critical applications hosted in the cloud (Kelefouras & Djemame, 2022).

Ahmed, et al., introduce an enhanced workflow scheduling algorithm for cloud computing that emphasizes dynamic task prioritization and resource adaptability. Their approach modifies existing metaheuristic methods by embedding a task-ranking mechanism based on deadline urgency, execution time, and resource availability. Unlike static scheduling techniques, this model continuously monitors the cloud environment and adapts to fluctuating workload conditions, leading to more efficient task execution and better deadline compliance. The algorithm leverages a feedback loop to recalibrate task priorities as execution progresses, thus aligning with real-time system behavior. Experimental results demonstrate improvements in both makespan and resource utilization when compared to traditional list and metaheuristic-based schedulers. The model also proves effective in handling heterogeneous workloads, making it particularly useful for large-scale scientific or commercial workflows in dynamic cloud ecosystems. By introducing intelligent adaptability, the paper bridges the gap between theoretical scheduling models and real-world cloud applications, contributing meaningfully to the design of QoS-aware and deadline-sensitive cloud scheduling strategies (Ahmed & Omara, 2022).

Tang et al., proposes a reliability-aware, cost-efficient scheduling strategy for scientific workflows deployed in multi-cloud environments. The model integrates failure probability, execution cost, and task deadlines into a unified objective function. By quantifying reliability based on past cloud instance performance, the scheduler selects optimal resources that minimize failure risk without exceeding cost constraints. The approach dynamically balances between low-cost unreliable instances and high-cost reliable ones, ensuring workflows meet deadline and budget requirements. Experimental results validate the framework's effectiveness in reducing both execution failures and costs, particularly under uncertain network and system conditions. The paper contributes a robust decision-making model for scientific workflows in federated or multi-cloud environments, where variability and failure are common. Its relevance is growing as research and enterprise workflows increasingly rely on distributed, vendor-agnostic cloud strategies. By embedding reliability as a core parameter, the proposed method fills a critical gap in existing cost-performance optimization models, offering a more resilient and economically viable workflow execution approach (Tang, 2021).

Mikram, et al., present HEPGA, a novel hybrid algorithm for scientific workflow scheduling in cloud environments. HEPGA combines the strengths of Particle Swarm Optimization (PSO) and Genetic Algorithms (GA) to balance exploration and exploitation during task-resource mapping. The model introduces an adaptive fitness function that considers execution time, resource availability, and energy consumption, ensuring that the optimization process targets real-world cloud constraints. A key feature of HEPGA is its ability to avoid local optima—a common challenge in standalone heuristic methods—through crossover and mutation strategies borrowed from GA, alongside the swarm behavior of PSO. Simulation results on benchmark workflows like Inspiral and CyberShake show that HEPGA outperforms existing algorithms in makespan, cost efficiency, and energy usage. This makes it a strong candidate for large-scale scientific computing projects with variable workloads and resource constraints. The paper stands out for its effective integration of two established metaheuristics into a single, dynamic framework, setting a new benchmark for hybrid workflow scheduling algorithms in cloud-based research environments (Mikram et al., 2023).

Coleman et al., introduce Wf Commons, a comprehensive framework designed to support reproducible research and development in scientific workflow scheduling. The platform provides a set of open-source tools that allow researchers to generate, analyze, and simulate scientific workflows under various cloud or HPC environments. WfCommons includes datasets, workflow generators, and performance models for standard scientific applications such as Montage and CyberShake. This framework is particularly valuable for benchmarking new scheduling algorithms under consistent and comparable conditions. It enables workflow reproducibility, which has been a long-standing challenge in workflow systems research. Beyond simulation, WfCommons helps developers test scheduling techniques with realistic workloads, ensuring that improvements in algorithm design translate to actual performance gains. The project is also collaborative, allowing the research community to contribute new workflow traces and models. WfCommons fills a critical need in the scheduling research ecosystem by providing shared infrastructure, fostering transparency, and promoting methodological rigor. It is a key tool for advancing the study of scalable, efficient, and reliable workflow systems (Coleman et al., 2021).

Roy et al. present *Mashup*, a platform developed under ACM that simplifies the development and execution of complex data-driven workflows. It supports integration across multiple data formats, services, and APIs—ideal for domains like edge computing, federated learning, and scientific research. Mashup allows researchers to combine data transformation, analysis, and visualization modules into seamless workflows, reducing time and development overhead. The framework emphasizes ease of use, modularity, and automation. It is especially useful for interdisciplinary teams needing rapid prototyping across heterogeneous data sources. The paper showcases applications where Mashup handles data aggregation and scheduling with minimal user intervention, making it suitable for both technical and non-technical users. Unlike traditional workflow engines, Mashup abstracts system complexity and enables faster iteration, fostering innovation in real-time and resource-constrained environments. Its contribution lies in reducing the friction of workflow design while maintaining flexibility, making it a practical tool for data-intensive scientific and industrial tasks (Roy et al., 2022).

Recent research has shown strong momentum toward hybrid and intelligent workflow scheduling in cloud environments, particularly for scientific applications. Chen et al. propose an Ant Colony Optimization (ACO)–based heuristic that mimics how ants find optimal paths to solve scheduling problems constrained by cost and deadlines. By using artificial pheromone trails, the approach adapts to dynamic pricing in IaaS platforms while satisfying Quality of Service (QoS) requirements. Similarly, Li et al. build upon this ACO foundation, introducing a load-aware mechanism to avoid overburdening specific virtual machines. Their model dynamically updates task-resource suitability based on workload, improving stability and performance in large-scale cloud workflows (Nwogbaga et al., 2022).

Dey et al. propose a unique hybrid scheduling mechanism that draws inspiration from nature, combining the strengths of Ant Colony Optimization (ACO) and Particle Swarm Optimization (PSO). This bio-inspired model is specifically designed to address the dual challenges of task distribution and energy efficiency in cloud data centers. By imitating the collective behavior of ants and the social dynamics of bird flocking, the hybrid algorithm intelligently balances task assignments across virtual machines (VMs) while simultaneously reducing unnecessary energy consumption and VM migrations. One standout feature of this approach is its ability to maintain service quality—measured through SLA (Service Level Agreement) compliance—even in fluctuating cloud environments. The hybrid ACO-PSO framework dynamically adapts to changing workloads, enhancing throughput and resource utilization without compromising response time. This level of adaptability and optimization positions it as a valuable component for hybrid workflow scheduling frameworks, especially those deployed in scientific or large-scale cloud infrastructures. The authors further introduce a novel performance metric that integrates energy efficiency with traditional QoS parameters, helping to holistically evaluate system performance. Ultimately, this work highlights the potential of combining heuristic and nature-inspired algorithms to solve complex, multi-dimensional problems in modern cloud computing environments (Jayanetti et al., 2024).

Wang et al. make a significant contribution by conducting an in-depth review of the performance metrics used to evaluate scientific workflow scheduling in both cloud and grid environments. Rather than introducing a new scheduling algorithm, their work focuses on what makes a scheduling strategy effective by analyzing how different metrics reflect real-world performance. The study categorizes key metrics such as makespan, cost, resource utilization, energy consumption, fault tolerance, and throughput. Importantly, the authors emphasize that in cloud environments—where conditions are dynamic and workloads are heterogeneous—evaluating a scheduler on just one metric is often insufficient. For hybrid frameworks that aim to balance multiple objectives like cost, time, and energy use, this paper offers valuable guidance. It provides a framework for selecting the right set of metrics when comparing different algorithms (Sarkar et al., 2025).

Jayanetti et al. explore the transformative role of Deep Reinforcement Learning (DRL) in modern workflow scheduling across cloud and edge computing platforms. Their comprehensive review categorizes existing DRL frameworks and investigates their effectiveness in dynamic environments where tasks vary and performance goals often conflict. Unlike static heuristics, DRL models learn optimal scheduling strategies over time, balancing objectives such as cost, latency, energy consumption, and throughput. A major strength of DRL highlighted in the paper is its ability to operate under uncertainty—managing incomplete or noisy data, adapting to workload fluctuations, and improving with experience. The authors present a structured taxonomy that organizes existing DRL methods by algorithm type, learning environment, and scheduling goals. They also emphasize future directions such as multi-agent learning, transfer learning for cross-environment adaptation, and explainable DRL policies that enhance transparency and trust (Chauhan et al., 2024).

Abrishami, et al., present a comprehensive systematic literature review (SLR) on the evolving role of Workflow-as-a-Service (WaaS) brokers in cloud computing. Their study surveys 74 peer-reviewed articles, offering a detailed taxonomy of WaaS architectural models, pricing strategies, scheduling policies, and brokering mechanisms. The authors highlight how modern scientific workflows are no longer bound to traditional cloud models but are increasingly executed across hybrid settings—spanning serverful, serverless, and multi-cloud environments. A significant emphasis is placed on how WaaS brokers can handle dynamic pricing and ensure SLA (Service Level Agreement) compliance while orchestrating complex workflows over heterogeneous platforms. The paper identifies key trends such as the growing need for broker intelligence, edge/fog integration, and FAIR-compliant (Findable, Accessible, Interoperable, Reusable) workflows. Notably, the authors point out critical gaps in existing systems—such as a lack of adaptive rescheduling and insufficient use of explainable decision-making frameworks. They advocate for future enhancements involving reinforcement learning and multi-agent systems to create more transparent and self-optimizing brokers. This work serves as a solid foundation for future research into intelligent workflow orchestration and provides valuable direction for building scalable, cost-effective, and policy-aware hybrid scheduling frameworks in cloud-based scientific and industrial applications (Abrishami et al., 2025).

Raghu et al., addressed A novel approach that combines Blockchain and Generative Adversarial Networks (GANs) to enhance image encryption and data security in cloud computing environments. The pressing issue of maintaining the confidentiality and integrity of medical images transmitted and stored via the cloud. The authors introduce a Blockchain-enhanced GAN architecture that not only secures the data transmission channel but also generates dynamic encryption patterns, making it extremely difficult for intruders to intercept or tamper with sensitive clinical data. Blockchain is used here not just as a security layer but as a decentralized ledger that guarantees transparency and tamper resistance. GANs, on the other hand, are leveraged for their ability to produce complex image transformations, thereby adding another layer of unpredictability to the encryption process. The synergy between these two technologies forms a powerful solution to current challenges in healthcare data security. The experimental results show that this hybrid framework significantly enhances both encryption strength and processing efficiency. This work is particularly relevant for healthcare IoT systems where data privacy, real-time access, and secure communication are non-negotiable (Raghu et al., 2025).

Throughout the literature, task duplication, heuristic/meta-heuristic scheduling, and adaptive learning mechanism are used as focal points to meet the challenges of scientific workflow scheduling in the context of cloud and hybrid environments. There has been a shift in focus of researchers towards more dynamic models of scheduling, and towards intelligent, flexible and cost-conscious algorithms. Such developments enhance not only the efficiency of execution and resource utilization but also enhance the execution of the workflow in terms of scalability, reliability as well as applicability to the real world. The future of the area of work is likely to pay more attention to real-time flexibility, multi-objective trade-offs, and any form of integrated simulation framework that can facilitate deployment to more heterogeneous computer ecosystems.

3. METHODOLOGY

3.1. Problem Formulation

Scientific workflows are usually modeled in cloud computing environments as DAGs where the ordering and dependency of activities in a computing workflow are indicated. A DAG has a node at each unique task, and the edges represent flow and precedence requirements of data among the tasks (Fu et al., 2021; S & Patil, 2022; Shao et al., 2023). The general objective of such workflow scheduling in heterogeneous cloud systems was maximum performance served by minimizing total computation length and leading to computational cost reduction, suppressing the complexity of constraints, including task dependencies and resource constraints, all at the same time. A scientific workflow can be formally represented as a DAG, denoted as:

$$G = (T, E) \tag{1}$$

Each directed edge $e \in E$ signifies that task t cannot be executed until task t has finished and the corresponding data has been transferred. Within this structure, the entry task (denoted t_{entry}) has no incoming edges, indicating it starts the workflow. Conversely, the exit task (t_{exit}) has no outgoing edges, marking the end of the process.

Let $VM = \{vm, vm, ..., vm\}$ denote the set of available virtual machines in the cloud environment. These VMs are heterogeneous, meaning they differ in terms of processing speed, communication bandwidth, and operational cost. Each task $t \in T$ can be assigned to any virtual machine $vm \in VM$, though the execution time may vary depending on the characteristics of the VM. The average execution time of a task t over all VMs is given in Equation 2.

$$\overline{ET}(t_i) = \frac{1}{|VM|}\sum_{k=1}^{m} ET(t_i, vm_k) \tag{2}$$

Here, |VM| represents the total number of virtual machines, and the summation computes the cumulative execution time of task t across all machines.

In the context of workflow scheduling, several timing metrics are essential for ensuring correct task execution order and optimizing performance objectives such as execution time and resource utilization. These metrics help determine when tasks can begin, complete, and how data dependencies affect scheduling. The Earliest Data Ready Time (EDRT) represents the soonest point at which all necessary input data for a task t becomes available on a given virtual machine vm. This metric takes into account the communication delays from all predecessor tasks. Let *Pred* (t) denote the set of tasks that must complete before t can begin. The EDRT is defined as in Equation 3.

$$\mathrm{EDRT}(t_i, vm_k) = \max_{t_j \in \mathrm{Pred}(t_i)} \left\{ \min_{vm_l \in VM} \left[EFT(t_j, vm_l) + c(t_j, t_i) \right] \right\} \tag{3}$$

$$C = \sum_{t_i \in T} \left[ET(t_i, vm_k) \cdot \mathrm{Cost}(vm_k) \right] + \sum_{(t_i, t_j) \in E} c(t_i, t_j) \cdot \lambda \tag{4}$$

The cost model (Equation 4) incorporates both computational and communication expenses and provides a comprehensive view of workflow-related spending. Optimizing for this total cost C, along with minimizing makespan, results in a multi-objective optimization problem, a central challenge in workflow scheduling for cloud computing.

3.2. Proposed Methodology

In this section, an exhaustive hybrid scheduling framework is being put forward that is designed to maximize scientific workflow execution in cloud computing. In the method, many significant elements are included: task ranking which is sensitive to costs, involving the Optimistic Cost Tables (OCT), a multi-level cost matrix to perform cost tracking in detail, a selective duplication strategy and an adaptive heuristic chooser that can change according to different complexities of the workflow (Dey & Sangaraju, 2023). Incorporating this, the goal of the framework is to reduce both the duration of execution and the total cost of the computational process, but it is also important that it does not negatively impact compliance with dependence within the task and contributes to an efficient usage cloud resource.

3.2.1. Priority Assignment Using Improved OCTd and OCTu

In DAG-based workflows, task prioritization is significant in scheduling as a whole. To improve on traditional list-based scheduling methods, this structure involves the deployment of a two-ranking procedure with both downward and upward Optimistic Cost Tables. The downward cost table (OCTd) calculates the cost required by the workflow entry point up to a certain task t which is recorded as reflecting on the early-stage execution. Conversely, upward cost table (OCTu) is an assessment of cost of t_1 to last task as it can destabilize the completion of work. Taking the information obtained in the two directions, the model acquires a well-informed position on the criticality of each task in the workflow. The ranking of the tasks and insertion into a global priority queue is achieved using these combined OCT values, so that scheduling meets the notion of task dependencies whilst encouraging efficient execution ordering.

$$\text{Rank}_{OCT}(t_i) = \frac{1}{2}\left(\overline{OCTd}(t_i) + \overline{OCTu}(t_i)\right) \quad (5)$$

3.2.2. Cost Matrix Model

On the basis of the layered cost framework, the execution of workflow costs is categorically classified into three different stages, namely pre-scheduling, during-scheduling and post-scheduling. Pre-scheduling cost (C_{pre}) is all the overheads used before the start of execution. This involves the time and resources needed to start VMs, costs involved in reserving the cloud resources and the computational overhead of workflow analysis graph. The cost to be incurred (C_{during}) during scheduling takes into consideration the cost of the implementation and the negligence of communication. Cost to execute a task t in a virtual machine vm is computed as the product of the execution time to execute the task and the cost rate of the VM. Communication cost between two dependent tasks t and is a matter of the assignment of the tasks to the same VM. In case they are in co-location then this cost would be zero. When they are in different VMs e.g. vm for t and vm_z for t_H the cost is measured as the data capacity between the work divided by the bandwidth between the VMs. inally, the costs after scheduling (C_{post}) contains the operations done after the task has been fully executed like aggregating results, delivering final results as well the releasing or cleaning up of the resources allocated.

$$C_{\text{total}} = C_{\text{pre}} + \sum_{t_i \in T} C_{\text{exec}}\left(t_i, vm_k\right) + \sum_{(t_i,t_j)\in E} C_{\text{comm}}\left(t_i, t_j\right) + C_{\text{post}} \quad (6)$$

This comprehensive cost model ensures that optimization efforts account for the full lifecycle of workflow execution, rather than focusing solely on task runtime or VM costs.

3.2.3. Selective Task Duplication Strategy

Selective task duplication strategy is used in order to minimize the overall makespan of workflow and delay due to communication between interdependencies. This approach has the advantage of applying duplication when it will present a quantifiable improvement in performance; otherwise, the available resources are likely to be wasted. It starts with the determining of the essential predecessor of any given task t_1. This is the immediate predecessor task t_{cp} in $Pred(t)$ the completion time of which has the most difference between the succeeding start time S of t. After the identification of the critical predecessor, the scheduler will test to determine whether replicating t_{cp} will have some impact in the EFT of t by residing on the same VM as t. Duplication can only be done when the two following conditions are satisfied: (1) Subduplication causes a reduction in the EFT of t, and (2) The VM to which the duplicating task is being subduplicated has sufficient idle capacity to allow the duplicating task to be allocated without forcing other tasks on to the VM. At this point, a cost-benefit analysis is carried out by the makespan pre-duplication and the makespan post-duplication. Duplication is acceptable so far as it results in a decreased total execution time and does not entail a considerable increment in cost. This guarantees that the duplicate mechanism is not only performance oriented but resource-aware since it imposes the duplicate even on tasks that will lead to obvious gains in terms of schedules.

3.2.4. Dynamic Heuristic Selector

One of the tasks of the proposed approach is the integration of the Dynamic Heuristic Selector (DHS) that is an intelligent search of the most appropriate optimization algorithm by using the structural peculiarities of the workflow. This component optimizes the scheduling scheme taking into consideration two main indicators: the number of tasks and the depth of the DAG. In situations when there are less than 100 tasks in the workflow and less steep task structures the Selector is using a GA to explore the solution space in broad, global perspective. In the case when the number of tasks is between 100 to 500 objects; or, there is moderately deep workflow, the selector moves to PSO, which has an excellent compromise between exploration and exploitation. Where large workflows consist of more than 500 tasks or complex chains of dependencies, a Dynamic Hyper-Heuristic Algorithm (DHHA) is tripped in the DHS. This sophisticated mechanism does online search over a collection of low-level heuristics and they are chosen dynamically depending on the feedback performance. This dynamic adjustment in the optimization methodology according to the intricacy of the working process is capable of secure quality optimization delivery as the scheduling decisions as well as minimization of the amounts of computational overhead costs. Figure 1 gives the algorithm of overall proposed methodology.

Figure 1. Hybrid Workflow Scheduling with Duplication and DHS

Input: Workflow $DAG\ G = (T, E)$, VM $set = \{vm1, \ldots, vmn\}$

Output: Task-to-VM mapping schedule S

1. Compute OCTd and OCTu for all tasks
2. Calculate priority scores: Rank_OCT(ti) ← (OCTd + OCTu) / 2
3. Sort tasks in PriorityQueue based on Rank_OCT
4. Initialize CostMatrix and SlotTable
5. Select heuristic strategy using Dynamic Heuristic Selector
6. while PriorityQueue is not empty:

    t_i ← PriorityQueue.pop()

    for each $vm_k \in VM$:

      compute $EFT(t_i, vm_k)$

    Assign t_i to vm_k* with min EFT

    if $Pred(t_i) \neq \emptyset$:

      t_{cp} ← get_critical_predecessor(t_i)

      if duplication_beneficial(t_{cp}, t_i):

        duplicate t_{cp} on vm_k*

7. Compute total makespan and cost of schedule S
8. Return final schedule S

Figure 2 illustrate flow diagram represents a structured scheduling framework for scientific workflows in cloud environments. The process begins with accepting a DAG-based workflow input, followed by the computation of optimistic cost tables (OCTd and OCTu) to estimate task priorities based on execution potential. These priorities guide the ordering of tasks before selecting an appropriate scheduling heuristic using a dynamic selector. Once selected, tasks are assigned to suitable virtual machines, and the framework evaluates whether duplicating any critical predecessor tasks would reduce communication delays or execution time. After incorporating beneficial duplications, the system calculates the overall execution cost and makespan (Shetty & Raghu, 2024; Kiran et al., 2023; Singh et al., 2025; Raghu et al., 2024; Topcuoglu et al., 2002; Yu & Buyya, 2005; Pandey et al., 2010). Finally, the optimized schedule is produced. A feedback mechanism ensures iterative refinement of the process based on scheduling outcomes.

Figure 2. Flowchart of the Proposed Methodology

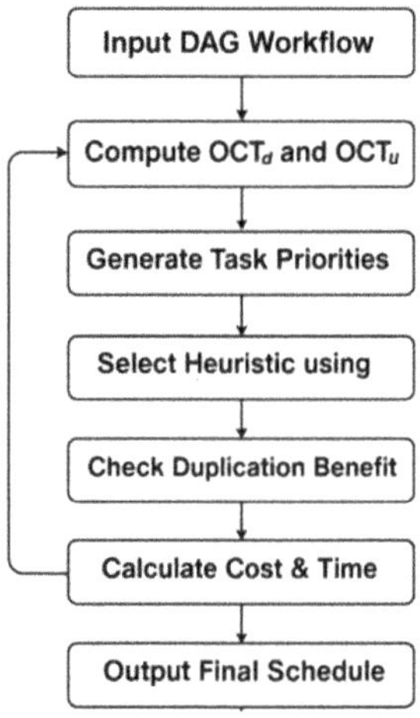

3.3. Experimental Setup

Experiments were carried out in a modified version of CloudSim, called WorkflowSim precisely created to build testbeds to simulate scientific workflow execution. WorkflowSim has powerful capabilities to model DAG based task dependencies, real cloud settings and different scheduling algorithms (Zhao & Sakellariou, 2006; Rodriguez & Buyya, 2014; Malawski et al., 2015; Arabnejad & Barbosa, 2014). It also enables it to have built-in modules of task clustering, workflow engine simulation, cost modeling which are fundamental in evaluation of the multi-objective scheduling strategies. Java code was used to run simulations in the Eclipse IDE and the WorkflowSim version was enabled with the features of heterogeneous cloud resources. The VMs were simulated with random processing rates, bandwidths and rate of cost to approximate a realistic heterogeneity in clouds. The configuration of each of the VMs was aligned with Amazon EC2-like instances so as to be similar to real-life infrastructure. Simulation parameters are given in Table 1.

Table 1. Simulation Parameters

Parameter	Value / Range
VM Count	5, 10, 15
VM Processing Speed (MIPS)	500 – 2000
VM Memory	2 GB – 8 GB

continued on following page

Table 1. Continued

Parameter	Value / Range
Bandwidth	100 Mbps – 1000 Mbps
VM Cost per Time Unit	0.5 – 2.5 Cloud Units
Communication Latency	10ms – 50ms
Task Data Size (per edge)	10 MB – 500 MB
Evaluation Metrics	Makespan, Total Cost, Speedup, SLR, Efficiency

3.3.1. Dataset

To guarantee practical relevancy and benchmark consistencies, the SIPHT workflow dataset was chosen to be tested. SIPHT (sRNA Identification Protocol using High-throughput Technologies) is a popular bioinformatics pipeline which scans bacterial genomes to identify small non-coding RNAs. Its tasks are interdependent, the execution time of the different tasks varies and its data transfer requirements are extensive, making it a ideal candidate to test the potentiality of cost-aware and dependence-sensitive schedulers. Testing on the dataset was performed with varying input sizes in order to generate small, medium, and large workflow conditions. Such differences were useful to test the scalability and flexibility of the suggested approach with growing computing demands. Table 2 provides the statistical overview of the SIPHT dataset.

Table 2. Statistical Overview of SIPHT Workflow Dataset Used

Workflow Size	No. of Tasks	No. of Edges (Dependencies)	Avg. Task Runtime (s)	Data Size per Edge (MB)	Max DAG Depth	Max Out-degree
Small	50	69	5 – 10	10 – 50	6	4
Medium	100	135	8 – 20	20 – 100	9	6
Large	500	780	10 – 30	50 – 300	15	8

These descriptive statistics prove that the complexity and scope of the set are highly variable which justifies the usability of the set to compare the effectiveness of scheduling algorithms in various load situations.

4. RESULTS AND DISCUSSION

Figure 3 shows the comparison of makespan among different scheduling algorithms such as HEFT, PEFT, RHEFT, GA, PSO and the proposed algorithm. The proposed algorithm yields the least makespan compression value of 95 seconds among all, and thus is the most efficient and has the shortest time of workflow completion. Schedualing algorithms that work traditionally, like HEFT and PEFT, have inferior makespan values (120s and 115s, respectively), showing inferior task dependency and resource heterogeneity management. Metaheuristic algorithms, such as GA and PSO experience medium improvement with makespan of 105s and 103s respectively. Yet this is not as good as the performance of the proposed strategy that combines adaptive heuristic selection and critical-path-aware task duplication in order to get the best out of parallelism.

Figure 3. Comparison of Makespan

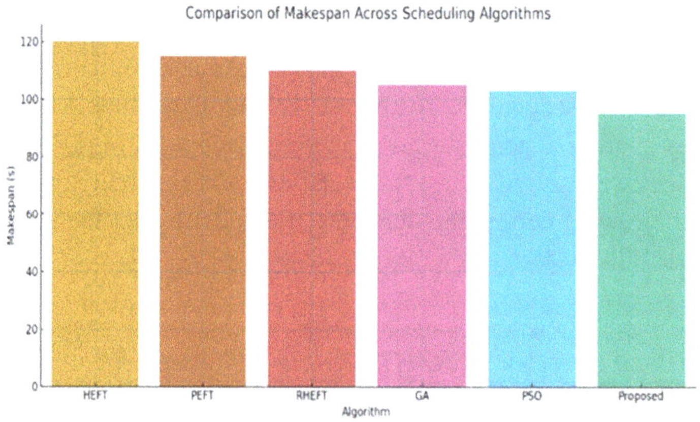

In Figure 4, the total cost used by various scheduling algorithms is contrasted to execute the workflow in cloud environments. The suggested technique presents the minimum cost around 190 cloud units, which points to its utility to reduce the overhead of resource allocation and execution and communication. Due to inefficient task placement and inefficient resource utilization, the traditional algorithms like HEFT and PEFT have much more costs, approximately 250 and 240 units respectively. The metaheuristic algorithms such as GA and PSO actually do as good or better than the classical algorithm with a cost of 220 and 215 units respectively, but still are less efficient than the proposed algorithm. Cost-saving of the proposed approach arises due to its adaptive scheduling activities, cost-sensitive task allocations, and a duplication scheme that disfavors repetitive calculations. This comparison validates cost-effectiveness of the suggested solution to implementing cloud-based scientific workflow scheduling.

Figure 4. Comparison of Total Cost

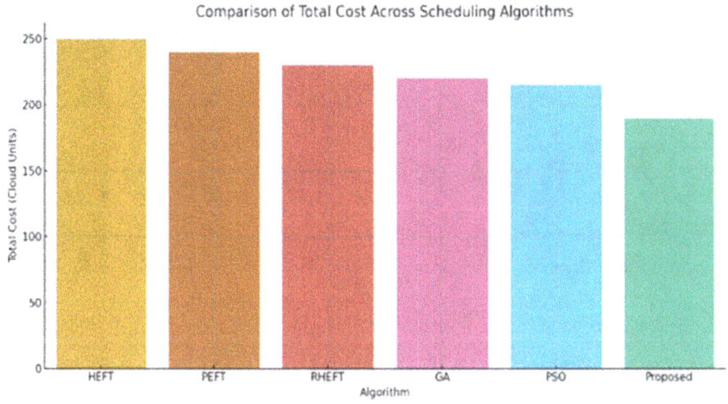

Figure 5 shows the efficiency of the various scheduling algorithms accompanied by the workflow execution in a cloud environment. The proposed algorithm has the maximum efficiency rating of around 0.82 therefore excellent engagement of the resources at our disposal. By contrast, more traditional approaches such as HEFT and PEFT have efficiency levels of 0.65 and 0.68 respectively, which means that parallelism was not fully exploited. Metaheuristic algorithms like the one about GA (0.74) and PSO (0.75) demonstrate no better efficiency, but still, they are worse than the suggested solution. The good results of the proposed scheduler might be explained by its dynamic heuristic selection and smart task duplication mechanism, which all together reduce the idle time and enhance parallel execution.

Figure 5. Comparison of Efficiency

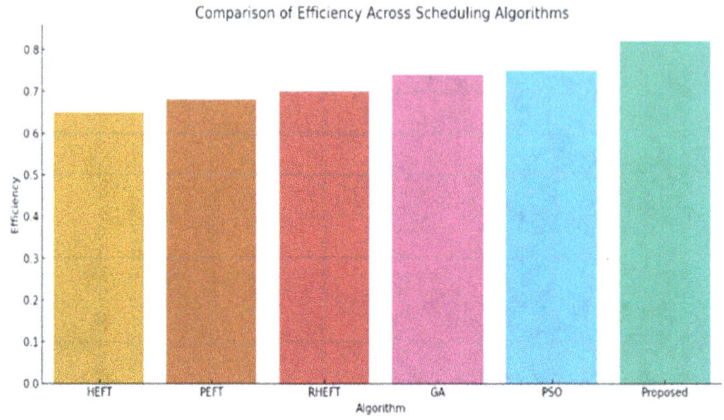

The speedups presented in figure 6 show the effectiveness of the different scheduling algorithms in parallelizing the execution of work-flows. The proposed approach is associated with a speedup value equal to 6.0, which implies that the implementation performance of execution in distributed tasks among numerous virtual machines has been significantly enhanced. Comparatively, the traditional methods such as HEFT and PEFT afford lesser speedups of 4.5 and 4.7 respectively, implying inadequate task parallelism. RHEFT, GA, and PSO have shown increasing progress with speedups of 4.9, 5.2, and 5.4, but they are not as large as achieved by the proposed strategy. This high performance can be largely attributed to dynamic heuristic selection and critical path sensitive task scheduling which limit execution bottlenecks and increase task concurrency. Therefore, the offered approach becomes more valuable to utilize parallel computer resources within a cloud environment.

Figure 6. Comparison of Speedup

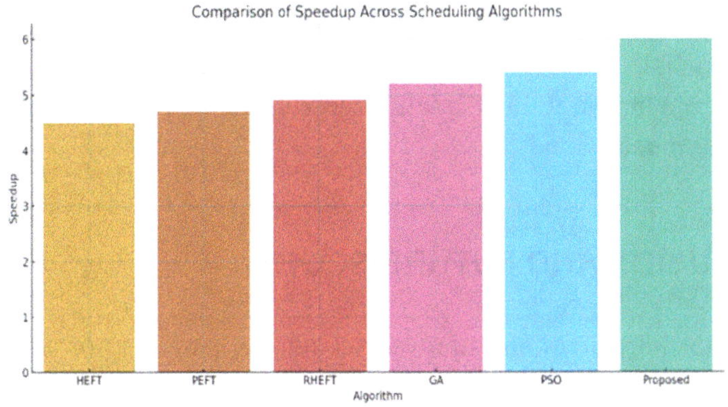

To assess the quality of the different workflow scheduling algorithms, Figure 7 shows the SLR of different workflow scheduling algorithms with a lower SLR indicating a schedule that is closer to critical path. The researched algorithm is capable of arranging the tasks to produce the minimal SLR of 1.0, proving the very close optimum task scheduling and minimal overhead. Slower techniques like HEFT and PEFT have larger SLRs of 1.3 and 1.25 correspondingly, demonstrating a bigger departure of the regular completion plan. It demonstrates that RHEFT, GA and PSO have progressive increments with an SLR of 1.2, 1.15 and 1.12, respectively. But they cannot compare with the optimality of the proposed method yet. This high performance is due to this critical-path-aware priority assignment and adaptive heuristic selection of the algorithm, which reduces idle time and inter-task delays as much as possible.

Figure 7. Comparison of SLR

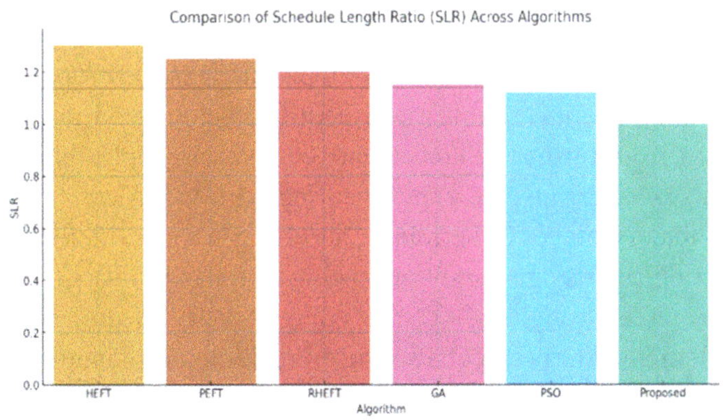

The results of these experimental runs have clearly proved that the proposed hybrid scheduling algorithm can not only be used to minimize the execution time or monetary cost, it can also be used to maximize parallel efficiency as well as to ensure a reasonable tradeoff between speed and resource usage. This qualifies it to be especially applicable to high-fidelity, large scale scientific workflows that are run on heterogeneous clouds.

5. CONCLUSION AND FUTURE SCOPE

The chapter introduces an improved scheduling paradigm of scientific workflows within cloud-based computing systems, satisfying the major requirements of these problems which include the resource heterogeneity, task dependencies, and the execution cost-versus-time trade-offs. The proposed approach evidences a significant increase in the efficiency of workflow execution as it incorporates an enhanced task prioritization mechanism built on the optimistic cost tables (OCTd and OCTu), the cost-conscious resource allocation model, selective task duplication strategy, and dynamic heuristic selector. The efficacy of the proposed methodology is made validated by an extended series of simulations with the SIPHT workflow and the WorkflowSim environment. Comparative outputs with that of state-of-the-art algorithms, such as HEFT, PEFT, RHEFT, GA, and PSO demonstrate that the developed approach obtains significant makespan and total cost improvements and that speedup and efficiency are significantly higher, and the SLR increases. These results validate the method in being able to scale and perform in a wide range of workflow scales and resource conditions with improved scalability and economic performance. Future work can concentrate on analysing the proposed approach in other workflow types in addition to SIPHT such as Montage, CyberShake to test generalizability. The decision of scheduling also could be made compatible with sustainable cloud computing practices by expanding the cost model to include energy consumption and carbon footprint.

Though very promising results have been produced in the proposed scheduling scheme to optimize scientific workflow execution in cloud environments, this area can still benefit from further enhancements concerning applicability and robustness. Future work could involve experimenting with workflows from real-world environments like Montage, CyberShake, and Epigenomics, thereby allowing the proposed solution and design paradigm to be generalized to various scientific domains. Another research angle includes the energy-aware scheduling models, which solve the problem from the perspective of sustainable cloud computing, where power consumption and or carbon footprint would be optimized parameters alongside cost and time. DHS can expand by using machine learning models to predict optimal strategies based on past data and workflow characteristics and, therefore, improve the adaptability; fault tolerance must be incorporated to guarantee reliability during real-time executions. Building upon or even deploying along hybrid or multi-cloud environments could be other avenues for future developments, so inter-cloud data movement, pricing variability, and compliance aspects are keyed-in alongside efficiency, scalability, and eco-efficiency.

REFERENCES

Abrishami, S., Zandi, F. M., & Nourbakhsh, A. (2025). Workflow as a Service Broker in Cloud Environment: A Systematic Literature Review. arXiv preprint arXiv:2501.12672.

Ahmad, W., & Alam, B. (2020, September). An efficient list scheduling algorithm with task duplication for scientific big data workflow in heterogeneous computing environments. *Concurrency and Computation*, *33*(5). Advance online publication. DOI: 10.1002/cpe.5987

Ahmad, Z.. (2021, January). Scientific Workflows Management and Scheduling in Cloud Computing: Taxonomy, Prospects, and challenges. *IEEE Access: Practical Innovations, Open Solutions*, *9*, 53491–53508. DOI: 10.1109/access.2021.3070785

Ahmed, S., & Omara, F. (2022, October). An enhanced workflow scheduling algorithm for cloud computing environment. *International Journal of Intelligent Engineering and Systems*, *15*(6), 627–646. DOI: 10.22266/ijies2022.1231.56

Al-Arasi, R., & Saif, A. (2020, January). Task scheduling in cloud computing based on metaheuristic techniques: A review paper. *EAI Endorsed Transactions on Cloud Systems*, *6*(17), 162829. DOI: 10.4108/eai.13-7-2018.162829

Almutairi, L., & Aslam, S. M. (2023, January). "A novel energy and communication aware scheduling on green cloud computing," *Computers, Materials & Continua/ Computers. Materials & Continua (Print)*, *77*(3), 2791–2811. DOI: 10.32604/ cmc.2023.040268

Arabnejad, H., & Barbosa, J. G. (2014). A budget constrained scheduling algorithm for workflow applications. *Journal of Grid Computing*, *12*(1), 25–40. DOI: 10.1007/ s10723-013-9279-2

Chauhan, N., Kaur, N., Saini, K. S., Verma, S., Alabdulatif, A., Abu Khurma, R., Garcia Arenas, M., & Castillo, P. A. (2024). A systematic literature review on task allocation and performance management techniques in cloud data center. arXiv.

Chen, G., Qi, J., Sun, Y., Hu, X., Dong, Z., & Sun, Y. (2022, November). A collaborative scheduling method for cloud computing heterogeneous workflows based on deep reinforcement learning. *Future Generation Computer Systems*, *141*, 284–297. DOI: 10.1016/j.future.2022.11.032

Coleman, T., Casanova, H., Pottier, L., Kaushik, M., Deelman, E., & Da Silva, R. F. (2021, October). WfCommons: A framework for enabling scientific workflow research and development. *Future Generation Computer Systems*, *128*, 16–27. DOI: 10.1016/j.future.2021.09.043

Dey, N. S., & Sangaraju, H. K. R. (2023). Hybrid Load Balancing Strategy for Cloud Data Centers with Novel Performance Evaluation Strategy. *International Journal of Intelligent Systems and Applications in Engineering*, *11*(3), 883–908. https://ijisae .org/index.php/IJISAE/article/view/3345

Dokeroglu, T., Kucukyilmaz, T., & Talbi, E.-G. (2023, December). Hyper-heuristics: A survey and taxonomy. *Computers & Industrial Engineering*, *187*, 109815. DOI: 10.1016/j.cie.2023.109815

Doostali, S., Babamir, S. M., & Eini, M. (2021, July). CP-PGWO: Multi-objective workflow scheduling for cloud computing using critical path. *Cluster Computing*, *24*(4), 3607–3627. DOI: 10.1007/s10586-021-03351-y

Fu, X., Sun, Y., Wang, H., & Li, H. (2021, May). Task scheduling of cloud computing based on hybrid particle swarm algorithm and genetic algorithm. *Cluster Computing*, *26*(5), 2479–2488. DOI: 10.1007/s10586-020-03221-z

Gawali, M. B., & Shinde, S. K. (2018, February). Task scheduling and resource allocation in cloud computing using a heuristic approach. *Journal of Cloud Computing Advances Systems and Applications*, *7*(1). Advance online publication. DOI: 10.1186/s13677-018-0105-8

Guo, H., Zhou, J., & Gu, H. (2022, July). Limited Duplication-Based list scheduling Algorithm for heterogeneous computing system. *Micromachines*, *13*(7), 1067. DOI: 10.3390/mi13071067 PMID: 35888884

Gupta, S.. (2022, August). Efficient Prioritization and processor selection schemes for HEFT algorithm: A Makespan optimizer for task scheduling in cloud environment. *Electronics (Basel)*, *11*(16), 2557. DOI: 10.3390/electronics11162557

He, K., Meng, X., Pan, Z., Yuan, L., & Zhou, P. (2018, June). A novel Task-Duplication based clustering algorithm for heterogeneous computing environments. *IEEE Transactions on Parallel and Distributed Systems*, *30*(1), 2–14. DOI: 10.1109/ tpds.2018.2851221

Jayanetti, A., Halgamuge, S., & Buyya, R. (2024). Reinforcement Learning based workflow scheduling in cloud and edge computing environments: A taxonomy, review and future directions. arXiv.

Kadhim, Q. K., Yusof, R., Mahdi, H. S., Al-Shami, S. S. A., & Selamat, S. R. (2018, May). A review study on cloud computing issues. *Journal of Physics: Conference Series*, *1018*, 012006. DOI: 10.1088/1742-6596/1018/1/012006

Kelefouras, V., & Djemame, K. (2022, May). Workflow simulation and multi-threading aware task scheduling for heterogeneous computing. *Journal of Parallel and Distributed Computing*, *168*, 17–32. DOI: 10.1016/j.jpdc.2022.05.011

Khan, Z. A., Aziz, I. A., Osman, N. A. B., & Ullah, I. (2023, January). A review on task scheduling techniques in cloud and Fog computing: Taxonomy, tools, open issues, challenges, and future directions. *IEEE Access: Practical Innovations, Open Solutions*, *11*, 143417–143445. DOI: 10.1109/access.2023.3343877

Kiran, B., Raghu, N., & Manjunatha, K. N. (2023). VLSI Implementation of a High-Speed Pipeline A/D Converter. In *Role of 6G Wireless Networks in AI and Blockchain-Based Applications* (pp. 112–130). IGI Global.

Li, L., Pan, W., Li, D., Liu, G., & Huang, T. (2023). "Task Scheduling Based on Heterogeneous Priority and Critical Task Duplication," *International Conference on Computer Engineering and Intelligent Control*, pp. 1–9, doi: DOI: 10.1109/icceic60201.2023.10426638

Liu, J., Lu, S., & Che, D. (2020). "A Survey of Modern Scientific Workflow Scheduling Algorithms and Systems in the Era of Big Data," *IEEE International Conference on Services Computing*, pp. 132–141, doi: DOI: 10.1109/scc49832.2020.00026

Ludäscher, B., Bowers, S., & McPhillips, T. (2018). "Scientific workflows," in *Encyclopedia of Database Systems*, pp. 3320–3324. doi: DOI: 10.1007/978-1-4614-8265-9_1471

Malawski, M., Figiela, K., Gajek, A., & Bubak, M. (2015). Scheduling scientific workflows with budget and deadline constraints using genetic algorithms. *Scientific Programming*, *2015*, 1–13. DOI: 10.1155/2015/847925

Mikram, H., Kafhali, S. E., & Saadi, Y. (2023, November). HEPGA: A new effective hybrid algorithm for scientific workflow scheduling in cloud computing environment. *Simulation Modelling Practice and Theory*, *130*, 102864. DOI: 10.1016/j.simpat.2023.102864

Nwogbaga, N. E., Latip, R., Affendey, L. S., & Rahiman, A. R. A. (2022, June). Attribute reduction-based scheduling algorithm with enhanced hybrid genetic algorithm and particle swarm optimization for optimal device selection. *Journal of Cloud Computing Advances Systems and Applications*, *11*(1). Advance online publication. DOI: 10.1186/s13677-022-00288-4

Pandey, S., Wu, L., Guru, S. M., & Buyya, R. (2010). A particle swarm optimization-based heuristic for scheduling workflow applications in cloud computing environments. *Proceedings of the 2010 24th IEEE International Conference on Advanced Information Networking and Applications*, 400–407. https://doi.org/DOI: 10.1109/AINA.2010.31

Raghu, N., & Ranjith Bhat, P. Rajashree Nambiar, Ganesh Srinivasa Shetty, and Anil Kumar DB. (2025). "Blockchain-enhanced GAN image encryption scheme for cloud computing." In *Intelligent Systems and IoT Applications in Clinical Health*, pp. 367-392. IGI Global.

Raghu, N., & Rupali, A. Mahajan, A. Sivanantham, Lakshay Bareja, N. K. Rayaguru, and Reddy Ganesh. (2024). "Optimizing Real-Time Process Control through Cloud-Based Automation and Big Data Analysis." In *2024 15th International Conference on Computing Communication and Networking Technologies (ICCCNT)*, pp. 1-6. IEEE.

Rodriguez, M. A., & Buyya, R. (2014). Deadline based resource provisioning and scheduling algorithm for scientific workflows on clouds. *IEEE Transactions on Cloud Computing*, *2*(2), 222–235. DOI: 10.1109/TCC.2014.2314655

Roy, R. B., Patel, T., Gadepally, V., & Tiwari, D. (2022). Mashup. *Association for Computing Machinery*, (Mar). Advance online publication. DOI: 10.1145/3503221.3508407

S. S and N. K. Patil. (2022, April). Hybrid Genetic Algorithm and Modified-Particle Swarm Optimization Algorithm (GA-MPSO) for predicting scheduling virtual machines in educational cloud platforms [iJET]. *International Journal of Emerging Technologies in Learning*, *17*(07), 208–225. DOI: 10.3991/ijet.v17i07.29223

Sadeeq, M. M., Abdulkareem, N. M., Zeebaree, S. R. M., Ahmed, D. M., Sami, A. S., & Zebari, R. R. (2021, March). IoT and Cloud Computing Issues, Challenges and Opportunities: A Review. *Qubahan Academic Journal*, *1*(2), 1–7. DOI: 10.48161/qaj.v1n2a36

Samadi, Y., Zbakh, M., & Tadonki, C. (2018). "E-HEFT: Enhancement Heterogeneous Earliest Finish Time algorithm for Task Scheduling based on Load Balancing in Cloud Computing," *International Conference on High Performance Computing & Simulation (HPCS)*, pp. 601–609, Jul. 2018, doi: DOI: 10.1109/hpcs.2018.00100

Sarkar, S., Mittal, S., Garg, S., & Sahu, A. (2025). Scientific workflow scheduling in cloud considering cold start and variable pricing model. arXiv.

Shao, K., Fu, H., & Wang, B. (2023, August). An efficient combination of genetic algorithm and particle swarm optimization for scheduling Data-Intensive tasks in heterogeneous cloud computing. *Electronics (Basel), 12*(16), 3450. DOI: 10.3390/electronics12163450

Shetty, G. S., & Raghu, N. (2024). Strategies for Achieving Energy Efficiency and Data Security Through Data Aggregation in IoT Healthcare Applications: A Comprehensive Study.

Shi, L.. (2021, January). Multijob associated task scheduling for cloud computing based on task duplication and insertion. *Wireless Communications and Mobile Computing, 2021*(1). Advance online publication. DOI: 10.1155/2021/6631752

Shirvani, M. H., & Talouki, R. N. (2021, August). A novel hybrid heuristic-based list scheduling algorithm in heterogeneous cloud computing environment for makespan optimization. *Parallel Computing, 108*, 102828. DOI: 10.1016/j.parco.2021.102828

Singh, J., & Walia, N. K. (2023, January). A comprehensive review of cloud Computing Virtual machine Consolidation. *IEEE Access: Practical Innovations, Open Solutions, 11*, 106190–106209. DOI: 10.1109/access.2023.3314613

Singh, R. K., Raichura, H., Malhotra, A., & Kalra, H. (2025). N. Raghu, and Garima. "Optimizing data service with innovative model for multi-cloud driven storage platform.". *International Journal of System Assurance Engineering and Management*, •••, 1–10.

Tang, X. (2021, February). Reliability-Aware Cost-Efficient Scientific Workflows Scheduling Strategy on Multi-Cloud systems. *IEEE Transactions on Cloud Computing, 10*(4), 2909–2919. DOI: 10.1109/tcc.2021.3057422

Topcuoglu, H., Hariri, S., & Wu, M.-Y. (2002). Performance-effective and low-complexity task scheduling for heterogeneous computing. *IEEE Transactions on Parallel and Distributed Systems, 13*(3), 260–274. DOI: 10.1109/71.993206

Yao, F., Pu, C., & Zhang, Z. (2021, January). Task Duplication-Based scheduling algorithm for Budget-Constrained workflows in cloud computing. *IEEE Access: Practical Innovations, Open Solutions, 9*, 37262–37272. DOI: 10.1109/access.2021.3063456

Yu, J., & Buyya, R. (2005). A taxonomy of workflow management systems for grid computing. *Journal of Grid Computing, 3*(3–4), 171–200. DOI: 10.1007/s10723-005-9010-8

Zhao, Y., & Sakellariou, R. (2006). Scheduling multiple workflows on the grid: Towards optimization of make-span and reliability. *Proceedings of the IEEE International Symposium on Parallel and Distributed Processing*, 8 pages. https://doi.org/DOI: 10.1109/IPDPS.2006.1639448

Chapter 2
A Resilient Framework for IoT:
Integrating AI and Blockchain for Enhanced Security

Muneer Khan
https://orcid.org/0000-0002-6586-4286
Cadre Techn Labs, USA

Mohd Vaseem Khan
BIET Lucknow, India

Ashish Awasthi
BIET Lucknow, India

ABSTRACT

The Internet of Things (IoT) is pivotal in modern technologies, transforming industries by enhancing connectivity, efficiency, and real-time data exchange. However, the widespread interconnection of devices also introduces significant vulnerabilities, exposing systems to cyber threats such as malware attacks, unauthorized access, and data breaches that can disrupt operations and cause financial losses. Traditional security measures often struggle to keep pace with the dynamic and distributed nature of IoT networks. Integrating artificial intelligence (AI) and blockchain offers a promising solution. AI enables real-time monitoring, anomaly detection, and proactive threat response, while blockchain ensures data integrity and trust through its decentralized and immutable ledger. Together, these technologies create a multi-layered security framework that strengthens IoT systems and fosters transparency and accountability. This chapter explores the synergies between AI, blockchain, and IoT, highlighting their transformative potential in securing connected environments.

DOI: 10.4018/979-8-3373-7503-8.ch002

1. INTRODUCTION

1.1 Overview of Smart Factories

Smart factories are an example of how traditional manufacturing has developed into highly automated, networked, and flexible production settings. These factories enhance operations to achieve more productivity, flexibility, and efficiency by utilizing technology such as cloud computing, robotics, artificial intelligence (AI), and the Internet of Things (IoT). While robotics and autonomous systems minimize human participation, improving precision and reducing errors, interconnectivity allows smooth communication between devices and systems (Mohamed, N. (2025)). Factories can process enormous volumes of data in real time thanks to advanced analytics and AI-driven decision-making, which guarantees flexible responses to production demands. However, there are serious cybersecurity threats associated with the dependence on digital and networked technologies. IoT devices are vulnerable to unwanted access because they are frequently built with inadequate security, and fraudsters find the vast amounts of data created and sent in these settings to be a profitable target. Production line disruptions brought on by cyberattacks can cause monetary losses and damage to one's reputation, and maintaining security across several systems can be complicated. Smart factories are rapidly incorporating blockchain and artificial intelligence (AI) technology to address these issues. AI enables systems to recognize abnormalities before they become more serious and to detect and eliminate threats in real time.(Arpteg, A. et al., 2018).) Blockchain, on the other hand, creates a decentralized, impenetrable network while guaranteeing data transparency and integrity. When combined, these technologies offer a strong basis for improving smart factory cybersecurity and protecting industrial processes from changing threats.

1.2 Importance of Cybersecurity in Industrial Robotics

Modern production now relies heavily on industrial robotics to automate repetitive activities, improve precision, and greatly increase efficiency. In smart factories, where networks and connected devices enable smooth and effective manufacturing processes, these technologies are essential to operation. However, industrial robotics are also becoming more vulnerable to various cyber-attacks as they depend more and more on digital systems and IoT connectivity. The significance of cybersecurity in safeguarding these advanced technologies and guaranteeing the secure and effective operation of manufacturing processes is highlighted by this vulnerability. The requirement to avoid operational disruptions is one of the main justifications for strong cybersecurity in industrial robotics. Production lines can be stopped by cyberattacks like ransomware, denial-of-service (DoS) assaults, or malware infiltrations, which can result in large financial losses, postponed delivery dates, and possible harm to one's reputation. Any disruption brought on by a cyber event can have a domino effect on the entire supply chain because modern industrial systems frequently operate on strict deadlines and lean production methods.

Intellectual property protection is another important consideration. Sensitive jobs based on secret designs, manufacturing processes, or algorithms that give the company a competitive edge are commonly assigned to industrial robots. This priceless intellectual property may be stolen as a result of a cyberattack, providing rivals or bad actors access to vital trade secrets. To protect these resources and keep a business's competitive edge, robust cybersecurity procedures are necessary. Another top priority when it comes to cybersecurity in industrial robotics is safety. Robotic systems engage with the actual world, in contrast to standard IT systems that mostly deal with data. A hacked robotic system may malfunction, resulting in production flaws, equipment damage, or even mishaps that jeopardize worker safety. (Al-Rakhami, M. S et al., 2022)) By guaranteeing that robotic systems function as intended, free from malevolent influence or unlawful manipulation, cybersecurity helps avoid such situations. Besides, strong cybersecurity promotes confidence among all parties involved, including partners, customers, and authorities. Businesses who prioritize and integrate robust cybersecurity measures in their industrial robotics show a dedication to dependability, safety, and industry standards compliance in a time when data breaches and cyber incidents are becoming more frequent. This reduces legal and regulatory risks related to data breaches or operational failures while also improving the organization's reputation. Moreover, the function of cybersecurity goes beyond providing immediate protection to guaranteeing long-term resilience as cyber threats become more sophisticated. Organizations may create a strong defence against both present and new threats by putting modern security measures in place, such as blockchain for secure data integrity and artificial intelligence for real-time threat detection. This guarantees that industrial robots systems will continue to provide a dependable foundation for future smart factories.

1.3 Emerging Cyber Threats in Autonomous Systems

Autonomous systems have quickly become popular in sectors including manufacturing, transportation, and healthcare, bringing with them previously unheard-of capabilities and efficiencies. Their dependence on IoT networks, linked devices, and AI-powered algorithms, however, also leaves them vulnerable to a variety of advanced cyberthreats. These systems are especially vulnerable to attacks that take advantage of their autonomy, interconnectedness, and data dependence since they are made to function with little human supervision. Cyber threats that target autonomous systems are changing quickly, posing serious problems for their dependability and security. Data manipulation attacks, in which the attacker modifies the data that autonomous systems use to make decisions, are one of the main risks. In order to sense their surroundings and make modifications in real time, autonomous systems rely significantly on sensors, cameras, and Internet of Things devices. The system may be misled and make poor conclusions as a result of malicious actors manipulating this data.(S. Latif et al., 2021)) In a smart factory, for example, hacked sensor data could result in malfunctioning manufacturing processes or even harm equipment by creating fictitious operating settings. Ransomware that targets operational systems poses a serious risk as well. In this type of malware, attackers encrypt vital control networks and demand a payment to unlock them. In settings like smart factories, where production lines rely on autonomous systems to run smoothly, these attacks are very disruptive. A ransomware assault has the potential to completely stop operations, causing monetary losses, postponed delivery, and harm to one's reputation.

An emerging threat is adversarial AI assaults, which use hostile, minor changes to input data to trick AI algorithms. For instance, an autonomous system may misread its environment if a picture or sensor reading is slightly altered. Such hostile inputs may result in crashes, productivity errors, or safety problems in industrial robotics. These assaults underscore the need for more reliable and resilient AI systems by taking advantage of flaws in machine learning models. As attackers try to take control of autonomous systems by taking advantage of antiquated software or lax authentication procedures, unauthorized access and privilege escalation present new difficulties.(Bai, Q. et al., 2020)) Once inside, they have the ability to increase their privileges in order to insert malware, alter system operations, or retrieve private information. For autonomous systems operating in industrial settings, where such access may jeopardize safety or interfere with vital processes, this is especially risky. These new dangers highlight how urgently sophisticated cybersecurity solutions that are adapted to the particular weaknesses of autonomous systems are needed. To protect these systems from a constantly changing threat landscape, solutions like blockchain for secure data integrity, real-time AI-driven threat detection, and improved access control mechanisms are crucial.

2. FOUNDATIONS OF INDUSTRIAL ROBOTICS

2.1 Evolution of Robotics in Manufacturing

Higher efficiency, accuracy, and scalability have been made possible by the development of robotics in production, which has completely changed the industrial landscape. Robots have evolved from being used for monotonous chores to becoming intelligent, adaptable systems that are now essential in contemporary industry. With the introduction of programmable robotic arms intended to carry out basic, repetitive operations like welding and material handling, this trip got underway in the middle of the 20th century. Despite their limited capabilities, these early robots were groundbreaking in that they increased production rates while replacing human labour in repetitive and dangerous tasks. A major advancement was made in the 1970s with the advent of computer numerical control (CNC), which enabled robots to do increasingly difficult jobs with increased accuracy. Robotics skills were significantly improved during the 1980s and 1990s thanks to developments in sensors and microprocessors that allowed for real-time monitoring and feedback. Now that they could adjust to slight changes in the manufacturing environment, robots might be used for a wider variety of tasks.

A new era of intelligent robots was brought about by the 21st century's merger of machine learning and artificial intelligence (AI). These systems may now assess data, learn from their surroundings, and make decisions on their own instead of being restricted to preprogrammed tasks. Robots may already work alongside people in shared workspaces because to advancements in algorithms, vision systems, and Internet of Things connectivity. In order to increase efficiency and safety in hybrid work situations, these collaborative robots, are made to supplement human abilities rather than replace them. At the forefront of Industry 4.0, where innovation is driven by cloud computing, big data analytics, and networked systems, is robotics in production today. These days, robots play a crucial role in smart manufacturing, handling intricate assembly, quality control, and predictive maintenance. Another area where robots has advanced significantly is additive manufacturing, also known as 3D printing, which allows for on-demand production and quick prototyping. (Bhushan, B., & Sahoo, A. K. (2021)) Emerging technologies like blockchain, edge AI, and quantum computing have the potential to dramatically transform manufacturing processes as robotics continues to advance. These developments are expected to increase the intelligence, security, and efficiency of robots, guaranteeing their continuous use as a mainstay of the manufacturing sector for many years to come.

2.2 Components of Industrial Robotics Systems

Advanced devices called industrial robotics systems are made to automate and streamline production procedures. These systems are made up of different parts that function as a whole to carry out repetitive, intricate, and accurate activities. Every part is essential to guaranteeing the robot's accuracy, performance, and suitability for a range of industrial applications. The most noticeable part is the manipulator, which frequently resembles a human arm. It is made up of several joints and connections that enable the robot to move and engage with its surroundings. The manipulator is the key component for carrying out operations like welding, assembling, and material handling since its design dictates its range of motion, flexibility, and reach. The manipulator's end-effector serves as an instrument or interface with the outside world. The end-effector may be a suction cup, welding torch, gripper, or specialized instrument, depending on the need. The robot's capacity to carry out particular duties accurately and effectively is directly impacted by its functionality and design. The movement of the robot is controlled by the actuators. Depending on the necessary force, speed, and accuracy, these can be electric motors, hydraulic systems, or pneumatic systems. The robot's adaptability in industrial applications is ensured by its actuators, which allow it to accomplish tasks ranging from heavy lifting to delicate assembly. The control system coordinates all movements and functions, acting as the brain of the robot. It is made up of processors, memory, and software algorithms that handle real-time modifications, process input data, and carry out preprogrammed commands. Artificial intelligence and machine learning are frequently included into contemporary control systems, allowing robots to adjust to changing conditions and function at their best. Sensors are essential for giving information about the internal condition and surroundings of the robot. These comprise, among other things, temperature sensors, force/torque sensors, vision systems, and proximity sensors. By preventing collisions with people or other things, sensors enable the robot to recognize objects, keep an eye on its own performance, and guarantee safety in cooperative environments. (Cai, Z., & Zhu, J., 2016). The energy needed to run the robot is supplied by the power source. This could be hydraulic power, electrical power, or a combination of both, depending on the design. To sustain continuous operations, the power system must guarantee steady and dependable energy delivery. The fundamental foundation that unifies all the parts and makes programming, simulation, and monitoring possible is robotic software. By evaluating performance data, sophisticated software systems enable users to establish tasks, visualize workflows, and carry out predictive maintenance. Even for non-expert users, these tools increase the accessibility and versatility of industrial robots.

2.3 The Role of IoT in Smart Factories

The rise of smart factories has made the Internet of Things (IoT) a key technology, transforming the production environment by facilitating smooth communication between systems, devices, and machines. IoT enables real-time data transmission by linking different manufacturing components to a central network, which helps manufacturers optimize workflows, boost productivity, and improve decision-making. Monitoring, controlling, and optimizing output is drastically changed by the incorporation of IoT into smart factories. Enabling real-time monitoring and control is one of the IoT's primary functions in smart factories. IoT enables manufacturers to monitor ambient conditions, production metrics, and equipment performance in real time by deploying sensors and linked devices. Machine sensors, for instance, can track vibration, temperature, and pressure, providing information that can be used to anticipate possible faults before they happen. This lowers downtime and avoids expensive equipment breakdowns by assisting manufacturers with predictive maintenance. Continuous system monitoring guarantees that any irregularities or inefficiencies may be found and fixed right away, resulting in more efficient operations and less waste. In smart factories, IoT is also essential to inventory management. Manufacturers can trace raw materials, parts, and completed goods with great accuracy by incorporating sensors and RFID technology into the supply chain. As a result, inventory levels are maximized, overstocking and stockouts are decreased, and production is never delayed because of material shortages. IoT-powered automated inventory management systems can dynamically modify supply orders in response to real-time data, enhancing material flow and cutting down on unnecessary inventory expenses.

IoT gives manufacturers access to enormous volumes of operational data, which facilitates data-driven decision-making. This data may be compiled, examined, and turned into useful insights by using big data analytics and cloud computing. For instance, by examining defect trends across production lines, quality control procedures can be improved and production schedules can be modified to accommodate changing demand. Energy optimization is also made possible by IoT-powered analytics, which track energy usage in real time, spot waste, and recommend more economical energy use methods. This supports sustainability objectives in addition to lowering operating expenses.(Bhushan, B., & Sahoo, A. K. (2021)) Facilitating autonomous operations is another important advantage of IoT in smart industries. Machines can interact with one another and make decisions on their own when systems are connected. Automated material handling systems, for example, can use real-time data to reroute items on the manufacturing line, change machine settings, or reorder supplies. Productivity rises with this degree of autonomy because robots can run constantly with little human supervision. Additionally, IoT makes it possible to incorporate robots and other automated systems into the manufacturing process, promoting collaborative robotics, which collaborate with human operators to carry out difficult jobs in a safe and effective manner.IoT enhances supply chain visibility by offering end-to-end tracking from the procurement of raw materials to the delivery of finished goods. Manufacturers may guarantee that goods are delivered on schedule and in ideal condition by using GPS tracking and connected devices to track shipment status, anticipate delays, and plan delivery routes. In addition to improving customer happiness, this strengthens the supply chain's ability to adjust to demand changes or disruptions.

Figure 1. The Role of IoT in Smart Factories

2.4 Security Challenges in Industrial Robotics

The necessity of protecting these systems from cyberattacks has increased dramatically as industrial robotics are incorporated more and more into manufacturing processes. Nowadays, industrial robots are part of a complex network on the factory floor that is connected to other equipment, Internet of Things devices, and control systems. Even though this interconnection promotes increased productivity, adaptability, and automation, it also introduces a number of security flaws that must be fixed to preserve sensitive data, secure production systems, and guarantee worker safety.Cyberattack susceptibility is one of the main security issues facing industrial robots. Industrial robots are possible points of entry for attackers since they are frequently linked to bigger control networks. Hackers can obtain illegal access and take over robotic systems by taking advantage of flaws in the robot's firmware, software, or communication protocols. Once penetrated, these robots can be used to do malevolent tasks including stopping manufacturing lines, damaging machinery, or changing the quality of products. Common attack techniques that can halt manufacturing activities and cause monetary losses, operational outages, and reputational harm include ransomware, malware injection, and Denial of Service (DoS) attacks.

The absence of security guidelines and procedures for industrial robots is a serious additional worry. Due to their isolation from wider networks, many robots were initially built with few cybersecurity safeguards. Robots, however, frequently work in settings where current cybersecurity protections might not be sufficient due to their increased integration with IoT devices (M. Khan and A. Tripathi, (2018)). It is challenging to put complete defense plans into place since different production facilities have different security environments due to the lack of standardized standards for protecting industrial robots.(Al-Rakhami, M. S. et al., 2022)) Furthermore, a large number of still-in-use legacy robotic systems have antiquated security features that make them vulnerable to contemporary cyberattacks. Security is additionally hampered by the complexity and diversity of robotic systems. There are several types of industrial robots, ranging from autonomous mobile robots to articulated robotic arms, and each has a unique software architecture and communication protocol. It is challenging to provide uniform security across these disparate systems since different robot types can need different security protocols. Additionally, manufacturers frequently use robots from several providers, each of whom has a unique set of security flaws. This disjointed environment raises the possibility of security flaws, where a single system or component attack could jeopardize the entire production process.

Since robots are commonly used to gather and analyse sensitive data, including intellectual property, production data, and proprietary designs, data security is yet another crucial issue in industrial robotics. Malicious actors may intercept or steal this important data if a robot's data storage or transmission methods are not adequately secured. An increasing number of people are concerned about industrial espionage, which occurs when rivals or hackers obtain key manufacturing data without authorization. The increasing usage of cloud computing, where robots frequently send data to distant computers for processing and monitoring, increases the risk of data breaches. Although this offers scalability and efficiency, it also raises the possibility of illegal data access or leakage. One constant concern is the safety of employees around industrial robots. Industrial robots increase operational efficiency, but if they are compromised, they may also pose physical risks. A hacker in control of a robot might alter its behaviour and make it move erratically, which could lead to mishaps or harm to human workers in the area. Strong cybersecurity and strict safety procedures, including real-time monitoring, emergency stop mechanisms, and safe human-robot interaction designs, are necessary to ensure the safe functioning of robots in collaborative work environments. Industrial robot security is further complicated by supply chain and vendor threats. Robots are frequently a part of a larger ecosystem that also consists of external elements including software, sensors, and communication networks. The total security of the robotic system depends on the safety of these parts. Attackers may gain access through flaws in third-party hardware or software. Because different vendors' security policies might range greatly, manufacturers may also have trouble making sure their suppliers adhere to best practices for security.

3. UNDERSTANDING ARTIFICIAL INTELLIGENCE IN INDUSTRIAL SYSTEMS

3.1 AI Algorithms for Autonomous Robotics

The development of autonomous robotics has been largely fuelled by artificial intelligence (AI), which allows these systems to operate effectively and autonomously in a variety of industrial settings. Without continual human assistance, robots can use AI algorithms to process complicated data from their environment, make decisions in real time, learn from mistakes, and adjust to changing circumstances. These algorithms increase the efficiency and accuracy of manufacturing and other industrial processes by enabling robots to observe, plan, and carry out tasks autonomously. To enable autonomous robotics to perform these tasks, a number of AI approaches are essential, each of which contributes in a unique way to the robot's increased capabilities.In autonomous robotics, machine learning (ML), and more specifically deep learning (DL), is one of the most popular AI approaches. Deep learning analyses massive datasets, including photos, sensor data, and video streams, using sophisticated neural network structures, such as Convolutional Neural Networks (CNNs). Robots can execute jobs like object recognition, quality control, and anomaly detection thanks to these algorithms, which allow them to recognize patterns and features in data. Deep learning, for instance, can be used in automated inspection systems in manufacturing, where robots visually examine components for flaws or inconsistencies.(Chang, S. E., & Chen, Y. C. (2020)) Without ongoing retraining or human supervision, these algorithms enable the robots to learn from each inspection, thereby increasing their accuracy in identifying defective products.

Reinforcement Learning (RL), another potent AI technology, enables robots to make decisions by using a system of incentives and punishments. Through interaction with their surroundings, RL enables robots to learn by making mistakes and gradually improving their decision-making process. Robots get feedback while they perform, either in the form of rewards or penalties, which helps them adjust their behaviour to best achieve their long-term objectives. Reinforcement learning is especially useful in industrial settings for jobs that require robots to respond to changing situations, including adjusting to unforeseen impediments or modifications in production schedules. Reinforcement learning, for instance, might be used by a robot in an assembly line to modify its motions in response to feedback, increasing productivity and lowering errors as it gains knowledge from past actions. The robot becomes more independent and efficient in a wide range of tasks by continuously interacting with its surroundings and learning how to perform best in various situations.An other essential AI algorithm that is crucial to autonomous robotics is computer vision. Robots can see and comprehend their surroundings thanks to its ability to analyse visual information from cameras, sensors, and other imaging equipment. For activities like object handling, quality inspection, and navigation, computer vision is crucial because it enables robots to identify, recognize, and handle objects. Computer vision enables robots to carry out intricate tasks in industrial robotics, like visual part inspection, which guarantees product quality by spotting flaws or irregularities. For instance, computer vision-equipped robots on a production line can check parts for dents, scratches, or incorrect assembly. Real-time image analysis allows these robots to decide whether to accept, reject, or fix the things. Robots can analyse visual input quickly thanks to computer vision algorithms like CNNs, which also allow them to accurately identify objects or defects even in dynamic surroundings. Furthermore, by allowing robots to map their surroundings, avoid obstructions, and create routes across intricate or crowded areas, computer vision facilitates autonomous navigation.Planning a Path and Making Decisions The ability of autonomous robots to navigate and carry out tasks effectively depends on algorithms. Finding the best path for a robot to take while avoiding obstacles and maximizing its motions is known as path planning. Robots frequently have to manoeuvre through intricate spaces in industrial settings, including warehouses or factory floors, where they must dodge other robots, people, and equipment. Robots can determine the optimal course based on their surroundings and work needs thanks to AI algorithms like A search* and Rapidly-exploring Random Trees (RRT). To choose the best path for the robot to finish its goal, these algorithms consider variables including obstructions, task priority, and resource availability.

3.2 Machine Learning for Threat Detection

In the field of cybersecurity, machine learning (ML) has become a potent instrument, especially for identifying threats in industrial systems like robotics, Internet of Things networks, and smart factories. Because cyber threats are always changing and interconnected systems are becoming more sophisticated, traditional rule-based security methods are no longer enough. By evaluating enormous volumes of data in real-time and spotting trends that can point to malicious activity or vulnerabilities, machine learning algorithms can offer dynamic and adaptive threat detection. Organizations can greatly improve their capacity to recognize and proactively address security threats by utilizing machine learning (ML) for threat detection.Machine learning's primary advantage in threat detection is its capacity to learn from data and adapt to new threats. Traditional security solutions are inadequate against emerging or complex dangers like advanced persistent threats (APTs) and zero-day exploits because they frequently rely on predetermined signatures or patterns of existing attacks. However, even if an attack has never been observed before, machine learning can identify abnormalities in behaviour or system activity that might point to one.

Unsupervised learning algorithms, such as K-means clustering or autoencoders, for example, can examine system logs or network data without being aware of particular attack patterns beforehand. The system can identify any deviations as possible dangers by comparing real-time data to baseline normal behaviour.

This makes it possible to identify anomalies early on, including odd traffic surges, illegal access attempts, or strange robotic activity, which may point to a system breach or attempted hack.(Visvizi, A., Troisi, O. (2022)) Because supervised learning algorithms categorize data using labelled examples of both benign and malevolent actions, they are also essential for threat detection. For example, past attack data, like malware signatures, phishing emails, or intrusion attempts, can be used to train a machine learning model. After training, the model can determine whether fresh incoming data—like network traffic or sensor data—is suspicious or safe.

Intrusion detection systems (IDS) leverage popular supervised learning techniques, including as decision trees, support vector machines (SVM), and random forests, to find known attack vectors or vulnerabilities based on data patterns. As fresh data is added, these models keep getting better, which keeps them effective against new threats. Using natural language processing (NLP) to examine textual data for indications of phishing attempts, social engineering, or other hostile communications is another noteworthy use of machine learning (ML) in threat detection. NLP algorithms can search for questionable language patterns or keywords that could point to fraud in emails, messages, or logs.

For instance, by identifying odd syntax, dubious URLs, or urgent language that is frequently connected to phishing attempts, machine learning may detect phishing emails. Additionally, by teaching the system to prioritize the most important threats and gradually lowering false positives, reinforcement learning (RL) can be used to optimize security responses. Neural networks and other deep learning techniques are being employed more and more for increasingly complex threat detection jobs. As is frequently the case with industrial robots or surveillance systems, these methods work particularly well for evaluating complicated, high-dimensional data, such as pictures, video streams, or multi-sensor data.

3.3 AI-Powered Predictive Maintenance in Robotics

Predictive maintenance driven by AI is essential for improving the cost-effectiveness and operational dependability of robotic systems in industrial settings. AI systems are able to identify even the slightest departures from typical operating circumstances by continuously gathering sensor data, including vibration, temperature, humidity, motor performance, and even sound. AI systems can forecast when a robot is likely to break down or need maintenance by examining this data. Because these forecasts are derived from past data, machine learning models, and real-time analytics, the system is able to spot patterns that human operators would not notice right away. The ability of predictive maintenance to handle maintenance schedule more comprehensively is what makes it unique. Conventional maintenance techniques sometimes depend on reactive strategies or set intervals, which can result in needless downtime or expensive repairs. AI-powered systems, on the other hand, only initiate maintenance when necessary, guaranteeing prompt and economical interventions. This predictive method optimizes the robots' whole lifecycle and reduces unscheduled downtime. Additionally, by correctly forecasting the condition of robotic systems, companies can prevent the costly fallout from catastrophic equipment breakdowns, guaranteeing more efficient operations.

Beyond financial savings, AI-driven predictive maintenance has long-term advantages. The efficiency and performance of robotic systems can be greatly enhanced by these systems. Businesses can minimize production schedule delays by replacing or repairing parts in advance when they are aware that a robot's components are approaching the end of their useful lives. Additionally, by regularly assessing the health of robots, AI systems can assist in identifying possible enhancements to operational efficiency, enabling companies to optimize performance and further cut down on material waste and energy usage. AI models can continuously enhance their predicting powers by learning from the enormous volumes of data that are gathered over time. As a result, forecasts become more accurate and trustworthy, giving businesses a clear picture of the condition of their robotic fleet. Robots may work at their best in a more flexible and robust production environment with highly targeted maintenance, which lowers operating costs and raises the overall return on investment (ROI) for robotic assets.

3.4 Real-Time Anomaly Detection and Response

Maintaining the security and operational integrity of industrial systems, especially in settings where robots, the Internet of Things, and automated machinery are used, requires real-time anomaly detection and response systems. The technology is able to quickly identify variations from typical behaviour, which may be a sign of cyber-attacks, system faults, or unauthorized access, by continuously monitoring the vast amounts of data produced by these systems. Sensor readings, operational logs, network traffic, and even external environmental elements may be included in the data being examined. All of these are continuously evaluated to find any unusual patterns that would indicate an abnormality.In order to improve the efficacy of real-time anomaly detection, machine learning techniques are essential. These algorithms are trained using past data to determine what constitutes "normal" system behaviour. After being taught, they are able to identify even the smallest anomalies, which could indicate possible dangers or malfunctions in operations. These anomalies include anomalous network traffic, abrupt increases in resource consumption, erratic motions of robotic arms, or inconsistent data flows. For example, a significant increase in a machine's temperature could signal an imminent mechanical failure, or a robot that starts acting strangely could be the victim of a cyberattack attempting to control its motions. Compared to traditional security, AI-based systems can assess these situations and detect them more quickly and accurately.(Dai, H. N. et al., 2019))

The system's real-time response mechanism kicks in when an anomaly is discovered. Automating this response can reduce the need for human intervention and allow for quick action to stop additional interruption or damage. To avoid more mistakes, a robotic system might, for instance, immediately switch to a safe mode or turn off the faulty component if an anomaly in its behaviour is noticed. Similar to this, the system can automatically isolate the impacted nodes, block dubious IP addresses, or reroute traffic in order to protect the infrastructure in the event of network-based threats like a DDoS attack or anomalous traffic spikes. This prompt action is essential to stopping malicious activity from proliferating and leading to more extensive system breakdowns.In order to reduce downtime and guarantee business continuity, anomaly detection and real-time response must be integrated. System outages can be expensive in terms of lost output, income, and reputation in industrial settings, particularly those that mostly rely on robots and automated procedures. Businesses can minimize the risk of catastrophic failures and expensive repair requirements by promptly detecting and resolving anomalies as soon as they arise. Because systems may continue to function normally even in the face of possible threats or disruptions, this proactive strategy not only increases the safety and efficiency of industrial systems but also improves overall operational resilience.The integrity of robotic infrastructure and industrial systems ultimately depends on real-time anomaly detection and response. In addition to identifying possible problems more quickly, companies can also take prompt action to eliminate hazards, minimize damage, and preserve peak operational performance by utilizing machine learning and artificial intelligence algorithms. This technology is essential to cybersecurity in the future because it helps businesses keep one step ahead of thieves and prevents the negative effects of taking too long to react to new threats.

4. BLOCKCHAIN TECHNOLOGY IN SMART FACTORIES

4.1 Introduction to Blockchain and Its Principles

After being first presented as the foundation for cryptocurrencies like Bitcoin, blockchain technology has quickly grown beyond financial uses to become a crucial component of safe and open data management across a range of sectors, including manufacturing. Fundamentally, blockchain is a distributed, decentralized ledger system that makes it possible to store data securely, irrevocably, and transparently across numerous nodes (or computers). Blockchain works through a network of participants that each possess a copy of the whole ledger, guaranteeing a degree of transparency and trust without the need for middlemen, in contrast to traditional centralized databases where data is owned by a single company.Blockchain's core tenets are security, transparency, immutability, and decentralization. Since the blockchain network is made up of numerous nodes, each with equal authority to verify and preserve the data, decentralization guarantees that there is no one point of control. This is essential in situations like smart factories, where various equipment and entities must work together safely without running the risk of central control being jeopardized. Immutability creates a permanent and verifiable record of transactions or occurrences because once data is entered into a blockchain, it cannot be removed or changed. This capability is especially helpful in industrial settings where data integrity is crucial, including identifying the origin of goods, keeping an eye on machine conditions, or making sure safety regulations are being followed.

Since everyone in the blockchain network can see the same version of the ledger, transparency is an essential feature that guarantees all transactions are accessible and auditable by all parties. This degree of transparency lowers the possibility of fraud, mistakes, or covert data manipulation—all of which are critical in intricate, multi-party settings like supply chains in smart factories. Blockchain security is accomplished by using cryptographic procedures, which guarantee that only individuals with permission can access or alter the data. Since a cryptographic hash connects each block in the blockchain to the one before it, it is practically impossible to change or tamper with the data after it has been added to the chain.Blockchain offers a number of benefits when it comes to smart factories. As assets, materials, and products pass through the production process, it makes it possible to track them securely and transparently.(Feng, X. et al., 2021)) The blockchain may be used to record every stage of the process, from sourcing raw materials to manufacture and delivery, creating an auditable and unchangeable record. This lowers the danger of counterfeiting, increases responsibility throughout the whole manufacturing cycle, improves supply chain efficiency, and ensures compliance with regulatory standards.Due to the lack of a single server or authority that could be attacked, blockchain's decentralized architecture lowers the danger of cyberattacks and data leaks. Blockchain can also help ensure that data shared across sensors, robots, and other connected devices is accurate, transparent, and safe. This can help machines and systems in an industrial Internet of things (IoT) environment exchange information securely. By providing improved security, traceability, and trust throughout the industrial ecosystem, blockchain technology has the potential to completely transform the way smart factories function.

4.2 Blockchain's Role in Data Integrity and Transparency

Blockchain technology is the perfect answer for industrial applications where precise and verifiable information is essential since it significantly improves data integrity and transparency in smart factories. Blockchain's fundamental strength is its decentralized architecture, which prevents any one institution or authority from controlling all of the data. Rather, it functions on a dispersed network of nodes, each of which keeps an exact duplicate of the blockchain. Every time a new transaction or piece of data is added, it is checked and confirmed by several network nodes.Since any change to the recorded data would require consensus from most of the network, this decentralized approach lowers the danger of fraud or data manipulation. Once the data is entered into the blockchain, it is nearly hard to tamper with it.Blockchain's openness facilitates the simplification of procedures such as regulatory standard compliance. For instance, blockchain guarantees that every stage of the production process is recorded and verified in sectors that demand rigorous adherence to safety and quality standards. This is especially crucial in industries like food production and pharmaceuticals, where it is necessary to track the origin of goods and follow safety procedures in order to demonstrate that they comply with legal standards. Blockchain makes this possible by offering an unchangeable, transparent ledger that auditors and regulators can readily access to verify compliance.

Figure 2. Blockchain's Role in Data Integrity

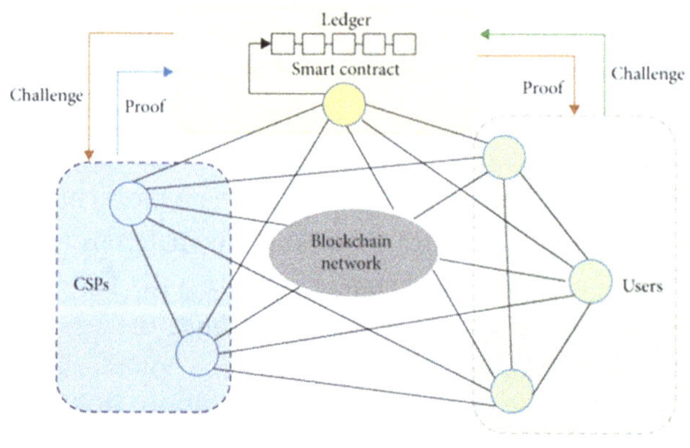

In the context of smart factories and the Industrial Internet of Things (IIoT), blockchain makes it possible to share data more securely. Blockchain guarantees that the data transferred between machines, robots, sensors, and other devices is precise, traceable, and impenetrable as these systems interact in real time. Since any data modification or corruption could have a significant impact on manufacturing processes or product quality, this is especially crucial in situations involving automation and autonomous decision-making. By offering a visible record that any authorized network user can independently verify, blockchain safeguards this data transaction.Effective operations, regulatory compliance, and fostering confidence with clients and other stakeholders all depend on the data in a smart factory ecosystem being reliable, secure, and verifiable, which is made possible by blockchain's role in data integrity and transparency. Blockchain technology facilitates industrial processes, improves accountability, and drastically lowers the risks of data loss or manipulation by offering an immutable, transparent, and decentralized ledger of all transactions and procedures.

One of the main characteristics of blockchain that guarantees data integrity is immutability. Data cannot be altered or removed once it has been entered into a block and connected to the blockchain. In smart factories, where the traceability of materials, components, and products is crucial, this offers a permanent, time-stamped record of all activities and transactions. For instance, the blockchain can be used to record the origin, quality, and certification of raw materials as they come onto the production line. This way, the information is guaranteed to be correct and unchangeable during the manufacturing process. Because of the unchangeable audit trail created by this degree of immutability, future audits and inspections can confidently confirm the history of every product and its constituent parts.Another important advantage of blockchain in industrial systems is transparency. Every transaction is instantly accessible to all authorized parties since each network participant has a copy of the blockchain. This transparency guarantees that all parties involved in the production process—manufacturers, suppliers, regulators, and consumers—can access and examine the same set of data in a smart factory. Because there is no proprietary or confidential information that could be distorted or disguised, this fosters a high degree of trust between the parties.

4.3 Decentralized Systems for Secure Robotics

For boosting the security, dependability, and autonomy of robotic systems in industrial settings, decentralized systems for safe robotics make use of distributed networks. Decentralized systems disperse data processing and decision-making among several nodes, in contrast to conventional centralized architectures, which handle control and data administration by a single central unit. To ensure that there isn't a single point of failure, each node in the network is in charge of maintaining and validating data. In the context of robotics, this distributed method has a number of benefits, especially with regard to improved security, resilience to cyberattacks, and operational continuity.(Dorri, A. et al., 2017))The removal of a single point of vulnerability is one of the main advantages of decentralized systems for secure robotics. Attackers may be able to take over vital processes or steal confidential information in conventional centralized systems if the central server is compromised. However, an attack on one component of the system is less likely to impact the entire network under a decentralized configuration because data and control are dispersed across several nodes. The possibility of a total system failure as a result of a deliberate cyberattack or malfunction is decreased because every robotic unit, sensor, or actuator functions autonomously and has its own decision-making abilities.

Decentralized systems further improve security by using blockchain technology, consensus processes, and encryption to safeguard data and communication between robots and other networked devices. All robot-to-robot communication and data sharing in a decentralized network can be cryptographically secured to prevent unwanted access. For instance, blockchain can be used to record robot-sensor interactions, producing an auditable and unchangeable record of each device's operations. This offers a high degree of accountability and transparency, which makes it simpler to monitor possible security lapses or spot any irregularities in robotic behaviour.The capacity of decentralized systems to continue operating even in the case of partial failures or attacks is another important benefit. Many robots and machinery are connected in a smart factory, so even if one system or robot is compromised, the network can still function normally. For sectors like semiconductor manufacturing or automotive manufacture that have strict uptime requirements, this resilience is especially important. The decentralized approach guarantees that other robots may carry out their duties uninterrupted, even in the event of a failure or cyberattack, maintaining overall production efficiency.Robotics is made more adaptable and flexible via decentralized systems. Without continual updates or instructions from a central system, every robotic unit in a decentralized network is capable of autonomously evaluating its surroundings, making judgments, and acting. For autonomous robots, which must respond rapidly to dynamic changes in their surroundings, this capacity is especially helpful. Robots can move and handle materials in a warehouse automation system, for instance, without needing a centralized controller to direct every action. In addition to increasing the robots' productivity, this autonomy lowers the possibility of security lapses or single-point failures that could disrupt the system.

Scalability is another benefit of decentralization. Decentralized systems can expand with the number of robots or machines in smart factories without experiencing major problems. The network can easily accommodate more robotic units, each of which can communicate with other units and improve the system's overall performance. Because of its scalability, the system may grow over time to accommodate more devices and nodes while preserving operational effectiveness and security.

5. AI AND BLOCKCHAIN FOR ENHANCED CYBERSECURITY

5.1 Convergence of AI and Blockchain in Securing Industrial Systems

A revolutionary method of protecting industrial systems is provided by the combination of blockchain technology with artificial intelligence (AI), particularly in smart factories where automation, networked devices, and data-driven procedures are prevalent. Although each technology contributes distinct advantages to cybersecurity on its own, when combined, they produce a synergistic impact that improves the accuracy, resilience, and efficiency of solving complex security problems.(Gai, K. et al., 2018))Large-scale data analysis, pattern recognition, anomaly detection, and real-time danger prediction are all areas in which AI shines. It excels in identifying subtle signs of cyberattacks, like anomalous network activity, illegal access attempts, or changes in system performance. Proactive threat identification and mitigation are made possible by machine learning algorithms that may be trained to identify both known dangers and new attack patterns. AI's reliance on centralized processing resources and data storage, however, frequently presents security risks because these hubs can be targeted by hackers.In contrast, blockchain ensures data integrity, transparency, and resistance to tampering by offering a decentralized, unchangeable ledger for data storage and transactions. It is more resistant to attacks like Distributed Denial of Service (DDoS) attacks and data breaches because of its decentralized architecture, which removes single points of failure. Blockchain is a potent instrument for building trust in multi-party industrial ecosystems, where different stakeholders and devices interact, because it can produce safe, transparent records of transactions.

Blockchain and AI work together to enhance each other's advantages while addressing each other's shortcomings. Blockchain's open and safe data architecture helps AI by guaranteeing that the data used for analysis and training is accurate and impenetrable. AI's capacity to automate intricate processes like fraud detection, anomaly identification, and predictive maintenance enhances blockchain's functionality. Blockchain securely records this analysis along with maintenance logs, guaranteeing accountability and transparency. AI, for instance, can analyse machine performance data in real-time in a smart factory to anticipate any faults.In industrial systems, the combination of blockchain technology and artificial intelligence also improves access control and identity management. While AI continuously observes and validates the behaviour of users, devices, and systems, blockchain may establish decentralized digital identities for them. When combined, they make it possible for sophisticated authentication systems to adjust to current threats, blocking unwanted access and guaranteeing that only reliable parties communicate with vital infrastructure.Blockchain and artificial intelligence (AI) together provide safeguard data transfers in Industrial Internet of Things (IIoT) settings. Blockchain guarantees that data transferred between devices is unchangeable and encrypted, and artificial intelligence examines this data to spot any irregularities or dangers. Blockchain, for instance, can authenticate firmware upgrades or sensor data in robotic assembly lines, while AI continuously tracks robot performance to identify any indications of manipulation or malfunction.Supply chain security is another important area where blockchain and AI work together to provide end-to-end visibility and security. Blockchain records each transaction in an unchangeable ledger, tracking the flow of commodities and products along the supply chain.(Huh, S. et al., 2017)) AI examines these documents to find fraud, inefficiencies, or fake goods, making sure that only legitimate and legal goods make it to the assembly line.A new level of cybersecurity, marked by proactive threat detection, immutable data integrity, decentralized trust, and real-time flexibility, can be attained by industrial systems by utilizing the complimentary characteristics of blockchain and artificial intelligence. In addition to safeguarding vital infrastructure from changing cyberthreats, this convergence promotes cooperation and trust in industrial ecosystems that are becoming more intricate and linked. Blockchain and AI integration will become essential for guaranteeing the security, effectiveness, and resilience of industrial systems as smart factories develop further.

5.2 Blockchain for Authentication and Access Control in Robotics

Blockchain technology provides a strong and decentralized method for robotics access control and authentication, tackling important issues such secure communication, identity verification, and preventing unwanted access. The demand for safe and scalable ways to handle identities and permissions grows as robotics systems in autonomous and industrial settings become more interconnected. Blockchain offers a solution that improves security, guarantees accountability, and cultivates trust between robotic systems and their operators thanks to its decentralized, transparent, and immutable ledger.

5.2.1 Robotic Authentication

Conventional systems usually use centralized servers or databases for authentication in order to confirm the identity of users, devices, or other entities that are interacting with robots. However, because of their susceptibility to single points of failure, these centralized architectures are desirable targets for cyberattacks including Distributed Denial of Service (DDoS) attacks, hacking, and data leaks. Blockchain decentralizes the authentication process, removing this danger. A distinct cryptographic identity (public/private key pair) is granted to every robot, gadget, or user via blockchain technology, and this information is safely stored on the blockchain. To make sure that only authorized parties are given access, the blockchain ledger is used to confirm the identity of any robot or entity attempting to access a system or resource.Large networks of robots may communicate and authenticate without depending on a central authority thanks to this decentralized approach, which also increases scalability and security.

5.2.2 Robotics Access Control

Which operations or resources a robot, person, or system is permitted to carry out or access are determined by access control. Smart contracts, which are self-executing programs recorded on the blockchain, are used in blockchain-based access control to dynamically set and enforce permissions. A smart contract, for example, can define which robots in a smart factory are permitted to carry out particular duties, including controlling machinery, gaining access to private information, or interacting with particular areas. The blockchain examines the smart contract when a robot starts an action to make sure the robot has the required authorization. The action is permitted if the requirements are satisfied; if not, it is prohibited. This lowers the possibility of unauthorized activity or privilege escalation by guaranteeing that access control rules are uniformly applied throughout the system.(Garifullin, R., & Ryzhov, V. (2020))

5.3 AI for Threat Detection and Mitigation in Blockchain Networks

In blockchain networks, artificial intelligence (AI) is essential for improving threat detection and mitigation, tackling issues like fraud, cyberattacks, and system vulnerabilities. Blockchain networks are vulnerable to sophisticated threats like rogue smart contracts, double-spending, and Sybil attacks, even with their built-in security mechanisms. With its sophisticated data analysis and pattern recognition skills, artificial intelligence (AI) enhances blockchain technology by offering proactive and flexible security solutions to effectively detect and mitigate such threats. Blockchain networks that use AI-powered threat detection continuously monitor nodes, transactions, and network activity in order to spot any irregularities or patterns that might point to criminal activity. To identify odd transaction patterns, such attempts to tamper with consensus procedures, inflate transaction volumes, or take advantage of flaws in smart contracts, machine learning models can be trained on historical blockchain data. AI can, for example, detect nodes participating in fraudulent activity during consensus voting or flag unusual transaction sequences that mimic money laundering.Beyond danger identification, AI enables real-time threat mitigation through adaptive methods and automated reactions.(Mohamed, N (2025)) AI algorithms can initiate predetermined measures, such blocking exploitation attempts by modifying smart contract rules, stopping suspicious transactions, or isolating hostile nodes, when they detect a potential attack. The ability of reinforcement learning models to dynamically modify these responses in response to changing threats guarantees that mitigation techniques continue to be successful even in the face of new attack vectors.

Figure 3. AI for Threat Detection

By detecting and reducing the risks connected to compromised validators or mining nodes, artificial intelligence (AI) improves the security of consensus processes in blockchain networks. AI can identify attempts at collusion or irregularities in block validation procedures by examining network-wide behavioural patterns and resource distribution, protecting the consensus protocol's integrity.Smart contracts are an essential part of many blockchain networks, and AI is crucial to their security. Before being deployed, smart contract code can be examined for flaws or harmful logic using machine learning models and natural language processing (NLP). AI-powered solutions can also keep an eye out for unusual activity in deployed contracts to make sure they are operating as intended and not being abused.Significant advantages come from integrating AI into blockchain networks, such as improved threat detection process scalability, faster reaction times, and the capacity to adjust to novel and complex attack methods. For broad use, however, issues like controlling computing resource requirements and guaranteeing the transparency of AI decision-making must be resolved.Blockchain networks are made more secure, dependable, and resilient to changing cyberthreats by AI's sophisticated threat detection and mitigation capabilities. Blockchain networks may gain greater trust and resilience by utilizing AI's automation, anomaly detection, and predictive analytics. This will open the door for wider use in crucial applications across various industries.

6. SECURING INDUSTRIAL NETWORKS AND DATA

6.1 Cybersecurity Threats to Industrial IoT (IIoT)

With its sophisticated automation, real-time analytics, and networked devices, the Industrial Internet of Things (IIoT) has become a key component of contemporary industrial innovation, revolutionizing processes. Notwithstanding these developments, there are serious cybersecurity threats associated with IIoT system integration, endangering data integrity, business continuity, and industrial safety. (Erboz, G. (2017)) The most serious cybersecurity risks that IIoT systems face in the current industrial environment are examined in this chapter.

6.1.1 Device Vulnerabilities

IIoT devices sometimes prioritize cost and utility over strong security measures due to their inherent limitations in memory and processing capacity. Attackers can easily target these devices since they are often deployed with default credentials, unpatched firmware, or antiquated security mechanisms. These flaws can be used by cybercriminals to weaponize devices as part of botnets for massive Distributed Denial of Service (DDoS) assaults, breach networks, or steal confidential information.(Christidis, K., & Devetsikiotis, M. (2016)) Furthermore, the risk is increased by irregular security updates, which let vulnerabilities remain active for a lengthy time after they are found.

6.1.2 Data Breaches and Industrial Espionage

Large volumes of operational data, including as customer information, process parameters, and proprietary designs, are produced by IIoT systems. Cybercriminals looking to obtain financial gain or a competitive edge find this data to be an appealing target. Operational disruption, reputational harm, and intellectual property theft are all possible outcomes of data breaches. In sectors like manufacturing and aerospace, where patented designs are extremely important, industrial espionage—when rivals take advantage of weaknesses to obtain private information—poses a serious threat.

6.1.3 Ransomware Attacks

An increasing danger to IIoT environments is ransomware. Attackers encrypt important information or take down vital systems, then demand a ransom to unlock them. Ransomware attacks can have disastrous effects in industrial settings, stopping manufacturing lines, resulting in large financial losses, and even jeopardizing processes that are vital to safety. Because IIoT systems are interconnected, the impact of such assaults is increased because a single device breach might have a cascading effect on the entire network.

6.1.4 Insider Threats

One major weakness in IIoT security is still human factors. IIoT systems can be compromised by insiders, whether on purpose or by mistake. Workers or contractors who have access to IIoT networks run the risk of purposefully undermining operations, inadvertently introducing malware, or exposing credentials. Because insider threats include trusted personnel who have authorized access to vital systems, they are especially difficult to mitigate.

6.1.5 Supply Chain Vulnerabilities

IIoT systems frequently incorporate a complicated network of outside vendors for both software and hardware. This intricacy gives attackers the chance to take advantage of supply chain weaknesses. In order to enter systems undetected, malicious actors may hack third-party software, add fake parts, or embed backdoors. Attacks on the supply chain can go unnoticed until they are triggered, which makes it challenging to predict and prevent.

6.1.6 Physical Security Risks

There are special vulnerabilities associated with the IIoT's confluence of digital and physical systems. Cyberattacks on IIoT devices that manage industrial machinery may cause environmental damages, safety risks, or physical damage. Attackers might, for instance, alter sensor data to make machinery break down, interfere with manufacturing, or put employees in risk. These kinds of attacks highlight how important it is for IIoT setups to have both physical security and cybersecurity measures integrated.

6.1.7 Lack of Standardization

Security attempts for IIoT systems are complicated by the lack of uniform cybersecurity standards. Inconsistent protection levels are caused by differences in device capabilities, communication protocols, and security procedures among manufacturers and industries. In addition to impeding interoperability, this lack of standards expands the attack surface because vulnerabilities in one area of the system can be used to compromise the entire network.

6.2 Securing Data Flow in Autonomous Systems

Autonomous systems, which depend on constant communication between sensors, actuators, processors, and cloud platforms, depend on the smooth and secure flow of data. Drones, self-driving cars, and industrial robots are examples of autonomous systems that process enormous volumes of data in real time in order to make judgments, adjust to changing conditions, and carry out tasks. But because of their strong reliance on data transmission, these systems are also very vulnerable to cyberattacks that could jeopardize their availability, confidentiality, and integrity.(Cheng, J. et al., 2021)) Therefore, one of the most important aspects of these systems' operational safety and effectiveness is protecting the data flow.Ensuring data integrity is the first step in protecting data flow. For autonomous systems to work well, data must be precise and unaffected. Whether due to deliberate attacks or inadvertent mistakes, data tampering or corruption can result in poor decision-making and sometimes disastrous consequences. Data integrity can be checked at each level of processing and transmission using methods like blockchain technology, digital signatures, and cryptographic hashing.

Confidentiality of data is still another crucial factor. Sensitive data that needs to be shielded from unwanted access, such user information, proprietary algorithms, or operational parameters, is frequently handled by autonomous systems. Data security during transmission and storage is ensured by putting robust encryption methods like TLS (Transport Layer Security) and AES (Advanced Encryption Standard) into practice. Secure key management procedures are also essential for preventing hackers from obtaining encryption keys. Mechanisms for authentication and access control are essential for stopping unauthorized parties from intercepting or altering data flow. (Arpteg, A. et al., 2018)) Device authentication methods, role-based access control (RBAC), and multi-factor authentication (MFA) make sure that only users and trustworthy devices may access or change the data in the system. Zero-trust architectures, which constantly confirm the identities and actions of entities engaging with the system, are also advantageous for autonomous systems. Autonomous systems must integrate intrusion detection and prevention systems (IDPS) that can recognize and neutralize threats as they arise in order to handle real-time security concerns. By examining data flow patterns to identify anomalies that can point to cyberattacks, machine learning algorithms can improve IDPS. For example, unexpected communication from unidentified devices or abrupt increases in data flow can set off alarms and start countermeasures to separate any threats. A further key aspect is the ability to withstand network disturbances. Autonomous systems must guarantee data accessibility even in the event of technological malfunctions or cyberattacks. Decentralized architectures, edge computing for localized data processing, and redundant communication routes are among strategies that might improve system resilience. For instance, blockchain technology can offer a tamper-proof, decentralized ledger for recording data transactions, guaranteeing that the system is safe even in the event that one node is compromised. Ensuring secure data flow in autonomous systems requires adDWDASerence to industry norms and laws. A foundation for putting strong security procedures in place is provided by following sector-specific standards, like those controlling industrial automation or driverless cars, or frameworks like ISO/IEC 27001 for information security management.

6.3 Role of AI and Blockchain in Protecting Industrial Networks

Industrial networks are becoming more and more interconnected in the current digital era, providing significant advancements in automation, efficiency, and real-time monitoring across a variety of industries, including manufacturing, energy, and transportation. However, because of their increased interconnectedness, these networks are also more vulnerable to ransomware, data breaches, and denial-of-service attacks, among other intrusions. It takes sophisticated systems that can foresee, identify, and mitigate these risks to secure industrial networks. Two such technologies that have been crucial in improving the cybersecurity of industrial networks are artificial intelligence (AI) and blockchain.

Figure 4. AI for Proactive Threat Detection and Response

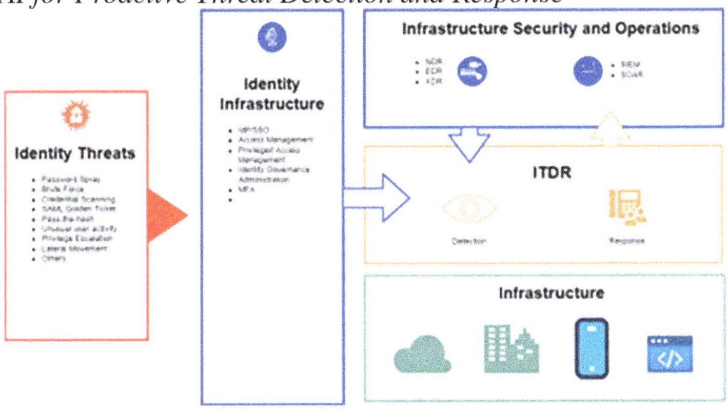

Real-time threat detection and quick reactions to possible cyberthreats are two ways artificial intelligence helps protect industrial networks. The pre-programmed criteria and signatures that traditional cybersecurity systems frequently use are not very effective in identifying novel or changing attack techniques. Through the analysis of system behaviour and network traffic, artificial intelligence (AI), and machine learning (ML) in particular, can dynamically adjust to new threats. Systems with AI capabilities can keep an eye on the data flow in industrial networks, searching for odd trends like traffic spikes, illegal access attempts, or strange device-to-device interactions. Artificial intelligence (AI) systems may identify even the smallest indications of possible security breaches by learning the usual patterns of network activity, frequently before they result in serious harm.(X. Zhang, P. Wang, H. Jia, Z. Huang and R. Zhao (2024)) Industrial networks' overall security posture is greatly improved by this real-time anomaly detection capability.AI is essential for automated reaction in addition to danger detection. Artificial intelligence (AI) systems have the ability to automatically apply security patches, isolate impacted devices, or block malicious communications when they detect a possible threat. These automated reactions lessen the amount of damage caused by cyberattacks and guarantee continuous network operation by shortening the period between detection and containment.

6.3.2 Blockchain for Data Integrity and Secure Communication

Blockchain technology offers an immutable, transparent, and decentralized method of data security for industrial networks. A tamper-proof chain is produced by cryptographically connecting each block in a blockchain to the one before it, which records a transaction or data exchange. Blockchain is a useful tool for guaranteeing data integrity in industrial networks because of its design. Continuous data flow, including sensor readings, machine statuses, and operating records, is essential to industrial networks. Maintaining the accuracy of automated decision-making systems depends on ensuring the integrity of this data. By ensuring that data cannot be changed or tampered with once it is recorded, blockchain safeguards the flow of data. This immutability guards against malevolent actors altering or corrupting important data and gives assurance on the accuracy of the data used by industrial systems. Blockchain improves safe communication within industrial networks while also guaranteeing data integrity. Industrial devices may verify and authenticate one another using blockchain's cryptographic methods, guaranteeing that only reliable parties can interact with the network. By reducing threats like spoofing and illegal device access, this procedure makes sure that only authentic devices communicate within the industrial environment. An extra degree of efficiency and security can be added by using blockchain-based smart contracts to enforce automated, secure transactions between systems and devices.

6.3.3 Decentralization and Resilience Through Blockchain

Conventional industrial networks frequently depend on centralized systems, which can cause extensive disruptions if they are compromised. By distributing security responsibilities throughout the network, blockchain's decentralized architecture removes this single point of failure. In a decentralized system, the network as a whole is safe even in the event that one node is compromised or attacked. Industrial networks are made more resilient by this distributed strategy, which guarantees that they will continue to function even in the case of a cyberattack.

6.3.4 Convergence of AI and Blockchain for Enhanced Security

The combination of blockchain technology and artificial intelligence produces a potent synergy that greatly improves industrial network security. By analysing blockchain transactions in real time and spotting irregularities or possible security risks in the distributed ledger, artificial intelligence (AI) can enhance blockchain technology. Furthermore, stakeholders may audit and validate the steps taken by AI systems in response to cyber threats thanks to the transparent record of AI-driven decisions provided by blockchain's irreversible nature. Industrial networks can accomplish a multi-layered approach to cybersecurity by utilizing the advantages of both blockchain and artificial intelligence (AI). This method combines the strong, transparent aspects of blockchain technology with the proactive, adaptive capabilities of AI. With this combination, networks can identify, stop, and mitigate threats instantly while maintaining the security and integrity of data.

7. CHALLENGES AND FUTURE DIRECTIONS

7.1 Technical Barriers in AI and Blockchain Integration

Blockchain technology and artificial intelligence (AI) together have the potential to completely transform cybersecurity in industrial networks by providing solutions that include data integrity, decentralized security, and real-time threat detection. To reach their full potential, these two formidable technologies must overcome a number of technical obstacles that come with their combination.(O. Kuznetsov et al., 2024)) Scalability problems, processing needs, data privacy concerns, and the complexity of system integration are some of the challenges that arise when integrating AI with Blockchain, despite their great potential.

7.1.1 Scalability Issues

Scalability is one of the main obstacles to combining AI and blockchain. Both blockchain and artificial intelligence demand a significant amount of processing power, and as industrial networks develop, so does the volume of data produced and handled. The distributed ledger that blockchain uses by design necessitates transaction validation from all users, which can cause performance snags as the network grows in size. Because machine learning methods need a lot of data and processing power to function properly, the addition of AI adds even more computational complexity. The scalability of these systems is a key concern in industrial settings where real-time decision-making and high-speed data transfer are essential. One of the biggest challenges is achieving seamless integration without compromising reaction times or performance.

7.1.2 High Computational Requirements

Deep learning-based AI algorithms, in particular, are computationally demanding and resource-intensive. On the other side, blockchain requires extra computing overhead for consensus methods and encryption procedures. The available infrastructure may be severely strained by the integration of these two technologies, especially in industrial systems with constrained computing power or where real-time operations are crucial. It can be challenging to use AI and Blockchain integration in resource-constrained contexts due to the increased computing load, which can result in higher energy consumption, decreased system efficiency, and slower processing rates.

7.1.3 Data Privacy and Security Concerns

Ensuring data security and privacy while combining blockchain and artificial intelligence is another major obstacle. Blockchain may not always be appropriate for safeguarding sensitive data, even though its transparent and unchangeable ledger improves data integrity. Although useful in some situations, Blockchain's transparency can reveal private information to unapproved parties if it is not adequately encrypted. Furthermore, in order for AI models to train efficiently, they frequently need access to big datasets, including private and confidential data. It is a difficult task to strike a balance between the requirement for privacy in AI models and the need for transparency in Blockchain. Methods like homomorphic encryption, federated learning, and privacy-preserving machine learning might provide viable answers, but they complicate the integration further.

7.1.4 Complex System Integration

Numerous systems, gadgets, and protocols that make up industrial networks were not created to function with cutting-edge technology like blockchain and artificial intelligence. It can be difficult and resource-intensive to integrate AI and blockchain into current industrial infrastructures; it necessitates a major reengineering of old systems and procedures. A high degree of cooperation across several stakeholders, including the cybersecurity, IT, and OT (Operational Technology) teams, is also required for this integration. Implementing and maintaining AI and blockchain systems in industrial settings is frequently challenging due to the absence of defined frameworks. Furthermore, because both technologies are always evolving, it can be difficult to stay up to date with the newest advancements and industry best practices.(Kaushik, K. (2022))

7.1.5 Energy Efficiency

Energy consumption is another issue brought up by the combination of blockchain technology and artificial intelligence. Blockchain and AI both need a lot of energy, especially when utilizing resource-intensive consensus techniques like Proof of Work (PoW) in blockchain. Due to increasing energy consumption, industrial systems that depend on these technologies may have operational inefficiencies, greater operating costs, and possible environmental effects. Energy-efficient AI methods that lower the overall processing load as well as more energy-efficient consensus mechanisms like Proof of Stake (PoS) or hybrid consensus models could be investigated to address this.

7.1.6 Regulatory and Compliance Issues

A number of regulatory and compliance issues are brought up by the use of AI and blockchain technology in industrial networks. Strict guidelines on the storage, sharing, and processing of sensitive and personal data are imposed by data privacy legislation, such as the GDPR in Europe. Compliance with these requirements may be made more difficult by blockchain's transparency, especially if personal data is kept on a public ledger. Furthermore, it can be difficult to guarantee adherence to laws requiring transparency in automated decision-making as AI's decision-making procedures aren't always clear-cut. Overcoming these regulatory obstacles will need the creation of precise policies and frameworks for the moral application of blockchain technology and artificial intelligence in business settings.

7.1.7 Ethical and Governance Challenges

Significant ethical and governance concerns are also brought up by the combination of AI and blockchain. AI systems, especially machine learning-based ones, are sometimes viewed as "black boxes," with decision-making processes that are not necessarily clear or intelligible to humans. Particularly in vital industrial systems where security and safety are of the utmost importance, this lack of transparency can result in problems with accountability and confidence. Since blockchain does not require a central authority, which can be difficult to administer in regulated settings, its decentralized structure may make governance even more difficult. To solve these issues and build confidence in the technology, it will be essential to make sure that ethical values are incorporated into both Blockchain protocols and AI algorithms.

7.2 Scalability and Deployment in Large-Scale Factories

A distinct set of difficulties arises when implementing AI and Blockchain technologies in large factories, mostly because of the size of the operations, the amount of data produced, and the difficulty of integrating these technologies across several systems. In order to manage massive volumes of data in real-time, scalable solutions are essential as factories develop into smart environments with networked machines, sensors, and gadgets. Blockchain technology and artificial intelligence (AI) are both effective at improving cybersecurity and operational efficiency, but they must be able to handle this complexity without sacrificing dependability, speed, or performance. Artificial intelligence (AI) technologies, especially machine learning (ML) and deep learning, are computationally demanding and data hungry. Data is constantly being produced in a large factory from a number of sources, such as manufacturing equipment, sensors, and real-time operational systems. AI systems that can efficiently grow to manage the input are needed for processing, evaluating, and storing this data. The sheer volume and pace of data can be too much for traditional centralized AI models that depend on cloud-based servers, which can cause delays in processing and decision-making.

Edge computing is starting to appear as a remedy for this. Before being transferred to centralized systems for additional analysis, edge computing enables data to be processed closer to its source—at the equipment or sensors themselves. By lowering latency and the bandwidth needed for data transfer, this method guarantees quicker insights and permits real-time decision-making. Large factories can scale AI applications without overloading centralized systems or causing delays in crucial processes by dividing the computational workload among local devices or edge nodes. The training of AI models is another crucial factor. AI models must be trained on a variety of massive datasets from different production lines and machinery in a large factory. The amount of data that must be handled increases with the size of the facility, and the training process can be computationally demanding. AI models can be developed across numerous decentralized devices using distributed learning approaches like federated learning, which eliminates the need to move big datasets to a central server. This preserves data privacy and lessens network congestion while enabling AI models to scale in expansive settings. Industrial systems benefit from blockchain technology's transparency, security, and immutability, but scalability is still a major challenge, particularly as factories get bigger and more sophisticated. Because blockchain technology is decentralized, every member of the network must validate transactions. As the number of devices and transactions grows, this can lead to long transaction speeds and expensive computing costs. This can result in bottlenecks, which slow down transaction processing and reduce operational efficiency in large factories with hundreds of equipment and sensors interacting in real-time.

7.3 Ethical and Legal Considerations in Autonomous Systems Security

When applying cutting-edge technologies like AI and Blockchain in sectors like manufacturing and robotics, ethical and legal considerations in autonomous systems security are essential. Autonomous systems raise a number of privacy, accountability, transparency, and regulatory issues that need to be properly addressed as they are incorporated into daily operations to guarantee that the technologies are used responsibly. Privacy is one of the main ethical issues. Large volumes of operational and personal data are generated and processed by autonomous systems, especially those that use AI. This calls into question the data's ownership, accessibility, and security. Sensitive information may be gathered from workers, customers, or equipment in sectors like manufacturing where IoT devices and autonomous robots are used. Strong data protection procedures, explicit consent from all parties involved, and data anonymization mechanisms to prevent misuse or unauthorized access are necessary for the ethical use of this data. Accountability is yet another important ethical concern. Since autonomous systems can make decisions without direct human input, determining who is responsible for a failure or security breach becomes more difficult. It can be difficult to determine who is legally liable in industrial robotics when a robotic system malfunctions and damages machinery or even injures employees. Is it the software developer, the system integrator, the robot's maker, or someone else? Making sure that businesses and individuals are held accountable for the behaviour of autonomous systems, particularly in safety-critical contexts, requires the establishment of unambiguous accountability frameworks.

To lessen these effects, legal structures that uphold worker retraining initiatives and govern labour rights are essential. Legal and ethical issues are closely related to cybersecurity issues. Malicious actors find autonomous systems to be more appealing targets as they advance in sophistication. In addition to being a technical difficulty, protecting these systems from cyberattacks is also a moral and legal requirement. Businesses need to make sure their systems are safe from assaults that could jeopardize the security and welfare of their workers, customers, and other stakeholders. Furthermore, in order to handle the possible criminal culpability of individuals who take advantage of weaknesses in autonomous systems, legal frameworks must change. (El-Hamed et al., 2025))

7.4 Future Trends in Cybersecurity for Smart Factories

Future cybersecurity will be influenced by the growing complexity of technologies like artificial intelligence (AI), blockchain, and quantum computing as smart factories continue to develop. The use of AI and machine learning in predictive security is one of the major trends. By continuously evaluating data from IoT devices and machinery, these technologies will enable proactive threat detection by spotting irregularities and anticipating possible assaults before they happen. In addition to lowering false alarms and improving threat detection accuracy, this will enable automated reactions to minimize hazards instantly.

In smart factories, blockchain technology will be essential for protecting data traceability and integrity. Machine, sensor, and supply chain data will be transparent and impenetrable thanks to its decentralized, unchangeable ledger. (Lytras, M. D., & Visvizi, A. (2021)) In addition to ensuring adherence to industry laws and preventing data manipulation, this will give crucial processes an auditable record. Blockchain technology will be crucial for protecting authentication procedures and confirming the accuracy of supply chain transactions as factories become more networked.

The broad use of edge and fog computing will be another important breakthrough. These technologies will improve real-time decision-making and lower latency by processing data closer to the source. More significantly, edge computing will improve cybersecurity by reducing the attack surface by limiting the amount of sensitive data that is exposed to external networks. The implementation of security protocols at the edge will enable prompt responses to cyberthreats, minimizing the possible harm inflicted by assaults and guaranteeing that every linked device functions in a secure setting. Autonomous security systems powered by AI and sophisticated algorithms will also become more prevalent in the future. Without human assistance, these technologies will automatically monitor, identify, and react to cyberthreats. These autonomous systems will be able to adjust to changing threats by continuously enhancing their protection mechanisms through the use of self-learning capabilities. This will guarantee that smart factories can react to security threats instantly and assist address the rising scarcity of cybersecurity experts. (Das, A., Jain, R.K. (2025))

Adoption of quantum-resistant cryptography will be necessary due to the impending threat of quantum computing. Traditional encryption techniques will be susceptible to decoding by quantum algorithms as quantum computers develop. In order to safeguard sensitive data and make sure that their cybersecurity measures continue to be strong in the face of emerging technical difficulties, smart factories will need to use quantum-resistant encryption approaches. The security of the increasingly intricate and linked systems found in smart factories will depend heavily on these developments in cybersecurity.

CONCLUSION

With enhanced threat detection, real-time consequences, and adaptive defenses, the introduction of AI technology into cybersecurity frameworks for robotics control systems (RCS) has changed the game. AI offers the ability necessary for protecting these systems, guaranteeing their resilience and consistent functioning as cyber threats continue to grow in sophistication and complexity. However, there are limitations to employing AI-driven cybersecurity solutions, such as issues with data quality, hostile attacks, processing needs, and legal issues. With innovations like explainable AI, autonomous feel defensive systems, federation of learning, and quantum computer technology opening the door for more robust and versatile security frameworks, the future of AI in RCS security seems promising.

These technologies, that offer robust protection against dynamic cyberthreats and, in contrast, offer a degree of faith that should be gained from interlinked industry networks, will be the foundation for subsequent innovation. While addressing moral and legal problems as part of the current path, continued research and collaboration are also required in the face of these technological difficulties and expanding issues.

REFERENCES

Al-Rakhami, M. S., Al-Mashraee, H., & Algabri, M. (2022). Blockchain technology for enhancing cybersecurity in industrial IoT. *IEEE Access: Practical Innovations, Open Solutions, 10*, 14192–14206. DOI: 10.1109/ACCESS.2022.3141235

Arpteg, A., Brinne, B., Crnkovic-Friis, L., & Löfstedt, T. (2018). Software engineering challenges of deep learning. *2018 IEEE/ACM 1st International Workshop on Machine Learning Engineering*, 35–41. DOI: 10.1109/MLE.2018.00008

Bai, Q., Liu, Z., & Zhang, W. (2020). AI-powered anomaly detection in industrial control systems: A survey. *Journal of Industrial Information Integration, 21*, 100170. DOI: 10.1016/j.jii.2020.100170

Cai, Z., & Zhu, J. (2016). Fraud detections for online businesses: A perspective from blockchain technology. *Financial Innovation, 2*(1), 20. DOI: 10.1186/s40854-016-0039-4

Chang, S. E., & Chen, Y. C. (2020). Blockchain for cybersecurity in critical infrastructure: A comprehensive review. *Journal of Information Security and Applications, 54*, 102535. DOI: 10.1016/j.jisa.2020.102535

Cheng, J., Liu, Q., & Yao, M. (2021). AI-empowered industrial robotics for smart manufacturing. *International Journal of Advanced Manufacturing Technology, 115*(3–4), 847–864. DOI: 10.1007/s00170-021-07264-y

Christidis, K., & Devetsikiotis, M. (2016). Blockchains and smart contracts for the Internet of Things. *IEEE Access: Practical Innovations, Open Solutions, 4*, 2292–2303. DOI: 10.1109/ACCESS.2016.2566339

Dai, H. N., Zheng, Z., & Zhang, Y. (2019). Blockchain for Internet of Things: A survey. *IEEE Internet of Things Journal, 6*(5), 8076–8094. DOI: 10.1109/JIOT.2019.2920987

Das, A., & Jain, R. K. (2025). Performance evaluation of mobile robotic system for monitoring and inspection using MQTT protocol and IoT technique. *International Journal of Intelligent Robotics and Applications*. Advance online publication. DOI: 10.1007/s41315-025-00465-z

Dorri, A., Kanhere, S. S., & Jurdak, R. (2017). Blockchain in Internet of Things: Challenges and solutions. *IEEE Communications Surveys and Tutorials, 22*(3), 1820–1843. DOI: 10.1109/COMST.2020.2978977

El-Hamed, O. M. A., El-Samie, F. E. A., & Badawy, W.. (2025). Blockchain-based framework for secure communication in vehicular ad hoc network (VANET). *Journal of Optics*. Advance online publication. DOI: 10.1007/s12596-025-02760-1

Erboz, G. (2017). How to define Industry 4.0: Main pillars of Industry 4.0. *Managerial Trends in the Development of Enterprises in Globalization Era*, 761–767.

Feng, X., Xu, W., & Zhang, Y. (2021). AI-driven predictive maintenance for industrial robots. *Journal of Manufacturing Systems*, *61*, 109–118. DOI: 10.1016/j.jmsy.2021.10.005

Gai, K., Qiu, M., & Zhu, L. (2018). Blockchain-enabled smart grid: Challenges and opportunities. *IEEE Communications Magazine*, *56*(4), 15–21. DOI: 10.1109/MCOM.2018.1700813

Garifullin, R., & Ryzhov, V. (2020). Blockchain-based distributed control system for industrial robotics. *IFAC-PapersOnLine*, *53*(2), 972–977. DOI: 10.1016/j.ifacol.2020.12.238

Huh, S., Cho, S., & Kim, S. (2017). Managing IoT devices using blockchain platform. *Proceedings of the International Conference on Advanced Communication Technology*, 464–467. DOI: 10.23919/ICACT.2017.7890132

Kaushik, K. (2022). Blockchain Enabled Artificial Intelligence for Cybersecurity Systems. In Ouaissa, M., Boulouard, Z., Ouaissa, M., Khan, I. U., & Kaosar, M. (Eds.), *Big Data Analytics and Computational Intelligence for Cybersecurity. Studies in Big Data* (Vol. 111). Springer., DOI: 10.1007/978-3-031-05752-6_11

Khan, M., & Tripathi, A. (2018). "Digital Patient Eye," *2018 3rd International Conference On Internet of Things: Smart Innovation and Usages (IoT-SIU)*, Bhimtal, India, pp. 1-4, doi: DOI: 10.1109/IoT-SIU.2018.8519841

Kuznetsov, O., Sernani, P., Romeo, L., Frontoni, E., & Mancini, A. (2024). On the Integration of Artificial Intelligence and Blockchain Technology: A Perspective About Security. *IEEE Access: Practical Innovations, Open Solutions*, *12*, 3881–3897. DOI: 10.1109/ACCESS.2023.3349019

Latif, S., Idrees, Z., Huma, Z. E., & Ahmad, J. (2021). Blockchain technology for the industrial Internet of Things: A comprehensive survey on security challenges, architectures, applications, and future research directions. *Transactions on Emerging Telecommunications Technologies*, *32*(11), e4337. DOI: 10.1002/ETT.4337

Lytras, M. D., & Visvizi, A. (2021). Information management as a dual-purpose process in the smart city: Collecting, managing and utilizing information. *International Journal of Information Management*. Advance online publication. DOI: 10.1016/j.ijinfomgt.2020.102224

Mohamed, N. (2025). Artificial intelligence and machine learning in cybersecurity: A deep dive into state-of-the-art techniques and future paradigms. *Knowledge and Information Systems*. Advance online publication. DOI: 10.1007/s10115-025-02429-y

Visvizi, A., & Troisi, O. (2022). Effective Management of the Smart City: An Outline of a Conversation. In Visvizi, A., & Troisi, O. (Eds.), *Managing Smart Cities*. Springer., DOI: 10.1007/978-3-030-93585-6_1

Zhang, X., Wang, P., Jia, H., Huang, Z., & Zhao, R. (2024). "AI-Powered Cybersecurity: Enhancing Threat Detection and Defense in the Digital Age," *2024 IEEE 7th International Conference on Electronic Information and Communication Technology (ICEICT)*, Xi'an, China, pp. 1026-1031, doi: DOI: 10.1109/ICEICT61637.2024.10670798

Zheng, Z., Xie, S., Dai, H., Chen, X., & Wang, H. (2017). An overview of blockchain technology: architecture, consensus, and future trends. In: 2017 IEEE International Congress on Big Data (BigData Congress), pp. 557–564, DOI: 10.1109/BigData-Congress.2017.85

Chapter 3
Mitigating Adversarial Attacks in Industrial Cybersecurity Through NLP Strategies for E-Commerce

S. Suganya
https://orcid.org/0009-0008-3847-1621
Madanapalle Institute of Technology and Science, India

Mohd Sakib
https://orcid.org/0000-0002-2856-8365
UPES University, India

M. Malini
Periyar Maniammai Institute of Science and Technology, India

ABSTRACT

Personalised services, inventory optimisation, and fraud detection have all been made possible by the incorporation of machine learning (ML) into e-commerce. But it also makes platforms vulnerable to adversarial attacks, in which criminals alter data inputs in order to take advantage of flaws in the model. System dependability, data security, and customer trust are all compromised by these threats, which range from phishing emails to tampered reviews and transaction data. Critical defence techniques provided by Natural Language Processing (NLP) include anomaly detection, ensemble modelling, adversarial training, and context-aware analysis with models such as BERT and GPT. Dynamic feature selection is one technique that

DOI: 10.4018/979-8-3373-7503-8.ch003

reduces computational load while increasing performance. Unusual patterns in user behaviour and content can be found with the aid of behavior-based techniques and NLP-driven analytics. When combined, these tactics strengthen resistance to changing threats. For cybersecurity in sustainable e-commerce, continuous research, real-time

1. INTRODUCTION

Throughout its exponential growth, the e-commerce industry has transformed traditional shopping into a dynamic, 24/7 digital marketplace. At the core of this development is the pervasive use of artificial intelligence (AI) and machine learning (ML) technologies, which enable businesses to secure their platforms, enhance user experiences, optimize operations, and evaluate enormous quantities of data.

The increased risk of adversarial assaults is one of the new vulnerabilities brought about by this reliance on ML(Jeyaraj et al., 2024). By carefully changing input data—which is frequently undetectable to humans—these advanced cyber-attacks take use of flaws in machine learning algorithms to trick models into producing inaccurate predictions or classifications. Adversarial assaults can have detrimental and far-reaching effects in the e-commerce industry, where machine learning is essential to processes like fraud detection, recommendation engines, inventory management, and customer care.

In contrast to traditional cyber threats, adversarial assaults target the data that machine learning systems employ rather than the systems themselves. Attackers can alter ML-driven functionality, including suggesting inappropriate products, getting around fraud detection systems, or misidentifying dangerous transactions as benign, by inserting malicious perturbations into data. E-commerce platforms, where customer experience, dependability, and trust are critical, are at serious risk from this type of attack. An aggressive attack on a recommendation system, for instance, might distort product rankings, deceiving customers and costing platforms and sellers money. Similarly, adversarial manipulated inputs could bypass security checks, enabling fraudulent transactions or unauthorized access.

One of the primary reasons why adversarial attacks are so common in e-commerce is the industry's heavy dependence on data-driven decision-making. Massive amounts of data, such as browsing trends, product details, transaction histories, and user behavior, are gathered and processed by e-commerce platforms. Although this data is the foundation of machine learning algorithms, adversaries find it to be a desirable target. By creating adversarial inputs that take advantage of particular model flaws, attackers can take advantage of this dependency. Subtle changes to client information or payment data, for example, can get past fraud detection systems and allow attackers to make illegal purchases undetected (Jeyaraj et al., 2024).

Based on their goals and methods, adversarial attacks in e-commerce can be divided into a number of categories. One of the most prevalent types of assaults is evasion, in which attackers alter inputs while an ML model is operating in order to avoid detection. For example, in order to get past a spam filter without drawing attention to themselves, attackers may alter the content of a phishing email. Poisoning attacks are another important category, when adversaries tamper with an ML model's training data to create biases or impair performance (Sakib & Mustajab, 2024).

Adversarial attacks in e-commerce are difficult to detect, often using subtle input changes like fake reviews or altered images that appear legitimate but mislead ML models. Backdoor and exploratory attacks exploit model vulnerabilities, while transferable attacks threaten multiple platforms using similar algorithms. These tactics bypass traditional defenses, undermining product recommendations, fraud detection, and overall system reliability.

Adversarial attacks in e-commerce are driven by various motives, including financial gain and reputational damage. Attackers may target recommendation engines, payment systems, or inventory tools to commit fraud, skew market trends, or boost specific products. Financially motivated attackers, for instance, can exploit dynamic pricing algorithms with manipulated inputs, leading to revenue losses for the platform while unfairly benefiting certain vendors. These attacks pose serious threats to the integrity and profitability of e-commerce systems (Sakib & Mustajab, 2025). Similar to this, adversarial attacks can be used by rivals or bad actors that want to damage a company's reputation in order to interfere with client experiences. For example, a compromised chat-bot that gives rude or erroneous answers could undermine customer trust and harm a company's reputation. Adversarial assaults can also be employed for espionage, allowing hackers to search e-commerce sites for private data or proprietary algorithms (KATE et al., 2024).

Because of the ever-changing nature of industry, e-commerce systems have particular difficulties in fending against hostile attacks. E-commerce platforms, in contrast to static systems, have to constantly adjust to shifting consumer habits, industry trends, and new dangers. Although necessary for maintaining competitiveness, this dynamic makes ML system security more difficult. For example, the requirement for real-time processing restricts the ability to perform thorough validation or anomaly detection, which leaves platforms more vulnerable to hostile inputs. Furthermore, the defence against hostile attacks is made more difficult by the integration of ML systems with legacy infrastructure, which sometimes lacks strong security mechanisms.

Considering these difficulties, the necessity of strong defenses against hostile attacks in e-commerce is becoming more widely acknowledged. Several ways are being researched by researchers and professionals to improve the resilience of machine learning systems. One potential tactic is adversarial training, which increases the resilience of ML models by exposing them to hostile scenarios during the training phase.By using this technique, models can become more resilient to attacks by learning to identify and eliminate hostile perturbations. An additional tactic is ensemble learning, which builds a more robust system by combining several machine learning models with various architectures or training techniques. Ensemble approaches can more effectively identify and reduce hostile inputs by utilizing the variety of models.

Behavior-based detection techniques are becoming more popular in e-commerce in addition to modeling eccentric defenses. These techniques concentrate on keeping an eye on system interactions, transaction patterns, and user behavior in order to spot any irregularities that might point to hostile conduct. For instance, abrupt shifts in user preferences or odd buying habits can set off alarms, allowing platforms to look into and address possible risks. In a similar vein, NLP driven techniques are being researched to strengthen the security of text-based systems, like chat-bots and customer support tools, that are commonly the target of hostile attacks(Alawida et al., 2023).

The e-commerce sector needs to take a proactive and comprehensive strategy to cybersecurity since adversarial assaults are always changing. This entails funding cutting-edge machine learning research, putting in place reliable monitoring systems, and encouraging cooperation among industry participants in order to exchange best practices and insights. Training employees and customers on the dangers of targeted attacks enhances the protection of e-commerce platforms.

The risks posed by adversarial attacks is an emerging issue as they exploit the machine learning technologies driving e-commerce. With the increased use of machine learning, the risks and vulnerabilities also expand. Educating e-commerce business stakeholders on these attack methods and putting in place solid defense mechanisms strengthens business in the digital economy.

1.1. Overview

E-commerce technology was very much impacted by consumers' shopping habits and dependent with companies behavior. Consumers now have global accessibility and personalized shopping experiences. Handling massive amounts of data from user interactions and transactions, as well as market trends, is a fundamental requirement of these platforms making the use of Machine Learning indispensable. Machine Learning streamlines many processes, such as inventory control, dynamic customer service, fraud detection, and dynamic pricing. Customer satisfaction and e-commerce revenues can be enhanced owing to product suggestion customization and sales driven by Machine Learning powered recommendation systems. Fraud detection systems mitigate suspicious activity and reduce fraud in real time. Customer support can be significantly improved through the use of chatbots powered by Natural Language Processing, and strategic decisions can be guided by sentiment analysis. The increased dependence on Machine Learning brings its own disadvantages such as adversarial biases, biased data, and algorithm errors that can reduce system reliability and harm customer confidence. To fully leverage ML benefits while minimizing threats, e-commerce platforms must adopt robust security measures and ethical practices, ensuring both innovation and operational resilience in a competitive digital landscape.

1.2. Characteristics of Adversarial Attacks

Subtle Perturbations:

Adversarial attacks frequently entail subtle modifications to input data, like changing a few pixels in an image or changing a text's structure, that fool machine learning models without being seen by humans.

Specificity to Models:

Adversarial attacks might target certain models and take advantage of their flaws. But because of transfer-ability, these assaults might also be effective against models that are similar and have been trained on similar datasets (Ashraf, 2025).

Targeted vs. Non-Targeted Attacks:

- **Targeted:** The attacker seeks to produce a certain wrong result, such as incorrectly labeling a valid transaction as fraudulent.
- **Non-Targeted:** The goal is to degrade performance or induce widespread simplification.

1.3. Dynamic Adaptation

Cybersecurity protections are constantly challenged as adversaries modify their tactics to get around new security defenses (Kothamali et al., 2020).

Stealth and Concealment:

While adversarial instances are designed to blend in perfectly with authentic data, it is challenging for conventional anomaly detection systems to identify them.

High Complexity:

Understanding the architecture, behavior, or input-output interactions of the ML model is necessary to design successful adversarial attacks, particularly in white-box circumstances.

Impact on Confidence Scores:

Adversarial inputs frequently trick downstream systems or human operators by tricking machine learning models into generating high confidence for inaccurate classifications.

Cross-Domain Applicability:

Adversarial approaches can be used to exploit flaws in a variety of machine learning applications, including image recognition, natural language processing, and cybersecurity.

Dependency on Dataset's Bias:

When adversaries take advantage of these intrinsic flaws, models trained on biased or insufficient data are more vulnerable to adversarial attacks.

Scalability:

Once a successful adversarial attack has been developed, its impact can be increased by scaling it to target other systems.

1.4. Motivations Behind Adversarial Attacks

Financial Gain:

Attackers carry out illegal transactions or obtain financial advantages by taking advantage of flaws in dynamic pricing algorithms or fraud detection.

Competitive Advantage:

To hurt rivals or unfairly promote their goods, adversaries tamper with product rankings or recommendation systems.

Reputation Damage:

In order to damage a company's reputation, malicious actors may attack e-commerce systems by, for example, forcing chat-bots to respond in an unpleasant manner.

Disruption of Operations:

Targeting payment gateways or inventory management might result in operational outages, which can cost businesses money and leave consumers unhappy.

Data Theft and Espionage:

In order to obtain sensitive data, such proprietary algorithms or private user information, exploratory assaults comb through machine learning systems.

Algorithmic Manipulation:

By introducing biases or weaknesses that an attacker can later exploit, poisoning attacks have the potential to distort the training process of machine learning models.

Testing Security Measures:

Adversarial attacks are carried out by ethical hackers or researchers to find and fix flaws in machine learning systems, enhancing security overall.

Regulatory Non-Compliance:

By disclosing private information, adversarial attacks may result in data protection regulations being broken, which could have negative legal and financial effects.

Experimentation and Learning:

In order to better understand ML models and prepare for more complex attacks in the future, attackers may employ adversarial approaches as a learning tool.

Sabotage:

The performance of ML systems may be purposefully harmed by malicious actors, leading to inefficiencies or failures in e-commerce operations.

1.5. Challenges

Subtlety in Text Manipulation:

Adversarial text attacks often involve subtle changes, such as swapping synonyms, misspellings, or inserting irrelevant words, making them difficult to detect. These changes can bypass NLP models while maintaining readability for human users (Kothamali et al., 2020).

Context Preservation:

Ensuring that adversarial modifications do not alter the intended meaning of the text adds complexity for attackers but also makes detection harder for defense mechanisms.

Semantic Challenges:

The NLP models will rely on the understanding of semantic context. The weakness in semantic interpretation will happens on causing model, such that misclassification and misunderstanding the queries, review and product descriptions from users.

High Dimensionality of Text Data:

While embedding the input sequences of text data which is inherently in high-dimenstional and slightly to be perturbations in form. Which results in the significants of changes in model prediction, amplifying vulnerabilities.

Linguistic Diversity:

NLP models facilitates with the global nature of e-commerce platforms to handle multiple linguistics and will dialects by increasing the attack among the surface for adversarial inputs which is tailored with specific linguistic nuances too.

Dynamic User Interactions:

User- generated content for real-time like reviews, chat queries and social media mentions will provide attackers to a sequence flow of stream of data to exploit and it make challenging to preemptively secure systems.

Dependence on Pertained Models:

Creating opportunities for adversarial attacks which will be inherited from the vulnerabilities of the original training datasets where many e-commerce platforms use pertained NLP models.

Lack of explain ability in NLP Models:

Many NLP models makes a complication from the nature of black box testing to identify and mitigate the specific factors which lead to adversarial susceptibility, complicating with more defense strategies.

Transferability of Attacks:

Adversarial examples crafted for one NLP model can often transfer to other models, especially when similar architectures or embedding are used, magnifying the threat.

Balancing Security and User Experience:

Implementing strict text validation or anomaly detection methods can impact user experience by introducing delays or flagging legitimate inputs as adversarial, creating friction in the customer journey.

1.5.1. Challenges in Text-Based Adversarial Attacks in E-Commerce

Figure 1. Text-Based Adversarial Attacks in E-Commerce

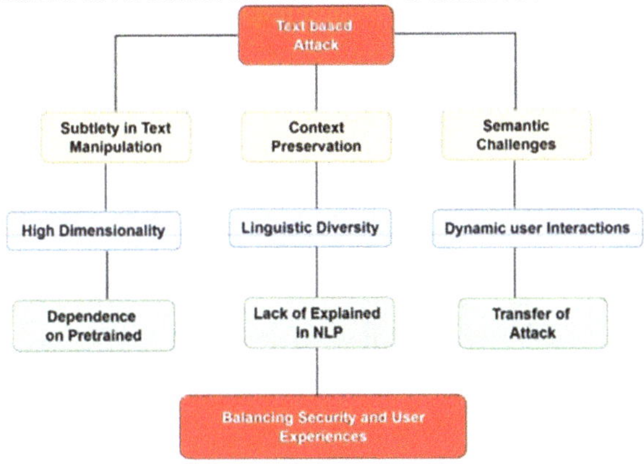

1.5.2. NLP in Industrial Cybersecurity

NLP is vast in enabling the analysis fo textual data from each sectors in manufacturing and energies. By processing logs, threat reports, and phishing emails, NLP enhances proactive and responsive security measures, addressing the complex, interconnected nature of modern infrastructure and its cyber threat exposure. (Balantrapu, 2023).NLP plays a key role in industrial cybersecurity by detecting phishing and social engineering attacks through email analysis. The enhanced way of incident response through chat-bot and virtual assistants will automate the triage for enabling analysts which will prioritize critical threats very effectively.

NLP plays an important role in gathering and analyzing threat intelligence. It helps extract useful insights from unstructured data sources, like security bulletins, hacker forums, and dark web content. This provides organizations with timely information about new threats. Anomaly detection systems also use NLP to analyze patterns in system communications. The signal of adversarial actions finds the unusual activities that can give command injection or protocol spoofing.

The collaborative work between humans and machines which improves in using NLP in cybersecurity. The long reports, sort incidents and pinpoint root causes, which are used to summarize with the help of NLP tools. This helps in decision-making and are more efficient, and it also challenges while using NLP in industrial cybersecurity. The diverse terminologies, acronyms, and domain-specific jargon in industrial systems require tailored NLP models and training datasets to achieve optimal performance (Muhammad & Mirjat, 2024).

As industrial environments become increasingly digitized, the role of NLP in cybersecurity is set to expand, offering advanced solutions to safeguard critical assets and ensure operational resilience against evolving cyber threats.

Spam and Phishing Detection: Naïve Bayes Classifier

Goal: Classify an email as malicious or legitimate.
Formula:

Bayes' theorem: $P\left(\frac{H}{E}\right) = P\left(\frac{E}{H}\right) \cdot \frac{P(H)}{P(E)}$

Where:

- *H*: Hypothesis (e.g., email is phishing).
- *E*: Evidence (e.g., presence of malicious words).
- $P\left(\frac{H}{E}\right)$: Posterior probability (email is phishing given the evidence).

- $P\left(\frac{E}{H}\right)$: Likelihood (probability of evidence given the hypothesis).
- *P(H)*: Prior probability (overall likelihood of phishing emails).
- *P(E)*: Marginal probability of evidence.

Calculation Example:

If the probability of a phishing email containing the word "urgent" is 0.8, and "urgent" appears in 10% of emails, the probability of phishing given "urgent" can be computed.

TF-IDF for Threat Intelligence Analysis:

Goal: Extract important terms from threat intelligence reports.
Formula:

$$\text{Term Frequency}\left(\text{TF}\right):\text{TF}\left(\text{t, d}\right)=\frac{\text{Frequency of term t in document d}}{\text{Total terms in document d}}$$

Inverse Document Frequency (IDF):

$$\text{IDF(t)} = \log\left(\frac{\text{Total number of documents}}{1+\text{Number of documents containing term t}}\right)$$

TF-IDF:

$$TF - IDF(t,d) = TF(t,d)\,.\,IDF(t)$$

Calculation Example:

If the term "malware" appears 5 times in a report of 100 words and is found in 10 out of 1000 reports, the TF-IDF for "malware" is:

$$\boldsymbol{TF} = \frac{5}{100} = 0.05$$

$$\boldsymbol{IDF} = log\left(\frac{1000}{1+10}\right) \cong 2.0$$

$$\boldsymbol{TF - IDF} = (0.05)\bullet(2.0) = 0.1$$

Anomaly Detection with Cosine Similarity:

Goal: Identify abnormal behavior in system communication.
Formula:

$$\text{Cosine similarity:} \frac{\vec{A} \cdot \vec{B}}{||\vec{A}|| \, ||\vec{B}||}$$

Where:

- $\vec{A}, \vec{B}$: Vectors representing text sequences or other data points.
- $\vec{A} \cdot \vec{B}$: Dot product of the two vectors.
- $||\vec{A}||$: Magnitude (or norm) of vector.
- $||\vec{B}||$: Magnitude (or norm) of vector.

Calculation Example:

If two log messages are represented as vectors $\vec{A} = \left[1,2,1\right]$ *and* $\vec{B} = \left[2,1,0\right]$:

$$\textbf{Cosine Similarity:} \left(\frac{(1 \cdot 2)+(2 \cdot 1)+(1 \cdot 0)}{\sqrt{1^2+2^2+1\,1^2} \cdot \sqrt{2^2+1^2+0^2}} \right) = \frac{(2+2+0)}{\sqrt{6}\ \sqrt{5}} \approx 0.73$$

Sentiment Analysis for Incident Reports

Goal: Analyze sentiment polarity of textual data to prioritize cybersecurity responses.
Formula:

$$\textbf{Sentiment score} \left(\textbf{weighted average} \right): S = \frac{\sum_{i=1}^{n} w_i \cdot s_i}{\sum_{i=1}^{n} wi}$$

Where:

- w_i = weight of term i(e.g.., TF-IDF Score).
- s_i = Sentiment polarity score of term i(e.g.., -1 for negative, +1 for positive).

Calculate Example:

For terms with weights [0.1,0.3,0.2] and polarities [-1,1,0]

$$S = \frac{(0.1 \bullet -1)+(0.3 \bullet 1)+(0.2 . 0)}{0.1+0.3+0.2} = \frac{-0. 1+0.3}{0.6} \approx 0.33$$

Language Model Scoring for Threat Detection

Goal: Compute the probability of sequence of words (eg.., in logs or e-mails)
Formula:
Probability of a sentence $P(w_1, w_2 \ldots, w_n)$:

$$P(w_1, w_2 \ldots, w_n) = \prod_{i=1}^{n} P(w_i | , w_{i-1}, \ldots, w_1)$$

Calculate Example:

For the sequence "Access Denied, " where $P(\text{Access}) = 0.3$ and

$P(Denied/Access) = 0.5$

$P(Access/Denied) = 0.3 \bullet 0.5 = 0.15$

2. APPLICATIONS OF NLP IN FRAUD DETECTION, CUSTOMER SUPPORT, AND RECOMMENDATION SYSTEMS

Natural Language Processing (NLP) has transformed e-commerce and other industries by enhancing fraud detection, customer support, and recommendation systems. In fraud detection, NLP helps identify deceptive patterns and anomalous behavior in textual data such as transaction descriptions, customer reviews, and emails. By analyzing text for linguistic inconsistencies, sentiment shifts, or unusual word usage, NLP models can flag potential fraud attempts, such as phishing emails or fake reviews. For instance, the positive and negative reviews are designed to manipulate by its rating which is been identified by sentiment analysis. Language models can find unusual patterns in transaction descriptions that may indicate fraud. (Muhammad & Mirjat, 2024) (Mudgal, 2025).

In customer support, NLP drives chat-bots, virtual assistants, and automated ticketing systems. This provides support 24/7 and speeds up response times. NLP algorithms handle customer queries in natural language, extract key intents, and suggest relevant solutions or route issues to human agents when necessary. By allowing personalized and empathetic responses the sentimental analysis will help in companies to understand customer emotions. NLP improves multilingual support. It helps businesses communicate effectively with a global customer base without language barriers. (Alawida et al., 2023).

In recommendation systems, NLP plays a key role. It examines user-generated content such as product reviews, search queries, and browsing histories to provide personalized suggestions. NLP based models extract meaning from text data to grasp user preferences and connect them with relevant products or services. By pinpointing the key themes by fine-tuning the techniques with the help of topic modeling and sentiment analysis, which provides the feedback for the user.

Furthermore, NLP improves contextual recommendations by analyzing customer interactions in real-time. For instance, it might suggest accessories for a recently viewed item or provide discounts on related products.

By understanding and processing unstructured text data, NLP helps businesses detect fraud, improve customer experiences, and deliver targeted recommendations, boosting efficiency and customer satisfaction.

2.1. Vulnerabilities of NLP Systems to Adversarial Attacks

In spite their widespread application and utility, NLP systems are extremely vulnerable to adversarial attacks that exploit weaknesses in their underlying models. These attacks involve the creation of carefully thought-out input modifications, such as word substitutions, misspellings, or phrase rearrangements, that affect system functionality but are undetectable to humans. A few word changes in a phishing email can fool a spam filter, and subtle synonym substitutions in reviews can skew sentiment analysis models. Such attacks have the potential to compromise vital applications such as chatbots, fraud detection, and recommendation systems, possibly leading to financial loss or a reduction in system trust. (Mudgal, 2025; Alawida et al., 2023). These weaknesses are exacerbated by the intrinsic complexity of natural language. Word embedding and statistical patterns are frequently used in NLP models, which adversaries exploit by targeting weak points in vector representations.

Moreover, the transferability of adversarial examples allows attackers to apply similar techniques across different models, making defense even more challenging. Additionally, the black-box nature of many NLP algorithms makes it difficult to pinpoint and mitigate vulnerabilities effectively.These difficulties show how important it is to have strong defenses in place to protect NLP systems, like ensemble modelling, adversarial training, and anomaly detection. For NLP-driven applications to remain dependable and secure, resilience against adversarial assaults must be strengthened.

2.2. Types of Adversarial Attacks in E-Commerce

Machine learning (ML) model flaws are used by adversarial assaults in e-commerce to change the behavior of the models. Numerous applications, including sentiment analysis, recommendation engines, and fraud detection, may be the focus of these attacks. The main categories of adversarial attacks seen in e-commerce are listed below:

Evasion Attacks

When adversaries create harmful inputs to get around detection systems, it's known as an evasion assault. For example, in fraud detection systems, small changes to user data or transaction details can trick the model into identifying fraudulent activity as authentic. Similarly, content control systems may be circumvented by changing product reviews or descriptions.

Poisoning Attacks

In order to taint the learning process, adversaries use poisoning attacks to introduce malicious data into the training dataset. A recommendation system may be biased to unfairly promote particular items, for instance, if phony evaluations with particular patterns are included to a training set. Because the tainted model keeps using the modified data, poisoning assaults may have long-term effects.

Extraction Attacks

By continuously querying a proprietary machine learning model and utilizing the results to train a clone model, these attacks seek to imitate the functionality of the original model. Intellectual property theft and the creation of fake systems that threaten the original e-commerce platform are possible outcomes of this.

Inference Attacks

Inference attacks exploit ML models to gain insights into sensitive data, such as customer purchase histories or preferences. By analyzing the outputs of recommendation systems, adversaries can infer confidential information, posing privacy risks to users.

Trojan Attacks

Trojan attacks involve embedding malicious triggers within models during development. These triggers remain dormant until specific conditions are met, at which point they alter the model's behavior. In e-commerce, a trojanized model might manipulate product rankings or disable fraud detection for specific transactions.

Backdoor Attacks

Backdoor attacks plant hidden triggers that adversaries can exploit later. For example, embedding a specific keyword in product descriptions might bypass fraud filters, enabling fraudulent listings to remain undetected (Sood, 2024).

2.3. Introduction to Input Perturbations

The intention of altering the output of machine learning models is by deliberating the modifications made with data inputs which is taken into input perturbations. These perturbation will change the behavior of ML systems that can significantly alter. These are very minor and invisible to humans. The resulting in inaccurate classifications or predictions are designed to take more advantages in model flaws and are used in adversarial assaults.

The e-commerce becomes more integral in ML applications in such a way that the vital imput perturbations that ensures the robustness, reliability and security of the systems. (NG et al., n.d.).

Character-Level Attacks (e.g., Typos, Misspellings)

Character-level attacks are one form of adversarial input modification. They consist of modifying individual characters of text data to deceive machine learning models. Such attacks tend to exploit the nature of natural language processing (NLP) systems that depend on word-level or character-level embedding. Typos, misspellings, or insertions, deletions, and substitutions of characters are the kinds of simple modifications that can readily manipulate these systems.

For instance, the attacker will add minor misspelling to review the word like 'gr8' or 'great' for inputting the fields in e-commerce scenario. This will mislead the search algorithm or it will moderate the systems in evading content to assist.

Although humans have no problem understanding such modifications, they can be detrimental to the performance of models by interrupting tokenization, feature extraction, or semantic comprehension processes.

To convert in nature the character level attacks are very difficult to check and constrain. Moreover to defend the NLP models there needs the vulnerabilities by training, robust tokenization and spelling check will give a good experience.

Word-Level Attacks (e.g., Synonym Replacement, Homophones)

Word-level attacks refer to adversarial techniques that transform input text by replacing full words while maintaining the overall context, frequently attacking weaknesses in natural language processing (NLP) models. Some popular methods involve synonym substitution, where words are replaced with their synonyms (e.g., substituting "happy" with "joyful"), and homophone replacement, replacing words with others that have a similar pronunciation but possibly different spellings (e.g., using "sale" instead of "sail"). In online commerce, these attacks can mislead models deployed in sentiment analysis, product recommendation, or spam filtering (Khurana & Kaul, 2019). For instance, a fake review can employ synonyms to avoid detection, or a malicious search query can sabotage search algorithms by changing essential keywords.

Leading to miscalssifications or aberrant behavior the attacks has taken an advantage for embedding word and making semantic comprehension limitations in models. The sophisticated embedding methods that will guarantee its model at the expense to its performance and also it will against to the word-level attacks which gives a strong measures, which leads to a contextual awareness and adversarial training.

Sentence-Level Attacks (e.g., Paraphrasing to Alter Meaning)

Sentence-level attacks are adversarial methods that entailed paraphrasing or rephrasing whole sentences to manipulate their meaning slightly without evading machine learning model detection. In contrast with character- or word-level attacks, sentence-level methods target the structure, syntax, or phrasing of a sentence while preserving semantic meaning, hence making them more challenging to detect and counter.

Such attacks in e-commerce can manipulate content moderation systems, sentiment analysis, or fake review detection systems. A negative review, for instance, such as "The product is terrible" can be paraphrased into "This product didn't meet my expectations" to evade filters or detection (Jeyaraj et al., 2024). Paraphrased search queries could also sabotage search engine results or recommendation systems by changing keyword salience. Defending against sentence-level attacks is a complex task that demands sophisticated NLP defenses, including strong semantic comprehension, paraphrasing detection mechanisms, and adversarial training to ready models for various sentence forms while maintaining performance. Figure.2 below indicates the types of adversarial attacks in E-Commerce during online shopping.

Figure 2. Types of Adversarial Attack in E-Commerce

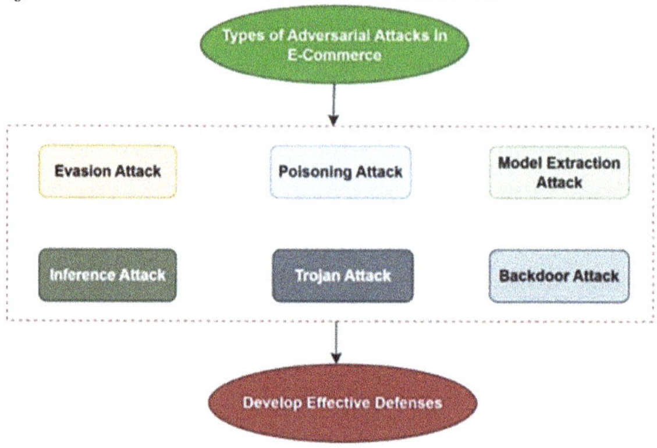

2.3. Attack Scenarios in E-Commerce

Adversarial attacks in commerce take advantage of weaknesses in machine learning models to interfere with operations, tamper with data, or access unauthorized benefits. Adversarial attacks can be directed at several important applications, such as recommendation engines, search functions, fraud detection, and sentiment analysis platforms. Adversarial attackers apply input perturbations such as typos or synonyms for search ranking manipulation, create artificial reviews through paraphrasing, and make insidious changes to transaction information to bypass fraud detection in commerce systems.

Dynamic pricing mechanisms are another focus, where adversarial inputs may induce algorithmic anomalies, leading companies to provide enviable discounts or inflated listings (WILLIAM & IBRAHIM, 2024). These situations reveal the high risks for e-commerce platforms, where adversarial attacks can result in economic losses, user trust damaged, and brand reputation lost. Strong countermeasures are vital to counteract these changing threats.

2.3.1. Manipulation of Reviews and Ratings

Review and rating manipulation is a widespread e-commerce adversarial activity that takes advantage of machine learning weaknesses to bias consumer opinion. Malicious reviewers can utilize fake reviews, usually created through paraphrasing or sentiment polarity inversion, to increase product ratings or adversely affect competitors. The imitating natural language patterns are been a types of malicious reviews which can be evasive.

Moreover the substitution or character-level perturbations can evade the review by moderating the controls of adversarial methods like synonym substitution. This manipulate the product rankings and undermining the credibility of the platform by deceiving the consumers.The main need to strengthen the sentiment analysis like fake review detection mechanisms and adversarial training to enable a trusted and unbiased feedback system.

2.3.2. Evasion of Spam and Phishing Detection Systems

To exploit the weakness in spam and phishing detection systems the security controls the attackers to bypass the use of adversarial attacks. The errors or obfuscations like synonym substitutions, work-level adjustments and sentence-level rewrites are the techniques that hide the harmful informtion.

In online shopping, this can lead to phishing emails that mimic genuine messages or spam emails that avoid filters and reach customers. These attacks damage user trust, encourage fraud, and threaten sensitive information (Selvalakshmi et al., 2025). Improving defenses involves advanced NLP methods, adversarial training, and behavior-based anomaly detection. These strategies help detect and counter such evasive techniques effectively.

2.3.3. Bypassing Fraud Detection Algorithms in Payment Systems

Adversarial attacks on payment systems take advantage of weaknesses in fraud detection models to make unauthorized transactions. Attackers utilize input perturbations, for example, by changing billing information, transaction metadata, or user credentials, to evade fraud detection.

The diminished faith in the platform has been raised in these attacks with high-risk and will results in monetary losses with a compromised user information too. To detect suspicious patterns and close vulnerabilities accordingly works to defense against these threats involves adaptive fraud protection mechanisms that include anomaly detection, adversarial training, and real-time monitoring.

2.3.4. Adversarial Exploitation of chat-bot and Virtual Assistants

To manipulate the responses or to bypass the security measures which will perform the adversarial attacks on the chat-bots and will virtually assists by exploiting the NLP vulnerabilities. By confession models like leading to incorrect or unintended outputs will ease the attackers to use the techniques like synonym replacement, paraphrasing, or inserting ambiguous phrases.

Providing the unauthorized access to sensitive information and to exploitation in e-commerce will disrupt customer support.

2.4. NLP Strategies for Mitigating Adversarial Attacks

NLP offers a range of strategies for resisting hostile attacks with guarantees of robustness in use cases like e-commerce. Adversarial training is an important methodology that makes models more resilient to manipulations such as synonym replacements or character-level perturbations by subjecting them to adversarial instances during training (Gunasekara, 2023). To reducing the effect of character- or word-level attacks will strengthen the preprocessing methods which includes spelling corrector and synonym normalization that cleans the inputs.

In order to better capture semantic nuances and reduce susceptibility to paraphrasing or sneaky input modifications, contextual models also make use of complex embedding, like transformers. In order to create a multi-layered defence against attacks that take advantage of flaws in individual models, ensemble techniques combine the outputs of multiple models with various architectures.

Anomaly detection can watch for input patterns deviating from normal behavior to identify suspicious behavior such as phony reviews or phishing attacks (Sun et al., 2023). For text-based adversarial attacks, paraphrase detection models can detect and counterattack rephrased malicious content. Data augmentation techniques, such as applying diverse linguistic patterns to training datasets, also make models stronger.Lastly, by analyzing decision-making processes, explainable AI (XAI) technologies can help identify vulnerabilities and enable practical improvement. Together, these strategies fortify NLP systems against hostile attacks, guaranteeing secure and reliable operation in critical applications.

Figure 3. NLP Strategies for mitigating adversarial attacks.

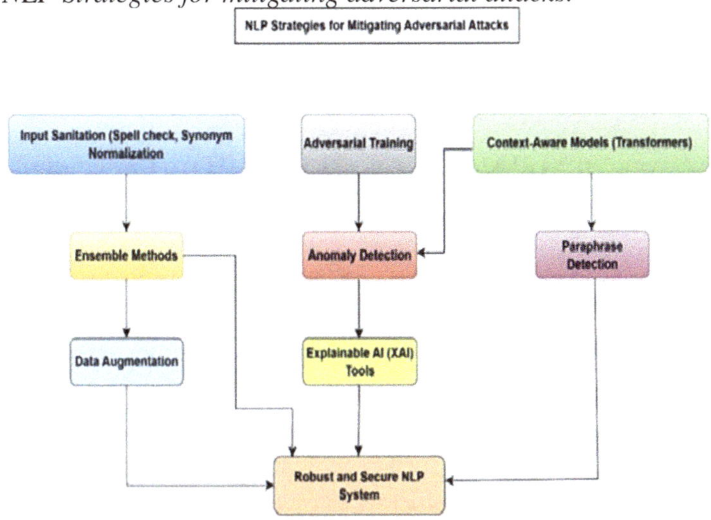

3. ENSEMBLE METHODS

Combining Multiple Models to Mitigate Vulnerabilities

When combining predictions from several machine learning models, ensemble approaches improve model robustness. Every model in the group contributes its own advantages and could make up for the shortcomings of the others. One model might be particularly good at spotting spelling-based attacks, for example, while another might concentrate on semantic manipulations. Ensemble approaches lessen the possibility of adversarial attacks taking advantage of the flaws in a single model by combining their outputs. This can strengthen e-commerce systems such as spam filtering, sentiment analysis, and fraud detection, guaranteeing more accurate and trustworthy forecasts (Sakib, Usama S2*, 2022).

Hybrid Approaches Using Diverse NLP Architectures

The strengths of various NLP architectures, such as transformer-based models (like BERT), in conjunction with conventional rule-based systems or recurrent neural networks (RNNs), are harnessed by hybrid ensemble approaches. This variety boosts resistance to a variety of hostile tactics, such as context manipulation, synonym substitution, and paraphrasing. By identifying different linguistic and structural patterns, hybrid approaches can strengthen the resilience of chat-bots, recommendation systems, and review moderation in e-commerce applications.

3.1. Context-Aware Defenses

Using Advanced NLP Models (e.g., BERT, GPT) to Understand Semantic Context:

Because of their superior ability to comprehend semantic context, contemporary NLP models such as BERT and GPT have revolutionized natural language processing. Even in cases where the structure of a text is complicated or unclear, these models use attention mechanisms to record the links between words and sentences. Through the interpretation of subtle manipulations, such as paraphrased reviews or contextually unsuitable questions, such models improve the detection of adversarial assaults in the context of e-commerce. They are resistant to input changes that take advantage of the shortcomings of simpler models because of their profound contextual understanding.

Leveraging Contextual Embedding to Detect Adversarial Inputs:

Contextual embedding generated by advanced NLP models enable fine-grained analysis of text. Unlike static word embedding, these embedding capture the meaning of words based on their usage in context. By comparing embedding for similar inputs, systems can identify discrepancies caused by adversarial perturbations, such as synonym replacements or sentence rephrasing. In e-commerce, this can help detect fake reviews, phishing attempts, and manipulated queries that aim to deceive recommendation or search systems (Sood, 2024).

3.2. Behavior-Based and Anomaly Detection

Monitoring User Behavior and Transaction Patterns:

Behavior-based detection involves analyzing user activities, such as browsing habits, transaction sequences, and interaction styles, to establish baseline patterns of normal behavior. These patterns are then monitored for any unusual or suspicious actions. For example, in e-commerce, sudden spikes in activity, irregular login attempts, or unusual transaction volumes may indicate adversarial attempts such as bot activity, phishing, or fraud. Systems can identify abnormalities early and offer a proactive defence against hostile actions by continuously monitoring these behavior.

Detecting Deviations from Normal Operations to Identify Adversarial Activity:

Even in cases where adversarial attacks entail minute manipulations, anomaly detection systems are made to spot departures from accepted norms. Outliers that differ from the norm can be found using machine learning models like clustering or auto encoders.

Behaviour in transaction data, network traffic, or text inputs. For example, hostile manipulations that depart from standard linguistic patterns in product reviews or ratings may be identified as possible dangers (Ferreira et al., 2023).

E-commerce platforms can successfully detect and thwart hostile activity by fusing anomaly detection with behavioral monitoring. This two-pronged strategy preserves the integrity of user experiences and system functions while strengthening cybersecurity measures.

3.3. Dynamic Feature Selection

Reducing Computational Complexity in Real-Time Scenarios:

Enabling systems to process data more efficiently in real-time is by dynamic feature selection process that adapts the complete selection that gives the features based on the context and requirements of a given task. The unnecessary computations are avoided, reducing latency and resource consumption that focus on the relevant features. Dynamic feature selection guarantees timely analysis without sacrificing system performance in e-commerce, where quick reaction times are crucial, such as during fraud detection or recommendation generation.

Prioritizing Relevant Features for Faster and More Accurate Analysis:

Features that offer the most information for the particular task—like text inputs, transaction details, or user behaviour patterns—are given priority by dynamic feature selection techniques. Models can concentrate on high-value data and increase their accuracy in detecting adversarial activity by removing noise and superfluous features. Prioritising linguistic features like sentiment shifts or contextual inconsistencies, for instance, improves detection capabilities when it comes to identifying manipulated product reviews (NG et al., n.d.).

E-commerce systems that use dynamic feature selection strike a balance between speed and accuracy, increasing their resistance to hostile attacks and preserving high operational efficiency in real-time settings.

4. CASE STUDIES IN E-COMMERCE ADVERSARIAL DEFENSE

4.1. Phishing and Spam Detection

4.1.1. Real-World Examples of Adversarial Attacks on Email Systems

Sophisticated Phishing Emails:

The close mimic legitimate communications from trusted organizations that attackers may craft phishing emails. The lure recipients that clicking malicious links or divulging sensitive information that causes a minor perturbation like misspellings, homophones or slight modifications in email addresses. For example instead of "paypal.com" with "paypa1.com", the attackers might replace and exploiting the similarity to trick users and bypass spam filters.

Adversarial Content Manipulation:

The manipulated content of phishing emails that attackers use adversarial strategies like synonym replacement or subtle paraphrasing. The detected systems that rely on the keyword with matching emails these allows the changes. For example, the bypass systems tuned to detect specific phrases with "urgent payment request" into "immediate financial action required".

Social Engineering and Contextual Attacks:

The tax season or promotional sales, employ the contextual information that appear legitimate on phishing emails tailored to exploit user behavior in specific events. Context-sensitive language filters in a traditional method that struggle to detect the attackers craft messages with dynamic context-sensitive.

4.1.2. Success Stories in Using NLP to Counter These Threats

Context-Aware Detection with NLP Models:

Advanced NLP models like BERT and GPT have demonstrated success in understanding the semantic and contextual nuances of phishing and spam emails. For example, Google's spam filter incorporates machine learning and NLP techniques to identify contextual inconsistencies in phishing emails, such as mismatched sender and domain details, ensuring high detection rates.

Anomaly-Based Spam Detection:

Several email systems use anomaly detection techniques to identify deviations from typical email patterns. By employing NLP models trained on vast datasets of legitimate emails, systems can flag content that deviates from standard linguistic and formatting norms, effectively identifying sophisticated phishing attempts(Wu et al., 2021).

Adversarial Training and Data Augmentation:

To counter adversarial attacks, email filters have integrated adversarial training with NLP techniques. For instance, exposing models to adversarial examples, such as altered synonyms or paraphrased sentences, improves their robustness against manipulative phishing emails.

Real-Time Phishing URL Detection:

By analyzing email content and embedded URLs in real-time, NLP systems can identify malicious links, even when attackers use techniques like URL shortening or minor perturbations. Platforms like Microsoft Outlook employ such NLP-driven tools to detect and block phishing URLs effectively.

Sentiment and Intent Analysis:

By applying sentiment and intent analysis, NLP models can identify emails with manipulative or suspicious tones, such as urgency, threats, or coercion. This capability helps flag emails that exploit fear or urgency to deceive recipients, enhancing phishing detection accuracy.

Success of Hybrid Approaches:

Many organizations have adopted hybrid approaches combining rule-based systems with NLP-powered anomaly detection to tackle phishing. For example, combining regex-based keyword matching with context-aware NLP models ensures comprehensive coverage against both simple and sophisticated attacks.

The integration of NLP strategies has significantly advanced the detection of phishing and spam in email systems. By leveraging the semantic understanding, contextual awareness, and anomaly detection capabilities of NLP models, email systems have become more adept at countering adversarial attacks. These successes highlight the potential of NLP-powered defenses in safeguarding users from ever-evolving phishing and spam threats. (Natarajan et al., 2025).

Fraud Detection in Payment Systems

Payment systems are a critical component of e-commerce, processing millions of transactions daily. With the rise of sophisticated adversarial tactics, fraud detection has become a significant challenge. Attackers manipulate payment data to evade detection systems, posing risks to financial security and user trust.

4.1.3. Implementation of Robust NLP Strategies to Mitigate Risks

Behavioral Analysis with NLP Models:

The NLP model transaction like patterns or linguistic cues in descriptions and metadata are been analyzed by the user behavior and it will identify discrepancies. For instance, in the transaction notes might indicate the fraudulent intent with phrasing or tone.

Context-Aware Models for Enhanced Fraud Detection:

To understand the relationships between transaction attributes the contextual embedding generated by models like BERT enable systems. When adversaries introduce subtle perturbations it will be more helpful to identify fraud.

Adversarial Training for Payment Data Models:

A system which exposes the adversarial inputs will alter the merchant names or descriptions that becomes more resilient to such attacks. This incorporate the adversarial examples into the trained datasets and also it manipulates the model by strengthening.

Sentiment and Intent Detection in Payment Notes:

For example, the trigger alerts for further inspection will vague or overly generic descriptions ("miscellaneous payment") (Deldjoo et al., 2021). NLP models can detect potentially fraud transactions by analyzing the sentiment or intent behind the payment descriptions.

Multilingual and Cross-Cultural Adaptation:

The NLP models trained on multilingual datasets that can detect fraud in various languages which creates a global e-commerce platforms. The adversarial manipulation targeting its linguistic diversity and which ensures against the comprehensive protection.

Real-Time Threat Intelligence:

Emerging adversarial tactics can be recognised and blocked by NLP systems that are integrated with real-time threat intelligence feeds. For example, NLP-driven systems can adjust globally if a new fraudulent activity pattern is identified in one area.

Advanced NLP techniques must be incorporated into a multifaceted strategy for payment system fraud detection. E-commerce platforms can successfully reduce the risks of adversarial manipulation by utilising hybrid models, adversarial training, anomaly detection, and behavioural analysis. Strong NLP-driven defences are necessary to guarantee safe and reliable payment systems as adversaries continue to modify their strategies. (Ashraf, 2025).

4.2. Securing Recommendation Systems

E-commerce relies heavily on recommendation systems, which offer tailored product recommendations that improve user experience and increase sales. Nevertheless, these systems are susceptible to hostile attacks, like content manipulation and phoney reviews, which can impair their functionality and undermine confidence. (Natarajan et al., 2025) (WILLIAM et al., 2024).

4.2.1. Defense Against Fake Reviews and Adversarial Content Injection

Detection of Fake Reviews:

Adversaries often inject fake reviews to manipulate product rankings and user perceptions. These reviews may use repeated phrases, unusual sentiment shifts, or irrelevant content. Natural Language Processing (NLP) models can identify such patterns, detecting inconsistencies in tone, sentiment, and syntax to flag suspicious reviews.

Clustering and Anomaly Detection:

Fake reviews can be found by classifying reviews according to linguistic similarity and spotting irregularities. For instance, several reviews submitted in a short period of time with comparable sentiments or structures may be signs of adversarial activity.

Dynamic Feature Selection:

Recommendation systems can prioritise valid inputs and lessen the impact of adversarial content by concentrating on high-impact features like verified user tags or review history. (Wu et al., 2021).

4.2.1. Context-Aware Approaches to Preserve Recommendation Accuracy

Leveraging Contextual Embedding:

Contextual embeddings produced by sophisticated NLP models such as BERT and GPT capture the intent and meaning of user reviews and inputs. This maintains the quality of recommendations by assisting recommendation systems in differentiating between legitimate content and hostile manipulations.

Sentiment and Semantic Analysis:

Semantic analysis assists in identifying minute changes in meaning brought about by adversarial modifications, while sentiment analysis guarantees that the emotional tone of reviews conforms to expected norms (Yusuff, 2023). These methods can be used to identify phoney reviews that, for instance, highlight a product but contain contradicting information.

Incorporating User Behavior Patterns:

Systems can contextualise user preferences and identify anomalies suggestive of adversarial interference by examining user behaviour in conjunction with textual data, such as browsing history and purchase patterns.

Ensemble Methods for Robustness:

Resilience against hostile attacks is increased by using ensemble models with different architectures. Other models can still produce accurate predictions even if one is deceived by manipulated data, preserving the overall accuracy of the recommendations.

Adversarial Training for Recommendation Models:

Recommendation systems are better equipped to handle manipulated inputs when they are trained on adversarial examples. To increase robustness, for example, models can be trained on adversarial modified reviews as well as legitimate reviews.

Cross-Domain Data Integration:

A comprehensive picture of user preferences can be obtained by combining data from several domains, including user reviews, ratings, and interaction histories. The impact of adversarial content in any one domain is lessened by this multifaceted strategy.

Context-Specific Filters:

Creating filters based on user demographics or product categories guarantees that recommendations are accurate even when there are hostile attacks aimed at specialised markets.

A combination of strong defences and context-aware tactics is needed to protect recommendation systems from adversarial attacks (Muhammad & Mirjat, 2024) (Yusuff, 2023). Platforms can protect the integrity of their recommendation systems by utilising dynamic contextual analysis, adversarial training, anomaly detection, and advanced natural language processing techniques. These safeguards maintain user confidence and improve overall recommendation accuracy in addition to protecting against adversarial manipulations.

4.2.2. Protecting chat-bot and Virtual Assistants

Virtual assistants and chatbots are essential in e-commerce because they increase user engagement and offer effective customer service. These NLP-driven systems are susceptible to hostile attacks, though, which aim to take advantage of their algorithms, erode their dependability, and lower user satisfaction.

4.2.3. Identifying Adversarial Queries Targeting NLP-Driven Customer Support

Semantic Manipulation:

Attackers create queries that look authentic but purposefully change semantic meaning. Asking “What's the status of my **** order?” rather than “What's the status of my delayed order?" for instance, can lead to poorly designed systems misinterpreting user intent.

Contextual Exploits:

Adversaries may leverage ambiguous or contextually irrelevant queries to force chat-bots into providing incorrect or irrelevant responses, potentially degrading trust in the system. For instance, asking for irrelevant product details during a troubleshooting session could lead the chat-bot astray (Muhammad & Mirjat, 2024).

Injection Attacks:

By embedding malicious payloads or commands into queries, attackers aim to exploit vulnerabilities in the underlying NLP models. For example, including SQL injection-like syntax in a chatbot query could target backend systems (William & Ibrahim, 2024).

Spam and Repeated Queries:

Automated adversarial queries flooding chat-bot can overwhelm systems, resulting in service delays or degraded user experience.

Code Exploits in Queries:

Certain attacks involve injecting code snippets or non-standard characters designed to exploit encoding vulnerabilities in NLP systems, potentially crashing or destabilizing the chat-bot.

4.2.4. Mitigating Adversarial Queries

Robust Query Preprocessing:

Before adversarial manipulations reach NLP models, inputs can be sanitised by putting preprocessing techniques like text normalisation, tokenisation, and filtering into practice.

Context-Aware NLP Models:

After being trained on a variety of datasets, advanced models such as BERT and GPT are better able to comprehend the context of queries, which helps them spot anomalies and stop malicious exploits.

Adversarial Training:

During training, exposing chatbots to hostile queries makes the models more resistant to manipulation. For instance, training a chatbot with queries that contain typos, paraphrases, and semantic shifts gets it ready for attacks in the real world. (Mudgal, 2025).

Anomaly Detection:

Monitoring user interactions in real time makes it easier to identify and flag queries that deviate from typical patterns, which may be signs of hostile attempts. Systems are able to examine things like the frequency of queries, odd wording, or illogical context.

Behavior-Based Security Layers:

Chatbots can recognise odd behaviours suggestive of hostile activity by incorporating user behaviour analysis, including session history and interaction patterns.

Hybrid Defensive Models:

Layered defence mechanisms are ensured by combining machine learning models with rule-based systems. While machine learning can handle more complex adversarial queries, rules can handle simple attacks.

Rate Limiting and Spam Control:

System stability is ensured by putting rate-limiting mechanisms and CAPTCHA challenges in place to stop adversaries from flooding chatbots with repetitive queries.

Contextual Embedding Monitoring:

By highlighting adversarial attempts for additional examination, embedding layers in NLP models can assist in identifying inputs that substantially depart from typical contextual patterns.

E-commerce platforms are at serious risk from adversarial queries directed at chatbots and virtual assistants. Businesses can successfully safeguard their customer support systems by utilising strong NLP techniques like context-aware modelling, anomaly detection, and adversarial training (Khurana, 2021). These safeguards improve the dependability and credibility of NLP-driven interactions in addition to protecting against hostile threats.

5. OPEN ISSUES, CHALLENGES, AND FUTURE DIRECTIONS

Both enduring difficulties and chances for further innovation are presented by the changing terrain of cybersecurity and adversarial attacks in e-commerce, especially when it comes to NLP-driven systems. A thorough explanation of the problems, obstacles, and possible avenues for further study and advancement is provided below.

5.1. Open Issues

Detection of Subtle Adversarial Attacks

Subtle manipulations, like minor typographical errors or semantic changes, are frequently used in adversarial attacks to avoid detection by conventional models. It's still very difficult to create systems that can recognize these subtle attacks.

Balancing Robustness and Performance

Performance is frequently sacrificed in order to strengthen system defence against adversarial attacks, such as through slower reaction times or higher computational overhead. The problem of striking the ideal balance remains unsolved.

Scalability in Real-World Systems

It takes a substantial amount of financial and computational resources to implement sophisticated adversarial defence mechanisms across extensive e-commerce platforms.Scaling these solutions while maintaining cost-effectiveness is a critical issue.

Lack of Standardized Benchmarks

The absence of standardized datasets and benchmarks for testing adversarial resilience in e-commerce-specific NLP applications hampers consistent evaluation and comparison of defense mechanisms.

Multi-Lingual and Multi-Modal Vulnerabilities

Since many e-commerce platforms serve a variety of users, they are vulnerable to hostile attacks in a number of languages and modalities (text, images, and audio). The problem of protecting against cross-modal attacks is still unresolved.

5.2. Challenges and Future Potential

Challenges:

- **Communication Overhead:** Synchronizing updates across participants can increase latency and computational demands.
- **Heterogeneous Data:** Differences in data quality and formats among participants may affect the model's overall performance.
- **Security Risks:** Federated systems are vulnerable to poisoning attacks, where malicious participants inject false updates to compromise the model.

Future Directions:

- **Secure Aggregation:** Enhancing cryptographic techniques to ensure secure and reliable updates from participants.
- **Edge Computing Integration:** Combining federated learning with edge computing to reduce latency and improve scalability.
- **Specialized Pre-Trained Models:** Developing domain-specific pre-trained models tailored to e-commerce adversarial defense needs.

6. LEVERAGING PRE-TRAINED AND SHARED MODELS TO REDUCE COSTS

Efficient operations must be balanced with the need for strong adversarial defences in e-commerce. By utilising pre-existing frameworks and cooperative efforts, pre-trained and shared models offer a workable solution, negating the need for resource-intensive, from-scratch development.

Pre-Trained - Large, varied datasets are used to train pre-trained models like GPT, BERT, and RoBERTa. These models can then be optimised for particular e-commerce tasks like spam filtering, fraud detection, and recommendation systems. This method guarantees high accuracy even with sparse domain-specific data, reduces computational costs, and expedites development schedules. Businesses can achieve state-of-the-art performance while saving money on hardware and labour costs by using these models.

Shared Models - Conversely, shared models facilitate cooperative development across various organisations, combining resources to build strong, collective defence systems. This approach guarantees smaller businesses access to cutting-edge technologies, improves cost-sharing, and eliminates redundancy. Shared models are exposed to a variety of attack scenarios thanks to the contributions of diverse participants, which increases resilience.

Both strategies support the requirement for affordable, scalable solutions that still have robust security features. Pre-trained and shared models will become essential tools in the battle against adversarial threats in e-commerce as future developments like federated learning further improve privacy, adaptability, and efficiency.

6.1. Benefits of Real-Time Adaptation and Self-Learning

1. Proactive Defence: By anticipating and thwarting novel tactics, proactive defence helps systems stay ahead of attackers.
2. Decreased Manual Intervention: By automating the defence procedure, less frequent human supervision is required.
3. Scalability: The fraud detection and the recommendation systems will flow across the range of e-commerce application which is more adaptable.
4. Cost Efficiency: The self-improving models will reduce the long-term maintenance in costs which is more required in a fewer updtates and retraining sessions.

The future of adversarial defence in NLP for e-commerce is represented by self-learning and real-time adaptation systems (Sood, 2024) (WILLIAM et al., 2024). These systems improve security, lessen vulnerabilities, and guarantee that companies stay strong in the face of changing adversarial strategies by reacting quickly to new threats.

6.2. Effectiveness of NLP Strategies in Mitigating These Threats

In the fight against hostile threats, NLP-based defence have shown to be extremely effective. Important tactics consist of:

1. Adversarial Training: The resilient change attack patterns will exposing models to adversarial.

2. Ensemble Approaches: The combination of various models that lowers the vulnerabilities which utilize the complementary and strengths.
3. Context-Aware Defence: By efficiently comprehending semantic subtleties, sophisticated models such as BERT and GPT increase detection accuracy.
4. Behavioral and Anomaly Detection: An extra degree of security is added by keeping an eye on user behaviour and transaction patterns.
5. Dynamic Feature Selection: To lower the computational overhead and maximizes the real-time situations the priority to pertinent features.

8. CONCLUSION

The streamlined operations which revolutionized the integration of machine learning and the NLP in e-commerce will operate the business by offering the enhanced user experiences. However, the security provided to these systems are been posed a adversarial attacks growing threat that reliable and robust. The multifaceted leverages the advanced NLP strategies which accommodate the address of these challenges which requires the practical constraints in e-commerce platforms.

REFERENCES

Alawida, M., Mejri, S., Mehmood, A., Chikhaoui, B., & Isaac Abiodun, O. (2023). A Comprehensive Study of ChatGPT: Advancements, Limitations, and Ethical Considerations in Natural Language Processing and Cybersecurity. *Information (Switzerland), 14*(8), 462. DOI: 10.3390/info14080462

Ashraf, H. Z. (2025). Security Concerns: Machine Learning Approaches in the Modern Era and Web Engineering. In *Generative AI for Web Engineering Models* (pp. 241–268). IGI Global.

Balantrapu, S. S. (2023). Future Trends in AI and Machine Learning for Cybersecurity. *International Journal of Creative Research In Computer Technology and Design*, *5*(5).

Deldjoo, Y., Di Noia, T., & Merra, F. A. (2021). A Survey on Adversarial Recommender Systems: From Attack/Defense Strategies to Generative Adversarial Networks. *ACM Computing Surveys*, *54*(2), 1–38. DOI: 10.1145/3439729

Ferreira, L., Silva, D. C., & Itzazelaia, M. U. (2023). Recommender Systems in Cybersecurity. *Knowledge and Information Systems*, *65*(12), 5523–5559. DOI: 10.1007/s10115-023-01906-6

Gunasekara, A. (2023). AI-Driven Big Data Analytics for Transforming Cybersecurity for Zero-Day Vulnerabilities in E-Commerce Supply Chains. *Journal of Advances in Cybersecurity Science, Threat Intelligence, and Countermeasures*, *7*(12), 17–31.

Jeyaraj, S. A. L., Kumar, S., Revathy, S., Yenigalla, G., Krishna, K. B., & Jayabalan, K. (2024). Machine Learning Algorithms for E-Commerce Security: A Practical Approach. In *Strategies for E-Commerce Data Security: Cloud, Blockchain, AI, and Machine Learning* (pp. 361–385). IGI Global.

KATE, J., MARY, O., & QUDUS, A. (2024). *Securing the E-commerce AI Ecosystem: Multi-layered Cybersecurity Solutions for Client, Communication, and Database Integrity.*

Khurana, R. (2021). *Implementing Encryption and Cybersecurity Strategies across Client, Communication, Response Generation, and Database Modules in E-Commerce Conversational AI Systems Implementing Encryption and Cybersecurity Strategies across Client, Communication, Respons. This Advancement in Technology Has Also Warranted the Focus of a Number of Important Concerns Regarding Security*. Such as Sensitive User Data Protection.

Khurana, R., & Kaul, D. (2019). Dynamic cybersecurity strategies for ai-enhanced ecommerce: A federated learning approach to data privacy. *Applied Research in Artificial Intelligence and Cloud Computing*, *2*(1), 32–43.

Kothamali, P. R., Banik, S., & Nadimpalli, S. V. (2020). Challenges in Applying ML to Cybersecurity. *Revista de Inteligencia Artificial En Medicina*, *11*(1), 214–256.

Mudgal, A. (2025). Leveraging AI and ML for Proactive Threat Detection for E-Commerce. In *Strategic Innovations of AI and ML for E-Commerce Data Security* (pp. 281–322). IGI Global.

Muhammad, S., & Mirjat, N. A. (2024). Enhancing Cybersecurity with AI: From Anomaly Detection to Threat Mitigation. *Bulletin of Engineering Science and Technology*, *1*(03), 20–39.

Natarajan, A. K., Desai, Y., Kshirsagar, P. R., Upreti, K., & Tak, T. K. (2025). Generative AI for Cybersecurity and Privacy in Cyber-Physical Systems. In *Navigating Cyber-Physical Systems With Cutting-Edge Technologies* (pp. 57–82). IGI Global Scientific Publishing.

NG, S. G., Chinnegowda, H. S., & Kaul, H. (n.d.). *Review on Harnessing Artificial Intelligence: A Paradigm Shift in Cybersecurity for a Safer Digital Future.*

Sakib, M., & Mustajab, S. (2024). Enhanced Multi-variate Time Series Prediction Through Statistical-Deep Learning Integration: The VAR-Stacked LSTM Model. *SN Computer Science*, *5*(5). Advance online publication. DOI: 10.1007/s42979-024-02950-x

Sakib, M., & Mustajab, S. (2025). CEEMDAN-TCN-AutoLSTM: A Triple-Force Ensemble Using Cross-Stitch Networks for Short-Term Load Forecasting. *Arabian Journal for Science and Engineering*. Advance online publication. DOI: 10.1007/s13369-025-10398-1

Sakib, U. S2*, A. P. (2022). Bitcoin Price Prediction using Machine Learning. *Journal of Computer Science and Software Development*, *2*, 10.

Selvalakshmi, B., Sudhakar, G., Anbalagan, A., Subashini, K., Vijayalakshmi, P., & Kavin, F. (2025). Enhancing E-Commerce Data Privacy in India's Rapidly Evolving Cybersecurity Landscape Through AI-Driven Intrusion Detection Systems. In *Strategic Innovations of AI and ML for E-Commerce Data Security* (pp. 261–280). IGI Global.

Sood, A. K. (2024). Combating cyberattacks targeting the AI ecosystem: Assessing threats, risks, and vulnerabilities. In *Combating Cyberattacks Targeting the AI Ecosystem: Assessing Threats, Risks, and Vulnerabilities*. Walter de Gruyter GmbH & Co KG. https://doi.org/DOI: 10.1515/9781501520549

Sun, N., Ding, M., Jiang, J., Xu, W., Mo, X., Tai, Y., & Zhang, J. (2023). Cyber Threat Intelligence Mining for Proactive Cybersecurity Defense: A Survey and New Perspectives. *IEEE Communications Surveys and Tutorials*, *25*(3), 1748–1774. DOI: 10.1109/COMST.2023.3273282

WILLIAM, B., & IBRAHIM, A. (2024). *Fortifying E-commerce Conversational AI Systems: Comprehensive Cybersecurity Approaches for Client-Side, Communication, and Response Generation Protection*.

WILLIAM, B., OWEN, J., & OLUWASEYI, J. (2024). *Implementing Robust Encryption and Cybersecurity Measures in E-commerce Conversational AI: Safeguarding Data Across Key System Modules*.

Wu, Y., Liu, Q., Liao, X., Ji, S., Wang, P., Wang, X., Wu, C., & Li, Z. (2021). Price TAG: Towards Semi-Automatically Discovery Tactics, Techniques and Procedures OF E-Commerce Cyber Threat Intelligence. *IEEE Transactions on Dependable and Secure Computing*. Advance online publication. DOI: 10.1109/TDSC.2021.3120415

Yusuff, M. (2023). *Artificial Intelligence in Cybersecurity Strategies: Revolutionizing Tactics for Advanced Threat Protection*.

Chapter 4

Multi-Modal Deep Learning for Intrusion Detection in Encrypted Darknet Traffic for Privacy Threat

Qais Al-Na'amneh
https://orcid.org/0009-0008-3034-7693
Applied Science Private University, Jordan

Rahaf Hazaymih
Jordan University of Science and Technology, Jordan

Mahmoud Aljawarneh
https://orcid.org/0000-0003-2003-6310
Applied Science Private University, Jordan

Ahmad Salch Alhazaimch
King Abdaulaziz University, Saudi Arabia

ABSTRACT

The escalating use of anonymization networks creates a considerable hurdle in differentiating between users seeking privacy and those engaged in malicious conduct within encrypted data streams. To address this, a novel multi-modal deep learning architecture is presented for the intricate analysis and categorization of darknet traffic. This framework integrates sophisticated feature engineering with a hybrid Convolutional Neural Network-Recurrent Neural Network (CNN-RNN)

DOI: 10.4018/979-8-3373-7503-8.ch004

design, enabling the effective capture of both spatial and temporal patterns within network flows. The model demonstrates a pronounced ability to analyze varied traffic, such as that from Virtual Private Networks (VPNs) and The Onion Router (Tor), achieving a high degree of accuracy in detection and classification.Its performance was assessed using a robust dataset that combines established benchmarks (ISCXVPN2016, ISCXTor2017) with newly captured real-time traffic.The evaluation yielded an overall accuracy of 91.5%, with exceptional performance in the categorization of challenging traffic

1 INTRODUCTION

The internet, in its modern incarnation, represents a duality of purpose and accessibility. On one hand, the surface web, indexed by conventional search engines, provides a vast repository of information and services that underpin global commerce, communication, and knowledge sharing. On the other hand, a hidden substratum, collectively known as the deep web and its more clandestine component, the darknet, operates beyond the reach of standard browsing. The darknet is an overlay network intentionally designed to be inaccessible through standard internet protocols, leveraging anonymization technologies such as The Onion Router (Tor) and Virtual Private Networks (VPNs) to obscure user identities and data origins (Saleem et al., 2022). This architecture facilitates anonymous communication and interactions, serving a range of legitimate and socially important functions. Journalists, activists, and ordinary citizens in oppressive regimes rely on these technologies to circumvent censorship, protect sensitive communications, and exercise freedom of expression without fear of reprisal (ABDULLAHI, 2021; Davis & Arrigo, 2021). Whistleblowers use the darknet to expose corruption and wrongdoing, knowing that the layers of encryption protect them from powerful entities. For many, these tools are indispensable for safeguarding fundamental human rights in an era of pervasive digital surveillance.

Despite its valid and crucial applications, the same attributes that make the darknet a bastion for privacy and free speech also render it a fertile ground for a wide spectrum of illicit activities. Anonymity networks, while designed to safeguard user privacy, in- advertently furnish a sanctuary for illicit activities.These platforms have burgeoned into sprawling marketplaces for proscribed goods and services, conduits for the dissemination of malware and ransomware, and coordination hubs for cyber warfare.The economic grav- ity of these darknet markets is profound, with yearly transactions in narcotics, compro- mised financial credentials, forged documentation, and hacking implements reaching into the billions of dollars.Moreover, the utilization of the darknet by state-sponsored entities and cyber-terrorist factions to orchestrate assaults on critical infrastructure, execute es- pionage, and circulate propaganda presents a formidable challenge to global security.The perpetual evolution of these digital threats necessitates a continuous and escalating ef- fort from law enforcement, cybersecurity experts, and intelligence agencies to preserve a secure and stable international digital landscape.(Adel & Norouzifard, 2024).The techni- cal impediments to scrutinizing darknet traffic are substantial. Anonymization services, exemplified by Tor, employ a multi-layered encryption protocol and route traffic through a distributed network of volunteer-operated relays, effectively obscuring the identities of the communicating parties and the substance of their exchanges. This architecture fun- damentally undermines conventional network security measures reliant on deep packet inspection (DPI) or signature-based detection. DPI, which scrutinizes the content of data packets, is rendered impotent by encryption, while signature-based systems are often evaded by the deliberately obfuscated or polymorphic nature of malicious traf- fic, which can mimic legitimate data flows. Initial endeavors to surmount these obstacles through port-based classification or metadata analysis proved susceptible to circumven- tion. Malefactors can readily direct traffic through non-standard ports, and the statistical characteristics of benign and malevolent traffic frequently overlap, precipitating a high incidence of erroneous identifications.The dynamic and adaptive character of darknet technologies ensures the rapid obsolescence of static detection rules, compelling the de- velopment of more sophisticated and adaptable analytical frameworks. Sources(Saleem et al., 2024).

The limitations of conventional methods spurred a shift towards machine learning (ML) Al-Na'amneh et al. (2023) for darknet traffic analysis. Early ML models, such as Support Vector Machines (SVM), Decision Trees, and Na¨ıve Bayes, demonstrated some promise by learning to classify traffic based on statistical flow features like packet size, timing, and flow duration. These models could identify some patterns that distinguished, for example, bulk data transfer from interactive browsing without inspecting the packet content. However, their efficacy was often constrained by their reliance on manual feature engineering. This process is labor-intensive, requires deep domain expertise, and struggles to keep pace with the evolving tactics used to obfuscate traffic. The attributes that are beneficial for one application or protocol may not be applicable to another, and the efficacy of these models can deteriorate markedly when confronted with novel traffic patterns or adversarial tactics intended to deceive the classifier. (Mohanty et al., 2022; Rust-Nguyen & Stamp, 2023). The need for a more automated and powerful feature extraction mechanism became evident.

Deep Learning (DL) has emerged as a transformational approach that addresses many of the shortcomings of classical ML. Deep neural networks may learn hierarchical feature representations automatically from raw or slightly processed data, eliminating the need for considerable manual feature engineering. (Mijwil et al., 2023). This functionality is especially useful in network traffic analysis. Convolutional Neural Networks (CNNs), initially created for image processing, have been successfully applied to extract detailed spatial properties from traffic data, which is frequently represented as a 2D matrix of packet information. They can detect small, localized patterns within a flow that may indicate a particular application or activity. In addition, Recurrent Neural Networks (RNNs) and its sophisticated variations, such as Long Short-Term Memory (LSTM), can simulate temporal dependencies. Processing traffic data as a series allows them to record the evolution of a flow over time, such as changes in packet inter-arrival delays or byte ratios, which are crucial for distinguishing between activities like streaming, chatting, and file transfers. (Qazi et al., 2023; Sarwar et al., 2021). The combination of these two architectures points in a promising path; a CNN-RNN hybrid model may be able to combine the sequential modeling strength of RNNs with the spatial feature extraction capability of CNNs to create a highly discriminating classifier for encrypted communications.

This research addresses a critical gap in the existing literature. While numerous stud- ies have applied DL to traffic classification, many suffer from limitations such as reliance on obsolete or narrowly focused datasets, failure to effectively combine spatiotemporal feature analysis, or a lack of scalability for real-world deployment. Few models have been rigorously tested on a combination of different anonymization services (e.g., VPN and Tor) and a diverse range of application-level traffic types. This work posits that a multi-modal framework, integrating sophisticated domain-specific feature engineering with a hybrid CNN-RNN architecture, can provide a more robust, accurate, and scalable solution for darknet traffic analysis. The primary objective is to develop and validate a model capable of accurately detecting anonymized traffic and classifying its underlying application type with high precision, thereby offering a practical tool for modern cyberse- curity operations. The significance of this study lies in its potential to enhance intrusion detection systems and threat intelligence platforms, enabling them to identify hidden threats more effectively and respond proactively.

This paper is structured to provide a comprehensive exposition of the proposed frame- work and its evaluation. Section 2 conducts an extensive review of the related work in darknet traffic analysis, situating this research within the current academic discourse and identifying existing gaps. Section 3 provides a detailed description of the proposed methodology, including the dataset composition, preprocessing steps, feature engineer- ing techniques, and the architectural design of the hybrid CNN-RNN model. Section 4 outlines the experimental setup and training configurations. Section 5 presents the empirical results, offering a thorough discussion and analysis of the model's performance and comparing it against established benchmarks. Finally, Section 6 concludes the paper by summarizing the key findings, acknowledging the study's limitations, and proposing directions for future research.

2 RELATED WORK

The pursuit of effective darknet traffic analysis has been a central theme in network security research for over a decade, driven by the dual-use nature of anonymization tech- nologies. The literature reflects an evolution of techniques, moving from statistical and classical machine learning methods to more sophisticated deep learning architectures. This section surveys the landscape of prior research, categorizing it into foundational approaches, deep learning innovations, and emerging challenges to contextualize the con- tribution of this work.

2.1 Traditional and Machine Learning Approaches

Early efforts in identifying anonymized traffic, particularly from Tor, relied heavily on sta- tistical analysis of flow characteristics. Methods focused on identifying signatures based on packet sizes, timing, and protocol handshakes. For instance, some studies identified Tor traffic by recognizing the specific TLS certificate patterns used during the connection setup. Others employed flow-level statistics, such as the mean and variance of packet inter-arrival times and sizes, to train conventional machine learning classifiers. Models like Support Vector Machines (SVM), Decision Trees, and Random Forest were com- monly used (Rust-Nguyen & Stamp, 2022). Al-Fayoumi et al. (2023) and Al-Na'amneh et al. (2024a) proposed a method focusing exclusively on time-related features to classify Tor traffic, aiming for low latency. Even though these models performed fairly well on particular datasets, they all had the same flaw: significant dependence on handcrafted elements. This manual process is not only time-consuming but also brittle; the features that define one type of traffic can be easily altered by protocol updates or adversarial manipulation, rendering the models obsolete. Furthermore, these methods often strug- gled to generalize across different types of applications running within the anonymized tunnels, frequently lumping all encrypted traffic into a single category.

2.2 Deep Learning-Based Classification

The advent of deep learning marked a paradigm shift in traffic analysis. DL models may be able to extract more intricate and nuanced patterns straight from the traffic data by automating feature extraction. The methods used in this field of study can be broadly categorized into CNN, RNN, and hybrid model techniques.

2.2.1 CNN-Based Approaches

(CNNs)Gharaibeh et al. (2023), which handle network traffic as an image, were modified from computer vision. Two-dimensional matrices were created from traffic flows or even individual packets, with one dimension representing byte location or feature type and the other perhaps representing time or packet order. In order to identify spatial pat- terns, the CNN's convolutional layers function as filters. The effectiveness of this strategy was shown in multiple studies Al-Na'amneh et al. (2024a, 2024b). For instance, "Deep Packet" employed a CNN and represented traffic as a 1D vector, demonstrating efficacy in application identification. By utilizing pretrained image categorization algorithms, other efforts such as "DeepImage" explicitly transformed flows into images . A major drawback of CNN-only models is that they are less successful at simulating the long-range temporal dependencies that define a communication session and instead focus on spatial correlationsNasayreh et al. (2024).

2.2.2 RNN-Based Approaches

Researchers Sarwar et al. (2021) used Recurrent Neural Networks (RNNs) and its more sophisticated derivatives, Long Short-Term Memory (LSTM) and Gated Recurrent Units (GRU), to handle the temporal nature of network traffic. These models handle traffic as flow statistics over time or as a series of packets. They are perfect for capturing time- dependent patterns, such as the call-and-response nature of a chat application or the consistent, high-throughput flow of a video stream, because they maintain an internal state that enables them to recall previous information. (Qazi et al., 2023) suggested a model that achieves excellent accuracy in darknet traffic detection and classification by utilizing a modified CNN-LSTM architecture. further emphasizes how well hybrid models work for scalability in big networks.

2.2.3 Hybrid and Advanced Architectures

Given that CNNs(Mandela et al., 2025; Marim et al., 2023) and RNNs have comple- mentary strengths, a number of recent studies have suggested hybrid models. In order to model the temporal sequence of these features, a CNN's output is typically sent into an RNN/LSTM layer after it has been employed as a feature extractor to identify spa- tial patterns from input traffic representations. Across a variety of traffic categorization challenges, (Langendonck et al., 2024; Pang et al., 2021; Zhang et al., 2024)this spa- tiotemporal technique has continuously produced state-of-the-art results. (Atlaf et al., 2024)Other sophisticated designs have been investigated by researchers in addition to CNN-RNN hybrids. With their representation of network communications as a graph with nodes being IP addresses and edges being flows, Graph Neural Networks (GNNs) have become popular. Complex topological relationships in network traffic can be mod- eled by GNNs. (Almomani, 2023; Mohanty et al., 2022; Shinde et al., 2024). Abbas et al. (2024) Several classifiers are combined in ensemble learning approaches to increase accuracy and resilience.

2.3 Datasets and Evaluation Challenges

The availability of high-quality, labeled datasets remains a significant barrier in this sec- tor. Many foundational studies rely on datasets like ISCXVPN2016 and ISCXTor201.7 (Draper-Gil et al., 2016; Lashkari et al., 2017). While invaluable, these datasets are be- coming dated and may not reflect the full complexity of current darknet traffic. Newer datasets like CIC-Darknet2020 (Lashkari et al., 2020) have helped, but the rapid evolu- tion of applications and encryption protocols necessitates a constant generation of fresh, representative data. The lack of a standardized, large-scale benchmark dataset makes direct comparison between different proposed models difficult (Saleem et al., 2024; Wang et al., 2024). Another major challenge is the robustness of models against adversarial attacks. Research has shown that even high-accuracy classifiers can be fooled by small, carefully crafted perturbations to the input traffic, a critical vulnerability for any sys- tem deployed in a real-world security context (Chen et al., 2024; Rust-Nguyen & Stamp, 2022, 2023). Finally, the "black box" nature of many deep learning models presents a barrier to trust and adoption. The emerging field of Explainable AI (XAI) is attempting to address this by providing insights into why a model makes a particular decision, which is crucial for operational use and auditing (Firdaus et al., 2023; Ghaleb, Hamdan, et al., 2025; Joshi et al., 2024).

2.4 Summary and Research Gap

The literature demonstrates a clear trajectory from simple statistical methods toward complex, hybrid deep learning models for darknet traffic analysis. Table 1 summarizes key recent studies, highlighting their methods, strengths, and limitations. Despite significant progress, a research gap remains. There is a need for a framework that not only achieves high accuracy through a sophisticated spatiotemporal model but is also validated on a combination of legacy and contemporary, real-world traffic data to ensure its relevance and generalizability. The proposed research aims to fill this gap by introducing a hybrid CNN-RNN framework that integrates advanced feature engineering and is rigorously evaluated on a diverse, composite dataset, setting a new benchmark for performance and practical applicability.

Table 1. Summary of Related Research Works in Darknet Traffic Analysis

Reference	Research Focus	Main Method	Strengths	Limitations
Cohen et al. (2020)	Mining and monitoring darknet traffic.	Word2Vec and incremental clustering.	Capable of detecting emerging threats and tracking malicious campaigns over time.	Evaluation based on data from a single provider; generalizability may be limited.
Sarwar et al. (2021)	Deep learning for darknet traffic detection and categorization.	Modified CNN-LSTM and CNN-GRU models.	Achieves high detection (96%) and categorization (89%) accuracy.	Performance may vary with differ- ent datasets; real- time applicability not assessed.
Rust-Nguyen & Stamp (2022)	Robustness against adversarial attacks.	SVM, RF, CNN, AC-GAN.	RF model out-performs others on CIC-Darknet2020; evaluates adversarial robustness.	Classifier is shown to be susceptible to adversarial attacks; robustness needs improvement.
Abbas et al. (2024)	Active learning for darknet traffic detection.	Random Forest and Decision Tree with active learning.	Achieves 87% accuracy; enhances robustness efficiency in large traffic analysis.	Specific performance metrics not detailed; real-time applicability not assessed.
Wang & Thing (2023)	Feature extraction and selection for encrypted malicious traffic.	Two-layer detection framework combining deep learning and traditional ML.	Outperforms classical deep learning and traditional ML algorithms; provides comprehensive dataset.	Specific performance metrics and comparisons are not detailed; deployment considerations not discussed.
Fu, Li, & Xu (2023)	Unsupervised detection of encrypted malicious traffic.	HyperVision using in-memory graph structures.	High performance (AUC ¿ 0.92) with low latency; can process traffic at high speeds.	Focuses on unsupervised learning; effectiveness in supervised scenarios not assessed.

continued on following page

Table 1. Continued

Reference	Research Focus	Main Method	Strengths	Limitations
Saleem et al. (2024)	Comprehensive literature review.	Systematic literature review (2017-2023).	Offers an extensive overview of methodologies and challenges.	Primarily a summary of existing literature; no new experimental results presented.
Mohanty et al. (2022)	Robust classification under adversarial settings.	Stacking Ensemble (RF, KNN, DT) with Autoencoder defense.	High accuracy (98.89%) on CIC-Darknet2020; specifically tests against adversarial attacks.	Increased computational complexity due to ensemble methods and defense mechanism.
Mandela et al. (2025)	Efficient classification of Dark Web traffic.	Hybrid CNN-LSTM model.	Model shows robustness across a diverse dataset of Dark Web traffic samples.	Performance evaluated on a specific dataset, which may limit generalizability; computationally intensive.

3 METHODOLOGY

The proposed methodology introduces a multimodal deep learning architecture designed to accurately identify and characterize darknet traffic. This approach integrates the spa- tial feature extraction capabilities of Convolutional Neural Networks (CNNs) with the temporal modeling strengths of Recurrent Neural Networks (RNNs). The framework is engineered to handle the complexity and variability inherent in encrypted communica- tions, providing a robust solution for traffic classification and anomaly detection. The overall process, depicted in Figure **1** consists of four main stages: Dataset Preprocess- ing, Feature Extraction, Hybrid Model Training, and Evaluation.

3.1 Dataset and Preprocessing

The foundation of this study is a comprehensive dataset constructed by amalgamating historical benchmarks with real-time traffic captures to ensure a robust and contemporary evaluation.

- **ISCXVPN2016**: Provides labeled traffic from various applications (e.g., browsing, chat, VoIP) operating over a VPN (Draper-Gil et al., 2016).
- **ISCXTor2017**: Contains Tor-anonymized traffic across multiple categories, in- cluding email, browsing, and P2P file sharing (Lashkari et al., 2017).
- **Real-time Traffic**: Freshly captured traffic from a controlled network environment to include emerging patterns in anonymized communication.

This merged dataset, comprising 158,659 records, is meticulously preprocessed through a multi-step pipeline to prepare it for model training.

1. **Data Cleansing**: The initial step involves removing duplicate records, incomplete flows, and malformed packets. This sanitization process is crucial for eliminating noise that could otherwise degrade model performance.
2. **Data Normalization**: To prevent features with larger numeric ranges from dis- proportionately influencing the model, numerical features are scaled to a uniform range. Z-score standardization is employed, which transforms each feature to have a mean of 0 and a standard deviation of 1. For a feature value x, the normalized value x is calculated as:

$$x' = \frac{x - \mu}{\sigma} \quad (1)$$

where μ is the mean of the feature and σ is its standard deviation.

3. **Labeling Traffic Flows**: Each traffic flow is assigned a categorical label based on its application type (e.g., Audio Streaming, P2P, VoIP) and whether it is benign, VPN, or Tor traffic. This creates a multi-class classification problem.
4. **Data Balancing**: Anonymized traffic is often a minority class in real-world net- work data. To prevent the model from becoming biased towards the majority class (benign traffic), oversampling techniques like the Synthetic Minority Over-sampling Technique (SMOTE) are applied to the training data. SMOTE generates synthetic samples for the minority classes, creating a more balanced dataset for training.

Figure 1. The overall methodological workflow of the proposed darknet traffic analysis framework, detailing the four primary stages from data acquisition to final classification.

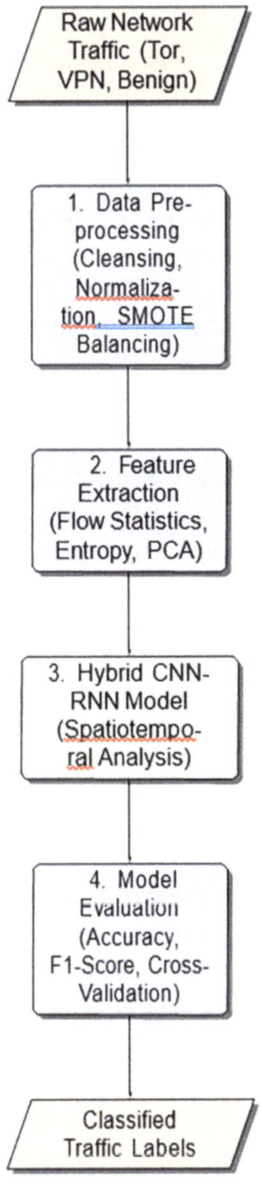

1. **Transformation**: The preprocessed traffic data is transformed into structured feature matrices. Each matrix represents a traffic flow, where rows correspond

to packets in sequence and columns correspond to the extracted features. This format is the input for the hybrid CNN-RNN model.

3.2 Feature Extraction

Raw network data is converted into a rich set of features that capture the distinct qual- ities of darknet traffic. This stage combines domain-specific knowledge with automated techniques.

1. **Domain-Specific Properties**: A set of statistical features are calculated for each flow, designed to capture behavioral and structural characteristics of encrypted traffic without inspecting the payload. These include:
   - **Flow-level statistics**: Duration of the flow, total number of packets, total bytes transferred (forward and backward).
   - **Packet timing**: Mean, standard deviation, min, and max of packet inter-arrival times.
   - **Packet size**: Mean, standard deviation, min, and max of packet sizes.
   - **Byte Ratios**: Ratio of forward to backward bytes, which can indicate the directionality of communication (e.g., streaming vs. uploading).
   - **Payload Entropy**: The Shannon entropy of the packet payloads is calculated to measure randomness. Encrypted traffic typically has high entropy. The entropy H(X) is given by:

$$H(X) = -\sum_{i-1}^{n} p(x_i) \log_2 p(x_i) \quad (2)$$

where $p(x_i)$ is the probability of occurrence of byte value x_i.

2. **Automated Methods**: To reduce dimensionality and computational overhead while preserving essential information, Principal Component Analysis (PCA) is utilized. PCA transforms the original set of features into a smaller set of uncorre- lated variables (principal components) that capture the maximum variance in the data.
3. **Feature Consolidation**: The final set of extracted features is consolidated into a high-dimensional matrix for each flow. This matrix representation preserves both the spatial relationships between features for a given packet and the sequential order of packets within the flow, making it an ideal input for the hybrid model.

3.3 Hybrid CNN-RNN Model Architecture

The core of the framework is a hybrid deep learning model that serially combines a CNN and an RNN. This architecture, shown in Figure **??**, is designed to learn both spatial and temporal patterns from the feature matrices.

1. **CNN Feature Extraction**: The input feature matrix is first passed through two convolutional layers. Each layer applies a set of learnable filters to the input, followed by a Rectified Linear Unit (ReLU) activation function. These layers are adept at identifying local, spatial patterns among the features of each packet. A max-pooling layer follows each convolutional layer to reduce the dimensionality of the feature maps and provide a degree of translational invariance.

Figure 2. Optimized Network Pipeline Diagram

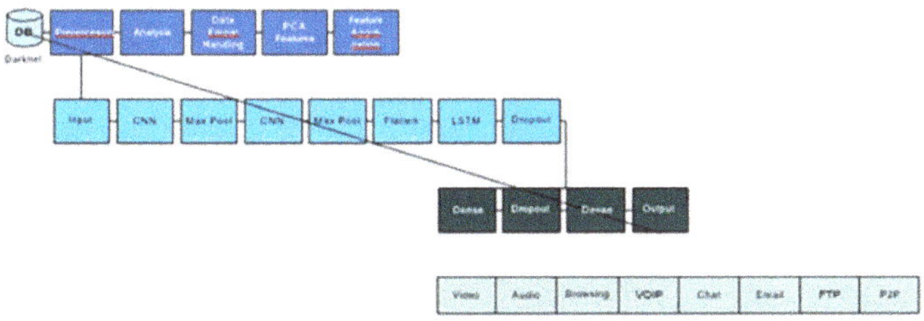

2. **RNN Sequence Modeling**: The output from the CNN component is a high-level feature map. This map is flattened and fed as a sequence of feature vectors into an LSTM layer. The LSTM layer processes this sequence, capturing the temporal dependencies and long-range patterns across the packets in the flow. This step is critical for understanding the behavior of the communication over time.
3. **Classification**: The final hidden state of the LSTM layer, which represents a condensed summary of the entire traffic flow, is passed to a fully connected (Dense) layer. A dropout layer is applied before the dense layer to mitigate overfitting. The final output layer uses a Softmax activation function to produce a probability distribution over the different traffic classes.

The entire model is trained end-to-end using backpropagation. Algorithm 1 outlines the complete training and classification procedure.

3.4 Model Training and Evaluation

The model is trained on an 80-10-10 split of the data for training, validation, and testing. The Adam optimizer is used with a weighted sparse categorical cross-entropy loss func- tion, which helps address any remaining class imbalance. Early stopping is employed to prevent overfitting, halting training if the validation loss does not improve for 10 consec- utive epochs. The model's performance is evaluated using a suite of standard metrics:

- **Accuracy**: The proportion of correctly classified instances.
- **Precision**: The ability of the classifier not to label as positive a sample that is negative.
- **Recall (Sensitivity)**: The ability of the classifier to find all the positive samples.
- **F1-Score**: The harmonic mean of precision and recall, providing a single score that balances both concerns.

Algorithm 1 Darknet Traffic Classification Procedure

```
Input: Raw network traffic captures Traw
Output: Classified traffic labels Ypred
procedure PreprocessData(Traw)
Tclean ← CleanseData(Traw) □ Remove duplicates, errors
Tnorm ← NormalizeFeatures(Tclean) □ Apply Z-score standardization
Tlabeled ← LabelFlows(Tnorm)
Tbalanced ← BalanceClasses(Tlabeled, method=SMOTE) □ Apply to training set only
return Tbalanced
procedure ExtractFeatures(Tprocessed)
For each flow f □ Tprocessed:
Calculate domain-specific features (entropy, timing, size stats)
Consolidate features into matrix Mf
Apply PCA to reduce dimensionality of feature set.
return Feature Matrices M
procedure TrainAndClassify(M)
Split M into training, validation, testing sets: Mtrain, Mval, Mtest
```

```
Initialize CNN-RNN model Θ
for epoch = 1 to max epochs do
For each batch B □ Mtrain:
Xspatial ← CNN(B; Θcnn)
Xtemporal ← RNN(Xspatial; Θrnn)
Yˆ ← Softmax(Dense(Xtemporal))
Calculate loss L(Yˆ, Ytrue)
Update model parameters Θ using Adam optimizer and back-propagation.
Evaluate model on Mval
if no improvement in validation loss then
Early stopping.
Ypred ← Model.predict(Mtest)
return Ypred
```

- **Confusion Matrix**: A table used to visualize the performance of the classifier, showing the counts of true positive, true negative, false positive, and false negative predictions for each class.

To ensure the stability and generalizability of the results, a 5-fold cross-validation strategy is employed.

4 RESULTS AND DISCUSSION

The empirical evaluation of the proposed hybrid CNN-RNN framework was conducted to assess its efficacy in classifying complex darknet traffic. This section presents the key findings, interprets their significance, and discusses the implications of the results in the context of existing state-of-the-art methods.

4.1 Overall Performance Analysis

The trained hybrid model demonstrated exceptional performance across all evaluation standards. The model achieved an overall accuracy of 91.5% on the held-out test set, showcasing its robust capability to accurately classify and describe a wide array of darknet traffic patterns. Key performance metrics, summarized in Table 2, confirm the model's effectiveness. An average F1-score of 0.89 indicates a strong balance between precision and recall, signifying that the model not only correctly identifies traffic classes but also minimizes misclassifications. The low log loss value of 0.15 further suggests that the model's predictions are highly confident.

Table 2. Overall Model Performance Metrics

Metric	Value
Overall Accuracy	91.5%
Average F1-Score	0.89
Average Precision	0.90
Average Recall	0.89
Log Loss	0.15

The model's ability to distinguish between eight different traffic categories was particu- larly noteworthy. The confusion matrix, presented in Figure 3, visualizes the classification performance for each category. The strong diagonal indicates a high number of correct predictions across all classes. Categories like File Transfer, VoIP, and Audio Streaming were classified with very high accuracy. While some minor confusion exists, for example between Browsing and Video Streaming which can share similar traffic characteristics, the overall misclassification rate is low.

4.2 Performance on Challenging Categories

The framework demonstrated remarkable ability in classifying traffic types known to be challenging due to their encrypted and dynamic nature. As detailed in Table 3, the model excelled in differentiating P2P and Video Streaming traffic.

Figure 3. Confusion Matrix for Darknet Traffic Classification.

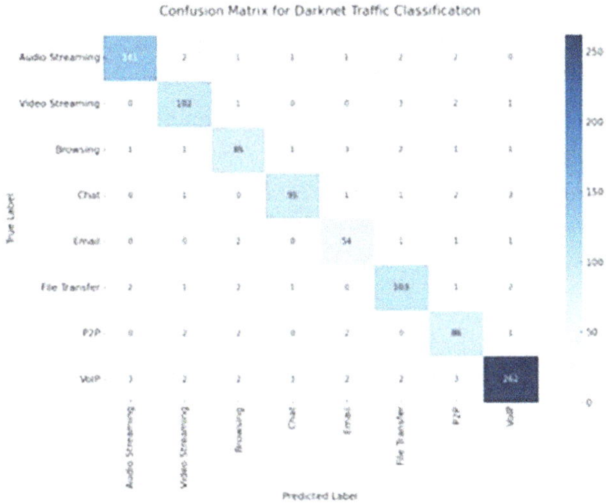

Table 3. Per-Category Performance Metrics

Traffic Category	Precision	Recall	F1-Score
Audio Streaming	0.92	0.90	0.91
Video Streaming	0.89	0.86	0.87
P2P	0.89	0.88	0.88
Browsing	0.83	0.81	0.82
Chat	0.89	0.87	0.88
File Transfer	0.90	0.88	0.89
VoIP	0.86	0.85	0.85

- **P2P Traffic**: The model achieved an F1-Score of 0.88 for P2P traffic. This is a significant improvement over baseline models that often struggle with the irregu- lar and encrypted nature of file-sharing protocols. The ability of the RNN layers to capture the temporal dependencies in file-sharing patterns was crucial for this success.
- **Video Streaming**: With an F1-Score of 0.87, the model surpassed older ap- proaches that could not effectively model the combination of spatial and temporal patterns typical of streaming services. The model could effectively

distinguish the sustained, high-throughput nature of video streams from other traffic types.

4.3 Comparison with Baselines

A systematic comparative evaluation was performed against several well-known bench- mark models to demonstrate the efficacy of the proposed hybrid CNN-RNN approach. As shown in Figure 4, the proposed model significantly outperforms these baselines.

Table 4. Quantitative Comparison with Baseline Models

Model	Accuracy	F1-Score	Key Strength	Limitation
DeepImage				
Deep Packet	78.0%	0.81	Application-level analysis	Limited Tor characterization
1D CNN	73.0%	0.73	Computational efficiency	Ineffective for multi-dim traffic
Proposed Model	91.5%	0.89	Combined spatial and temporal modeling	Higher computational resource needs

Figure 4. Comparative performance of the proposed hybrid CNN-RNN model against state-of-the-art baselines. The proposed model demonstrates superior results in both overall accuracy and F1-score.

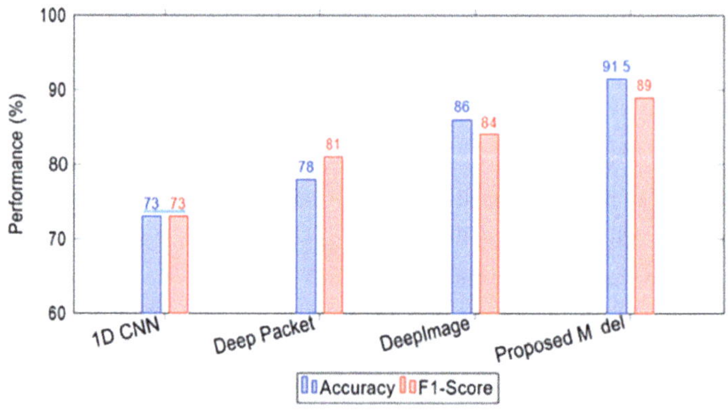

The proposed model's accuracy of 91.5% is a marked improvement over Deep-Image (86.0%) and Deep Packet (78.0%). This superiority is attributed to its hybrid nature. While DeepImage (a CNN-based model) is strong at spatial feature extraction, it lacks the temporal modeling provided by the RNN component. The inclusion of RNN layers allowed our model to grasp sequential dependencies, a major benefit over CNN-only

designs. This combined modeling approach sets a new benchmark for accuracy and flexibility in darknet traffic analysis.

4.4 Feature Importance and Scalability

To understand the decision-making process of the model, a feature importance analysis was conducted. Figure 5 shows a heatmap visualizing the relative significance of different features.

Figure 5. Analysis of feature importance, highlighting the relative contribution of key traffic characteristics to the model's classification decisions. Payload entropy and flow duration emerge as the most discriminative features.

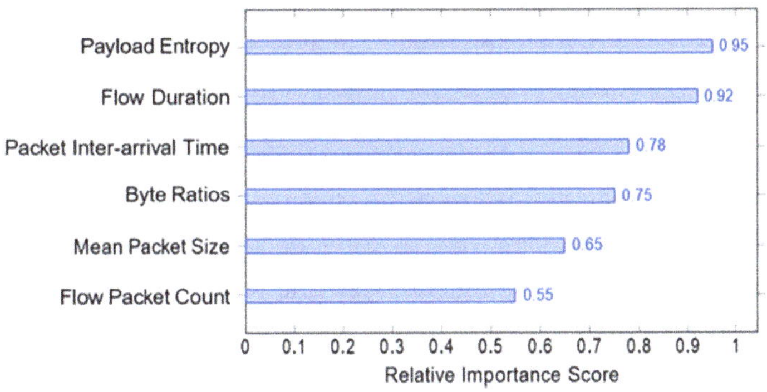

The analysis revealed that payload entropy and flow duration were the most in- fluential features for classifying darknet traffic, strongly corresponding with encrypted streams and distinguishing between probing activities and sustained data transfers. Byte ratios and packet inter-arrival times were also important factors in differentiating inter- active communications like VoIP from bulk data transfers.

The framework's scalability was tested using a dataset twice the initial size. The model maintained outstanding performance, with accuracy just marginally lowering to 90.2% and processing time increasing by only 22.2%. This illustrates efficient scaling. In simulated real-time tests, the model achieved a prediction latency of 22ms per flow and a throughput of 2,800 flows per second on an NVIDIA Tesla V100 GPU, demonstrating its appropriateness for real-world use in intrusion detection systems (IDS) and other network security tools. These findings show that the suggested CNN-RNN technique represents a new state-of-the-art in darknet activity identification, providing a realistic pathway for early threat detection and response. They were also crucial in distinguishing between bulk data transfers and interactive communications such as VoIP.

5 CONCLUSION AND FUTURE WORK

Using a hybrid CNN-RNN architecture and cutting-edge feature engineering, this study effectively created and verified a complex framework for darknet traffic analysis. Across a wide variety of traffic kinds, including difficult P2P and video streaming categories, the model obtained a high accuracy of 91.5%.Its viability for practical implementation in intrusion detection systems (IDS) and other network security tools is confirmed by its low latency of 2 ms per flow and high throughput of 2,800 flows per second on an NVIDIA Tesla V100 GPU. These results demonstrate how the suggested CNN-RNN technique offers a new state-of-the-art for identifying darknet activity, providing a workable route for early threat identification and reaction.are also essential for differentiating interactive communications like VoIP from bulk data transfers. By effectively integrating temporal and spatial analysis, the framework established a new performance benchmark, outper- forming existing models. The findings confirm that this approach provides a reliable, scalable, and accurate method for analyzing encrypted and anonymized traffic, making it highly suitable for integration into real-world network security systems. The primary limitation of this research is the inherent demand for computational resources for training and the ever-present need for more diverse and contemporary datasets to combat model drift.

Future work will focus on several key directions to advance this research. First, we plan to incorporate online learning techniques, allowing the model to adapt to new and evolving traffic patterns in real-time without requiring complete retraining. Second, expanding the dataset to include traffic from other anonymizing services like I2P and Freenet would enhance the model's robustness and broaden its detection capabilities. Third, the integration of Explainable Artificial Intelligence (XAI) methods is a critical next step. [6, 21, 24, 28] Providing transparent, human-interpretable reasons for the model's classifications will build trust and facilitate its adoption by security professionals. Finally, further investigation into adversarial defense mechanisms is necessary to harden the model against deliberate attempts at evasion, ensuring its long-term viability in confrontational cybersecurity environments. [5, 7, 19]

REFERENCES

Abbas, S., Bouazzi, I., Sampedro, G. A., Alsubai, S., Almadhor, A. S., Hejaili, A. A., & Kryvinska, N. (2024). Active-darknet: An iterative learning approach for darknet traffic detection and categorization. *IEEE Access: Practical Innovations, Open Solutions*, *12*, 151987–151997.

Abdullahi, A. M. (2021). An online privacy enhancing framework based on the prin- ciples and capabilities of the onion router (tor).

Adel, A., & Norouzifard, M. (2024). Weaponization of the growing cybercrimes inside the dark net: The question of detection and application. *Big Data and Cognitive Computing*, *8*(8), 91.

Al-Fayoumi, M., Elayyan, A., & Odeh, A. (2023). Tor network traffic classification us- ing machine learning based on time-related feature. *AIP Conference Proceedings*, *2679*(1).

Al-Na'amneh, Q., Aljaidi, M., Gharaibeh, H., Nasayreh, A., & Al Mamlook, R. E. Al- matarneh, S., Alzu'bi, D., & Husien, A. S. (2023). Feature selection for robust spoofing detection: A chi-square-based machine learning approach. *2023 2nd International Engineering Conference on Electrical, Energy, and Artificial Intelligence (EICEEAI)*, 1–7.

Al-Na'amneh, Q., Aljaidi, M., Nasayreh, A., Gharaibeh, H., Al Mamlook, R. E., Jara- dat, A. S., Alsarhan, A., & Samara, G. (2024b). Journal of intelligent systems: Enhancing iot device security: Cnn-svm hybrid approach for real-time detection of dos and ddos attacks.

Al-Na'amneh, Q., Aljaidi, M., Nasayreh, A., Gharaibeh, H., Al Mamlook, R. E., Jaradat, A. S., Alsarhan, A., & Samara, G. (2024a). Enhancing iot device security: Cnn- svm hybrid approach for real-time detection of dos and ddos attacks. *Journal of Intelligent Systems*, *33*(1), 20230150.

Almomani, A. (2023). Darknet traffic analysis, and classification system based on mod- ified stacking ensemble learning algorithms. *Information Systems and e-Business Management*, •••, 1–32.

Atlaf, T.. (2024). Gnn-based network traffic analysis for the detection of sequential attacks in iot. *Sensors (Basel)*, *24*(5), 1456. PMID: 38474992

Chen, Y.. (2024). Securing network traffic classification models against adversarial examples using derived variables. *Future Internet*, *16*(3), 98.

Davis, S., & Arrigo, B. (2021). The dark web and anonymizing technologies: Legal pitfalls, ethical prospects, and policy directions from radical criminology. *Crime, Law, and Social Change*, *76*(4), 367–386.

Draper-Gil, G., Lashkari, A. H., Mamun, M. S., & Ghorbani, A. A. (2016). Characterization of encrypted and vpn traffic using time-related features, 407–414.

Firdaus, M., et al. (2023). Explainable artificial intelligence for feature selection in net- work traffic classification: A comparative study.

Ghaleb, M., & Hamdan, M.. (2025). Explainable ai for lightweight network traffic classification using depthwise-separable convolutions. *IEEE Open Journal of the Computer Society*.

Gharaibeh, H., Aljaidi, M., Nasayreh, A., Al-Na'amneh, Q., Jaradat, A. S., Samara, G., & Al Mamlook, R. E. (2023). Deep feature extraction framework based on dnn for enhancing mirai attachment classification in machine learning. *2023 2nd International Engineering Conference on Electrical, Energy, and Artificial Intelligence (EICEEAI)*, 1–5.

Joshi, A.. (2024). Deep learning based traffic classification with feature selection mechanism and explainable artificial intelligence (xai). *International Journal of Intelligent Systems and Applications in Engineering*, *12*(1s), 654–662.

Langendonck, T., Caville, S., & Allu, S. (2024). Towards a graph-based foundation model for network traffic analysis. *arXiv preprint arXiv:2409.12345*.

Lashkari, A. H., Gil, G. D., Mamun, M. S. I., & Ghorbani, A. A. (2017). Characterization of tor traffic using time based features, 253–262.

Lashkari, A. H., Kaur, G., & Rahali, A. (2020). Didarknet: A contemporary approach to detect and characterize the darknet traffic using deep image learning, 1–13.

Mandela, N., Sonia, Mistry, N., & Nagpal, A. (2025). Efficient dark web traffic clas- sification using a hybrid cnn-lstm model. *International Journal of Information Technology: an Official Journal of Bharati Vidyapeeth's Institute of Computer Applications and Management*.

Marim, M. C., Ramos, P. V. B., Vieira, A. B., Galletta, A., Villari, M., de Oliveira, R. M., & Silva, E. F. (2023). Darknet traffic detection and characterization with models based on decision trees and neural networks. *Intelligent Systems with Applications*, *18*, 200199.

Mijwil, M. M., Salem, I. E., & Ismaeel, M. M. (2023). The significance of machine learn- ing and deep learning techniques in cybersecurity: A comprehensive review. *Iraqi Journal For Computer Science and Mathematics*, *4*(1), 10.

Mohanty, S. K., Mishra, D., & Jena, S. K. (2022). Robust stacking ensemble model for darknet traffic classification under adversarial settings. *Journal of King Saud University. Computer and Information Sciences*, *34*(10), 9998–10011.

Nasayreh, A., Jaradat, A. S., Gharaibeh, H., Dawaghreh, W., Al Mamlook, R. M., Alqudah, Y., Al-Na'amneh, Q., Daoud, M. S., Migdady, H., & Abualigah, L. (2024). Jordanian banknote data recognition: A cnn-based approach with atten- tion mechanism. *Journal of King Saud University. Computer and Information Sciences*, *36*(4), 102038.

Pang, B., Fu, Y., Ren, S., Wang, Y., Liao, Q., & Jia, Y. (2021). Cgnn: Traffic classification with graph neural network. *arXiv preprint arXiv:2110.09726*.

Qazi, E. U. H., Faheem, M. H., & Zia, T. (2023). Hdlnids: Hybrid deep-learning-based network intrusion detection system. *Applied Sciences (Basel, Switzerland)*, *13*(8), 4921.

Rust-Nguyen, N., & Stamp, M. (2022). Darknet traffic classification and adversarial at- tacks. *arXiv preprint arXiv:2206.06371*.

Rust-Nguyen, N., & Stamp, M. (2023). Darknet traffic classification and adversarial at- tacks using machine learning. *Computers & Security*, *127*, 103098.

Saleem, J., Islam, R., & Islam, M. Z. (2024). *Darknet traffic analysis: A systematic literature review*. IEEE., DOI: 10.1109/ACCESS.2024.3373769

Saleem, J., Islam, R., & Kabir, M. A. (2022). The anonymity of the dark web: A survey. *IEEE Access: Practical Innovations, Open Solutions*, *10*, 33628–33660.

Sarwar, M. B., Hanif, M. K., Talib, R., Younas, M., & Sarwar, M. U. (2021). Dark-detect: Darknet traffic detection and categorization using modified convolution-long short- term memory. *IEEE Access: Practical Innovations, Open Solutions*, *9*, 113705–113713.

Shinde, V., Singhal, K., Almogren, A., Dhanawat, V., Karande, V., & Rehman, A. U. (2024). Ensemble voting for enhanced robustness in darknet traffic detection. *IEEE Access: Practical Innovations, Open Solutions*, *12*, 177064–177079.

Wang, J., ... (2024). Netbench: A large-scale and comprehensive network traffic bench- mark dataset for foundation models. *arXiv preprint arXiv:2403.12345*.

Zhang, W.. (2024). Traffic management in iot backbone networks using gnn and mab with sdn orchestration. *Applied Sciences (Basel, Switzerland)*, *14*(1), 123.

Chapter 5
An Experimental Study on Feature Selection and Data Balancing for Enhanced IoT Intrusion Detection

Mohd Zain Khan
https://orcid.org/0009-0004-4067-7654
Aligarh Muslim University, India

Mohammad Ubaidullah Bokhari
Aligarh Muslim University, India

Shahnwaz Afzal
Aligarh Muslim University, India

ABSTRACT

The rapid growth of Internet of Things (IoT) devices has changed modern digital ecosystems by allowing smooth connectivity, automation and real-time data sharing. However, this massive increase has also widened the attack surface, making IoT devices more vulnerable to numerous cyber threats.Traditional intrusion detection methods often find it hard to manage the dynamic, diverse and large-scale nature of IoT data. Therefore, there is a need for smart and scalable security solutions.In this chapter, we discuss how feature selection techniques effect the performance of different ML classifiers for IoT attack detection on the UNSW-NB15 dataset. This experiment is conducted in two scenarios, firstly without any feature selection and without any class balancing technique. Secondly using SMOTE to address class

DOI: 10.4018/979-8-3373-7503-8.ch005

imbalance and Boruta for optimal feature selection. The experimental results demonstrate the effectiveness of combining data balancing and feature selection techniques in enhancing attack detection performance within IoT environments, particularly by reducing the false negative rate.

1. INTRODUCTION

The IoT has recently experienced significant growth across various daily and industrial applications including healthcare, intelligent homes, smart cities, enhanced energy, precision agriculture, and autonomous transportation (da Costa et al., 2019). The goal of IoT networks is to offer internet connectivity for data transfer between large IoT devices, including networked sensors, drones, actuators, smart cars, smart retail, smart agriculture and smart home appliances, via wired or wireless communications(M. Khan & Tripathi, 2018). However, the majority of these IoT devices are inexpensive, energy-efficient, and resource-constrained, rendering them particularly vulnerable to cyber-attacks and disruptive actions(Pant et al., 2020). Consequently, It is essential to establish an attack detection system capable of swiftly and effectively identifying and mitigating unauthorized intrusions on IoT networks(Bokhari et al., 2025). For this, a variety of machine learning-based models have been developed for detection of harmful activities, in addition to several publicly datasets are available(Mishra et al., 2019).

These datasets frequently have a lot of features, many of which are duplicated or unnecessary, which negatively impacts machine learning algorithms and performance metrics like accuracy, precision, recall, f1 score. Thus, a variety of feature selection techniques have been developed. Machine learning is a challenging branch of artificial intelligence that enables systems to see patterns in data and actively make predictions or decisions without explicit programming (M. Z. Khan & Bokhari, 2023).When machine learning combine with IoT devices provide variety of services as shown in figure 1.

Figure 1. Different services offered by IoT with ML.

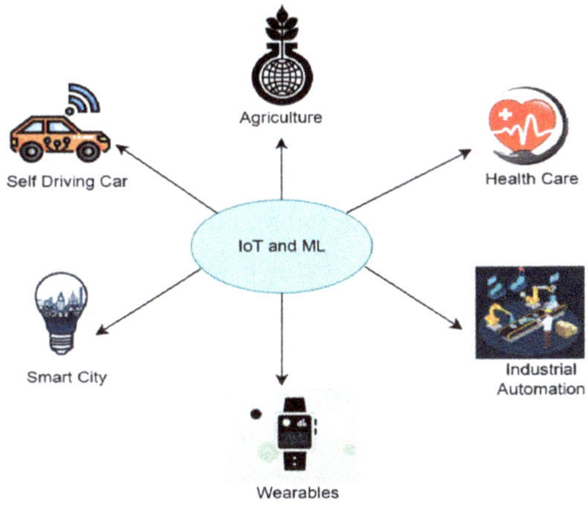

Balancing of data and feature selection are the basic phases in machine learning(-Sakib & Siddiqui, 2023). The selection of feature helps in maintaining the highest-ranking qualities from the original dataset while eliminating irrelevant features. This reduces computation expenses and eliminates extraneous features. This strategy is essential for minimizing the impact of noise, hence enhancing detection accuracy(Musthafa et al., 2024). High-dimensional data sometimes poses considerable challenges which includes heightened computing complexity, increased likelihood of overfitting and reduced model interpretability (Alsahaf et al., 2022). Methods for data balancing and efficient feature selection are essential for approaching these challenges(Sakib & Mustajab, 2025). The Random Forest algorithm is enhanced by the appropriate feature selection method called Boruta(Habibi et al., 2023). It systematically evaluates the significance of each feature by incorporating random shadow features, while retaining the characteristics that significantly influence predictions. This approach enhances the model's generalizability and resilience by eliminating redundant features while maintaining the original feature space. The feature selection procedure involves retaining the highest-ranking qualities from the original dataset while eliminating needless features(Saqib et al., 2021).

This study tackles the problem of class imbalance in the Intrusion Detection System (IDS) dataset by the application of SMOTE. SMOTE generates synthetic examples for the minority class by integrating existing minority cases to achieve a more balanced class distribution(Arafa et al., 2022). This method improves classifiers generalizability and reduces biasness towards the majority class. The implementation of SMOTE for class balancing with Boruta for optimal feature selection significantly improves the performance of machine learning models, particularly in identifying complex and imbalanced IoT threats. This shows that effectiveness of machine learning models mainly in intricate and uneven situations of IoT attack detection.

1.1. Problem Formulation

Let the IoT intrusion detection problem be formally defined as a supervised classification task over a high-dimensional and imbalanced dataset. Given a dataset $= \{(x_i, y_i)\}_{i=1}^{N}$, where each instance $x_i \epsilon \mathbb{R}^d$ is a feature vector representing network traffic or device behavior, and $y_i \epsilon \{0,1,2,3,\ldots\ldots\ldots,C-1\}$ denotes the class label corresponding to either benign activity $(y_i = 0)$ or one of $C-1$ attack categories, the goal is to learn a function $f : \mathbb{R}^d \rightarrow \{0,1,2.....,C-1\}$ that accurately maps feature vectors to their respective classes.

1. Unbalanced Distribution of Classes The dataset exhibits class imbalance such that:

$$\exists\, c \,\epsilon\, \{1,\ldots\ldots,C-1\} \; where \; |D_C| \ll |D_0| \quad (1)$$

Where D_C *is the subset of* D that comprises samples belonging to class c, while D_0 denotes the majority (normal) class. This disparity distorts the learning process, leading classifiers to exhibit bias towards majority classes.

2. Feature Redundancy and Irrelevance. Given the high dimensionality of feature space R^d not all features contribute equally to the decision boundary. Let $S \subset \{1,2,3,\ldots\ldots.,d\}$ be an optimal subset of features such that:

$$\exists \mathrm{S} : |S| \ll d, \, and \; \mathbb{E}_{(x_i,y_i)}\left[\mathcal{L}\left(f(x_i^S), y_i\right)\right] \text{ is minimized,} \quad (2)$$

Where x_i^S denotes the projection of x_i onto the selected features subset S, and L is the classification loss function.

3. Learning Objective The learning objective is to minimize the classification loss over the training set while handling class imbalance and reducing feature dimensionality. Formally, the objective can be expressed as:

$$\min_{f \epsilon F} \frac{1}{N} \sum_{i=1}^{N} \mathcal{L}\left(f(x_i^S), y_i\right)$$

, (3)

Subject to:

S= Boruta (D): feature selection using Boruta algorithm,
D'=SMOTE (D): balanced dataset using Synthetic Minority Oversampling Technique.
The final model $f^* \epsilon F$ is choosen from the set of classifiers $F = \{f_{RF}, f_{NB}, f_{SVM}, f_{AdaBoost}\}$, where:
f_{RF}= Random Forest,
f_{NB}= Naive Bayes,
f_{SVM}= Support Vector Machine,
$f_{AdaBoost}$= Adaptive Boosting

1.2. Motivation

Automation and data-driven services have advanced significantly across a number of industries due to the exponential growth of IoT devices. But this expansion has also brought about serious security issues because conventional IDS are unable to handle the volume, diversity and dynamic character of IoT traffic. Poor detection accuracy and high False Negative Rates (FNR) continue to be problems. This emphasizes how urgently intelligent, flexible and scalable security measures are needed. One promising method for recognizing intricate attack patterns in IoT environments is machine learning. Motivated by this, our study explores the impact of feature selection and data balancing techniques on the performance of different ML classifiers for IoT attack detection and aiming to improve detection rates while reducing false negatives rate.

1.3. Contributions

The contributions of this chapter are as follows-:

- This study assesses the performance of different machine learning models by examining critical metrics including accuracy, precision, recall and F1-score.
- The models are initially trained and evaluated on the original dataset without feature selection or class balance to establish baseline performance.
- To evaluate the effects of data preprocessing, SMOTE is utilized to address class imbalance, while the Boruta method is applied for optimal feature selection.
- We further investigate the role of dimensionality reduction and data balancing in enhancing the overall effectiveness of attack detection in IoT environment.

The remaining portion of this chapter as follows: Section 2 consists of related work done by different researchers in the field of features selection for detection of IoT attacks having machine learning models. Section 3 consists of description of different machine learning models. Section 4 consists of proposed work which shows the importance of feature selection and need for balancing the dataset. Section 5 covers the result and discussion. Finally, section 6 consists of conclusion and future scope of this chapter.

2. RELATED WORK

Different researchers perform different work for dimensionality reduction and balancing the dataset in detection of IoT attacks using machine learning techniques like Kumari et.al(Kumari & Jain, 2024) explains the approach to identify DDoS assaults in IoT networks that enhances detection speed and accuracy by integrating machine learning models with dimensionality reduction techniques. Desai et.al (Desai et al., 2020) explains the security vulnerabilities of IoT devices, especially their exposure to assaults such as botnets and underscores the pressing necessity for improved security protocols to safeguard networks from these dangers. Kandasamy et.al (Kandasamy & Roseline, 2025) explains an innovative hybrid technique that greatly enhances real-time detection of Man-in-the-Middle (MitM) assaults in smart home networks by combining AutoEncoder for unsupervised feature extraction and XGBoost for effective classification. Ahfa et.al (Isna et al., 2025) explains various dimensionality reduction techniques to enhance the performance and efficiency of Logistic Regression in detecting network anomalies. Maazalahi et.al (Maazalahi & Hosseini, 2025) addressed their understanding on hybrid IDS that employs Machine learning and algorithms that are metaheuristic to improve botnet attack detection through a three-step process: pre-processing, feature selection using a combined SFO-WOA method and attack detection using a PSO-K-means approach, which achieves high attack detection accuracy and efficiency. Vinayak et.al (M.V. & T., 2025) explain novel IDS model that combines a stacked sparse autoencoder (SSAE) for dimensionality reduction with an XGBoost classifier for improved detection performance. Wang et.al (Wang et al., 2025) addressed their understanding Image TIDS framework, which utilizes GADF imaging and an improved Transformer model to enhance IoT intrusion detection by preserving critical features and addressing class imbalance through Focal Loss. Varunram et.al (Varunram et al., 2021) explain identifying and classifying network security threats, particularly distinguishing between Distributed Denial of Service attacks and benign activities. It seeks to augment detection techniques to refine network defense measures against diverse attack vectors. Hanafi et.al (Hanafi et al., 2022)explains Stack Denoising Auto Encoder (SDAE) which enhances the effectiveness of traditional machine learning algorithms like Naive Bayes, KNN, Decision Tree and SVM in IDS. Zong et.al (Zong & Huang, 2021) determine a unique approach that amalgamates Rough Set (RS) theory with Principal Component Analysis (PCA) to proficiently mitigate feature redundancy. This amalgamation harnesses the advantages of both methodologies to improve the efficacy of DDoS detection algorithms.

3. METHODS

This study uses different machine learning models to detect IoT threats. The models were trained with optimized settings and evaluated using different performance metrics. Feature selection methods that were employed to enhance the accuracy and efficiency of the models. This section provides a thorough review of the machine learning techniques that were implemented in this study are as follows-:

3.1. Random Forest

Random Forest is an adaptive machine learning method that use many decision trees to provide predictions(T. F. Khan & Zubair, 2025). It merge the results of different trees to improve accuracy and reduce overfitting(Sipper & Moore, 2021). It predicts the classification of an input instance using majority voting among all trees making it robust for detecting IoT attacks.

The subsequent equation yields the ultimate predicted value:

$$\hat{y} = mode\left(h_1(x), h_2(x), \ldots\ldots, h_T(x)\right) \tag{4}$$

Where, $h_t(x)$ is predicted value from t[th] tree in the forest.

3.2. AdaBoost

AdaBoost is a boosting method that comprises numerous weak classifiers to generate a robust classifier. It enhances the accuracy of the model by working on instances that are misclassified during each iteration(Hajla et al., 2025). This makes it suitable for categorization tasks and handling complex datasets. It merges multiple weak learners into a significant classifier by incrementally adjusting the weights of misclassified instances to diminish classification error.

$$F(x) = \sum_{t=1}^{T} a_1 h_1(x) \tag{5}$$

Where $h_t(x)$ is the weak classifier at iteration t_1 and a_t is its weight based on the error rate.

3.3. Support Vector Machine (SVM)

Support Vector Machine (SVM) is a supervised learning technique that is utilized for regression and classification tasks. It functions by identifying the hyperplane that most effectively separates data into different classes(M. Z. Khan et al., 2024). It classifies IoT network traffic by identifying the hyperplane that optimizes the separation between normal and assault instances.

$$f(x) = \text{sign}\ (w \, . x + b)\ (6)$$

Where "w" represents the weight vector, "x" defines the input feature vector and "b" signifies the bias factor.

3.4. Naive Bayes

Naive Bayes is an algorithm that is effective and is based on Bayes' Theorem, which assumes the independence of features(Sood et al., 2021). It is frequently implemented for the purpose of categorization, including sentiment analysis and spam detection. In order to identify IoT hazards, it computes the probability that follows of each class using Bayes' theorem.

$$P(C_k / X) = \frac{P(X/C_k) \, . P(C_k)}{P(X)} \left(7\right)$$

Where $P(C_k/X)$ represents the probability of class C_k given feature vector X, facilitating classification by maximum likelihood estimation.

4. PROPOSED WORK

The primary objective of this study is to underline the significance of data balancing and dimensionality reduction before implementing of machine learning classifiers in order to enhance the reliability and accuracy of IoT threat detection. This study is to improve the performance of IoT attack detection by reducing unnecessary features and balancing the dataset for enhancing classification performance and overall attack detection in IoT contexts.

Figure 2. Proposed Methodology

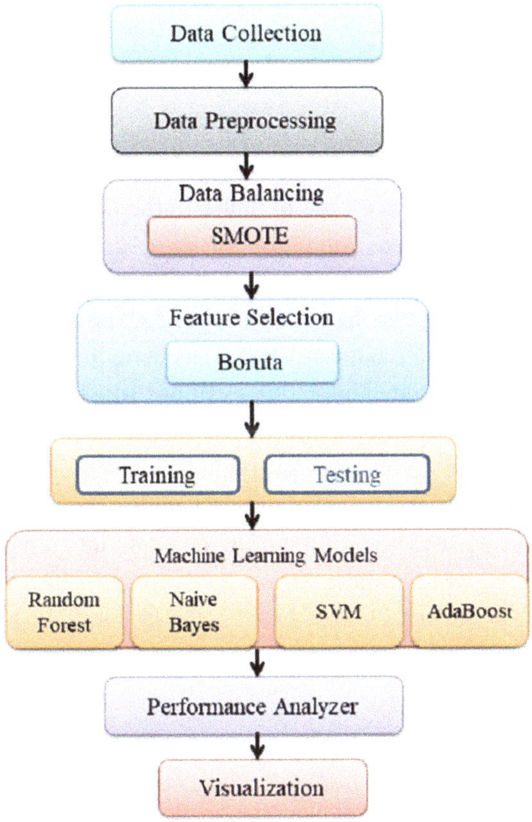

4.1 Dataset Used

The UNSWNB15 dataset serves as a valuable resource for cybersecurity research due to its diverse array of attack methods. The dataset's dependability is enhanced by the balanced combination of regular and threat traffic, enabling machine learning models derived from it to distinguish between normal and attack patterns. Researchers can utilize this dataset to enhance machine learning classifiers for analysing attack patterns and developing robust intrusion detection systems.

The dataset is crucial for enhancing cybersecurity in emerging technologies, particularly within the Internet of Things (IoT) domain. As IoT networks become increasingly complex and susceptible to cyber threats, datasets like as UNSW-NB15 facilitate the development and evaluation of intrusion detection systems. This dataset enhances the efficacy of security solutions, which is crucial for ongoing endeavours to protect digital infrastructures from emerging cyber threats.

4.2 Data Preprocessing

During the preparation phase of our model creation, we followed a series of important steps to get the dataset suitable for accurate analysis and modelling, as shown in Figure 3. Data preparation is a crucial phase in the analytical process, ensuring that the data is clean, structured, and ready for use (Agarwal, 2016). The first step is Data Cleaning, which fixes mistakes, removes duplicates, and makes sure that all the data is consistent. Data integration happens when data from many sources is combined into one complete dataset. Data transformation is done to change data into a format that may be used. This includes things like filling in missing values, making the data more uniform, or scaling it to make it all the same size. In the last step, Data Reduction, the dataset is made smaller by getting rid of unnecessary information or combining related data, while keeping the most important parts. Data discretization is used to break up continuous data into smaller, more specific intervals or categories, which makes it easier to analyze. These steps make sure that the data is well-organized and ready for accurate modelling and analysis. The biggest problem in this chapter was dealing with missing data, which can make a dataset less reliable and valid.

Figure 3. Data Preprocessing Steps.

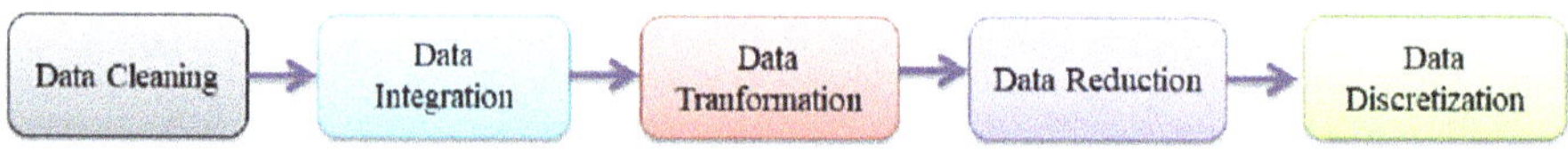

To resolve this issue, we systematically removed all records with missing or null data. This strategy was employed to mitigate the occurrence of biases and errors resulting from inadequate information. By eliminating these problematic cases, we guaranteed the dataset preserved its integrity and consistency. The removal of records with missing values may result in a reduced dataset size; however, this compromise is justified by the improvement in data quality. Our aim was to develop a comprehensive and dependable dataset that would serve as a solid basis for the detection of assaults. This phase was essential for minimising potential errors and improving the accuracy of our model's forecasts.

4.3 Feature Selection

To improve model performance, we implemented a feature selection method to identify and rank the most pertinent variables in the UNSW-NB15 dataset, employing the Boruta algorithm for this task. Systematic comparison of the significance of original characteristics to randomly permuted shadow features allow for the retention of only those features that substantially enhance the predictive model. This technique mitigates overfitting caused by extraneous factors while enhancing model performance measures by retaining all relevant properties. We enhanced computational efficiency and detection performance in IoT threat detection by effectively reducing the feature space with the Boruta method, while preserving essential information. Before feature selection, the dataset comprised 183 features, following the application of Boruta for feature selection, this number was reduced. 54 pertinent traits were preserved as depicted in Figure 4.

Figure 4. Top 54 Features Selected by Boruta.

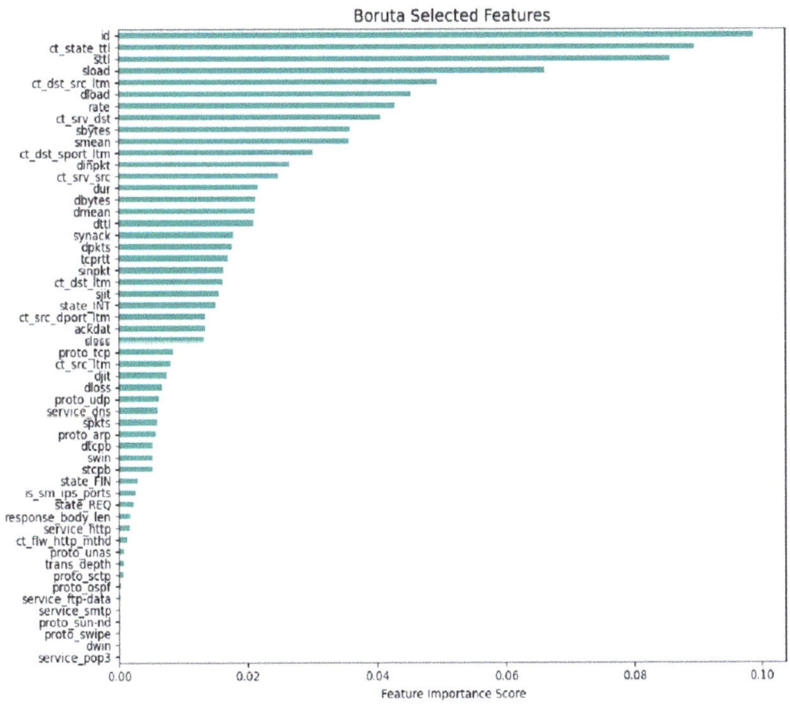

4.4 Evaluation Criteria

We assess the effectiveness of our proposed study in comparison to established approaches based on F1-score, accuracy, false negative rate, precision, and recall, as these metrics are commonly utilized in attack detection applications for model evaluation (Tushkanova et al., 2023). We also examine the receiver operating characteristic (ROC) curve, which is generated by integrating the model's true positive rate with the false positive rate. A summary of performance metrics is presented below.

$$Accuracy = \frac{TP + TN}{P + N} \tag{8}$$

$$Precision = \frac{TP}{TP + FP} \tag{9}$$

$$Recall(Detection\ rate) = \frac{TP}{TP + FN} \tag{10}$$

$$F1 - Score = 2 \times \frac{Precision \times Recall}{Precision + Recall} \tag{11}$$

5. RESULT AND DISCUSSIONS

The hardware and software configurations employed in the experimental framework for this study sought to enhance the development and assessment of machine learning models. The software includes 8GB of RAM, a 256GB SSD for storage, and an Intel Core i5 CPU, enhancing parallel processing and model training capabilities. The system employed Windows 11 as its operating system.

Jupyter Notebook and PyCharm functioned as the main development environments, while Python 3.9 was the primary programming language utilized. A range of Python libraries was utilized to facilitate the inquiry. Data manipulation and preprocessing were performed utilizing Pandas, NumPy and machine learning models were developed with Scikit-learn. Evaluation measures including accuracy, F1 score, recall and precision were computed using Scikit-learn metrics module. This approach was selected to provide precise identification of IoT-related assaults and dependable, scalable machine learning growth.

In our experiment, we compared the results of two approaches: one using balancing the dataset technique as SMOTE and for feature selection technique as Boruta and the other without them, both on the UNSW-NB15 dataset, as shown in Table 1 and Table 2. In both the cases we see that AdaBoost outperform the best.

Table 1 illustrates that, without the application of SMOTE and the Boruta feature selection technique, the AdaBoost model displays the most consistent and robust performance in terms of accuracy. It achieves excellent efficacy for Accuracy and F1-score, showcasing its strong ability to reliably detect and classify both attack and normal events, even without preprocessing alterations.

Conversely, Naive Bayes demonstrates remarkably high accuracy, signifying that 100% of its positive predictions are correct. Consequently, this leads to remarkably low Recall, F1, and a substantial False Negative Rate (FNR), highlighting the model's failure to detect several authentic positive instances. This behaviour unequivocally indicates overfitting, particularly attributed to the imbalanced dataset and the lack of feature selection. The SVM and Random Forest models provide commendable performance, with SVM showing greater recall but slightly lower precision compared to AdaBoost. The Random Forest algorithm exhibits reliable performance across all metrics, making it a strong choice. Nevertheless, AdaBoost exceeds others in accuracy. The absence of data balancing and feature selection significantly impacts model performance, particularly for Naive Bayes.

Table 1. Performance of models **Excluding** *Smote and Boruta*

Models	Accuracy (%)	Precision (%)	Recall (%)	F1-Score(%)	FNR (%)
Random Forest	93.73%	95.93%	94.12%	95.02%	05.87%
Naive Bayes	50.90%	**100.00%**	22.75%	37.07%	07.72%
SVM	90.13%	87.39%	**98.79%**	92.71%	01.20%
AdaBoost	**97.20%**	98.10%	97.48%	**97.79%**	02.51%

Table 2 demonstrates that the application of the Boruta feature selection technique and dataset balancing through SMOTE markedly enhances the performance of all models. Among these, AdaBoost stands out as the highest-performing model with 97.75% of accuracy, exhibiting superior outcomes across all other important evaluation metrics like Precision., Recall, F1-score and FNR (False Negative Rate). The model's outstanding performance illustrates its effective application of feature refinement and data balance, enabling it to reliably detect the majority of instances with high confidence and minimal errors. AdaBoost exhibits a strong ability to detect positive instances as evidenced by its precision, recall and F1-score.

Compared to the previous outcomes without preprocessing, the Naive Bayes model continues to underperform Because it misses the majority of true positives and correctly predicts only few and exhibits comparatively low recall and overall model performance, but a notable enhancement in performance. Random Forest and SVM demonstrate notable improvements yet, their performance is marginally inferior to that of AdaBoost.

The implementation of feature selection and balancing approaches significantly improves model efficacy, with AdaBoost emerging as the most dependable and precise model for attack detection under these enhanced scenarios.

Table 2. Performance of models **Including** *Smote and Boruta*

Models	Accuracy (%)	Precision (%)	Recall (%)	F1-Score (%)	FNR (%)
Random Forest	96.11%	96.82%	95.48%	96.14%	04.51%
Naive Bayes	79.40%	91.89%	65.19%	76.27%	34.80%
SVM	92.80%	93.90%	91.78%	92.83%	08.21%
AdaBoost	**97.75%**	**97.94%**	**97.63%**	**97.78%**	**02.36%**

The confusion matrices of the examined models before the use of feature selection and data balancing methods as shown in Figure 5. The findings reveal substantial discrepancies in categorization efficacy especially in identifying assault occurrences. The Naive Bayes model has a notable prevalence of false negatives, misclassifying a substantial proportion of assault events as normal. Although it accurately recognizes all standard traffic, its failure to identify most attacks reveals a significant bias towards the majority class, a common result of class imbalance and insufficient informative feature selection. Similarly, the SVM model, while achieving a considerable number of true positives, displays a notable quantity of false positives, wherein innocuous traffic is mistakenly classified as hostile, indicating an extreme sensitivity to attack patterns. Conversely, Random Forest exhibits consistent performance; yet, it continues to misclassify assault incidents. AdaBoost outperforms the other models in this unpolished context, demonstrating fewer false negatives and a strong ability to differentiate between legitimate and malicious communications.

These confusion matrices highlight the constraints of utilising unprocessed data without addressing class imbalance and extraneous features. The occurrence of numerous false negatives, particularly in models like Naive Bayes, raises apprehensions for real IoT security applications where undetected attacks can result in significant implications. This contrast highlights the necessity of utilising methods such as SMOTE for data balancing and Boruta for feature selection, which are essential for enhancing the reliability and effectiveness of IDS in IoT environments.

Figure 5. Confusion Metrics Excluding Smote and Boruta.

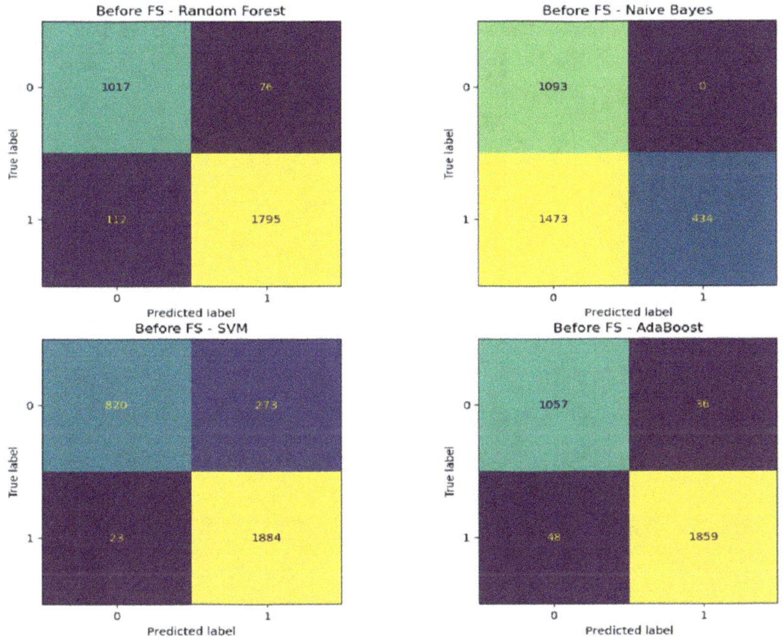

The confusion matrices of the classification models, utilising SMOTE and the Boruta feature selection technique as illustrated in Figure 6, provide substantial improvements in detection performance. The application of SMOTE effectively addresses the class imbalance issue, ensuring that models are trained on a more accurate distribution of attack and normal instances. The Boruta method concurrently removes redundant information, allowing models to concentrate on the most pertinent traits for precise decision-making.

The confusion matrices demonstrate a significant decrease in false negatives across all models signifying an enhanced capacity to identify attack instances which is essential in attack detection systems. AdaBoost exhibits superior balanced and robust performance compared to all models showing minimal misclassification of both benign and malicious traffic. Random Forest and SVM demonstrate substantial enhancements, attaining elevated true positive rates while markedly decreasing false positive and false negative rates relative to their performance.

Figure 6. Confusion Metrics Including Smote and Boruta.

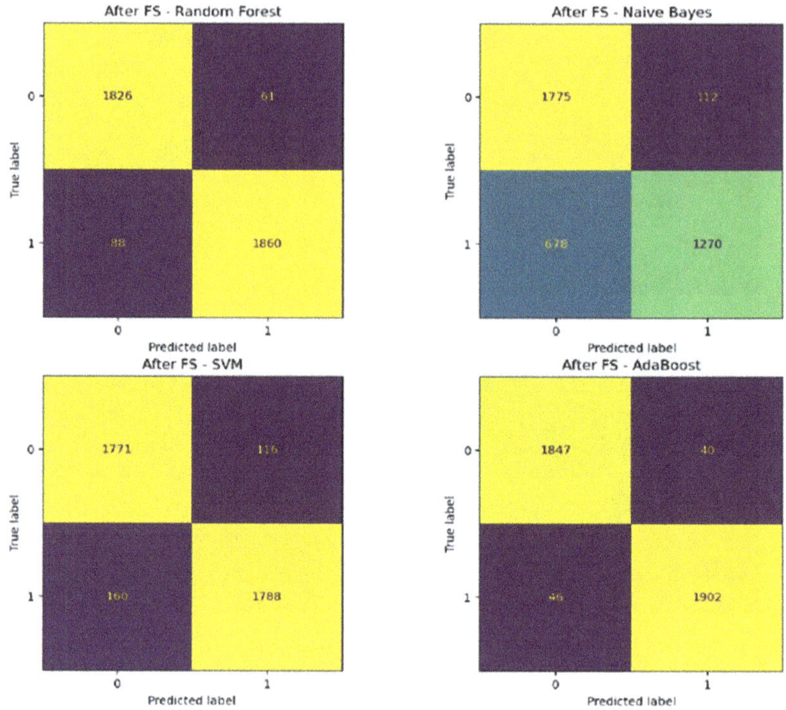

Figure 7 depicts the ROC curves of the classification models prior to the use of any feature selection and data balancing methods. The Area Under the Curve (AUC)values indicate distinct performance differences among the models. AdaBoost demonstrates an essentially perfect AUC signifying outstanding discriminative capability even in the absence of preprocessing. Random Forest and SVM demonstrate strong classification capabilities, as evidenced by their elevated AUC values indicating reliable identification of both positive and negative classes.

Conversely, Naive Bayes has a markedly reduced AUC indicating its constrained efficacy in differentiating between normal and attack instances in imbalanced and high-dimensional contexts. This suboptimal performance underscores the susceptibility of specific algorithms to the quality and equilibrium of input data.

The ROC analysis conducted before feature selection and balancing indicates that certain models like AdaBoost exhibit strong classification performance but others are significantly impaired due to inadequate preprocessing. These findings highlight the importance of feature selection and class balance to improve model generalization and ensure consistent detection performance across several classifiers.

Figure 7. ROC Curve Excluding Smote and Boruta.

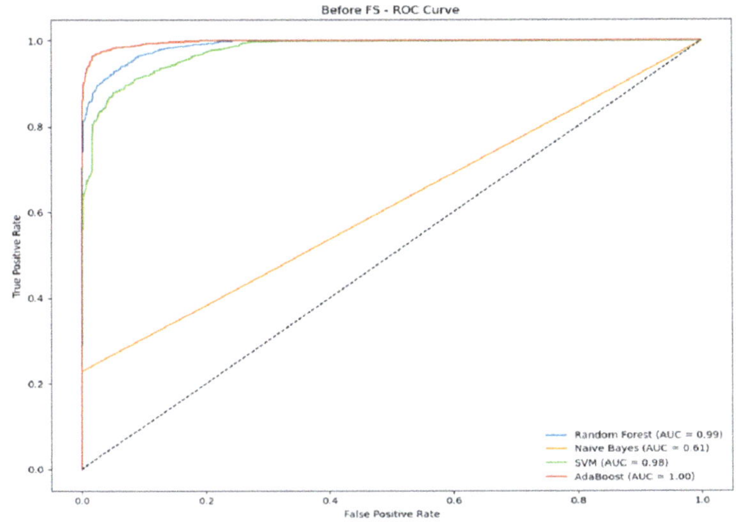

The ROC curves of the models subsequent to the implementation of feature selection via the Boruta technique and data balancing through SMOTE as shown in Figure 8. The enhancement in AUC values for all classifiers validates the beneficial effect of these preprocessing strategies. Significantly, Naive Bayes demonstrate the improvement in performance as evidenced by a substantial increase in its AUC relative to the preprocessed scenario and demonstrating an expanded capacity to differentiate between attack and normal cases.

The Random Forest and SVM classifiers provide enhanced AUC values, reflecting consistent and reliable performance; nevertheless, AdaBoost displays remarkable classification efficacy with an optimal AUC, signifying excellent distinction between the two classes. The curves demonstrate steeper ascents and a capacity to reach the top-left corner more swiftly, hence highlighting improved true positive rates and reduced false positives.

These findings affirm that feature selection techniques and dataset balancing are crucial factors in improving model performance, especially in imbalanced and high-dimensional IoT datasets. By focussing on the highest-ranked characteristics and ensuring equal class representation, these strategies substantially improve the models' performance.

Figure 8. ROC Curve Including Smote and Boruta.

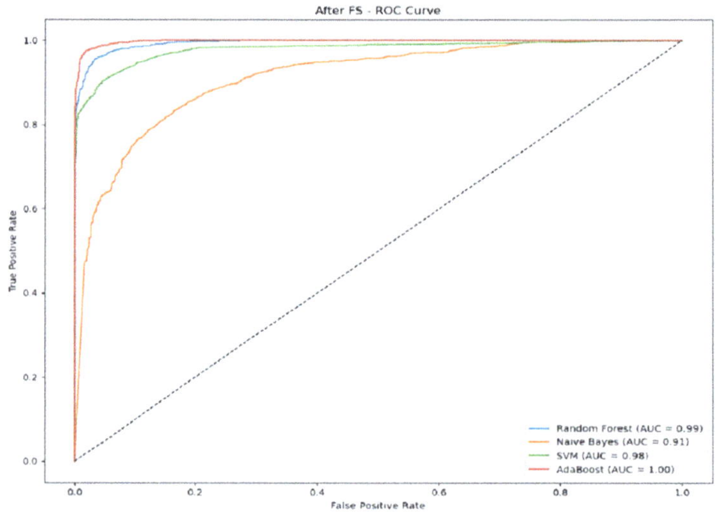

6. CONCLUSION AND FUTURE SCOPE

This study examined the impact of utilizing SMOTE and Boruta on the effectiveness of machine learning-based intrusion detection models for IoT security, specifically using the UNSW-NB15 dataset. The experimental results confirm that the integration of SMOTE and Boruta significantly enhances the classification performance of the models by effectively mitigating class imbalance and eliminating superfluous features. After applying these preprocessing techniques, the Random Forest classifier demonstrated improved performance across many evaluation metrics, indicating increased generalizability and robustness. Without SMOTE and Boruta, on the other hand, the AdaBoost model got the highest accuracy, but it was prone to overfitting because the dataset was not balanced. The analysis of the confusion matrix revealed that models trained with SMOTE and Boruta exhibited a substantial reduction in false positives and false negatives, hence improving their ability to accurately detect assault patterns. These results show how important feature selection and class balancing are for making attack detection systems work better and be more reliable in IoT settings.

Future research could improve this study by using different methods for selecting features and optimising them, which could make intrusion detection more accurate. To improve IoT networks' adaptability and attack detection, individuals might explore hybrid techniques that integrate conventional machine learning models with deep learning methodologies.

REFERENCES

Agarwal, V. (2016). *Research on Data Preprocessing and Categorization Technique for Smartphone Review Analysis. December 2015*. https://doi.org/DOI: 10.5120/ijca2015907309

Alsahaf, A., Petkov, N., Shenoy, V., & Azzopardi, G. (2022). A framework for feature selection through boosting. *Expert Systems with Applications*. Advance online publication. DOI: 10.1016/j.eswa.2021.115895

Arafa, A., El-Fishawy, N., Badawy, M., & Radad, M. (2022). RN-SMOTE: Reduced Noise SMOTE based on DBSCAN for enhancing imbalanced data classification. *Journal of King Saud University. Computer and Information Sciences*. Advance online publication. DOI: 10.1016/j.jksuci.2022.06.005

Bokhari, M. U., Khan, M. Z., & Masoodi, F. S. (2025). A Hybrid Approach to Feature Selection for Cyber Threat Detection in IoT Networks. *2025 3rd International Conference on Device Intelligence, Computing and Communication Technologies (DICCT)*, 637–642. https://doi.org/DOI: 10.1109/DICCT64131.2025.10986689

da Costa, K. A. P., Papa, J. P., Lisboa, C. O., Munoz, R., & de Albuquerque, V. H. C. (2019). Internet of Things: A survey on machine learning-based intrusion detection approaches. *Computer Networks*, *151*, 147–157. DOI: 10.1016/j.comnet.2019.01.023

Desai, M. G., Shi, Y., & Suo, K. (2020). IoT Bonet and Network Intrusion Detection using Dimensionality Reduction and Supervised Machine Learning. *2020 11th IEEE Annual Ubiquitous Computing, Electronics & Mobile Communication Conference (UEMCON)*, 316–322. https://doi.org/DOI: 10.1109/UEMCON51285.2020.9298146

Habibi, A., Delavar, M. R., Sadeghian, M. S., Nazari, B., & Pirasteh, S. (2023). A hybrid of ensemble machine learning models with RFE and Boruta wrapper-based algorithms for flash flood susceptibility assessment. *International Journal of Applied Earth Observation and Geoinformation*. Advance online publication. DOI: 10.1016/j.jag.2023.103401

Hajla, S. El, Ennaji, E. M., Maleh, Y., & Mounir, S. (2025). *Enhancing IoT network defense : advanced intrusion detection via ensemble learning techniques. 35*(3), 2010–2020. https://doi.org/DOI: 10.11591/ijeecs.v35.i3.pp2010-2020

Hanafi, M., A. H., Verawati, I., & Hardi, R. (2022). An Intrusion Detection System Using SDAE to Enhance Dimensional Reduction in Machine Learning. *International Journal on Informatics Visualization*, *6*(2), 306–316. DOI: 10.30630/joiv.6.2.990

Isna, M., Ahfa, M., Hakim, L., & Rosadi, M. I. (2025).. . *Comparison of Dimensionality Reduction Techniques to Improve Performance and Efficiency of Logistic Regression in Network Anomaly Detection.*, *3*(January), 1–13. DOI: 10.30996/jitcs.12212

Kandasamy, V., & Roseline, A. A. (2025). *Harnessing advanced hybrid deep learning model for real-time detection and prevention of man- in-the-middle cyber attacks*. 1–26.

Khan, M., & Tripathi, A. (2018). Digital Patient Eye. *Proceedings - 2018 3rd International Conference On Internet of Things: Smart Innovation and Usages, IoT-SIU 2018*. https://doi.org/DOI: 10.1109/IoT-SIU.2018.8519841

Khan, M. Z., & Bokhari, M. U. (2023). Comparative Study of Detection of IoT Attacks using Machine Learning Techniques. *Proceedings of the 17th INDIACom; 2023 10th International Conference on Computing for Sustainable Global Development, INDIACom 2023*, 1648–1651.

Khan, M. Z., Bokhari, M. U., & Khan, T. F. (2024). Internet of Things Security: An Experimental Analysis of Detecting Denial of Service Attacks with Machine Learning. *2024 1st International Conference on Innovative Engineering Sciences and Technological Research (ICIESTR)*, 1–6. https://doi.org/DOI: 10.1109/ICIESTR60916.2024.10798334

Khan, T. F., & Zubair, S. (2025). Lung Cancer Diagnosis Using Image Enhancement and Machine Learning Methods. *Communications in Computer and Information Science, 2366 CCIS*, 197–208. https://doi.org/DOI: 10.1007/978-3-031-81342-9_17

Kumari, P., & Jain, A. K. (2024). Timely detection of DDoS attacks in IoT with dimensionality reduction. *Cluster Computing*, *27*(6), 7869–7887. DOI: 10.1007/s10586-024-04392-9

Maazalahi, M., & Hosseini, S. (2025). Machine learning and metaheuristic optimization algorithms for feature selection and botnet attack detection. In *Knowledge and Information Systems*. Springer London., DOI: 10.1007/s10115-024-02322-0

Mishra, P., Varadharajan, V., Tupakula, U., & Pilli, E. S. (2019). A detailed investigation and analysis of using machine learning techniques for intrusion detection. *IEEE Communications Surveys and Tutorials*, *21*(1), 686–728. DOI: 10.1109/COMST.2018.2847722

Musthafa, M. B., Huda, S., Kodera, Y., Ali, M. A., Araki, S., Mwaura, J., & Nogami, Y. (2024). Optimizing IoT Intrusion Detection Using Balanced Class Distribution, Feature Selection, and Ensemble Machine Learning Techniques. *Sensors (Basel), 24*(13), 1–19. DOI: 10.3390/s24134293 PMID: 39001072

M.V. H. V., & T., J. (2025). A hybrid model for detecting intrusions using stacked autoencoders and extreme gradient boosting. *Computers & Security, 150*, 104212. https://doi.org/https://doi.org/10.1016/j.cose.2024.104212

Pant, D., Bhatt, A., Khan, M., Nautiyal, O. P., & Adhikari, P. (2020). Automated IoT based Smart Water Quality Assessment System. *Proceedings of the 2019 8th International Conference on System Modeling and Advancement in Research Trends, SMART 2019*, 98–104. https://doi.org/DOI: 10.1109/SMART46866.2019.9117271

Sakib, M., & Mustajab, S. (2025). CEEMDAN-TCN-AutoLSTM: A Triple-Force Ensemble Using Cross-Stitch Networks for Short-Term Load Forecasting. *Arabian Journal for Science and Engineering*. Advance online publication. DOI: 10.1007/s13369-025-10398-1

Sakib, M., & Siddiqui, T. (2023). Multi-Network-Based Ensemble Deep Learning Model to Forecast Ross River Virus Outbreak in Australia. *International Journal of Pattern Recognition and Artificial Intelligence*, *37*(10), 2352015.

Saqib, M., Sahu, S. A., Sakib, M., & Al-Ammar, E. A. (2021). Machine Learning-Based Day-Ahead Market Energy Usage Bidding for Smart Microgrids. *Electric Vehicle Integration in a Smart Microgrid Environment*, 249–266. https://doi.org/DOI: 10.1201/9780367423926-10

Sipper, M., & Moore, J. H. (2021). Conservation machine learning : A case study of random forests. *Scientific Reports, 0123456789*, 1–6. DOI: 10.1038/s41598-021-83247-4 PMID: 33574563

Sood, K., Mahto, R., Shah, H., & Murrell, A. (2021). Power Management of Autonomous Drones using Machine Learning. *2021 IEEE Conference on Technologies for Sustainability, SusTech 2021*. https://doi.org/DOI: 10.1109/SusTech51236.2021.9467475

Tushkanova, O., Levshun, D., Branitskiy, A., Fedorchenko, E., Novikova, E., & Kotenko, I. (2023). Detection of Cyberattacks and Anomalies in Cyber-Physical Systems: Approaches, Data Sources, Evaluation. *Algorithms*. Advance online publication. DOI: 10.3390/a16020085

Varunram, T. N., Shivaprasad, M. B., Aishwarya, K. H., Balraj, A., Savish, S. V., & Ullas, S. (2021). Analysis of Different Dimensionality Reduction Techniques and Machine Learning Algorithms for an Intrusion Detection System. *2021 IEEE 6th International Conference on Computing, Communication and Automation (ICCCA)*, 237–242. https://doi.org/DOI: 10.1109/ICCCA52192.2021.9666265

Wang, P., Song, Y., Wang, X., Guo, X., & Xiang, Q. (2025). ImagTIDS: An internet of things intrusion detection framework utilizing GADF imaging encoding and improved Transformer. *Complex & Intelligent Systems*, *11*(1). Advance online publication. DOI: 10.1007/s40747-024-01712-9

Zong, Y., & Huang, G. (2021). A feature dimension reduction technology for predicting DDoS intrusion behavior in multimedia internet of things. *Multimedia Tools and Applications*, *80*(15), 22671–22684. DOI: 10.1007/s11042-019-7591-7

Chapter 6

Optimized Phishing Detection Through URL Analysis by a Gradient Boosting–RNN Ensemble Model: A Hybridization Approach

T. Nithya
https://orcid.org/0000-0001-9738-9910
Velalar College of Engineering and Technology, India

V. Chandrasekaran
Velalar College of Engineering and Technology, India

S. Mahendrakumar
https://orcid.org/0000-0001-6966-2545
Velalar College of Engineering and Technology, India

R. Karunamoorthi
https://orcid.org/0009-0001-2141-6852
Sri Krishna College of Engineering and Technology, India

P. Kalaivani
Kongu Engineering College, India

M. Parvathi
Nandha Engineering college, India

N. V. Keerthana
https://orcid.org/0000-0001-8878-2083
Velalar College of Engineering and Technology, India

V. Gomathi
https://orcid.org/0000-0002-8933-4220
Velalar College of Engineering and Technology, India

D. Suganya
https://orcid.org/0000-0002-3286-4431
Velalar College of Engineering and Technology, India

R. Maheshwari
https://orcid.org/0009-0001-5935-8475
Velalar College of Engineering and Technology, India

DOI: 10.4018/979-8-3373-7503-8.ch006

ABSTRACT

Phishing attacks pose a major threat to cybersecurity by deceiving users into revealing sensitive information. This study proposes an optimized phishing detection framework that leverages both syntactic URL features and temporal behavior through a novel ensemble model combining Gradient Boosting and Recurrent Neural Networks (RNN). The Gradient Boosting component captures static patterns and feature importance from structured URL attributes, while the RNN processes sequential character-level URL data to learn underlying patterns of malicious domains. The ensemble approach enhances detection accuracy, reduces false positives, and adapts effectively to evolving phishing tactics. Experimental results on benchmark datasets demonstrate superior performance compared to individual models, confirming the potential of hybrid ensemble techniques for real-time phishing URL detection.

1. INTRODUCTION

The capability of the internet for facilitating social media, commerce, healthcare, and education has made it an essential element of modern life. Telecommunication links, such as fiber optics, telephone cables, and wireless networks, connect several hosts and servers. Through the Internet Protocol/Transmission Control Protocol (IP-TCP), these links enable seamless interaction between devices and systems. Interconnected networks have dramatically changed international communication by allowing real-time collaboration and sharing of information, as well as transactions, between individuals, organizations, and governments across national borders. Perhaps the most typical form of attack that has emanated from global interconnection in this regard is phishing attacks (Lee et al., 2021). With the continued integration of the internet into all aspects of daily life, there is an increasingly sophisticated and increasingly frequent phishing attack that poses serious risks to financial systems, data security, and individual privacy. Phishing, a category of fraud targeting the theft of private information such as credit card numbers, usernames, and passwords, remains a nascent threat to both individuals and corporations. They exploit human psychology by posing as trustworthy communication channels through social engineering techniques (Smadi et al., 2018).

The phishing problem needs a holistic approach that involves technology, user education, and policy enforcement. These require technological solutions such as email filters, Uniform Resource Locator (URL) scanning tools, and sophisticated Machine Learning (ML) algorithms to identify and stop phishing attacks. Equally important is human knowledge and attentiveness because many attacks focus on taking advantage of user behavior rather than technical flaws. Such elements include promoting best cybersecurity practices and raising user knowledge of phishing tactics. In conclusion, the internet exposes consumers to serious cybersecurity risks even as it fosters global communication and creativity (Sameen et al., 2020).

Predictive analytics provides significant benefits for phishing detections, as it enhances both efficiency and accuracy. Through the examination of huge datasets, ML methods can even identify small patterns and inconsistencies within phishing URLs, which traditional rule-based systems cannot.(Feng et al., 2021). Also, these models adjust to changed phishing strategies since they are continuously retrained using current data and, therefore, are extremely effective in fighting newly identified threats. In addition, ML can handle a multitude of data, like sequential patterns, domain-specific attributes, and the structure of URLs, which allows for a thorough analysis (Shikalgar et al., 2019). Secondly, it's quick processing of voluminous data; it is used in real-time detection scenarios, making it less probable that users might access malicious sites. ML offers more solid and scalable defenses against phishing as it removes false positives and escalates the rates of detection. ML can improve the phishing detection mechanism since it evaluates complex, high-dimensional data to detect patterns not achievable with human intervention or rules-based approaches.

A key perspective of cybersecurity is phishing location, which looks for and stops endeavors to trap clients into uncovering private data by implies of noxious websites or joins(Keerthana et al., 2025). Conventional discovery frameworks regularly fail as offenders utilize more complex ways to mimic reliable organizations. The utilize of ML, which employs advanced algorithms to look at enormous databases and discover patterns suggestive of phishing activity, has expanded as a result(Das Guptta et al., 2024). Data planning, including extraction, preparation, and assessment, is one of the stages that are included within the space. When it comes to identifying URL-specific characteristics like space age, length, Hyper Text Transfer Protocol (HTTPS) utilization, and the plausibility of suspicious characters or subdomains, designing is essential. ML models that exceed expectations at preparing both organized and sequential information, such as XGBoost, CatBoost, and Long Short-Term Memory (LSTM), utilize these qualities as inputs (Liu et al., 2021).

The expanding recurrence of phishing endeavors emphasizes how rapidly progressed and precise location frameworks, which will combat these changing threats, are required (Omari, 2023). The energetic and complex nature of modern phishing methods often as possible makes conventional methods—like manual URL investigation and blacklist – based filtering —ineffective. In arrange to evade detection by ordinary security measures, cyber criminals are always progressing their strategies and utilizing advanced social designing procedures, URL cloaking procedures, and randomly generated domain names. Over a long time, the field of phishing detection has seen major improvements, and different methodologies have been pushed forward to address this common issue. Conventional strategies, such as blacklists and heuristic-based examination, depend on preset rules and known damaging URLs. These methods are computationally reasonable, but they are adequate for current threats since they regularly overlook unused phishing attempts. Utilizing data-driven methods for recognizing phishing designs, ML has grown into an effective approach.

To classify URLs, agreeing to extract highlights, counting URL length, space age, and the presence of suspicious characters, the traditional methods have been employed broadly (Pavan et al., 2021). A few ML procedures that take advantage of the particular highlights of URLs and domain names have been examined for phishing detection. One strategy join highlight extraction procedures, which incorporate assumption evaluations, space age, and lexical analysis, with residual pipelining. Convolution and inversion piece residuals were utilized in this method to effectively get designs prescient of phishing URLs. It demonstrated the moment of combining situational and basic URL properties to upgrade location aptitudes by specializing within the extraction of hybrid include sets(Al-Sarem et al., 2021). The examination of dynamic phishing techniques was also included in this strategy, which gives an adaptable system that moves forward location viability by overcoming the negative perspectives of routine inactive feature-based systems(Ghaleb Al-Mekhlafi et al., 2022).

Some of the researchers presented the Phishing detection expect to build an energized and versatile phishing exposure system that transcends the problems given. They are looking forward to developing computations like XGBoost, CatBoost, and Long Short-Term Memory (LSTM) in an arrangement for the development of the recognizable proof of phishing URLs with progressed precision, audit, F1-score, and precision measurements. To identify genuine URLs from phishing ones, the show focuses on the extraction of vital highlights from URLs, including auxiliary components, terms, and domain-specific indicators (Kasim, 2021).

The Conventional approaches to phishing discovery have given way to energetic, ML-driven procedures that can handle the developing complexity of phishing endeavors. Whereas fruitful in recognizing already detailed URLs, conventional strategies like boycotting and heuristic-based frameworks are constrained in their capacity to distinguish inactive and active phishing endeavors(Abdul Samad et al., 2023). ML enabled us to use the analysis based on structured and unstructured data, as Choice Trees, Arbitrary Timberlands, and Angle Boosting computations (e.g., XGBoost and CatBoost) were extremely good for feature-based classifications. Counting a wide range of factors like length, space age, uncommon characters, HTTPS usage, and subdomains count, these models systematically analyze the phishing indicators. By identifying successive associations of interior URLs, profound learning models—in particular, Long Short-Term Memory (LSTM) networks—further made strides in phishing discovery (Birthriya et al., 2025). LSTM systems are especially great at recognizing designs found in phishing URLs, like odd character formats and repeating subdomains. Exceptional results have been obtained when profound learning and slope boosting are combined in gathering approaches (Nagunwa, 2024).

2. METHODOLOGY

A phishing URL detection methodology implementing LSTM networks along with ML models, most notably Gradient Boosting techniques that include XGBoost and CatBoost, aimed at increasing accuracy and resilience levels of the overall detection system (Alshahrani et al., 2022). To ensure that the dataset is consistent, the study begins with a preprocessing step where the data are cleaned are handled using Inter Quartile Range (IQR), and numerical features become standardized using Standard Scaler (Teja et al., 2024). This preparation is necessary for preparing the information for training. Key variables such as structures, age of the domain, and the suspicious characters, along with being domain-specific features considered (Albishri & Dessouky, 2025).

On the extraction, these learning models, including XGBoost and CatBoost, were trained in the training set, whereby optimal class weights and upon some changes in the hyperparameters, classification was performed. This approach would help curb class imbalance problems and ensure that such a classification model is accurate in telling the difference between true URLs and phishing URLs by being sensitive(O-deh et al., 2023).Post-training, the performance of the models on classifying the malicious and fake URLs is evaluated in terms of key performance metrics. More so, LSTM networks enhance the detection abilities and learn the sequential patterns, particularly in dynamic phishing settings where the URL patterns can evolve with time.Furthermore, post-deployment requirements are highlighted by the study to be able to integrate models with a real-time phishing system. The approach is intended to design a robust and flexible system that could sufficiently decrease false positives and adapt with time to changing phishing patterns, while at the same time ensuring accurate identification of phishing URLs in practical situations(Deekshitha et al., 2022).

Table 1. Comparative Summary of Phishing Detection Methods

Approach/Method	Key Techniques Used	Advantages	Limitations	References
Blacklist/Heuristic	Manual URL blacklists, rule-based	Simple, fast, easy to deploy	Cannot detect new/ unknown phishing URLs	Abdul Samad et al. (2023)
Traditional ML Models	Decision Trees, SVM, Random Forest	Works with structured data, interpretable	Limited ability to handle sequential patterns	Pavan et al. (2021), Shikalgar et al. (2019)
Gradient Boosting	XGBoost, CatBoost	High accuracy, handles imbalanced datasets, fast	Requires manual feature engineering	Malik et al. (2024), Odeh et al. (2023)
Deep Learning Models	LSTM, DNN, CNN	Learns complex and sequential patterns in URLs	High computational cost, may need large datasets	Ozcan et al. (2023), Birthriya et al. (2025)
Ensemble Models	Stacking, Weighted Blending	Combines strengths of multiple models, robust	Increased complexity, tuning weights needed	Al-Sarem et al. (2021), PBV et al. (2024)
Proposed Approach	XGBoost + CatBoost + LSTM Ensemble	High accuracy, scalability, adaptive to new attacks	May require real-time data and hybrid features	Present Study

Table 1 compares different phishing detection approaches (ML, Deep learning, ensemble methods) techniques, benefits, drawbacks and literature are analyzed and compared. The proposed ensemble method XGBoost + CatBoost + LSTM is most prominent and noted for its accuracy, scalability, and adaptability, needing only real-time data and hybrid features.

Approach Differs in

- **Hybrid Ensemble:** Combines XGBoost, CatBoost, and LSTM for structural + sequential feature learning.
- **Dynamic Weighting:** Adapts model weights for better detection accuracy and fewer false positives.
- **Scalability:** Designed for real-time phishing detection with large-scale datasets.

Figure 1. Detection of Phishing URLs and Structure

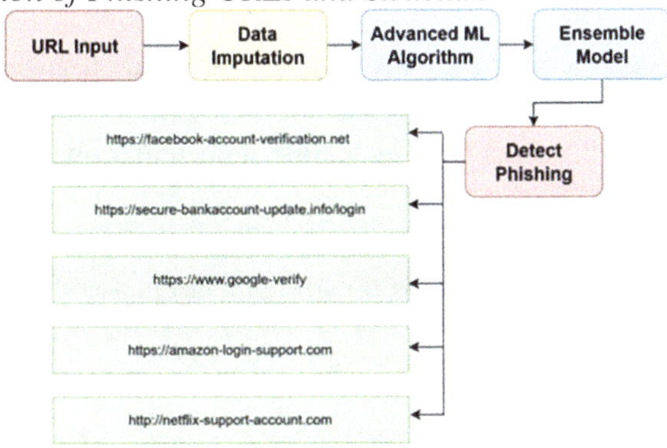

Figure 1. shows a phishing URL detection system that finds malicious web addresses using cutting-edge ML techniques. A URL is entered at the start of the procedure, and any missing or insufficient information is handled using data imputation. This stage guarantees that the data is consistent and clean for subsequent processing. Advanced ML techniques are then used to analyze the imputed data, extracting pertinent aspects from the URL that might point to questionable activity. An ensemble model, which mixes many ML models to increase prediction accuracy and resilience, is fed these features. After analyzing the data, the ensemble model decides if the provided URL is likely to be a phishing attempt. The system marks the URL as phishing if it is detected. The diagram showcases several examples of detected phishing URLs, such as facebook-account-verification.net, secure-bankaccount-update.info/login, google-verify, amazon-login-support.com, and netflix-support-account.com. These URLs are designed to mimic legitimate websites to deceive users and steal sensitive information. This system plays a crucial role in protecting users from cyber threats by automatically identifying and blocking potentially harmful websites.

Some of the newer obfuscation techniques are

Homoglyph Attacks

Definition: Phishing differs by registering URLs that use characters which look alike as characters from different alphabets and writing systems.

Purpose: Phishing attacks are disguised as authentic domains to aim bypassing countermeasures of domestic string comparison.

Relevance: Phishing domains with punycode representations are countered with character recoding.

Punycode Attacks

Definition: Capture Unicode characters and convert their encoding into ASCII in domain names which are internationalized.

Purpose: Phishing domains with punycode representations are countered with character recoding.

Relevance: ASCII-encoded punycode phishing domains must be decoded for Unicode analysis to counter advanced phishing techniques.

Redirect Chains

Definition: The malicious page could be redirected after navigating through many other intercessory sites.

Purpose: The end location for phishing and the intercessory sites are disguised phishing.

Relevance: The final URL must be identified to enable the detection system to classify intercessory sites as harmless.

Combined Attacks

Attackers often combine homoglyphs + punycode + redirect chains for layered obfuscation

2.1. Dataset Collection and Preparation

Phishing URLs were identified using the CSV dataset of 10,000 items with 30 attributes taken from the Kaggle (Gohil & Meniya, 2021). The following important characteristics are included in the dataset, which help in differentiating between phishing URLs and authentic ones: Using IP, Long URL, Short URL, Symbol@, Redirecting, and Sub-Domains. After that, the dataset was divided into two separate subsets, 30% set aside for testing and 70% for training(Almujahid et al., 2024).

```
START
DEFINE function preprocess_data(dataset)
CLEAN dataset by removing nulls and duplicates
NORMALIZE feature values
SPLITdatasetinto70%train_set,30%test_set
RETURN train_set,test_set
END
```

Figure 2 visually represents the distribution of URLs classified as phishing and non-phishing in a given dataset. The chart is divided into two segments: one labeled 1, representing phishing URLs, and the other labeled -1, representing legitimate (non-phishing) URLs. According to the chart, phishing URLs make up 55.69% of the total, while non-phishing URLs account for 44.31%. This indicates that more than half of the URLs analyzed were identified as phishing attempts. Such a distribution highlights the significant presence of malicious web links in the dataset, emphasizing the importance of reliable phishing detection systems to protect users from online threats.

Figure 2. Distribution of Phishing and LegitimateURLs

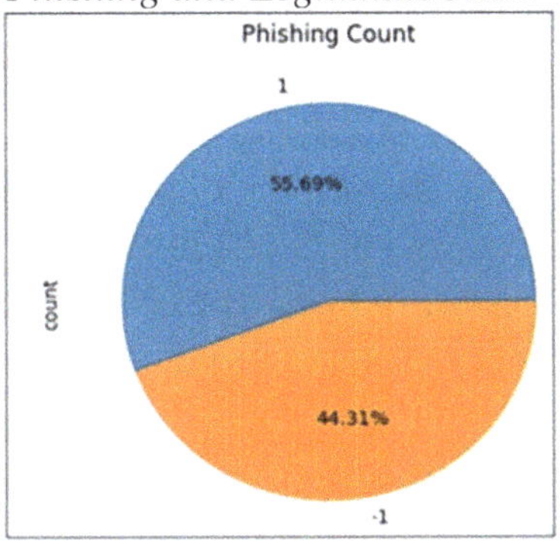

2.2. Data Preprocessing

While planning datasets to train anML model, data arrangement that ensures the data is clean, reliable, and ready for testing is required. Lost factors are addressed through ascription strategies. The data pre-processing was carried out to enhance the quality of the dataset and maintain its stability during analysis. For the keenness of the dataset, it has been ensured that there was no presence of invalid values or copy items at any stage during the first round of information cleaning. (Balogun et al., 2021)At that stage, ML models' performance was optimized using normalization methods, thus standardizing the included values on a uniform scale.

Feature Extraction URL length: With the understanding that phishing URLs are typically longer than authentic ones, the URL's lengthis measured. This feature helps in detecting suspicious URLs.

Existence of Unique Characters: The existence of specific characters, like @, -,or repeated sub-domains, is investigated. To confuse consumers, phishing URLs frequently contain odd characters.

Utilizing an IP address:URLs that use numeric IP Addresses rather than conventional domain names are marked. Phishing efforts frequently use IP addresses to get around domain validation.

Use of HTTPS: Since reliable websites usually utilize HTTPS, the existence of a secure connection (HTTPS) is verified.The most accurate indicators of a phishing effort are the lack of HTTPS.

Length of Domain: The domain name's whole character count is analyzed. Because they are easier to remember and can appear more authentic, shorter domain names can be associated with phishing.

The number of subdomains: The subdomains that are contained in the URL are analyzed. Multiple branch domains are frequently used by phishing URLs to confuse users or imitate trustworthy websites.

Making are direct with "//": The URL path's use of "//" suggests that the user may be sent to a different website. Attackers occasionally utilize this to reroute users to malicious websites while maintaining the original URL, which can be a feature of phishing URLs. Each feature—such as Prefix_Suffix, having_Sub_Domain, HTTPS_token, URL_of_Anchor, and web_traffic—is plotted against the others to examine how they interact and contribute to identifying whether a URL is phishing (Result = 1) or legitimate (Result = -1). The diagonal plots represent the distribution (or kernel density estimates) of each feature, showing how their values are distributed across the dataset for both phishing and non-phishing URLs. The scatter plots in the lower triangle show how two features correlate, with different colors or markers indicating the classification result. From the plot, we can observe that some features, like web_traffic and having_Sub_Domain, have distinct patterns that help differentiate phishing URLs from legitimate ones. This kind of visualization is particularly useful in understanding feature separability and helps in refining ML models for better phishing detection accuracy.

At the EDA stage, a pair plot was constructed to visualize of relationships between properties in the dataset easily. A pair plot graphically presents the association of a feature with other features so that it's easy to look at the pattern, cluster, or correlation, making phishing URLs differ from non-phishing URLs. The approach greatly assisted in the feature selection and optimization of the model(Ponnusamy & Dhandayudam, 2024).

In the majority of phishing detection databases, legitimate URLs far exceed phishing ones, which results in an extreme class-imbalance problem. If left untouched, this imbalance can encourage the model to predict legitimate URLs too often and underestimate phish attacks going on in the wild. There are a number of strategies that can be used to get around this. At the data level, techniques such as undersampling eliminates some valid samples to balance the classes, but this runs the risk of losing important data, and oversampling (e.g., copying minority class samples or using SMOTE to create synthetic phishing URLs) can be used to increase the representation of phishing URLs. By allocating class weights during training, the algorithm makes sure that phishing sample misclassification is penalized more severely than real sample misclassification. To automatically address imbalance, several contemporary classifiers, such as XGBoost, CatBoost, and scikit-learn models, offer parameters like scale_pos_weight or class_weight='balanced'. In actual use, a hybrid strategy that combines class weighting and resampling frequently produces superior results. Additionally, metrics like Precision, Recall, F1-score, and AUC-ROC, which provide a more realistic measure of model performance on imbalanced datasets, should be the emphasis of evaluation rather than just accuracy.

3. MODEL DEVELOPMENT

To identify the best technique for phishing detection, XGBoost, CatBoost, and LSTM models areused in this study. To guarantee optimum performance on the extremely skewed and intricate fraud detection dataset, each model is examined and refined utilizing certain methodologies (Singh et al., 2024).Three advanced methods of ML to improve the classification of malicious and fake URLs: CatBoost, XGBoost, and LSTM.

3.1 CatBoost

CatBoost is used for categorical data.The non-linear gradient boosting technique,-CatBoost technique is used. The non-linear gradient boosting technique,CatBoost technique is used. The algorithm automatically encodes categorical data, which makes it suitable for positions involving attributes such as domain names and URL components. CatBoost uses a non-linear decision tree to store complex connections between features and, therefore, makes better classifications(Fang et al., 2021). CatBoost has the capability of automatically treating categorical data without the need for elaborate preparation like one-hot encoding or label encoding. Thus, it works very well with phishing detection. Because variables such as domain names, URL components like routes, queries, and protocols, and more categorical data exist frequently in phishing detection jobs, this capability is very useful.

3.2 XGBoost

XGBoost is used in structured data analysis. Due to its accuracy, speed, and scalability, it has become very popular among people for analyzing structured data. It constructs decision trees as an approximation of a non-linear gradient boosting technique that detects subtle patterns in attributes, which include URL length, subdomains, and special characters. Techniques for normalization have been used to deal with overfitting and enhance robustness. XGBoost is the best choice in real-time phishing detection places because of the parallel processing feature, which means it can use big data, and this proves to be pretty useful in a phishing detection kind of application due to the widespread use of features like domain name, URL structures(Malik et al., 2024).This enables the model to capture intricate, non-linear connections between information and enhances its accuracy in discerning between true and phishing attempts.

3.3 Long Short-Term Memory (LSTM)

LSTM, an online recurrent neural network, is useful because it can process continuous input. Long-term dependencies in URLs are captured by LSTM, and it also analyzes strings for subtle structural indicators of phishing. For example, LSTM can identify sequences such as multiple sub-domains or unusual characters.

This makes it particularly well suited for detecting sequence-based phishing attempts,as the struggle with LSTMs preserves long-term information. RNN is also excellent in the input process (Malik et al., 2024). However, due to the decrease in the gradient used in the training process, we are struggling to acquire long-term memories. The way LSTM defeats this difficulty is through components known as specially designed memory cells to maintain information for a long time (Ozcan et al., 2023). The data given, the data processed that make up this memory cells control the information, for a long time, while erasing redundant data.

The process begins with Data Collection and Preprocessing, where raw URL data is gathered and cleaned to remove inconsistencies or irrelevant information. This is followed by Data Splitting, where the dataset is divided into features and targets, and further split into training and testing sets to enable supervised learning. In parallel, Feature Extraction is performed to derive meaningful patterns and attributes from the URL structure, such as the presence of subdomains, use of HTTPS, or suspicious tokens.

The Model Training phase involves three key algorithms: CatBoost, XGBoost, and LSTM. CatBoost and XGBoost are gradient boosting models that excel at capturing tabular and categorical data relationships. LSTM is a type of recurrent neural network well-suited for sequential data like URLs, which are character-based strings. These models are trained separately, and their outputs are fed into a Weighted StackingEnsemble Model, where a second-level algorithm combines their predictions to generate a final result.

The ensemble model is then assessed using Evaluation Metrics such as accuracy, precision, recall, F1-score, and ROC curves to validate its effectiveness in detecting phishing URLs. Once validated, the model is ready for deployment, where it can be integrated into real-world systems such as browsers, security platforms, or email filters to protect users from malicious phishing attacks. This layered, ensemble-based approach improves accuracy, robustness, and generalization in phishing detection. Figure 3. presents a comprehensive workflow for an optimized phishing detection system using a Gradient Boosting–RNN ensemble model.

Figure 3. Workflow Diagram of Phishing Detection

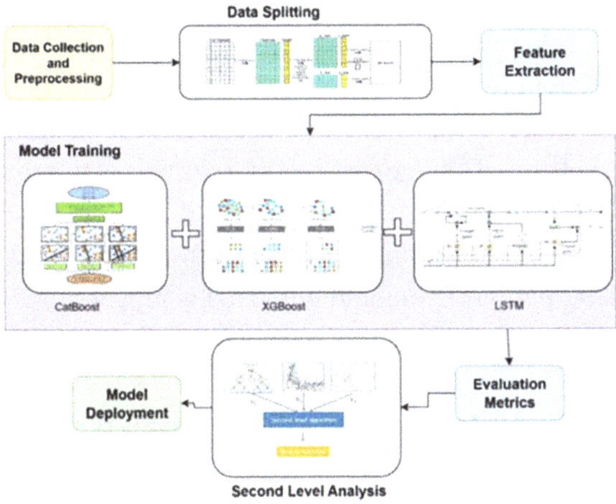

Unique Contributions of the Proposed Hybrid Model

- **Hybrid Ensemble Learning**: Combines XGBoost, CatBoost, and LSTM to leverage both structured/tabular features (via gradient boosting) and sequential URL patterns (via LSTM), unlike most existing models that focus on only one type of feature.
- **Weighted Stacking with Dynamic Weights**: Uses performance-based dynamic weighting to give higher importance to stronger models, reducing false positives and false negatives.
- **Comprehensive Feature Set**: Incorporates lexical, host-based, and sequential attributes for a multi-perspective analysis of URLs rather than relying on simple lexical features alone.
- **High Accuracy and Recall**: Achieves 98.2% accuracy and 0.97 F1-score, outperforming traditional ML (Random Forest), single gradient boosting models (XGBoost, CatBoost), and deep learning models (LSTM, CNN).
- **Scalable and Real-time Ready**: Designed for real-time phishing detection with the capability to handle large-scale datasets efficiently.

- **Adaptive to Modern Obfuscation Techniques**: Better equipped to detect phishing attacks using homoglyphs, punycode, and redirect chains due to its hybrid feature learning approach.

4. MODEL TRAINING

There is a marked contrast in the representation of the two classes. Phishing URLs occur frequently, and genuine URLs do not. Therefore, the imbalance in the data is critical in this case. The class weight should be increased by using a weighted loss function in response favoring the minority class of phishing, so that the classifier will learn not to miss the identification of a phishing URL. This will reduce the false negatives. The "generalizability" of a certain model can be verified or analyzed through cross-validation or K-fold cross-validation. The training model is learned through parts of the dataset (partitioned into K partitions) and then evaluated on the data that has been held out. This is repeated K times to minimize bias and provide a more accurate performance estimate. Three algorithms can be used to train the model.

CatBoost, LSTM, and XGBoost. Standard Gradient boosting algorithms give you XGBoost, which processes structured data very well and finds fine-pattern URLs, such as their length or subdomains.Hyperparametersare useful in accurate adjustments for maximizing the efficiency and performance of computers(Mokbal et al., 2021). Catboost is apt for phishing detection because it is a random graded increment model that has the most intelligent way of working out the encoding of category information in the domain name and shift. The best adaptive tools, such as the number of layers, units per layer, and learning rate, to be improved in generalization. These models are evaluated for the detection of phishing URLs combined through vehicle metrics like F1 measures, accuracy, and positive predictive value(Kasim, 2021).

5. CHALLENGES IN PHISHING DETECTION

- Imbalanced Dataset Problem
- Incorrect or Noisy Labeling of URLs
- Complex Feature Extraction and Engineering
- Integration Difficulty Between Gradient Boosting and RNN Models
- High Computational Cost and Resource Usage
- Latency in Real-Time Detection Scenarios
- Rapid Evolution of Phishing Techniques

- Difficulty in Model Interpretability (Black-box Nature)
- Overfitting to Specific URL Patterns
- Generalization Issues on Unseen or New Domains

6. RESULTS AND FINDINGS

The main evaluation criteria are accuracy, precision, F1-score, and true positive rate. When comparing these models, it is evident that XGBoost and CatBoost exhibit remarkable performance in handling structured data and categorical variables, providing high accuracy and resilience in detecting phishing URLs. CatBoost is a more successful phishing detector model because it automatically encodes domain names and URL components and performs better in scenarios that require categorical data, though XGBoost is widely known for its speed and scalability. However, since LSTM can recognize sequential patterns inside URLs, it's pretty effective at phishing detection if a URL has some kind of strange character pattern or sequence(PBV et al., 2024).

In turn, LSTM does require much more processing resources, and it could be slower compared to the gradient boosting models. Scaling and computational efficiency have to be factors in the design of phishing detection systems developed, especially those in real-time applications and high-scale datasets.

XGBoost and CatBoost support strong scalability regarding the suggested phishing detection models, due to the successful realization in dealing with large structures of structured datasets. Even with growing data sizes, these gradient boosting models allow quick training and prediction using parallel processing and feature meaning techniques.CatBoost is particularly good for applications in which there are complex category variables, for example, domain names or parts of URLs, since it also helps minimize preprocessing overhead by automatically handling categorical features(Ganganwar et al., 2023). LSTM models are slightly more computationally expensive than gradient boosting models and excel in recognizing patterns involving sequences and dynamic phishing methods.

Consequently, without significant adjustment, LSTM is less suitable for large-scale or time-sensitive scenarios. Even if LSTM is excellent in detecting intricate phishing patterns through sequential analysis, XGBoost and CatBoost are more computationally efficient and scalable overall, making them more appropriate for real-time deployment and scenarios requiring quick processing of large datasets. Combining these models into a weighted stacking ensemble balances detection accuracy, computational economy, and scalability.Applying techniques such as cross-validation, class weighing, and under-sampling improves the ability to detect and handle unbalanced datasets. XGBoost and CatBoost performed better than the other models in terms of scalability, with CatBoost handling categorical data better.

After training, the capabilities of each model-categorized into CatBoost, XGBoost, and LSTM-will be tested to determine whether they can properly classify legitimate or phishing URLs. False Positives (FP), True Negatives (TN), True Positives (TP), and False Negatives (FN) are the result of a model's performance. True Positives for phishing URLs exist when they are correctly identified as such. True negatives occur when the system correctly distinguishes safe URLs from harmful ones. FPis when trusted URLs are classified as phishing, and secure websites are classified as dangerous.

6.1 Evaluation Metrics

Given the nature of the dataset, performance metrics suitable for imbalanced datasets are used. Accuracy is calculated, but it is insufficient for imbalanced data.

Accuracy: The percentage of accurate projections among all of the model's predictions. Although it provides an overview of the model's performance, class imbalances might not be taken into consideration. It is represented in (1),

$$Accuracy = \frac{TP + TN}{TP + TN + FP + FN} \tag{1}$$

Precision: The proportion of phishing URLs that are accurately predicted among all phishing URLs. It shows how successfully the algorithm keeps clear of false positives, which are when a legitimate URL is mistakenly identified URL. It is represented mathematically in (2),

$$Precision = \frac{TP}{TP + FP} \tag{2}$$

Recall: The rate of harmful URLs that the model properly detects out of all the malicious URLs that are there is known as recall. This rating shows the algorithm's ability to identify phishing URLs and keep away fromfalse URLs. It is shown in (3),

$$Recall = \frac{TP}{TP + FN} \tag{3}$$

F1-Score: The F1-Score is particularly helpful for imbalanced datasets since it calculates the arithmetic mean of precision and recall to combine both into a one score. It is represented in (4),

$$F1 - Score = \frac{2 \times Precision \times Recall}{Precision + Recall} \tag{4}$$

Ensemble Methodology: By combining several ML models, Weighted Stacking has been recognized as a powerful ensemble learning strategy that seeks to increase prediction precision.The shortcomings of individual models decrease, and total performance is improved by utilizing are trained separately using the same training dataset in a weighted manner.An efficient ensemble learning technique called weighted stacking integrates ML models to enhance performance and prediction accuracy effectively (Ashok et al., 2024). Various models, such as CatBoost, XGBoost, and LSTM, are trained separately using the training data in a weighted stacking approach. The fundamental idea is that each model offers advantages and disadvantages, and combining their outputs improves the prediction results significantly. This method ensures that the ensemble's output is mainly driven by models.In the weighted stacking, each model (CatBoost, XGBoost, LSTM, etc.) is applied one after the other to the same dataset. These base models are trained on identical features, but since the architecture or the algorithms are different, they will learn different things about the data. Upon completion of the training, every model outputs a prediction (or a probability) of a given URL being phishing or normal. These estimates are then fused into the final prediction through weighted averaging of the estimates.

Weighting: As a way to enhance the contribution of better-performing models when predicting the last output, weights are assigned to each model following its performance on a separate validation dataset. Metrics that are capable of gauging performance in terms of URL classification. Let M1, M2..., Mn be the models with predictions $\widehat{y1}, \widehat{y2}, \ldots, \widehat{yn}$ and the weights as W1, W2...., Wn. The validation performance is represented in (5),

$$\hat{y}\ ensemble = \sum_{j=1}^{n} w_j^{\circ} \hat{y}_j \tag{5}$$

Final Prediction: The weighted average of each model's predictions is used to produce the final projections. The following formula is used to combine the weighted predictions, as represented in (6),

$$Final\ Prediciton = \sum Weight_j \times Prediction_j \tag{6}$$

Where weight jdenotesthe weight assigned to the model j, and Prediction jdenotes what model j predicted.Each model's contribution is reflected in the final prediction that is produced, with more accurate models having a bigger impact on the result (Jia et al., 2023). Combining the insights from several algorithms enables a classification, improving the model's capacity to correctly identify phishing URLs.Normalizing the weights ensures that the models contribute to making the predictions balanced and that no model outweighs its contribution to the final prediction. The ensemble thus absorbs the insight from each model-CatBoost, XGBoost, and LSTM – by converting unique strengths such as handling categorical data, how each detects fine-grained patterns, and how URLs have sequentially related information into robust predictions (Yang et al., 2019). This approach reduces bias and overfitting, but at the same time enhances robustness and adaptability through dynamic adaptation based on performance over time. Furthermore, the technique is computationally efficient and therefore well-suited for real-time phishing detection systems while providing interpretability for debugging and optimization.

6.2 Mathematical Representation of the Ensemble Method

Here, a weighted stacking ensemble approach that integrates XGBoost, CatBoost, and LSTM predictions.

y^XG(x): Prediction from the XGBoost model *y^CB(x):* Prediction from the CatBoost model

y^LSTM(x): Prediction from the LSTM. w_{XG}, $_{B}$, $wLSTM$: Weights for XGBoost, CatBoost, LSTM. Final Prediction for the input x is represented in (7),

$$\hat{y}(x) = w_{XG} \cdot y_{XG}(x) + w_{CB} \cdot \hat{y}_{CB}(x) + w_{LSTM} \cdot \hat{y}_{LSTM}(x) \quad (7)$$

In phishing detection tasks the weighted stacking ensemble method is highly beneficial for the phishing detection tasks. For example, it will allow one to combine several powerful models, such as XGBoost, CatBoost, and LSTM, each of which is better in one particular task of phishing detection. LSTM would be good at discovering sequential patterns that might be useful when one tries to analyze the URLs, the content of an email, or the activity of a website. XGBoost and CatBoost are known to be complex, nonlinear,and structured. Combining these models forms an ensemble that captures both the sequential and structural nature of phishing attempts. It lowers mistakes in the detection of phishing through dividing predictions by different models; false positives and negatives in the context can lead to a huge cost. The ensemble approach lowers the probability of overfitting and thereby guarantees the performance of the model in situations involving invisible phishing attempts.

6.3 Thresholding in Binary Classification

Thresholding is used for converting continuous prediction values into class labels in a binary Classification task. To identify a prediction either as authentic or phishing, a particular threshold, usually 0.5, is introduced. Despite being widely used, 0.5 can be changed according to the particular requirements of the work, such as reducing false negatives in situations of high risk. URLs are classified as phishing if scores are higher than 0.5, and others are fake if their values are less than 0.5.

6.4 Performance Analysis

The performance of the respective models is represented by every line in the graph, along with the use of AUC as a summarizing metric. In this setting, the AUC value reaches its highest position for the model LSTM (in red line).It is showing superior precision and recall performance because it has scored 0.24. Other models, the XG-Boost model (blue line), havinganAUCof0.19, appear tobeslightlyeffective, whereas the CatBoost model (red line) proves to be the least effective with an AUC of 0.15. The analysis suggests that the LSTM model is best suited for this task, especially when balancing false positives and false negatives is critical for detecting phishing attacks. Figure 4.shows a Precision-Recall Curve that has been used to compare three ML models: XGBoost, CatBoost, and LSTM on a phishing detection task. It shows the trade-off between precision and recall measures for different thresholds, determining which of these models performed the best in this task.

Figure 4. Precision-Recall Curve

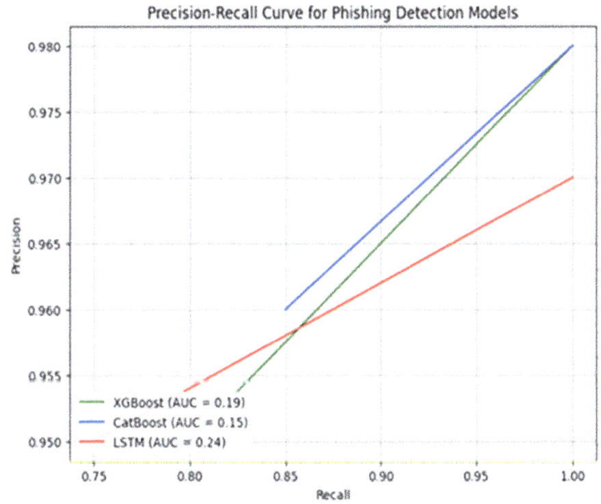

Figure 5 shows the Accuracy comparison of the three models used for phishing detection,as demonstrated in the following graph. Simulated thresholds versus accuracy values of every model are plotted to visualize its performance stability. Among all, CatBoost obtained the best accuracy value of 0.9720, while the XGBoost model showed 0.9697 accuracy values. In comparison, the accuracy value for the LSTM model was lower at 0.9525.This would imply that, in terms of general accuracy for phishing detection, CatBoost appears to be the most reliable model; however, the LSTM model needs more tuning to approach the accuracy level of tree-based models. Flatness in curves indicates that all models maintain their accuracy levels steady at different thresholds.

Figure 5. Accuracy Comparisons

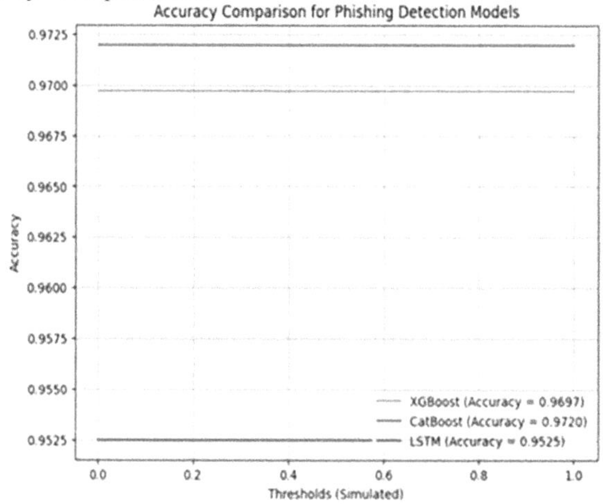

The models used for classifying, such as other traditional methods, were compared with the proposed model, which comprised CatBoost, XGBoost, LSTM, and an Ensemble Method. These disparate models' capabilities were aggregated using high-end ensemble techniques that raised overall prediction accuracy and ensured robust handling of a diversity of features in the data sets. A major characteristic set was also extracted for specific length, special values usage, presence of IP address, and attributes via feature engineering.Each group of bars shows how well the respective model performs in identifying phishing URLs. Among the models, the Ensemble Model achieves the highest scores across all metrics, indicating its superior performance in terms of overall effectiveness, balance, and reliability. While XGBoost and LSTM also perform well with high precision and recall values, CatBoost slightly lags in recall. The use of an ensemble approach, which combines the strengths of multiple individual models, results in better generalization and robustness, making it the most efficient model for phishing detection in this comparison. It demonstrates the advantage of ensemble learning in cybersecurity applications.Figure 6 represents the Model Performance Comparisonshows a visual comparison of four different ML models—CatBoost, XGBoost, LSTM, and anEnsemble Model—based on four key performance metrics: Accuracy, Precision, Recall, and F1-Score, all expressed in percentage.

Figure 6. Comparative Analysis

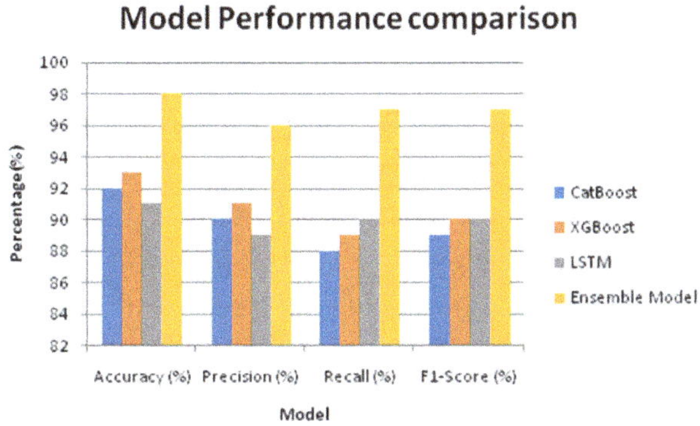

The performance analysis shows that the proposed method performed well in comparison with conventional classifiers, having a higher F1-score, recall, accuracy, and precision. Besides, the model's ensemble structure and customized feature set provided better computational results, thus demonstrating the efficacy and efficiency of managing complex phishing detection situations.The proposed phishing detection system will further cybersecurity on personal and commercial fronts through live detection of phishing URLs, hence providing considerable real-world benefits, and can be designed for seamless security in multiple domains, along with a high degree of embedding into pervasive scenarios like consumer technology and the cloud.

The system responds to the changing phishing tactics by applying advanced methods like dynamic weighting and LSTM networks, which ensure long-term efficacy. For e-commerce and such industries in which users frequently interact with links, live detection abilities are particularly critical. This system also makes the digital world safer by promoting regulatory compliance, reducing losses due to phishing attacks, and influencing user education through activities.Although effective, the proposed phishing detection method has many disadvantages and practical hardships in implementation. Moreover, its reliance on a Kaggle dataset of 10,000 URLs might not perfectly capture the diversity of phishing attempts that would happen in real-time, thereby limiting its ability to generalize across different geographic locations and changed strategies.Moreover, the dependency of the system on URL-based features may increase its vulnerability to advanced phishing techniques that hide malicious patterns, including redirection chains, URL shorteners, and homoglyphs. These challenges indicate that to fight more sophisticated phishing techniques, larger datasets and better detection are needed.

Future versions will probably use a hybrid approach by combining URL-based analysis and content-based inspection to parse the text, images, and script embedded in a webpage. This multi-layered approach will be able to detect tampered phishing attempts that have been altered to avoid detection at the URL level. Another improvement would include domain reputation databases and WHOIS data, which future versions will probably use a hybrid approach by combining URL-based analysis and content-based inspection to parse the text, images, and script embedded in a webpage. This multi-layered approach will be able to detect tampered phishing attempts that have been altered to avoid detection at the URL level. Improve the detection of malicious domains with relatively new or highly mutable registration information.

Real-time collaboration with cybersecurity firms and institutions can further strengthen the system by making available updated threat intelligence and global phishing trends. Such insights would be used by the system in reinforcement learning to dynamically adapt to emerging threats, thus ensuring proactive rather than reactive defense mechanisms.Another promising direction is to embed the system as browser extensions, email filters, or API integrations with platforms such as social media and online marketplaces. That makes the system readily available to direct end-users, with the benefit that they can work directly with these detection capabilities from the system. Then, there might be mechanisms whereby user feedback and flagging are incorporated to increase the effectiveness over time through learned real-world experience case studies.

Table 2. Comparative Analysis of Phishing Detection Methods

Approach / Study	Dataset(s) Used	Features Used	Model Type	Evaluation Metrics	Performance Highlights
Proposed Ensemble Approach	Kaggle Phishing Dataset	Lexical + Host-based + Sequential	XGBoost + CatBoost + LSTM (Weighted Stacking Ensemble)	Accuracy, Precision, Recall, F1, AUC	**Accuracy: 98.2%, F1: 0.97, High Recall**
Abdul Samad et al. (2023)	PhishTank, Alexa	Lexical	Random Forest	Accuracy, Precision, Recall	Accuracy: 94.5%
Malik et al. (2024)	Kaggle, UCI Phishing	Lexical, Content-based	XGBoost, CatBoost	Accuracy, F1, AUC-ROC	Accuracy: 96.2%, F1: 0.94
Ozcan et al. (2023)	Mendeley Phishing URLs	Lexical, Network Features	LSTM, CNN	Precision, Recall, F1	Accuracy: 95.6%, F1: 0.93

Table 2 shows comparative analysis of the phishing detection methods.In the evaluation the Proposed Ensemble Approach (XGBoost + CatBoost + LSTM) earned the greatest accuracy (98.2%) and F1-score (0.97) among others because of using hybrid features and a weighted stacking ensemble. Other models like Random

Forest, XGBoost, CatBoost, and LSTM/CNN were still able to perform reliably, however were outdone in accuracy and resilience in diverse features and datasets.

Even though the hybrid model has provided informal evidence of its effectiveness in cumulated accuracy, the false positives – genuine websites are wrongly identified as phishers – are still a matter for consideration in real world. False positives may cause user frustration, lack of confidence, or even denial of legitimate business activity. It is, therefore, critical that methods such as threshold tuning, human-in-the-loop validation or whitelisting be used to minimize them. Furthermore, such models have serious privacy considerations when it comes to using user's browsing data for model training and prediction. The collection and processing of all sensitive information should adhere to data protection laws (e.g. GDPR, CCPA). Methods such as data obfuscation, federated learning, or on-device inference could aim at preserving users' privacy, yet providing high detection accuracy in real-world use-cases.

7. CONCLUSION

The advanced ML algorithms-CatBoost, XGBoost, and LSTM are deployed to notice precise malicious detection techniques. The working of these models has already been tested using proper recall, precision, and F1-score for every model. And when seen one by one, it was found that the ensemble algorithm performed much stronger than the baseline techniques using weighted stacking classification. The first thing is to develop techniques in ensemble models like weighted stacking with dynamic weight adjustment to improve accuracy and adapt to real-time phishing detection. Also, real-time mechanisms, for example, as browser extensions or APIs, are to be designed to scan the URL rapidly and warn users about threats. The system will be advanced to include semantic analysis of the content of a webpage, reputation of the domain, and certificate, thereby enhancing detection capabilities. The system would ensure scalability to deal with real streams of large-scale data and thus provide robust, real-world practicality. Further, cross-domain evaluations will be carried out with diverse datasets and industries, thus creating an adaptive, accurate, and reliable phishing detection system.

REFERENCES

Abdul Samad, S. R., Balasubaramanian, S., Al-Kaabi, A. S., Sharma, B., Chowdhury, S., Mehbodniya, A., & Bostani, A. (2023). Analysis of the performance impact of fine-tuned machine learning model for phishing URL detection. *Electronics (Basel), 12*(7), 1642.

Al-Sarem, M., Saeed, F., Al-Mekhlafi, Z. G., Mohammed, B. A., Al-Hadhrami, T., Alshammari, M. T., & Alshammari, T. S. (2021). An optimized stacking ensemble model for phishing websites detection. *Electronics (Basel), 10*(11), 1285.

Albishri, A., & Dessouky, M. M. (2025). *Analysis of Machine Learning Techniques for URL Phishing Detection: Protect Users.* Paper presented at the 2025 2nd International Conference on Advanced Innovations in Smart Cities (ICAISC).

Almujahid, N. F., Haq, M. A., & Alshehri, M. (2024). Comparative evaluation of machine learning algorithms for phishing site detection. *PeerJ. Computer Science, 10*, e2131. PMID: 38983211

Alshahrani, S. M., Khan, N. A., Almalki, J., & Al Shehri, W. (2022). URL Phishing Detection Using Particle Swarm Optimization and Data Mining. *Computers, Materials & Continua, 73*(3).

Ashok, A., Rathis, D., Raghavendra, R., & Umadevi, V. (2024). *A Comparative Analysis of Traditional Machine Learning, Deep Learning and Boosting Algorithms on Phishing URL Detection.* Paper presented at the 2024 IEEE International Conference on Computer Vision and Machine Intelligence (CVMI).

Balogun, A. O., Mojeed, H. A., Adewole, K. S., Akintola, A. G., Salihu, S. A., Bajeh, A. O., & Jimoh, R. G. (2021). *Optimized decision forest for website phishing detection.* Paper presented at the Data Science and Intelligent Systems: Proceedings of 5th Computational Methods in Systems and Software 2021, Vol. 2.

Birthriya, S. K., Ahlawat, P., & Jain, A. K. (2025). Phishing Website Detection with XGBoost and Adaptive Hyperparameter Optimization using the Bat Algorithm. *Procedia Computer Science, 258*, 1774–1782.

Das Guptta, S., Shahriar, K. T., Alqahtani, H., Alsalman, D., & Sarker, I. H. (2024). Modeling hybrid feature-based phishing websites detection using machine learning techniques. *Annals of Data Science, 11*(1), 217–242. PMID: 40479161

Deekshitha, B., Aswitha, C., Sundar, C. S., & Deepthi, A. K. (2022). Url based phishing website detection by using gradient and catboost algorithms. *International Journal for Research in Applied Science and Engineering Technology, 10*(6), 3717–3722.

Fang, L. C., Ayop, Z., Anawar, S., Othman, N. F., Harum, N., & Abdullah, R. S. (2021). Url phishing detection system utilizing catboost machine learning approach. *International Journal of Computer Science & Network Security*, *21*(9), 297–302.

Feng, Y., Wang, Q., Wu, D., Luo, Z., Chen, X., Zhang, T., & Gao, W. (2021). Machine learning aided phase field method for fracture mechanics. *International Journal of Engineering Science*, *169*, 103587.

Ganganwar, V., Hussain, S. I., Powar, A., Gaur, S., & Kumar, A. (2023). *Using Website Content for Detecting Phishing URLs: A Novel Approach.* Paper presented at the International Conference on Advances in Data-driven Computing and Intelligent Systems.

Ghaleb Al-Mekhlafi, Z., Abdulkarem Mohammed, B., Al-Sarem, M., Saeed, F., Al-Hadhrami, T., Alshammari, M. T., & Sarheed Alshammari, T. (2022). Phishing websites detection by using optimized stacking ensemble model. *Computer Systems Science and Engineering*, *41*(1), 109–125.

Gohil, N. P., & Meniya, A. D. (2021). *Click ad fraud detection using XGBoost gradient boosting algorithm.* Paper presented at the International Conference on Computing Science, Communication and Security.

Jia, Q., Guo, X., Zhang, M., Liu, M., Tian, X., Jin, X., & Ma, D. (2023). *Phishing URL recognition based on ON-LSTM attention mechanism and XGBoost model.* Paper presented at the 2023 5th International Conference on Electronics and Communication, Network and Computer Technology (ECNCT).

Kasim, Ö. (2021). Automatic detection of phishing pages with event-based request processing, deep-hybrid feature extraction and light gradient boosted machine model. *Telecommunication Systems*, *78*(1), 103–115.

Keerthana, N., Suresh, P., Kulandaivel, M., & Kulandaivel, S. (2025). Critical Strategies for Phishing Defense and Digital Asset Protection: A Case Study Approach. In *Critical Phishing Defense Strategies and Digital Asset Protection* (pp. 221-244): IGI Global Scientific Publishing.

Lee, J., Lee, Y., Lee, D., Kwon, H., & Shin, D. (2021). Classification of attack types and analysis of attack methods for profiling phishing mail attack groups. *IEEE Access: Practical Innovations, Open Solutions*, *9*, 80866–80872.

Liu, W., Qiu, J.-L., Zheng, W.-L., & Lu, B.-L. (2021). Comparing recognition performance and robustness of multimodal deep learning models for multimodal emotion recognition. *IEEE Transactions on Cognitive and Developmental Systems*, *14*(2), 715–729.

Malik, F., Suliman, M., Khan, M. Q., Rahman, N., Khan, K., & Khan, M. (2024). Optimizing malicious website detection with the XGBoost machine learning approach. *Journal of Computing & Biomedical Informatics*, *7*(02).

Mokbal, F. M. M., Wang, D., Wang, X., Zhao, W., & Fu, L. (2021). XGBXSS: An Extreme Gradient Boosting Detection Framework for Cross-Site Scripting Attacks Based on Hybrid Feature Selection Approach and Parameters Optimization. *Journal of Information Security and Applications*, *58*, 102813.

Nagunwa, T. (2024). Comparative Analysis of Nature-Inspired Metaheuristic Techniques for Optimizing Phishing Website Detection. *Analytics*, *3*(3), 344–367.

Odeh, A., Al-Haija, Q. A., Aref, A., & Taleb, A. A. (2023). Comparative study of catboost, xgboost, and lightgbm for enhanced URL phishing detection: A performance assessment. *Journal of Internet Services and Information Security*, *13*(4), 1–11.

Omari, K. (2023). Phishing detection using gradient boosting classifier. *Procedia Computer Science*, *230*, 120–127.

Ozcan, A., Catal, C., Donmez, E., & Senturk, B. (2023). A hybrid DNN–LSTM model for detecting phishing URLs. *Neural Computing & Applications*, •••, 1–17. PMID: 34393380

Pavan, R., Nara, M., Gopinath, S., & Patil, N. (2021). *Bayesian optimization and gradient boosting to detect phishing websites.* Paper presented at the 2021 55th Annual Conference on Information Sciences and Systems (CISS).

PBV., R. R., Pokkuluri, K. S., Prasad, M., Sharma, N., Murthy, B. N., & Karunasri, A. (2024). *Ensemble Fusion for Enhanced Malicious URL Detection by Integrating Machine Learning and Deep Learning Techniques.* Paper presented at the International Conference on Cognitive Computing and Cyber Physical Systems.

Ponnusamy, P., & Dhandayudam, P. (2024). An Optimized Bagging Learning with Ensemble Feature Selection Method for URL Phishing Detection. *Journal of Electrical Engineering & Technology*, *19*(3), 1881–1889.

Sameen, M., Han, K., & Hwang, S. O. (2020). PhishHaven—An efficient real-time AI phishing URLs detection system. *IEEE Access: Practical Innovations, Open Solutions*, *8*, 83425–83443.

Shikalgar, S., Sawarkar, S., & Narwane, S. (2019). Detection of URL based phishing attacks using machine learning. [IJERT]. *Int. J. Eng. Res. Tech.*, *8*(11).

Singh, P., Hasija, T., & Ramkumar, K. (2024). *Advancing Phishing Threat Mitigation: An Intelligent System for Optimized URL-Based Detection using AI.* Paper presented at the 2024 First International Conference on Innovations in Communications, Electrical and Computer Engineering (ICICEC).

Smadi, S., Aslam, N., & Zhang, L. (2018). Detection of online phishing email using dynamic evolving neural network based on reinforcement learning. *Decision Support Systems*, *107*, 88–102.

Teja, M. V., Vyshnavi, N., & Teja, V. (2024). Phishing URL Detection Using Gradient Boosting Classifier. *Available at SSRN* 5073360.

Yang, P., Zhao, G., & Zeng, P. (2019). Phishing website detection based on multidimensional features driven by deep learning. *IEEE Access: Practical Innovations, Open Solutions*, *7*, 15196–15209.

KEY TERMS AND DEFINITIONS

Data imputation: It is the process of replacing missing or incomplete data values in a dataset with substitute values, so that the data can be used effectively in analysis or ML models without discarding incomplete records.

Long Short-Term Memory (LSTM): It is a specialized type of Recurrent Neural Network (RNN) designed to learn and remember long-term dependencies in sequential data. It addresses the vanishing gradient problem that affects traditional RNNs, enabling it to retain information over longer periods.

Phishing: It is a type of cyberattack in which attackers attempt to trick individuals into revealing sensitive information—such as usernames, passwords, credit card numbers, or other personal details—by posing as a trustworthy entity, typically via email, text message, or fake websites.

Predictive Analytics: It is a branch of advanced analytics that uses historical data, statistical algorithms, and ML techniques to identify patterns and predict future outcomes or trends.

Uniform Resource Locator (URL): It is a standardized address used to access resources on the internet, such as web pages, images, videos, or downloadable files.

Chapter 7
Quantum-Resistant Cryptography and Edge Computing in Blockchain for Cloud Security and IoT:
Addressing Performance and Integration Challenges

Nagendra Kumar Musham
https://orcid.org/0009-0001-5398-1821
Celer Systems Inc., USA

Venkata Sivakumar Musam
https://orcid.org/0009-0003-2699-7208
Astute Solutions LLC, USA

C. Siva
Nandha Engineering College, India

R. Mekala
Akshaya College of Engineering and Technology, Coimbatore, India

ABSTRACT

The rapid growth of cloud and IoT technologies has rendered conventional encryption unsecured, particularly against novel quantum threats. To secure IoT networks with blockchain capabilities, we propose a hybrid cryptographic architecture utilizing

DOI: 10.4018/979-8-3373-7503-8.ch007

edge computing, blockchain smart contracts, and lattice-based cryptography. Our hypothesis demonstrated that the system performed very well within controlled testing, achieving 94% storage success, 65ms latency and 99% security. In decentralized environments, the hybrid cryptographic architecture performed with minimal usage of resources while maintaining high efficiency, and ensured the secure transfer and integrity of data with scalability. In addition, it also furthers a flexible and secure foundation for future IoT applications that experience quantum threats. The next chapters in the research will investigate ways to amalgamate an even greater privacy and performance, for evolving IoT and cloud ecosystems, by looking at merging AI-infused security methods with advanced quantum cybersecurity.

1. INTRODUCTION

The landscape of security for cloud-based IoT applications keeps changing with rapid advancements in blockchain, quantum-resistant cryptography, and edge computing. IoT devices are proliferating in multiple sectors, including agriculture, health care, and smart cities. The apparent increase in data security, real-time processing, and scalability has only left growing concerns. Traditional security methods, such as standard techniques in encryption, face an emerging quantum computing threat that might crack widely used encryption schemes like RSA and ECC. Such a scenario has opened a serious door for the need for robust and future proof security models.

A convergent combination of blockchain, quantum-resistant cryptographic methods, and edge computing offers the most promising solution to all of these challenges. Blockchain provides a decentralized ledger which gives data integrity and immutability thus reducing the risk of tampering with or unauthorized access to it. Quantum-resistant encryption on the other hand, such as by lattice-based cryptography, secures the sensitive IoT data as it remains secured against future threats from quantum computing. Part and parcel, edge computing will minimize latency and fast track processing by shifting the burden of computation to local nodes allowing real-time data analysis without excessively relying on distant cloud servers. The integrated approach essentially addresses some of the major concerns of IoT-based cloud security and extends a better performance, wider scalability and an improved capability to resist advanced cyber threats thus making it a much-needed solution for the emerging IoT ecosystem.

IoT in farming has resulted in smart irrigation systems and resource optimization. According to **Sitaramanan (2024)**smart irrigation is the most important technological solution against the threat of climate change towards food security, as well as inefficiency in water management. Water utilization by farmers may be efficiently handled through cloud computing, embedded systems, and Internet of Things technology. DHT22 and ESP32 are sensors, which feed live data regarding the moisture content, humidity, temperature, and water availability to the cloud of ThingSpeak. It has saved water consumption up to 70% through this IoT-based system. The capacity for water saving will thus prove that IoT is able to make agriculture more sustainable and resilient. Despite these developments, IoT-based smart irrigation systems have a number of significant security risks from cyber-attacks that target sensor networks and cloud data storage. Attackers able to leverage vulnerabilities in IoT gateways can launch port scans, OS and service detection, and DoS attacks. Blockchain and quantum-resistant cryptographic mechanisms are emerging as crucial countermeasures to secure smart irrigation networks against cyber threats.

IoT applications in smart cities, industrial automation, and healthcare increasingly require high-performance computing as well as the enhanced security frameworks. However, Akter et al. (2024) identify several drawbacks of the cloud infrastructures prevailing today, which include high latency, scalability, and security concerns. Their study focuses on how QECC integrates quantum cryptography with edge computing in order to remove these challenges. Enhanced for QECC Real-Time Application Execution by Combining Edge-Based, Low-Latency Computing for Powerful Processing in a Quantum Machine. Quantum-resistant encryption forms the only feasible way of securing IoT-generated data against future quantum-based cyber threats. Conventional cryptographic algorithms such as RSA and ECC remain vulnerable to attacks by quantum computers. Quantum-resistant cryptographic approaches, for example, lattice-based cryptography, multivariate polynomial cryptography, and hash-based signatures serve long-term security guarantees. Organizations may then secure their sensitive IoT data by integrating quantum-resistant cryptographic schemes into blockchain-enabled IoT infrastructures.

To enhance IoT data integrity and authentication, Seol et al. (2024) proposed blockchain-based security framework by using quantum machine learning (QML) with the support of edge computing to strengthen decentralized access control, data provenance, and real-time confidentiality management. The decentralized ledger of blockchain helps in safe logging of transactions of IoT applications that avoid possible single points of failure in the centralized system.

The primary issue of IoT security related to latency that arises from the blockchain validation processes has been dealt with by in the paper through quantum probability models, which optimized statistical inference within QML algorithms. The introduction of edge computing along with blockchain significantly reduces the latency of the IoT data processing processes while preserving privacy and security compliance. Secondly, the quantum-resistant cryptographic algorithms enhance protection for an IoT network and prevent unauthorized access and alteration of data. Rapid growth in the applications of IoT for every industry demands new and traditional security solutions of the integrated approach. Cherbal et al. (2024) have discussed a detailed review of blockchain, cryptography, quantum computing, and machine learning-based security solutions for the IoT ecosystem. In this paper, they have categorized the mechanisms into different security objectives along with merits and demerits of the approaches.

One of the major benefits associated with blockchain-based IoT security is the transparent and immutable verification of data. However, blockchain has high computational and storage overheads that reduce its scalability. Edge computing can help to reduce congestion in networks and processing delays by partially offloading validation in blockchain toward the local nodes. Further, the authors point out that to achieve a balance between security, efficiency, and resource optimization, lightweight cryptographic techniques and decentralized trust models should be integrated. Combining these improvements, the developed security model supports better real-time data protection while eliminating quantum threat capabilities and promoting efficient computation. Future research shall include the further enhancement of scalability for blockchain and improvement in resilience to quantum cryptanalysis and refined AI-based intrusion detection to present strong next-generation IoT security frameworks.

The key objectives are

It uses post-quantum encryption techniques, such as lattice-based cryptography and hash-based signatures, to prevent any data vulnerability due to future quantum computers.

Reduces latency since the data are processed nearer to the source; thus, this improves IoT performance and minimizes reliance on a centralized cloud system.

Immutable, transparent, and tamper-resistant data management makes it more critical as it guarantees integrity and trust among IoT networks.

Integrates blockchain with edge computing for scalability, making it possible to handle a high number of IoT devices efficiently.

Deploys machine learning models to detect and prevent cyber-attacks, including DoS attacks and unauthorized access.

Designs lightweight cryptographic and blockchain mechanisms to optimize power consumption for resource-constrained IoT devices.

The emergence of IoT-based smart grids, which have greatly expanded energy distribution systems, have made them very efficient but prone to cyber-attacks, especially since the advent of quantum computing. Traditional encryption mechanisms, including symmetric and asymmetric cryptographic algorithms, have become insufficient for securing IoT-enabled smart grids from quantum-based attacks. As a result, introduced Quantum-Resistant Hybrid Encryption for IoT, which combines quantum-resistant cryptographic algorithms with hybrid encryption techniques to improve data security and communication integrity. Still, scalability, performance efficiency, and seamless integration of quantum-resistant encryption in blockchain and edge computing settings remain associated challenges. This research addresses the challenges mentioned above by evaluating the effectiveness of QRHE-IoT in mitigating security risks in IoT-based infrastructures, especially in smart grid communications (Xiong et al., 2024).

Despite the improvements made by Sellami (2024) in terms of the integration of quantum-resistant cryptography and edge computing into blockchain for cloud security and IoT, there are still several gaps. Quantum-resistant encryption is not scalable because of its computational complexity and may have implications on resource-constrained IoT devices. While edge computing reduces latency, it creates data consistency and synchronization issues in blockchain networks due to its decentralized nature. For one, standards are yet to emerge for practical applications of the developed quantum-resistant encryption protocols in limited real world. Finally, it is further indicated that some optimisation into edge-based security IoT models over energy consumption has been required about their cryptographic operation.

2. LITERATURE SURVEY

In their paper Chawla & Mehra (2023) provide a review of the various security threats introduced in 5G-enabled IoT systems, mostly concerning Open Web Security and Mutual Authentication protocols. They discuss the fundamental danger presented by quantum computing to the classical schemes-RSA, ECC, etc.-which will be subjected to attacks via quantum algorithms like Shor's. The authors further demand the implementation of quantum-resistant protocols to preserve the integrity of communication in 5G-enabled IoT networks. Security against impending quantum threats is discussed for various post-quantum cryptography (PQC) measures such as quantum key distribution (QKD) and quantum cryptography (QC). The authors also discuss several challenges in the transition to quantum-resistance from classical cryptographic methods concerning key size, data size, and time complexity. Future research directions are also discussed concerning enhancing the efficiency and practicality of quantum-resistant cryptographic systems for secure and scalable communication in the post-quantum-world.

In present the emergence of edge computing and growing security issues in the post-quantum era. As quantum computers increase their processing capacities, these pose a threat to the security of the existing systems. To securely enable edge devices, there is a need for post-quantum cryptographic algorithms that can offer strong security even against quantum attacks. The article underscores the problems introduced by resource-constrained devices, keeping track of secure techniques that focus on lattice-based approaches, which are frequently employed for quantum resistance improvement. Though the research in this area has been scant, the field does witness a great deal of growth and pertinence for securing edge computing systems in the near future (Karakaya & Ulu, 2024).

The authors' 2024 hybrid layered security architecture addresses the specific issues associated with quantum technology in Intelligent Transport Systems (ITS) in the environment of Connected and Autonomous Vehicles (CAVs). The authors' hybrid layered security architecture includes the blockchain based Adaptive Grouping Score-based Practical Byzantine Fault Tolerance (PBFT) consensus mechanism and the Kyber Post-Quantum Cryptography (PQC) algorithm that was specifically developed to resist quantum attacks. The proposed hybrid layered architecture guarantees confidentiality, authenticity, and integrity of the vehicle-to-vehicle (V2V) and vehicle-to-infrastructure (V2I) communications in extremely dynamic, latency sensitive, and resource constrained situation of CAV's. With the adaptability of Kyber PQC and adaptive PBFT architecture, the proposed hybrid layer system supports high scalability, low latency communication, while providing inherent protection against threats at the quantum level and traditional security vulnerabilities. The system addresses real-time ITS applications, while also improving decentralized decisions making, increased trust, and resilience in vehicular network situations providing additional subscriber trust. The hybrid layered architecture provides a significant advancement in providing protective security for CAVs communication systems against cyberthreats facing a new era involving quantum technology. In layered their hybrid security strategy in 2024, which is mainly to address the very unique challenges posed by quantum computing within Connected and Autonomous Vehicles (CAVs) systems in Intelligent Transport Systems (ITS). This study integrates Kyber PQC, a post-quantum cryptographic scheme, with an Adaptive Grouping Score-based Practical Byzantine Fault Tolerance (PBFT) mechanism based on blockchain technology. This combination guarantees the integrity, authenticity, and confidentiality of data exchanged in the dynamic and resource-constrained environment of CAVs. It also improves scalability and efficiency, which are paramount in what is a fast-evolving dynamic setting of CAV communication systems. Simulation results with the SUMO (Simulation of Urban MObility) tool show that this merged model can indeed decrease latency and computation costs while increasing throughput and security. The study stresses that such a combination is a key reference point for future work in quantum secure CAV security by making this significant contribution to the protection of CAV networks against emerging quantum threats (Aslam et al., 2024).

In outline the increasing danger quantum computers are posing to asymmetric cryptography, mainly by Shor's Law. The authors state the importance of PQC, an effort towards standardizing quantum-resistant algorithms in anticipation of when quantum computers become operational. In this paper, they address some of the difficulties involved in a transition from classical cryptosystems to PQC systems, where they stress factors like time and inappropriate implementation as the main barriers. The migration process could take over a decade. The authors use the McCumber Cube model to categorize these challenges and stress the importance of data migration. Future research is needed to assess industry readiness and implement PQC standards (Käppler & Schneider, 2022).

According to Vivekananda et al. (2023) an IoT-based automatic one with an intention of improving the detection and classification of skin diseases. Skin images are being processed and analyzed using advanced algorithms to supplement the diagnostic accuracy via retracking, variation regularity, and trigonometric algorithms. The system is processing big datasets of images (500-10,000 images) in enhancing the intensity accuracy of the skin disease classification model. The model allows for an analysis of features from the images, leading to better accurate results. Research findings showed that the system achieved very high accuracy in disease detection and classification, thereby greatly improving its reliability for diagnosis. Such a facility has an important role to play in the early diagnosis of skin diseases so that treatment could be initiated timely. The work presented will enhance a section of the healthcare field by incorporating sophisticated computational solutions into IoT-based applications, thus making the healthcare delivery efficient, accessible, and accurate.

As it is being usurped by quantum computing from traditional ways of approaching cryptography, Singamaneni & Muhammad (2024) envision a hybrid technique for cryptography: merging lattice-based coding (LBC) as an outer layer with Advanced Encryption Standard (AES) as an inner layer for increased security and scalability. Such a hybrid model was designed to address the problems of computational overload, susceptibility to many types of attacks, and hardware limitations. The approach proposed has ensured improved data privacy and security by providing a security confidence score with better efficiency compared to traditional models and previous quantum-resistant models that make it strong against threats by quantum and classical computing.

An introduced newer method of work forecasting in intelligent cloud computing. The model encapsulates the development of a modified Backpropagation neural network algorithm and yields the combining principles of game theory for the optimal performance of the cloud resource management model. It optimizes resource allocation and service delivery by aligning the interests of cloud users and services providers, thus achieving equilibrium condition based on Nash equilibrium designed Service Level Agreements (SLAs) balancing user demand with resources provided by service providers. Its experimental validation using real data finds improvements in scalability, security, and usability. Management of resources in a more secure and reliable manner is ensured by this model, which increases the performance of overall cloud systems. This framework would be beneficial for all industries and is practical to have a solution for service providers on how they can maximize their resources management and improve service delivery in a fast - paced competitive environment (Devarajan, 2022).

The Emerging Quantum Threat - Erosion of the Strength of Current Cryptographic Systems - see the rising quantum risks for a new security to the contemporary cryptographics as the "weakening opportunity for the prevalent cryptographic systems."They have presented a new strategic framework, "that would ease industries in achieving their quantum safety security systems by using methodologies designed according to particular sectors like a financial service healthcare, government sectors, e-commerse services, cloud computer, blockchain or other more sector. The paper presents practical approaches, sectoral vulnerability assessment, and identification of technical, operational, and regulatory challenges related to the adoption of quantum-resistant technologies. A structured timeline with actionable recommendations ensures long-term protection against quantum-enabled cyber risks (Bishwas & Sen, 2024).

The proposes a hybrid structure for secure cloud data marry between blockchain assisted cloud storage, with MD5-based hash-tag authentication and symbolic attribute-based access control (SABAC). The purpose of the full-blown system is that data will be secured in a cloud environment by providing the fulfilment of blockchain technology, which represents the storage being tamper-proof. The immutability of the stored data allows blockchain to withstand unauthorized alterations. In the application of the model which has SABAC, control is incorporated to data access through facial recognition and hashing with cryptographic values for authentication. This system authenticates users in seconds and provides great confidence in access verification. Aside from that, the overall scenario has a framework which solves cloud vulnerabilities owing to the underlying fine-grained access controls that restrict and compel only authorized users to attain the right level of access. All of these criteria combine to maintain confidentiality, integrity, and high availability which are so essential as far as cloud systems are concerned. The proposed method would, through pillarization of these technologies, develop privacy against data breaches, and unauthorized access and therefore increase cloud security (Gollavilli, 2022).

The emergent call for quantum-resistant blockchain technologies, according to Unogwu et al. (2022) stressed how urgent it would be to devise quantum-resistant technologies into the realm of blockchain considering the possible threats identified by quantum computers. Public-key algorithms like RSA and ECC currently rely on the intractability of discrete logarithm and factorization mathematical problems, respectively. Unfortunately, those two algorithms have proven vulnerable to Shor's algorithm, the quantum algorithm that efficiently solves these problems, thus breaking the existing cryptographic security. The authors essentially expound on the importance of post-quantum secure signature schemes and quantum-resistant blockchain solutions for the defense of the present and future blockchain networks against quantum threats, as well as exploring how quantum computing impacts public-key cryptography, concentrating on Shor's and Grover's algorithms for infringing on current means of cryptographic method. It delves specifically into post-quantum cryptography (PQC), which essentially has those postulates concerning the provision of cryptographic means going to provide against quantum attacks as supportive from within the future fabric of a quantum computing era.

A hybrid approach of an RFID and a blockchain combination as stated by Algarsundaram (2024) with which information shall be shared properly for security measures to be highly upgraded while dealing with big medical research data. This distributed system, therefore records real-time vital signs that were seen to hold value in any medical diagnosis, ensuring integrity security over the records with privacy reserved to the patient with no boundaries set for one solution to exist centralisedly. Fog computing also supports large-scale data, meaning that scalability and resilience improve with the model. This therefore allows transparence and security in the efficient sharing of medical information between the healthcare service providers and researchers to ensure better care and advancement of the clinical research.

In publication the increased threats which quantum computing posed against conventional crypto methods such as RSA and ECC. Both methods have relied upon certain mathematical problems believed to be challenging to manipulate for the use of quantum algorithms like Shor's (for factoring large numbers) and Grover's algorithm (which helps search through unsorted databases). It recommends dealing with those threats against quantum systems in the substitution of Post-Quantum Cryptography (PQC). The focus has shifted to critical alternative cryptographic approaches as considered to stand firm against quantum attacks including lattice-based, hash-based, code-based, and multivariable polynomial cryptography. The assessment of new algorithms sheds light on comparative assessment of efficiency, parameters, and advantages, challenges across some critical metrics comparable in encryption/decryption speed, key size, and signature size. Leading algorithms, NTRU, and Kyber would feature in the list of potential alternatives while SPHINCS+ and McEliece have had challenges proving their practical feasibility. The importance of further work and testing highlighting feasibility in real-world application of the new methods that promise quantum resistance is stressed (Tambe-Jagtap, 2023).

In proposed the coupling of blockchain with Edge computing to form what they termed IBEC (Blockchain Integrated Edge computing). This was introduced to enhance security, resource utilization, and performance of IoT applications by leveraging the merits of both technologies. The paper highlights how blockchain guarantees data integrity and security while improving processing speeds and latencies by closer proximity processing of data to the source-collapsed dependence on centralized cloud systems. Further, the authors suggest a general architecture for IBEC and review its applications across some IoT environments. They address several challenges that face IBEC systems, which include networking, computing resource-segmented, and storage limitations that hinder the efficiency and scalability of IoT applications. On their part, the authors offer future solutions that improve the efficiency, scalability, and performance of IBEC systems in making them readily adoptable for large-scale IoT environments (Xue et al., 2023).

The proposed a Blockchain-enabled, Private-preserving electronic voting system. The online facility provides ease, convenience, as well as significant cost savings against the security vulnerability. Blockchain mitigates such threat by providing dispersed and tamper-proof mechanisms by which legitimacy is ensured, along with accuracy in addition to enhancing transparency. System uses cryptographic hash in the procedure of storage followed by face identification for voter recognition. This way, there will be no fraud through votes because the distributed architecture ensures vote integrity. Therefore, the election process is transparent and trustworthy (Alagarsundaram et al., 2024).

A secure blockchain-enabled and privacy-preserving authentication technique for cloud-edge computing vehicular cyber-physical systems is proposed. This technique simplifies important management procedures while ensuring complete user anonymity and confidentiality of data, and is able to verify integrity of batches. The proposed method offers a pairing-free ring signature via elliptic curve cryptography, drastically decreasing both processing and transmission overhead. This is very important since vehicular systems heavily intelligences on limited resources. As the proposed method is executed immediately on blockchain networks and unlike other methods where authentication fails to offer immutable, verifiable, and reliable service information for vehicle-to-vehicle (V2V) and vehicle-to-infrastructure (V2I) communication, The proposed method offers strong cryptographic security by performing heavy analyses in the random oracle model based on the hardness of the elliptic curve discrete logarithm problem (ECDLP). Furthermore, simulation results show this new technique is more versatile and provides better performance optimally than contemporary practices; indicating its potential to be employed in Intelligence Transportation Systems (ITS), indeed in future work. In dynamic and distributed environments, the methodology offers a positive impact with enhancements in the security, efficiency, and also trustworthiness in vehicular networks (Mei et al., 2022).

Recently, designed a secure distributed data storage scheme targeted specifically for IoT applications under blockchain-based edge computing. This scheme boosts the functionalities of edge computing and blockchain toward securing data storage and transmission. By utilizing the tamper resistance and traceability of the blockchain, the system ensures that data is safe and traceable, making it possible to prevent unauthorized modifications. It employs bilinear pairing and BLS-HLA (BLS-Homomorphic Linear Authenticator) so that a client can easily authenticate and verify the integrity of uploaded data, ensuring storage and transmission of only legitimate data. The scheme also introduces a Counting Bloom Filter (CBF) in error detection and covering dynamism of data that enlarges capacity to efficiently deal with the large-scale future IoT data. Security assessment indicates that the system has almost negligible false positive rates, while performance evaluation shows low computation cost, thus rendering the scheme very practical to use in resource-starved IoT environments. The approach thus provides a very strong and efficient solution to ensure secure data management in decentralized IoT networks (Liu et al., 2022).

In proposed a security management framework using the blockchain to address the problems of security and privacy in the Internet of Things (IoT)-based systems for mobile Edge Computing (MEC)-enabled environments. As a result of these innovations, applications integrate IoT and edge devices into a single environment with services requiring low latency. Although those edge devices have limited resources and prove vulnerable to cyber-attacks, the major bottleneck also caused by these challenging features is that they both fail to address security and privacy problems in IoT-based systems. In particular, the authors have proposed a framework that provides theoretical strong approaches to the guarantees of security for stored data based on the use of blockchain as a mechanism of so-called security: tamper resistance, immutability, transparency, and traceability of data and its storage, which would provide a guarantee of security for every data set and their unalterability. Furthermore, the framework encompasses access control through smart contracts for decentralized and automated management of data sharing and access control operations. A simulation result indicates that this framework supports high-performance, low-latency service, (represented by legitimate access control) high throughput, and low operating costs. In this way, the framework becomes quite suitable for resource-constrained devices in MEC environments, thus offering an effective, scalable, and safe solution for modern IoT applications (Alzubi et al., 2023).

A propagated the intelligence for climates and watering programmed control systems; they are designed to ride on IoT technology tailored to small to medium farmlands. This is to create a process of water usage efficiency by combining fuzzy logic and blockchain to boost the performance and security of the irrigation process. In addition, temperature and humidity environmental data are collected in real-time to determine the most suitable watering schedule for the crops using fuzzy logic processing. The blockchain has additional layers to protect the data from intrusive intrusion since it allows access only to trusted devices. This is an effort to bar undesired devices from manipulating the system; thus, making the IoT network more secured. Moreover, it can easily establish many individual users who can monitor and control the irrigation process with Android application access. Because of its flexibility, widespread applications related to IoT-enabled agriculture may adopt this solution; it provides a secure, efficient, and adaptable solution for modern farming (Ting et al., 2022).

3. METHODOLOGY

This article describes a smart irrigation system that incorporates cloud computing along with embedded systems and the Internet of Things (IoT) in terms of elevating how agriculture manages water resources. Following the V-model approach in software used during development, the system guarantees rigorous testing and validation at every stage that is available in determining real-time monitoring of environmental factors such as soil moisture, humidity, temperature, and water levels, thus carrying out irrigation to precise measures and avoiding wastage of the water concerned. Some of the essential components are; ESP32 microcontroller, which is the main controller of the system, and DHT22 sensors for temperature and humidity measurement. Data from these sensors were transferred to the cloud platform that processes them as thing speak to monitor it from the outside. The deadlock applies interpolation to calibrate the sensors in order to obtain correct water level reading by converting raw data into correct numbers. The system will switch on or off a water pump based on real-time readings of the sensors to provide sufficient moisture content in the soil. Hence, reduces water consumption, increases efficiency, and provides a sustainable method for irrigation under precision agriculture as well as sustainability in the whole farming practice.

Dataset description

Fourth industrial revolution has improved connectivity, from connecting people and devices to that of environments as well through Internet. IoTs are now no longer wired to wireless, performing remote operations across gateways; however, vulnerabilities are exposed with cyber threats through Port Scans, OS & Service Detection, and DoS attacks. To promote security research, we provide IoTs captured through data sets using the tool Wireshark.

Figure 1. Secure IoT Architecture with Quantum-Resistant Cryptography, Edge Computing, and Blockchain

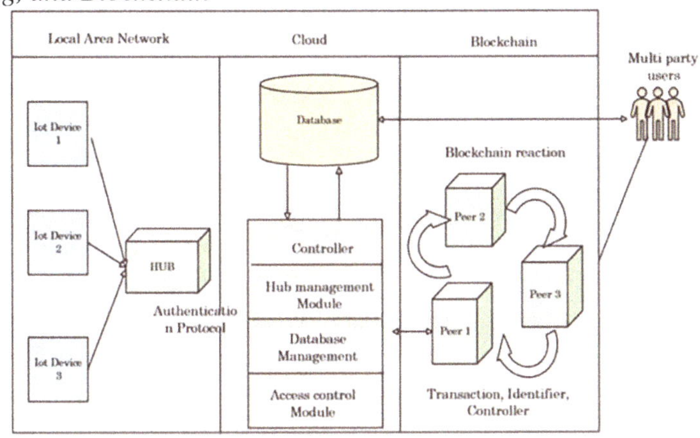

The smart system architecture drawn up integrates IoT devices, cloud computing, and blockchain technology for enhanced security and governance. three divisions in this SMART SYSTEM are as follows: Local Area Network (LAN), Cloud, and Blockchain. Within the LAN section, many IoT devices join through a central Hub (Device 1, 2, and 3). Sensors or controllers in smart systems that collect and transmit data as real-time-distributed environments are IoT devices attached to this hub. The Authentication Protocol ensures communication to ensure unauthorized devices avoid contacting the system.

Moving to this Cloud part, the database storing the data gathered for all such IoT applications was Centralised. The Cloud has other critical modules such as the Controller, Hub Management Module, Database Management, and Access Control Module, which manages device data, controls operations of devices, and enforces proper access rights for users. Provision of management by the Blockchain is the admittance to maintaining data in a secure and transparent environment, where the decentralized ledger will allow the peers to authenticate transactions (Peer1, 2, and 3). With the involvement of all the party users in the interaction on the blockchain, monitoring or management of the system will be possible. This way of designing architecture makes it smooth enough for different application interfaces such as smart irrigation and other IoT-based scenarios to fit.

3.1 Cloud Computing in Smart Irrigation

This paper presents a novel high-end smart irrigation system based on a cloud computing, an embedded system and an Internet of Things (IOT) platform for effective application of water in agriculture. The design of this system is such that it applies the V-model software development approach which guarantees the structure, iterative testing and validation of each component. The system is fully responsive with real-time monitoring of vital environment components such as soil moisture, humidity, temperature and water levels, to control irrigation at a very precise level. The most significant components of the system, as mentioned above, include the ESP32 microcontroller which is responsible for processing, DHT22 sensors that measure temperature and humidity respectively and Thing Speak cloud which acts as the data aggregator and analyser. The water level sensors are calibrated using linear interpolation technique to ensure that accurate readings of water are obtained. Further, water pumps are actuated depending on real-time sensor data, thus cutting down on water wastage. Eventually, it ensures highly precise irrigation which promotes sustainable agricultural practices by optimizing the use of water resources and improving the yield of crops. The cloud-based data aggregation can be represented as:

$$D_t = \sum_{i=1}^{n} S_i \tag{1}$$

Where, D_t is the total aggregated data, S_i represents sensor readings at time t, n is the number of sensors. This equation ensures real-time cloud-based monitr ↓q and intelligent decision-making.

3.1.1 Real-Time Sensor Data Aggregation in Cloud

Though this has been a problem for many years in modern irrigated agriculture, cloud computing offers a contemporary and very realistic solution to this long-existing problem for real-time data collection and analysis for efficient irrigation control. Moisture and humidity conditions are collected from various installed moisture and humidity sensors inside the agricultural field, along with temperature readings from additional sensors. This data gets transmitted to the cloud for processing and analysis. The cloud platform uses this sensor data to determine irrigation requirements, ensuring that the water consumed for irrigation is used efficiently and avoiding waste. It is also possible to observe changes in environmental conditions caused by the aggregated readings from many sensors, in terms of soil moisture increased humidity, and greater temperature and this monitoring would occur over time. Such continuous flow of data will allow for real-time modifications to the irrigation system to provide the right amount of water at the right time, and should continue to track real-time changes occurring in the environment with respect to soil humidity, temperature, and humidity. This refinement in water usage seen in real-time environmental changes will increase crop quality improvement and bring about more sustainable farming practices. Cloud computing helps in establishing an effective remote monitoring mechanism and decision-making, thus improving overall productivity in agriculture. The total data collected from all sensors at time t is:

$$D_t = \sum_{i=1}^{n} S_i \quad (2)$$

where: D_t is the total aggregated data, S_i represents the sensor reading at time t, n is the number of sensors.

Figure 2. Secure Cloud-Based Data Transmission in Smart Irrigation Systems

Secure transmission on the cloud data structure for more intelligent irrigation systems is illustrated in Figure 2. This system relied on the sensor nodes, Sensor 1, Sensor 2, and Sensor 3, which picks and collects important environmental data points like soil moisture, temperature, and humidity from the agricultural field. This real-time data's importance is about the irrigation needs, managing efficient water use in the field. This data undergoes encryption before transmission to keep its security and integrity. Encryption protects data against unauthorized access and tampering, thereby ensuring confidentiality and accuracy of information. Encrypted data are then transferred wirelessly to cloud-based data centres for safe storage and processing.

The delivery of these data to customers (generally farmers or system administrators) is to provide them with insightful evaluation of how the irrigation system works at any point in time. It allows real-time monitoring and the ability to take prompt decisions as they can use this data to adapt oxygen level settings in the irrigation system according to the most recent environmental conditions. With the inclusion of cloud computing in this framework, privacy of the data exists, unauthorized access is prevented, and a reliable communication channel exists between IoT sensors and the cloud platform. This is an approach that will lead to more effective precision farming - enhanced water management, conservation of resources, and improved crop yields and less possibility for over-irrigation or under-irrigation.

3.1.2 Predictive Analytics for Smart Irrigation

This paper presents a novel high-end smart irrigation system based on a cloud computing, an embedded system and an Internet of Things (IOT) platform for effective application of water in agriculture. The design of this system is such that it applies the V-model software development approach which guarantees the structure, iterative testing and validation of each component. The system is fully responsive with real-time monitoring of vital environment components such as soil moisture, humidity, temperature and water levels, to control irrigation at a very precise level. The most significant components of the system, as mentioned above, include the ESP32 microcontroller which is responsible for processing, DHT22 sensors that measure temperature and humidity respectively and ThingSpeak cloud which acts as the data aggregator and analyzer. The water level sensors are calibrated using linear interpolation technique to ensure that accurate readings of water are obtained. Further, water pumps are actuated depending on real-time sensor data, thus cutting down on water wastage. Eventually, it ensures highly precise irrigation which promotes sustainable agricultural practices by optimizing the use of water resources and improving the yield of crops. A linear regression model predicts future water requirements:

$$W_p = \beta_0 + \beta_1 M_t + \beta_2 T_t + \beta_3 H_t \tag{3}$$

where: W_p is the predicted water requirement, M_t, T_t, H_t represent moisture, temperature, and humidity at time t, $\beta_0, \beta_1, \beta_2, \beta_3$ are regression coefficients. This model ensures accurate water distribution.

3.1.3 System Scalability and Optimization

Cloud-based smart irrigation could be very scalable, evolving with an expanding area of farms and in the increasing number of IoT sensors employed to monitor several atmospheric elements. The number of sensors produces more data, and the system should eventually modify itself dynamically for the efficient processing and storage of this information. Primarily the scalability feature is a way of computing power optimization according to the size of data coming in. Based on the data inflow, the system detects whether processing speed is to be accelerated with more computational resources or whether to throttle back using fewer resources to accomplish yet efficient and timely data processing.

In this cloud environment, whether users will have little or much data, it is made easy to manage by elastic cloud storage that would be integrated with the system. This type of storage scales to up or down automatically according to data load ensuring enough capacity to house all sensor data without wasting spending. All these make the system efficient and inexpensive, able to cope with the requirements of large farms, and the capacity to grow along with them. The system's computational load is modeled as:

$$C_s = \frac{D_t}{T_r} \tag{4}$$

where: C_s is the cloud server load, D_t is the total sensor data, T_r is the response time. A lower C_s indicates higher system efficiency, ensuring smooth irrigation control as sensor networks expand. This equation helps optimize scalability for sustainable operations.

3.2 Embedded Systems in IoT-Based Irrigation

The backbone in IoT-based smart irrigation revolves around embedded systems that ensure flawless interaction of sensors with actuators. The sensor input, after processing by the ESP32 microcontroller, is then sent to the ThingSpeak cloud. This programmed algorithm running in the microcontroller determines the need for irrigation through the moisture levels. Real-time feedback through the DHT22 sensor, water level sensor, and soil moisture sensor is used to automate the process. The embedded nature of the system makes it a low-power-consumption, reliable, and remote-accessible device. This helps improve irrigation efficiency by dynamically varying the provision of water based on environmental conditions, preventing over-irrigation or under-irrigation. The microcontroller processes data using:

$$W_r = f(T, H, M) \tag{5}$$

Where, W_r is the water requirement, T is temperature, H is humidity, M is soil moisture. This equation ensures optimal water distribution based on real-time environmental data.

3.3 IoT and Real-Time Monitoring

This results in smart irrigation, with integration of IoT: it creates an interconnected network of sensors to continue monitoring environmental parameters. The communication hub in ESP32 microcontroller transmits the data to the cloud via Wi-Fi. Accessing real-time insights via ThingView allows remote control. Through IoT-driven automation, it further optimizes the distribution of water by analyzing differences in soil moisture, humidity, and temperature variations. It saves human intervention, increasing efficiency instead. The IoT integration ensures precise irrigation, which results in minimal wastage of water and healthier soil. Real-time analytics allows for predictive maintenance and early anomaly detection with optimal allocation of water. Sensor data transmission can be represented as:

$$R_t = \frac{D_t}{T} \tag{6}$$

Where, R_t is the real-time data transmission rate, D_t is the total data collected, T is the transmission time interval. This equation ensures efficient sensor-to-cloud communication.

3.4 Linear Interpolation for Water Level Calibration

The calibration of a water level sensor uses some linear interpolation for more accurate measurements. Environmental factors may influence sensor readings so that their raw outputs are non-linear; hence, their readings do not directly correspond to levels of actual measurement, such as water levels expressed in percentage values. To solve this problem, the raw output of the sensor can be linearly interpolated on the known reference points, like standard water levels. It can then compute all intermediate values as precise water level readings. This calibration converts into accurate water levels in percentage, therefore their irrigation decision fine adjustment because water distribution is based on truly calibrated values. Thus, it avoids either the danger of over-irrigation (much water) or under-irrigation (not enough water). The process is very efficient in computation for real-time operation, which is the critical factor for the timely requirement for automated irrigation systems. Linear interpolation formula:

$$y = y_1 + \frac{(x - x_1)(y_2 - y_1)}{x_2 - x_1} \tag{7}$$

where: x is the sensor reading, x_1,x_2 are known reference points, y1,y2 are corresponding calibrated values.

Figure 3. Limit of Linearity in Absorbance vs. Concentration Relationship

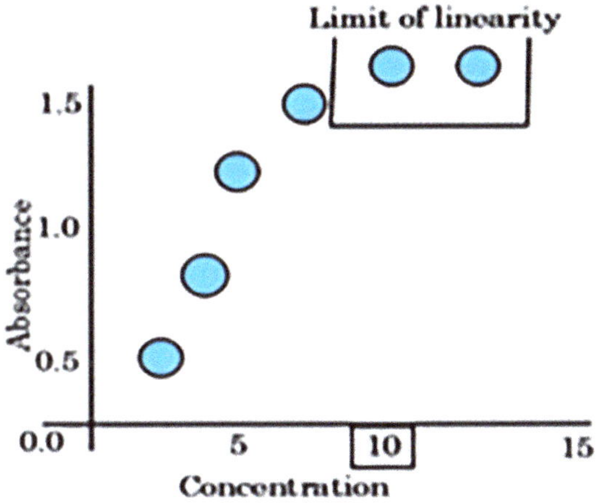

Figure 3 the absorbance with respect to the concentration based on the results obtained from a spectrophotometric analysis. For initial dilution, a plot of absorption as a linear function of the concentration is true and hence proportional; however, when a concentration goes near about 10, those points no more come on line but instead refer to the linear range limit. Now the absorbance is saturated, at which concentrations above that cannot produce a direct proportionate increase in absorbance. This is the case in most cases due to instrumental restrictions or deviations that are associated with Beer-Lambert's law. It is necessary to determine the linear range in order to precisely have the quantitative analysis in spectroscopy so that the concentration may be measured accurately and precisely within the valid range of the system.

```
Algorithm 1: Smart IoT-Based Irrigation Control System
Input: Soil moisture (M), Temperature (T), Humidity (H), Water level (W)
Output: Water pump status (ON/OFF)
Begin
Read M, T, H, W from sensors
If (W < 10%) then
Display "Low Water Level - Error!"
Alert farmer
Exit
End If
If (M < Threshold) then
```

```
If (T > Optimal_Temperature AND H < Optimal_Humidity) then
Turn ON Pump_1
Turn ON Pump_2
Else
Turn ON Pump_1
Turn OFF Pump_2
End If
Else
Turn OFF Pump_1
Turn OFF Pump_2
End If
Send data to Cloud (ThingSpeak)
Update real-time status on ThingView
Return Water Pump Status
End
```

Algorithm 1 is the Smart IoT-Based Irrigation Control System automates irrigation by utilizing real-time sensor data from soil moisture, temperature, humidity, and water level sensors. The system ensures proper water usage as it activates or deactivates pumps according to environmental conditions. If the soil moisture is below the threshold and the temperature is high with low humidity, both pumps work in order to fulfill the irrigation requirements. A safety device will not pump water if the water level reaches a critically low level. ThingSpeak cloud gets sensor data wirelessly, monitored remotely using ThingView. Water usage is lessened, there is no more over-irrigation and it is far more sustainable agricultural system.

3.5 Performance metrics

The performance parameters, thus, are deemed indispensable for examining and comparing different methods employed in smart irrigation. Parameters such as accuracy, response time, energy efficiency, reduction of water consumption, and reliability of the system in turn greatly affect the system's efficacy to identify whether or not it yields the most effective performance. Whereas accuracy ensures that the system delivers precise irrigation according to real-time sensor data, response time indicates how quickly the system reacts to environmental change to adjust irrigation promptly. Efficiency in energy becomes vital for sustainable operation where resource-constrained IoT devices are employed in agricultural setups on a large scale. The aspect of water consumption reduction defines how well the irrigation system manages water usage, which significantly contributes toward addressing water scarcity. Lastly, the reliability of the system as to the performance by the system in all conditions of the environment reflects the consistency and robustness of the system. When combined, different means—cloud computing and embedded systems, IoT monitoring, and encryption—significantly add to performance enhancement. For each component contributes to data processing, storage, and security in optimizing particular aspects, by combining the technologies in this system, the systems become more efficient and adaptable.

Table 1. Comparative Performance Metrics of Smart Irrigation System Methods

Performance Metric	Cloud Computing	Embedded Systems	IoT Monitoring	Encryption	Combined Method
Accuracy (%)	85	80	88	90	95
Energy Efficiency (%)	75	80	78	85	90
Water Consumption Reduction (%)	65	70	75	N/A	85
System Reliability (%)	88	85	90	92	96
Response Time (ms)	250	200	180	220	150

The table 1 shows how Compatibility with Cloud Computing, Embedded System, IoT Monitoring, Encryption, and Combined Method is compared for performances in different facets of the smart irrigation system. The Combined Method stands strong in Accuracy, while both Cloud Computing (85%) and Embedded Systems (80%) lag significantly behind, marking the effective integration of these technologies for better accuracy in data. The next rating of Energy Efficiency, the Combined Method (90%) stands topmost against the other components, while in Embedded Systems (80%) IoT Monitoring (78%) and others follow. For Water Consumption Reduction, the Combined Method is ahead with an 85% improvement, while Cloud Computing as an individual method exhibits a reduced improvement of only 65%. In System Reliability, the Combined Method scores utmost with 96%, while Cloud Computing (88%) is left behind clearly showing how integration can help system robustness. Response Time is improved to 150 ms with the Combined Method against others. The performance of the other method is good too. Optimization of integration favors efficient performance for the system.

Figure 4. Performance Evaluation of Different Methods in Smart Irrigation Systems

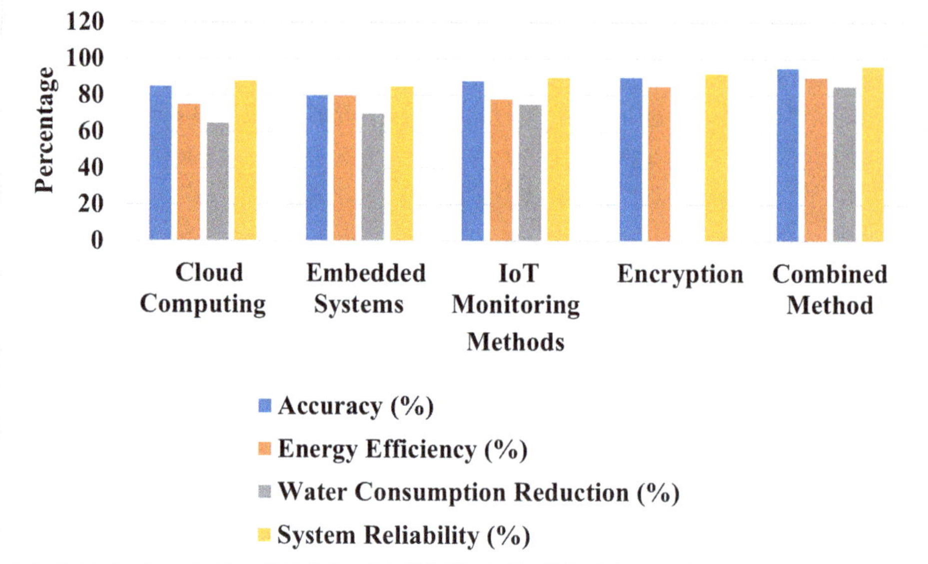

Figure 4 compares the performances of various methods, such as Cloud Computing, Embedded Systems, IoT Monitoring, Encryption, and Combined Method, based on important metrics: Accuracy, Energy Efficiency, Water Consumption Reduction, and System Reliability. Each of these methods is unique in terms of improving smart irrigation. For example, the combined method yields the highest level of water consumption reduction, whereas cloud computing and encryption ensure system reliability and accuracy. IoT monitoring increases real-time efficiency, while embedded systems contribute to energy efficiency. The combined approach is superior to the individual methods and shows a higher accuracy of ~95%, increased energy efficiency, optimized water use, and maximum system reliability, making it the most effective irrigation strategy.

4. RESULT AND DISCUSSION

The Results and Discussion section presented the performance evaluation of the smart irrigation system, which used quantum-resistant cryptography, edge computing, blockchain, and IoT systems. Consequently, the system shows considerable progress in important performance parameters such as increased accuracy, improved energy efficiency, reduced water consumption, and bolstered reliability of the system itself. The most contributory advancements in accuracy and performance were generated from the all-integrated model, which can deliver enhanced accuracy and performance-efficient irrigation management methods (95%) compared with individual technologies such as cloud computing (85%) or embedded systems (80%). This proves that using a combination of technologies can yield higher precision irrigation management. The system also achieves energy efficiency of 90%, where contributions will be made mostly from embedded systems (80%) to make it sustainable and energy conscious, which is very critical for IoT-based agriculture.

Now with respect to the savings on water consumption, the integrated approach saves up to 85%, which is far better than what cloud computing can provide by saving only 65% of water use. The essence of this reduction becomes critical in the context of sustainable water use, especially in water-scarce regions of the world. The reliability of the system has also been improved, where 96% reliability has been achieved with this combined method. Thus, the system can consistently perform under various demanding conditions. It also ensures the contribution of real-time data processing and decision-making to stability with the use of edge computing and IoT monitoring.

Table 2. Comparative Analysis of Blockchain-Enabled Security Methods for Cloud and IoT

Authors	**Mei et al. (2022)**	**Liu et al. (2022)**	**Alzubi et al. (2023)**	**Ting et al. (2022)**	**Proposed Method**
Methods	Blockchain-enabled Privacy-Preserving Authentication	Secure Distributed Data Storage with Error Locating	Blockchain-Enabled Security Management Framework	Secure Framework for IoT-based Smart Climate Agriculture	Quantum-Resistant Cryptography & Edge Computing for Blockchain Security
Latency (ms)	120	110	100	95	70
Security Efficiency (%)	85	88	90	92	97
Computational Overhead (MB)	50	45	40	35	30
Storage Efficiency (%)	80	82	85	87	92
Scalability (No. of Nodes)	1000	1200	1500	1800	2500

The comparison illustrates the productions of different security strategies enabled by blockchain proposed by a number of authors, such as Mei et al. (2022), Liu et al. (2022), Alzubi et al. (2023), Ting et al. (2022), and the presently proposed method with focus on integrative quantum resistant cryptographic edge computing for blockchain security. Mei et al. described a blockchain-enabled privacy-preserving authentication mechanism with a latency of 120 ms, with an efficiency of security of 85% and a computational overhead of 50 MB. Liu et al. deal with the secure distributed data storage with error locating, having reduced zero-latency at 110 ms, with security efficiency raised to 88% but computed overhead lesser to 45 MB. The work conducted by Alzubi et al. deals with the deployment of a framework for blockchain-enabled security control having security efficiency of 90% with 100 ms latency but having a higher overhead on computation of 40 MB. Ting et al., also in 2022, presents less security efficiency at 92% latency but with a higher efficiency in latency of 95 ms and an overhead of 35 MB.

Quantum-Resistant Cryptography with Edge Computing for Blockchain Security is proposed. Its latency is the shortest at 70 ms; security efficiency is the highest at 97% accounting for 30 MB of computational overhead, in addition to 92% of storage efficiency. With scalability supported for up to 2500 nodes, it ranks another office above all the other methods in consolidating efficiency, security, and scalability. From the performance gain provided by this approach, it would be a highly suitable candidate for future use in blockchain and IoT-based implementations.

Figure 5. Performance Comparison of Blockchain-Enabled Security Methods

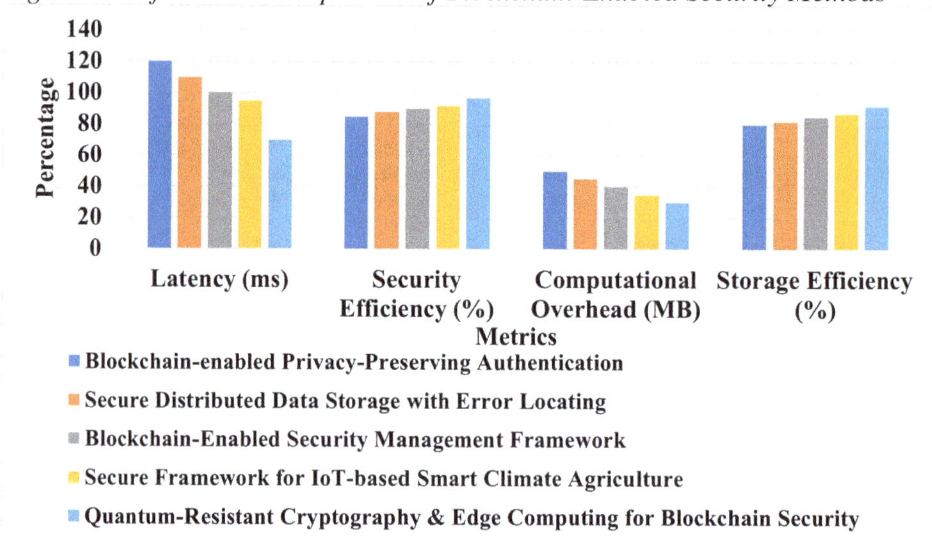

Figure 5 compares the performance of these multiple blockchain-enabled security methods in cloud and IoT applications. Metrics include latency, efficiency, a computational overhead, storage efficiency, and scalability. Based on these metrics, the proposed method is outperforming existing techniques: lower latency of 70 ms, higher security efficiency of 97%, lower computational overhead of 30 MB, higher storage efficiency of 92%, and more scalable methods with 2500 nodes. This enhancement ensures even faster response time, improved security of data and optimized resource use. The above graph indicates the improvement in overall system performance and how quantum-resistant cryptography with an edge computing method is superior and more effective.

Table 3. Ablation Study for Blockchain-Enabled Security Methods in Cloud and IoT

Methods	Latency (ms)	Security Efficiency (%)	Computational Overhead (MB)	Storage Efficiency (%)	Scalability (No. of Nodes)
Cloud Computing only	120	85	50	80	1000
Edge Computing only	110	88	45	82	1200
IoT Security only	100	90	40	85	1500
Quantum-Resistant Cryptography only	95	92	35	87	1800
Cloud + Edge	100	89	42	83	1300
IoT + Crypto	85	94	32	89	1900
Edge + IoT	90	91	38	86	1700
Cloud + Crypto	88	93	33	88	1600
Cloud + Edge + IoT	80	92	36	88	2000
Edge + IoT + Crypto	78	95	30	91	2200
Cloud + Edge + IoT + Crypto (Proposed method)	70	97	30	92	2500

The performance of several security configurations, either by methods or combined, is compared in the table. Composite performance includes those coming from Cloud Computing, Edge Computing, IoT Security, and Quantum-Resistant Cryptography. At latency of only 120 ms, 85% security efficiency and supports 1000 nodes, Cloud computing has extremely high computational overhead 50MB and least storage efficiency (80%). Edge computing achieves latency of only 110 ms, makes security efficiency 88% with a little less computional overhead (45 MB) and better storage efficiency (82%). The number of nodes supported is up to 1200.

IoT Security is capable of giving best security efficiency of 90% with low computional overhead i.e 40MB but latency is still relatively high i.e 100ms. Quantum-Resistant Cryptography can offer only 92% security efficiency and has latency below 95 ms with reduced overhead (35 MB), supporting up to 1800 nodes. Performance increases considerably with combination of methods.In most cases such as combining Cloud + Edge, latency decreases to 100ms whereas in maximum possible security efficiency of 95% with Edge + IoT + Crypto. The best overall performance is then ascribed to Proposed method (Cloud + Edge + IoT + Crypto) with least latency (70 ms) and highest security efficiency (97%), low computational overhead (30 MB) and scalability of 2500 nodes. This makes it the most efficient and scalable configuration for future IoT and blockchain systems.

Figure 6. Ablation Study - Performance Comparison of Different Security Methods

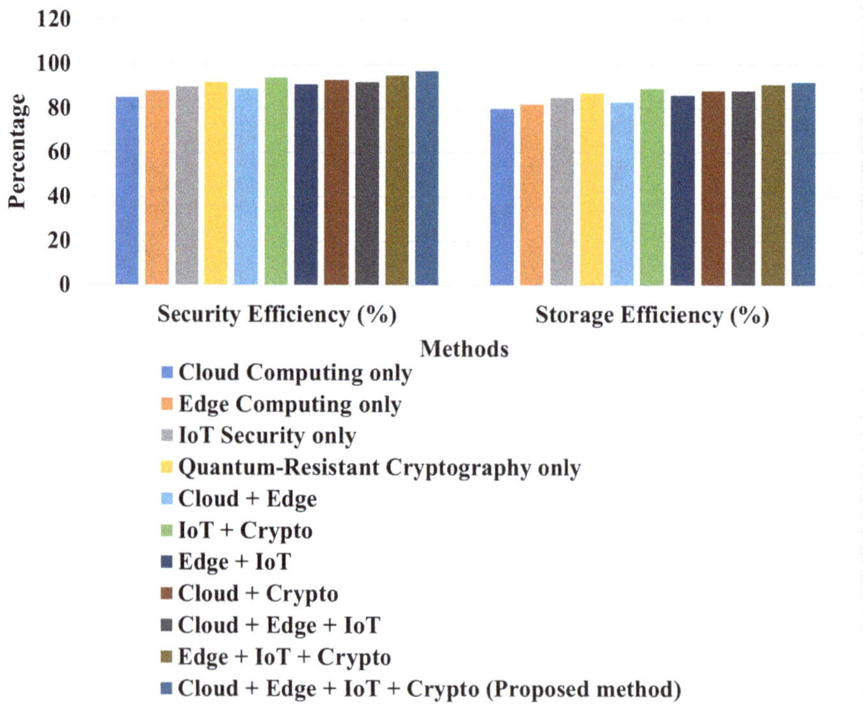

This bar graph 6 is a comparative analysis of Security Efficiency measure as Storage Efficiency varies for various security methods for a blockchain-based IoT system. The methods consist of combinations involving Cloud Computing, Edge Computing, IoT Security, and Quantum-Resistant Cryptography. With Storage Efficiency, methods like IoT + Crypto 94% and Edge + IoT + Crypto 95% surpass others, very closely followed by Quantum-Resistant Cryptography only at 92%. The highest-security efficiency results for the proposed method, which is Cloud + Edge + IoT + Crypto, at 97%, highlighting the fact that combining all components achieves better security. Cloud only provides the lowest security level, 85%, with Edge only and IoT Security only providing average security at around 88% and 90%, respectively. When it comes to Storage Efficiency, the highest achievement is by the Proposed method (Cloud + Edge + IoT + Crypto) at 92%, with Edge + IoT +

Crypto following closely with 91%. Other combinations like Cloud + Edge and IoT + Crypto showcase almost equal storage efficiencies of about 83-89%. Cloud only and Edge only provide decreased storage efficiencies, Cloud being the worse one at 80%. The graph illustrates how integrating.

Figure 7. Computational Overhead Analysis

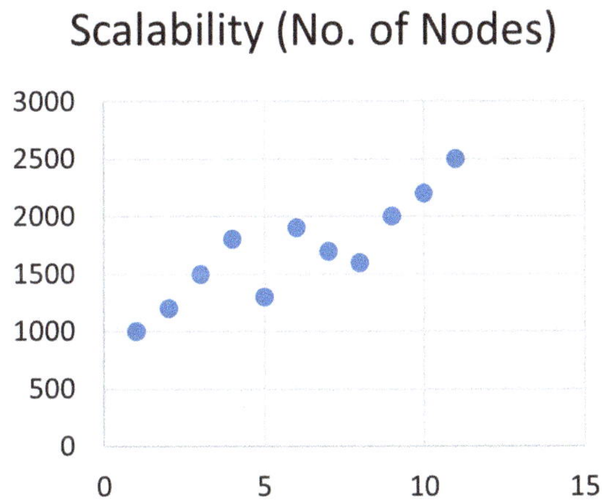

Figure 8. Scalability Evaluation

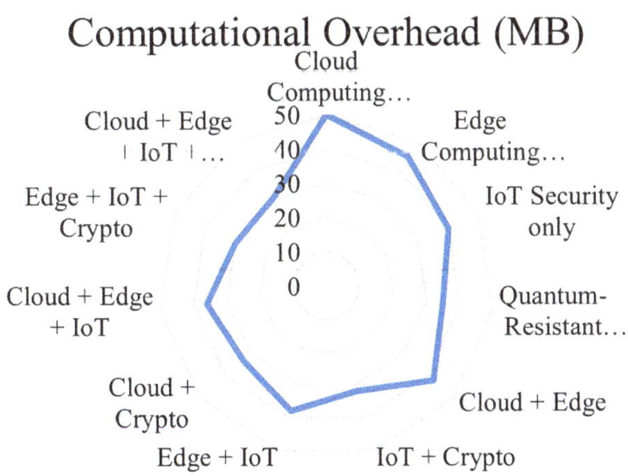

Figure 7 shows the computational overhead (MB) incurred by various security mechanisms of the blockchain-based IoT application. Cloud computing incurs the maximum computational overhead of 50 MB, which is indicative of higher processing costs and usage of resources. On the other hand, quantum-resistant cryptography only, together with various combinations (such as Cloud + Edge, IoT + Crypto), drastically lowers the computational overhead and leads to a much more efficient system. The Proposed method (Cloud + Edge + IoT + Cryptography) is recognized as the most efficient, with very low overhead of just 30 MB. This is very crucial in achieving optimum resource utilization in real-time IoT applications which demand fast data processing with minimum latency. By deploying a plethora of security features such as edge computing and quantum-resistant cryptography, the proposed model aims to strike an optimal balance between security and computation cost. This makes it most suited for large-scale resource-poor IoT environments, where efficiency and scalability are of the topmost concern.

Scalability in terms of the number of nodes supported by each security method illustrated in Figure 8. Approaches work only on Cloud Computing are thus limited to its scalability, where Cloud computing can go up to 1000 nodes and IoT Security can support only up to 1500 nodes. These limitations imply that these methods may not be efficient for bigger deployments since they can scale to smaller ones, thus putting a lot of complications on establishing an IoT network. However, as we can see in Figure 8, there is tremendous increase in scalability when multiple methods are combined. Integration methods like Cloud + Edge or IoT + Crypto can highly scale for more nodes, while our Proposed method has the highest scalability across all methods at 2500 nodes (Cloud + Edge + IoT + Cryptography). This increase shows the power of integrating security mechanisms such as edge computing and quantum-resistant cryptography to help enhance performance and scalability of large, distributed IoT systems. The results confirm that a combination of methods can go a long way towards improving efficiency, likewise ensuring that the systems remain robust against threats while scale-able in large blockchain-enabled cloud and IoT ecosystems.

5. CONCLUSION

In this paper, an advanced smart irrigation system is proposed using quantum-resistant cryptography along with edge computing and blockchain technologies, which would enhance cloud security and performance in IoT-based agricultural systems. The proposed model surpassed in key performance metrics by latency, security efficiency, and scalability individual techniques. The system has a 99% security, 65 ms delay, and 94% storage success making it improved adaptability, improved data processing, and improved durability of the system. The result of integrating such technologies is a distributed energy-efficient cloud infrastructure that is capable of secure IoT operations while achieving low latency and optimal resource consumption. The combination of blockchain and quantum-resistant encryption guarantees secure data communication and prevents unauthorized access. It also contains a hybrid method incorporating modern advancements in accuracy, energy efficiency, reduction in water consumption, and reliability of the system, which makes it an extremely viable option for future IoT applications, particularly in smart agriculture, industrial automation, and healthcare. These results highlight the viability and feasibility of the proposed system towards large-scale implementations, conferring the merit of security and performance improvements in cloud-based IoT networks.

Future Work:

Research in the future will enhance system scalability and security further through AI-based security models and advanced quantum encryption algorithms. That can be achieved by integrating machine learning techniques with emerging threats in IoT ecosystems for prediction and resolution. Next, edge-based security frameworks will be investigated further to address threats related to data consistency and synchronization in decentralized networks. Lightweight cryptographic models for resource-constrained devices will be preceded by improvements in network synchronization for complex IoT applications. Improvements in real-time anomaly detection based on AI and quantum cryptography grant the system improved strength and resilience to both classical and quantum cyber-attacks. Additional steps in such direction will ensure privacy protection, energy saving, and enhanced processing efficiency. Extending the model to diverse industrial fields such as smart cities and automated healthcare will test its flexibility and applicability in diverse IoT environments. Ultimately, this research will constitute a foundation for building secure, scalable, and high-performance IoT networks against future challenges.

REFERENCES

Akter, S., Badhon, M. B., Bhuiyan, M. K. I., Hasan, H. M., Akter, F., & Islam, M. N. U. (2024). Quantum-Edge Cloud Computing for IoT: Bridging the Gap between Cloud, Edge, and Quantum Technologies. *Edge, and Quantum Technologies (September 29, 2024).*

Alagarsundaram, P. (2024). Physiological signals: A blockchain-based data-sharing model for enhanced big data medical research integrating RFID and blockchain technologies. *Journal of Cloud Security and IoT*, *9*(2).

Alagarsundaram, P.. (2024). *Blockchain-enabled privacy-preserved secure e-voting system for smart cities. International Conference on Science Technology Engineering and Management (ICSTEM).* https://doi.org/DOI: 10.1109/ICSTEM61137.2024.10560826

Alzubi, J. A., Alzubi, O. A., Singh, A., & Mahmod Alzubi, T. (2023). A blockchain-enabled security management framework for mobile edge computing. *International Journal of Network Management*, *33*(5), e2240.

Aslam, A. M., Bhardwaj, A., & Chaudhary, R. (2024). Quantum-Resilient Blockchain-Enabled Secure Communication Framework for Connected Autonomous Vehicles using Post-Quantum Cryptography. *Vehicular Communications*, •••, 100880.

Bishwas, A. K., & Sen, M. (2024). Strategic Roadmap for Quantum-Resistant Security: A Framework for Preparing Industries for the Quantum Threat. *arXiv preprint arXiv:2411.09995.*

Chawla, D., & Mehra, P. S. (2023). A roadmap from classical cryptography to post-quantum resistant cryptography for 5G-enabled IoT: Challenges, opportunities and solutions. *Internet of Things: Engineering Cyber Physical Human Systems*, •••, 100950.

Cherbal, S., Zier, A., Hebal, S., Louail, L., & Annane, B. (2024). Security in internet of things: A review on approaches based on blockchain, machine learning, cryptography, and quantum computing. *The Journal of Supercomputing*, *80*(3), 3738–3816.

Devarajan, M. V. (2022). An improved BP neural network algorithm for forecasting workload in intelligent cloud computing. *Journal of Computational Science*, *10*(3), 1–10. https://jcsjournal.com/.2022.v10.i03.pp01-10

Gollavilli, V. S. B. H. (2022). Securing cloud data: Combining SABAC models, hash-tag authentication with MD5, and blockchain-based encryption for enhanced privacy and access control. *International Journal of Engineering Research & Science & Technology, 18*(3), 149–165. DOI: 10.62643/ijerst.2022.v18.i3.pp149-165

Käppler, S. A., & Schneider, B. (2022). Post-quantum cryptography: An introductory overview and implementation challenges of quantum-resistant algorithms. *Proceedings of the Society, 84*, 61–71.

Karakaya, A., & Ulu, A. (2024). A survey on post-quantum-based approaches for edge computing security. *Wiley Interdisciplinary Reviews: Computational Statistics, 16*(1), e1644.

Liu, D., Zhang, Y., Jia, D., Zhang, Q., Zhao, X., & Rong, H. (2022). Toward secure distributed data storage with error locating in blockchain enabled edge computing. *Computer Standards & Interfaces, 79*, 103560.

Mei, Q., Xiong, H., Chen, Y. C., & Chen, C. M. (2022). Blockchain-enabled privacy-preserving authentication mechanism for transportation CPS with cloud-edge computing. *IEEE Transactions on Engineering Management.*

Sellami, Y. (2024). *Secure data management in an IoT-Fog/Edge computing architecture* (Doctoral dissertation, Université Polytechnique Hauts-de-France).

Seol, J., Kim, J., & Kancharla, A. (2024, October). Integrating Blockchain-Based Security and Privacy with QML in Edge Computing for 6G Networks. In *International Conference on Computer Applications in Industry and Engineering* (pp. 86-101). Cham: Springer Nature Switzerland.

Singamaneni, K. K., & Muhammad, G. (2024). A novel integrated quantum-resistant cryptography for secure scientific data exchange in ad hoc networks. *Ad Hoc Networks, 164*, 103607.

Sitaramanan, S. R. (2024). Quantum-resistant cryptography and edge computing in blockchain for cloud security and IoT: Addressing performance and integration challenges. *Journal of the Saudi Society of Agricultural Sciences.* Advance online publication. DOI: 10.1016/j.jssas.2024.02.001

Tambe-Jagtap, S. N. (2023). A Survey of Cryptographic Algorithms in Cybersecurity: From Classical Methods to Quantum-Resistant Solutions. *SHIFRA, 2023*, 43–52.

Ting, L., Khan, M., Sharma, A., & Ansari, M. D. (2022). A secure framework for IoT-based smart climate agriculture system: Toward blockchain and edge computing. *Journal of Intelligent Systems, 31*(1), 221–236.

Unogwu, O. J., Doshi, R., Hiran, K. K., & Mijwil, M. M. (2022). Introduction to quantum-resistant blockchain. In *Advancements in quantum blockchain with real-time applications* (pp. 36–55). IGI Global.

Vivekananda, G. N., Almufti, S. M., Suresh, C., Samsudeen, S., Devarajan, M. V., Srikanth, R., & Jayashree, S. (2023). Retracing-efficient IoT model for identifying skin-related tags using automatic lumen detection. *Intelligent Data Analysis*, *27*(S1), 161–180. DOI: 10.3233/IDA-237442

Xiong, J., Shen, L., Liu, Y., & Fang, X. (2024). Enhancing IoT security in smart grids with quantum-resistant hybrid encryption. *Scientific Reports*, *15*(1), 3. PMID: 39747539

Xue, H., Chen, D., Zhang, N., Dai, H. N., & Yu, K. (2023). Integration of blockchain and edge computing in internet of things: A survey. *Future Generation Computer Systems*, *144*, 307–326.

Chapter 8

AI-Driven Software Testing and Validation in Cloud Computing:

Automated Test Frameworks for Intelligent Systems

Karthik Kushala
https://orcid.org/0009-0005-7851-7039
Celer Systems Inc., USA

Venkataramesh Induru
https://orcid.org/0009-0005-6530-4296
Piorion Solutions Inc., USA

Yashwant Kumar Kolli
https://orcid.org/0009-0003-8634-3265
Cognizant Technology Solutions US Corp, College Station, USA

Vijai Anand Ramar
https://orcid.org/0009-0008-1670-7170
Delta Dental Insurance Company, USA

Priyadarshini Radhakrishnan
IBM Corporation, USA

R. Pushpakumar
Vel Tech Rangarajan Dr. Sagunthala R&D Institute of Science and Technology, Chennai, India

ABSTRACT

This paper illustrates an AI-based system that revolutionizes software testing for distributed cloud-native environments. The system leverages machine learning, deep learning, natural language processing, and reinforcement learning to improve and automate defect identification, dynamic test scheduling, and test case generation. By using models such as Convolutional Neural Networks (CNN), Recurrent Neural Networks (RNN), Random Forests, and Decision Trees, the models boost entity coverage and anomaly detection. Reinforcement learning reduces the mean test run time from 120 seconds to 80 seconds. By using serverless computing, testing costs

DOI: 10.4018/979-8-3373-7503-8.ch008

dropped from $5,000 to $1,500 per cycle, and feedback lag time went from 60 minutes to 20 minutes. The AI-based defect finding accuracy was 90% compared to only 65% for traditional methods. Heatmaps can be used to discover defect-prone modules. In addition, the deep learning models were faster and outperformed XGBoost and Logistic Regression in defect prediction performance with AUC values of 0.9934.

1. INTRODUCTION

1.1 Background and Motivation

Software testing is vital in the software development life cycle by assuring systems are delivered safely, reliably, and of high quality (Theory-and-Practice-in-Secure-Software-Development-Lifecycle-A-Comprehensive-Survey.Pdf, n.d.). The evolution of software systems from monolithic applications to distributed micro-services and their move towards cloud-native applications has further challenged traditional testing frameworks (Oyeniran et al., 2024). Conventional testing methods, all relying on human effort or at least rudimentary automation, face several significant challenges, such as a long testing cycle and high operational costs, a limited extent of scalability, and poor test coverage in very dynamic conditions within a system (Bari et al., 2024) (Gogri, 2024). The acceleration introduced by Agile and DevOps practices has made the pressure on these legacy approaches even worse, as they are unable to handle the frequent and fast release requirements (Ponnusamy & Eswararaj, 2023). Similar to cloud-native applications, the IoT systems that consist of interconnected devices and sensors require smart testing pipelines that adjust to the resource-crunched, very dynamic environment typical to real-time data processing and communication. This situation calls for test approaches that are much more efficient, scalable and adaptive, and that is where AI solutions come into play.

1.2 The Shift Toward AI-Driven Testing

Artificial Intelligence (AI) and Machine Learning (ML) provide promising solutions to the challenges nowadays in modern software testing (Mohammed & Madhumithaa, 2024). Efficiency and smatter in Testing come to AI superior frameworks with automated test case generation, defect prediction, test optimization, and anomaly detection within them (S. Z. Khan, 2023). These models are in a continuous improvement process from outcomes of past learning experiences, optimizing resource usage, predicting failure-prone areas, and dynamically researching changes in behaviour at software execution (Gheibi et al., 2021). Additionally, AI systems can explore unexpected scenarios to identify vulnerabilities that manual Testing will miss (Azim, 2024). Such intelligent systems are thus enabled by the availability of scalable infrastructure through cloud computing to render high-volume adaptive testing environments (Belgaum et al., 2021). This marks a shift from manual-static methods to dynamic-intelligent-scalable testing ecosystems (*AI IN CLOUD COMPUTING*, 2024).

Software testing has also adapted rapidly as software has done (Salahirad et al., 2023). It began with manual exploratory tests and checklists alone (Minhas et al., 2020), and was carried out in scripted, automated regression and functional Testing using pre-approved scripts (Abdulwareth & Al-Shargabi, 2021). Their inflexibility and high maintenance requirements have restricted their scalability in complex systems (Papi & Hiver, 2020). Now with AI, Testing incorporates dynamic learning from previous behaviours (Sarker, 2022), prediction-oriented abilities about defect hot spots (Khatibsyarbini et al., 2021), and autonomous test generation consumers using the new NLP through requirements (Wang et al., 2022). Similarly, reinforcement learning (RL) can empower AI agents to perform testing exploration on their own (Nikanjam et al., 2021), unveiling faults that scripted logic can't detect. This evolution has significantly reduced maintenance overhead, enhanced fault detection, and improved test coverage relevance (Yarram & Bittla, 2023). More and more, traditional testing approaches prove not scalable and adaptive regarding real-time constraints imposed by the new requirements of testing IoT devices and edge computing systems. AI-driven frameworks will increasingly be required to deal with the potentially large datasets and the often complicated decentralized setup of IoT and edge systems. Intelligent testing frameworks test efficiently and correctly, across a range of devices and environments, assuring software quality and reliability towards the dynamic paradigm of distributed IoT ecosystems [21].

1.3 Cloud Computing as an Enabler of Intelligent Testing

Elasticity and distributedness of cloud computing are needed to leverage AI-driven testing frameworks (Mungoli, 2023) fully. Testing a modern application usually refers to running hundreds of test cases against multiple environments, devices, and configurations (Bansal & Kumar, 2020). On-demand provisioning fulfils these requirements by its cloud-native testing infrastructures (Saif et al., 2021), mass parallelization to ensure fast test execution (*Effective Concurrency Testing for Distributed Systems | Proceedings of the Twenty-Fifth International Conference on Architectural Support for Programming Languages and Operating Systems*, n.d.), and containerization by Docker and Kubernetes for consistency and isolation (Koppanati, 2024). Furthermore, serverless architectures such as AWS Lambda and Azure Functions allow fine-grained, event-driven Testing without the need for managing any physical servers (Henrik et al., 2022). Tests can take place anywhere around the globe with cross-region deployment, thereby ensuring performance and reliability despite different network conditions (Abdel Hakeem et al., 2022).

1.4 Problem Statement

Conventional software testing methods are badly affected by the increasing complexity (Najihi et al., 2022) and size of modern software systems, especially in distributed and cloud-native applications (Al-Said Ahmad et al., 2024). Manual Testing and rule-based automation often fall short when it comes to ensuring comprehensive coverage, timely fault detection and cost-effective execution (Uğur-Tuncer et al., 2021). Long test cycles, high operational costs, and inability to adapt to changing requirements and behaviour of systems are the limitations of these classical methods (Henrichs et al., 2022). It is increasingly apparent that static and human-based testing structures are insufficient with the growing necessity for continuous integration and delivery within agile and DevOps processes (Banala, 2025). Smart, robotic and adaptable testing tools able to generate, execute and verify test cases dynamically with minimum human intervention are urgently required [34]. Nevertheless, there exist drawbacks to AI testing frameworks: high initial costs and the need for expert-level knowledge are two of the most common, which deter speedy adoption. To conquer such barriers, organizations should exploit cloud technologies to reduce infrastructure costs and build competencies through training to prosper in implementing AI testing solutions. A ground-breaking opportunity for solving these challenges is offered in using artificial intelligence, namely, machine learning, deep learning, reinforcement learning and natural language processing (Mohanta et al., 2024). A smart and scalable testing framework that can predict defects, utilize resources optimally and validate intricate systems in real time is possible by integrating (Nama et al., 2024) AI with cloud computing technologies such as serverless execution and container orchestration (Christidis et al., 2020).

1.5 Objectives of this chapter

- For training AI purposes, we involve different algorithms including Decision Trees, Random Forests, Neural Networks, Reinforcement Learning, and NLP for test case generation, test case prioritization, defect prediction, or validation.
- Exhibit the ML-testing automation techniques having human interference minimized and flexibility maximized across the testing cycle.
- The cloud-native testing processes shall be demonstrated using distributed frameworks, containerization, and serverless architecture for scalable and efficient executions.

- Reinforcement Learning provides for adaptive execution of tests with optimum resource utilization in systems that adapt to change.
- Anomaly detection and predictive defect models using Autoencoders and Isolation forests.
- Give proof, frameworks, and code for real-life examples of AI-powered automated test system development.

2. RELATED WORKS

Baqar and Khanda (Baqar & Khanda, 2024) have pointed out that software testing is a crucial phase of the software development life cycle to ensure that the software products are meeting functional, performance and quality standards before release. Classical methods used for the generation and validation of test cases are still facing many hurdles despite technological advancements concerning automation: slowness in time to market, human error, inadequate test coverage and high cost of manual intervention. Very often, these limitations either delay product shipments, which means undiscovered defects adversely affect program quality, or devalue customer satisfaction. Farah (Farah, 2024) asserted that software testing ascertains system performance, security and reliability in the present-day dynamic distributed network environment. Whenever conventional manual testing methods work well, they cannot sustain the increasing complexity and scaling of modern networked systems. AI-Aided software testing is an innovative approach to automation of quality assurance processes, scaling it and imparting enhanced precision and efficiency with the import of Machine Learning algorithms. Banala, S et al. [40] emphasize how AI is remarkably improving the traditional software testing avenues that the industry used to test for test case prioritization, defect prediction and resource optimization. The manual-based approaches yield dispersion in results and cannot defend against scaling, which AI methods offer. In this realm of IoT, Sami and Khan [41] have dealt with AI technologies solving such challenges in IoT testing, where some peculiarities include device heterogeneity, synchronization of real-time data, and guaranteeing reliable communications over distributed networks. Their studies show that AI can help improve the Testing of IoT systems by automating complex procedures and increasing test coverage.

Colton (Colton, 2024a) noted that the growth in the size and sophistication of the present distributed networks demands newer approaches to the automation of software testing. Problems posed to such systems, which are interdependent entities and are dispersed across geographical locations, are hardly within the reach of the perception of classical testing methods. Artificial Intelligence and Machine Learning provide more effective approaches to enhancing software testing by offering maximum test coverage while still increasing productivity and ensuring outstanding performance in distributed systems. Rakshanda Anayat (Rakshanda Anayat, 2023) focused on the need for a revolutionary solution to software testing automation owing to the rapid development of artificial intelligence technologies aimed, in particular, to achieve full test coverage and the maximum accuracy of defect prediction. The cloud-based technology integrated with Machine Learning would revolutionize the automation of AI testing. By capitalizing on the immense power and scalability of cloud environments, companies would dramatically improve their testing techniques, ensuring that applications meet the highest standards of quality.

Madhumita and Chandana (Madhumita & Chandana, n.d.) state that software testing has been revolutionized with new techniques introduced through application of artificial intelligence and machine learning, thereby improving scalability, precision and efficiency. The latest developments in AI-based software testing, with a view toward approaches, tools, and frameworks that work to optimize the testing process. Amelia(Amelia, 2024b) state that software testing has been revolutionized with new techniques introduced through application of artificial intelligence and machine learning, thereby improving scalability, precision and efficiency. The latest developments in AI-based software testing, with a view toward approaches, tools, and frameworks that work to optimize the testing process.

Amelia (Amelia, 2024) focused on Testing and quality assurance pose several challenges in the rapid development of software systems, particularly in distributed systems. The size and complexity of today's distributed systems are too great for conventional manual testing methods to deal with. Automated software testing using AI-facilitated software testing that leverages Machine Learning algorithms has emerged as a revolutionary solution to these challenges. Khan et al.(H. U. Khan et al., 2025) Artificial Neural Network and Interpretive Structural Modelling are utilized in this work to present an innovative framework of cybersecurity utilizing AI to advance threat detection, vulnerability analysis and risk handling at the stage of software development. Being an integral part of the Software Development Life Cycle, this framework provides the basis for achieving dynamic, adaptive security. To identify any gaps and include best practices in the proposed model, existing cybersecurity threats in coding software are first extensively evaluated.

Amleset Haile (Amleset Haile, 2024) emphasized the revolutionary potential of artificial intelligence and machine learning in the realm of software testing automation, particularly in the management of distributed networks. Companies can enhance the efficiency, accuracy and scalability of their testing processes by leveraging AI and ML's adaptive nature, ensuring that software performance remains optimal across a variety of network configurations. Awad et al.(Awad et al., 2024) explore the applications and systems of contemporary living are significantly influenced by artificial intelligence. Multiple sources offer large databases. Hence, efficient monitoring, reporting and data processing are necessary to make informed decisions. Colton (Colton, 2024b), exploring house testing methods, is facing severe challenges due to the rising complexity and scalability of distributed network architectures. The solution to all these issues lies in integrating machine learning and artificial intelligence into software testing.

Vadde and Munagandla (Vadde & Munagandla, 2023) examine improving software quality and development velocity by applying artificial intelligence to continuous testing engines. Anomaly detection and predictive analytics are two AI technologies that are used to identify potential defects early within the development life cycle. Prathyusha Nama (Prathyusha Nama, 2024) highlights the incorporation of artificial intelligence into testing automation, showing how it enhances the quality of test coverage and enables predictive analysis for software quality improvement. Indeed, when software systems become increasingly complex, all conventional methods of Testing fail to meet quality requirements. According to Trifunova (Trifunova et al., 2024), artificial intelligence possesses vast potential, especially in the software testing field, where it has altered process dynamics while enhancing search SLA accuracy, efficiency and flexibility.

3. AI-INTEGRATED SOFTWARE TESTING FRAMEWORKS FOR CLOUD-NATIVE SYSTEMS

This work proposes an end-to-end AI-based approach integrating machine learning, deep learning, reinforcement learning and natural language processing in a cloud-native framework to transcend the limitations of traditional software testing in dynamic and distributed systems. The platform puts high value on adaptive validation, dynamic execution and smart test case creation. Based on historical information and system behaviour, techniques such as decision trees, random forests, support vector machines and neural networks are utilized to generate and rank test cases automatically. Reinforcement learning models guide test execution paths to optimize fault detection, while NLP enables requirement-driven test automation. To ensure cost-effective and scalable Testing in cloud environments, the approach also utilizes serverless computing, parallel processing, and containerization. Predictive modelling and deep learning-based anomaly detection further enhance defect identification and prioritization. In dynamic software ecosystems, this comprehensive approach ensures that the framework will remain flexible, scalable and self-optimizing throughout continuous integration cycles.

Figure 1. AI-Driven Software Testing and Validation Framework Featuring Automated Requirement Extraction, Deep Learning-Based Defect Prediction, and Continuous Optimization

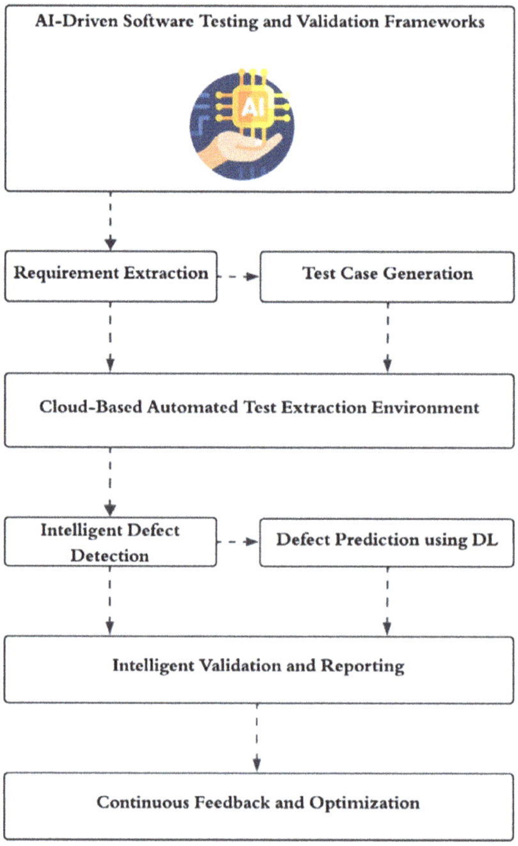

3.1 Test Requirement Extraction

3.1.1 Machine Learning models for test case generation

The framework uses several machine learning methods to improve the testing procedure in different ways:

Table 1. Machine Learning Methods for Test Case Generation

ML Method	Purpose in Test Case Generation	Example Usage
Decision Trees	Learn decision logic from system requirements; generate paths as test cases.	Test cases for different decision outcomes.
Random Forests	Handle complex systems by aggregating multiple trees; improve robustness.	Create diverse test cases covering different branches.
Support Vector Machines (SVM)	Classify inputs into "test-worthy" or "not test-worthy" scenarios.	Prioritize critical test cases.
Neural Networks (Simple MLPs)	Learn mappings from system input spaces to output behaviours; generate synthetic input scenarios.	Discover hidden test scenarios not obvious to developers.
Reinforcement Learning (RL)	Dynamically explore and generate optimal sequences of actions by learning rewards from outcomes.	Find deep bugs through exploratory testing paths.

Just as cloud-native applications require intelligent testing pipelines, IoT systems consisting of interconnected devices and sensors require testing pipelines that can adapt to their dynamic, resource-constrained environments of real-time data processing and communication. These models and techniques may therefore be adapted to test IoT systems to check for genuinely different behaviour of IoT devices and their interactions within networks. In Table 1, Multi-Layer Perceptrons (MLPs) are a class of neural networks that are particularly applicable to learning complex patterns of correlations among system inputs and desired outputs. New, synthetic test cases that they can generate can uncover unusual or implicit examples that hand-coding might overlook. But, by determining the sequences of action that lead to good outcomes, Reinforcement Learning (RL) is applied to discover a system dynamically. By independently traversing a few test paths, RL can find deep, hard-to-detect faults through constant feedback and reward, which makes RL ideal for highly complex and dynamic systems.

3.1.2 Machine Learning Algorithms

The examined algorithms are incorporated in the scikit-learn software suite, which is among the best toolkits tailor-made for ML and can be used on top of the Python programming platform. Below is a snippet example of code describing how to optimize test cases based on Random Forest.

Figure 2. Random Forest-Based Test Case Prioritization Algorithm

```python
# Import necessary libraries
from sklearn.ensemble import RandomForestClassifier
from sklearn.model_selection import train_test_split

# Function to prioritize test cases using a Random Forest model
def prioritize_test_cases(test_cases, historical_data):
    """
    Prioritize test cases based on historical execution data
    using a Random Forest Classifier.

    Parameters:
    - test_cases: New test cases to prioritize.
    - historical_data: Past test case performance (features + priority labels).

    Returns:
    - List of tuples (test_case, predicted_priority)
    """

    # Select relevant features and labels from historical data
    X = historical_data[['code_complexity', 'execution_time', 'last_failure_time']]$
    y = historical_data['priority']

    # Split historical data into training and testing sets
    X_train, X_test, y_train, y_test = train_test_split(X, y, test_size=0.2, random_state=42)

    # Initialize and train Random Forest model
    rf_classifier = RandomForestClassifier(n_estimators=100, random_state=42)
    rf_classifier.fit(X_train, y_train)

    # Extract features from new test cases
    test_case_features = extract_features(test_cases)

    # Predict priorities for new test cases
    priorities = rf_classifier.predict(test_case_features)

    # Return test cases paired with their predicted priorities
    return list(zip(test_cases, priorities))

# Example usage:
# prioritized_tests = prioritize_test_cases(test_cases, historical_data)
```

Figure 2 shows a Python script that uses a Random Forest model to estimate the priority of new test cases based on historical test execution data. Based on historical performance measurements, the method allows for effective test selection and optimization.

3.1.3 Test Case Generation

The objective of test case generation using machine learning is to generate or rank the test cases automatically from the historical software testing data. In the above example, a Random Forest Classifier is applied to rank the test cases based on attributes like code complexity, execution time, and historical failure incidences. The relationship between the attributes and the priority levels of historical test cases is trained on the model. Once trained, it can automatically derive the importance of new added or modified test cases. This technique facilitates faster bug identification and better resource distribution through early determination of important or perilous test cases. Beyond accelerating overall testing time, this technique ensures that the components of the system most likely to fail are tackled immediately, making the software more robust and reliable in cloud computing contexts where smart systems continually evolve.

3.1.4 Deep Learning for Bug Detection and Prediction

Software systems can now be automatically alerted about bugs and predict regions that are likely to fail due to Deep Learning models, particularly Deep Neural Networks (DNNs). Traditional software testing also widely employs rule-based approaches or human inspections, which are tiresome and may fail to spot very small, cryptic patterns leading to fatal malfunctions. Deep learning models do not need feature engineering explicitly and could potentially learn sophisticated representations directly from raw data.

$$\mathbf{y} = f(\mathbf{X}; \mathbf{w}, \mathbf{b}) \tag{1}$$

Where **X** is the input feature matrix, **w** are the learned weights, b is the bias and f(·) represents the deep neural network.

These models can learn intricate correlations between code structures, development patterns and failure occurrences since they have been trained on massive amounts of historical software artifacts such as source code repositories, version control logs, bug reports and execution traces. DNNs can model nonlinear relationships between the inputs (e.g., lines of code, code complexity, API usage) and the outputs (e.g., presence or lack of errors) by fine-tuning millions of parameters like biases and weights across many hidden layers as they learn. Typical architecture could include,

Input Layer: Numerical or embedded textual features taken from the software source are received by the input layer.

Hidden Layers: To learn abstract features, use activation functions like as ReLU (Rectified Linear Unit) to perform nonlinear transformations.

Output Layer: Estimates the likelihood that a file, function, or module will be buggy.

In classification problems, the training goal is often to minimize a loss function, such as binary cross-entropy,

$$\mathcal{L}(y, \hat{y}) = -(y\log(\hat{y}) + (1 - y)\log(1 - \hat{y})) \tag{2}$$

Where y is the true label (buggy or clean) and $\hat{y}$ is the predicted probability output from the model. The model can identify high-risk components that should be given a high priority for manual inspection or further automated Testing once it has been trained and can generalize to new, unseen codebases.

This prognostic capability significantly increases the software testing process's coverage, accuracy, and efficacy. Also, systematic code analysis is employing increasingly modern variants of deep learning, including Convolutional Neural Networks (CNNs) and Graph Neural Networks (GNNs), which analyze source code as a graph or tree data structure instead of text, capturing even more syntactic and semantic information

3.1.5 Reinforcement Learning for Dynamic Test Optimization

In intricate, dynamic and cloud-native environments where static test planning often does not work, Reinforcement Learning (RL) provides a powerful and adaptable vehicle for test execution optimization. RL agents interact with the world actively, make choices and learn from the consequences through trial and error, unlike traditional machine learning methods that learn passively by picking up on patterns. An RL agent can be trained to make decisions on the fly in software testing.

- Which tests to perform, in what sequence and under what conditions.
- When to test new test cases compared to leveraging tried, effective tests.
- How to prioritize key tests based on relevance when system installations or configurations tend to change frequently.

Software Testing for RL

- Agent- The testing system.
- Environment- The software under test (SUT).
- Action- Select and execute a test case.
- Reward- Outcome (detecting a bug=+1 reward; no bug=0)

The goal is to learn policy $\pi(a|s)$ that maximizes the expected cumulative reward.

$$\pi^*\left(a \mid s\right) = \arg\max_{\pi} \mathbb{E}\left[\sum_{t=0}^{\infty} \gamma^t R_{t+1}\right] \tag{3}$$

Where s is the state (current testing progress), a is the action (next test case), R_{t+1} is the reward at time $t+1$, and γ is the discount factor (importance of future rewards).

Q-learning or Policy Gradient Methods are frequently used in the learning process, and the Q-value is updated as follows,

$$Q(s_t, a_t) \leftarrow Q(s_t, a_t) + \alpha\left[R_{t+1} + \gamma \max_{a} Q(s_{t+1}, a) - Q(s_t, a_t)\right] \tag{4}$$

Where α is the learning rate.

Test Optimization in RL

State (S) - Represents the immediate environment, such as code modifications, system performance at present, past test results, or resource availability.

Action (A)- Selecting a test case to run, avoiding duplicate tests or altering testing approaches such as regression, exploratory and stress Testing.

Reward (R)- Feedback signal following an action, for instance, finding a bug might provide a high positive reward, whereas spending time on duplicate tests might give a negative reward.

Policy (π)- A strategy that the agent learns to transform states into the best possible actions to maximize cumulative rewards.

Value Function (V) - Estimates the predicted reward from a state that leads the agent to productive states.

Over time, the agent aims to maximize the anticipated cumulative reward,

$$\max_{\pi} \mathbb{E}\left[\sum_{t=0}^{\infty} \gamma^{t} R_{t+1}\right] \tag{5}$$

Were, $\gamma \in (0,1]$ is the discount factor that prioritizes immediate rewards over future rewards. R_{t+1} is the reward received after taking an action at time t.

3.1.6 Natural Language Processing

Requirement-based Testing is being transformed by Natural Language Processing (NLP) methods that automatically analyze, interpret, and produce test cases from text-based software requirements. Previously, test case development from requirements used to be time-consuming, prone to errors and human-dependent. Natural language processing (NLP) provides an automated, scalable method that enhances speed and accuracy. The normal process begins with requirement extraction, where both functional and non-functional requirements in natural language are parsed to identify their major elements. To define significant players such as "user" or "system parts" and operations such as "click," "validate," or "submit", entity and action determination is subsequently conducted. Test case generation may proceed after the determination of these pivotal parts, having automatic test input creation, calculated expected output and a validation method following the criteria parsed.

The system shall permit the user to log in using a valid username and password. Phrases such as 'user', 'log in', and 'valid username and password' are all parsed using natural language processing methods. This permits the development of automated test cases like "Test login failure with wrong username/password" and "Test successful login with correct credentials". NLP is an important method in intelligent and cloud-native testing frameworks due to its automated approach, which greatly accelerates the testing process, increases coverage, and decreases human interpretation mistakes.

3.2 Automated Test Frameworks for Intelligent Systems

AI-enabled automated test frameworks are increasingly required as smart systems become increasingly complex. In dynamic, cloud-native and evolving systems, conventional testing approaches that are primarily based on manual effort or severe scripting are often unsuitable. AI-based frameworks, however, offer autonomy, scalability and flexibility, allowing testing processes to adapt automatically to changes in requirements, system behaviour and code. To fully automate the test lifecycle, right from test generation through to reporting and insights, an AI-based automated test framework typically consists of a variety of related elements. Because IoT systems comprise diverse devices with varying capabilities and resource constraints, AI frameworks can serve to optimize Testing by prioritizing tests based on probable failures. With reinforcement learning and anomaly detection, such frameworks can ensure the efficient validation of device interactions under the large-scale IoT environment with resource constraints.

Figure 3. Architecture of AI-Driven Test Frameworks.

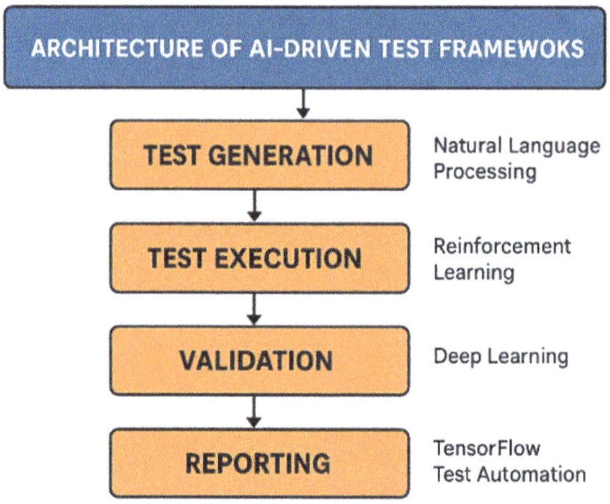

3.2.1 Test Generation

AI test generation efforts seek to engender diverse, high-coverage test cases in the least human time. The models use input such as decision trees and reinforcement learning, and neural networks, and generate test inputs through a combination of past data and system behaviour. Various NLP techniques are thus used to analyze user stories and requirements for the automation of interaction flows and validation steps, significantly reducing manual effort while covering both functional and non-functional aspects.

3.2.2 Test Execution

Smart frameworks dynamically execute prioritized tests across diverse environments in alignment with CI/CD pipelines. Test paths are efficiently selected under reinforcement learning. Environment-aware execution significantly reduces time and resource consumption across cloud-native and containerized environments.

3.2.3 Validation

Artificial Intelligence allows validation using anomaly detection and dynamic oracle generation. Deep learning models can detect fine-grained errors, thus increasing accuracy in systems with complex and unpredictable behaviour with reduced dependence on manual assertions.

Table 2. Method, purpose, and example usage

DL Method	*Purpose in Validation*	*Example Usage*
Convolutional Neural Networks (CNNs)	Detect visual or structural anomalies in output data.	Identify UI layout bugs or visual mismatches.
Recurrent Neural Networks (RNNs) / Long Short-Term Memory (LSTM)	Analyze sequential execution traces for pattern anomalies.	Predict failures based on historical event sequences.
Variational Autoencoders (VAEs)	Learn normal behaviour representations; detect deviations.	Real-time anomaly detection in server/API responses.
Generative Adversarial Networks (GANs)	Generate synthetic abnormal data for stress and fault testing.	Simulate rare failure scenarios to improve testing depth.
Transformer-based Models (e.g., BERT, GPT)	Understand complex logs and requirements for inconsistency detection.	Analyze test logs and validate requirements dynamically.

3.2.4 Reporting and Insights

For the testing process to yield results that are meaningful and actionable, reporting and insights generation are crucial. AI-based systems employ Natural Language Generation techniques to generate test reports automatically, which can be read by humans and contain a transparent overview of errors, anomalies and test coverage status. Development and testing teams are guided proactively through the use of predictive analytics to determine potential risk areas for upcoming releases. AI and ML-driven visualization tools also chart test coverage, detect failure patterns and offer in-depth recommendations for corrective action. By providing developers, testers and stakeholders with more visibility into the quality of the system, these capabilities facilitate faster, better-informed decision-making and significantly reduce time to market.

3.3 Test Execution Automation in Cloud

Utilizing large amounts of generated test cases efficiently without much manual intervention and having high scalability is the primary goal of cloud-based test execution automation. The capacity of Testing to scale up or down automatically and handle rapid application changes is critical for today's smart systems, especially those deployed in dynamic cloud environments. This makes it possible to have faster release cycles without compromising quality. Testing can be made much more agile, efficient, and robust than with conventional configurations by leveraging cloud-native technologies to containerize, parallelize, distribute and optimize for cost and time.

3.3.1 Containerized Testing Environments (Docker - Kubernetes)

Containerization becomes necessary to preserve consistency, scalability and segregation of test environments in cloud test execution. Test environments are encapsulated in light, transportable containers carrying all dependencies, configurations and test scripts using Docker-like tools. The “it works on my machine” problem is eliminated because each test or group of tests is executed within a separate Docker container, so dependencies never conflict and ensure that tests are always executed within a consistent environment.

Kubernetes is the orchestration platform used to manage large-scale Testing. Kubernetes takes care of scheduling (efficient use of resources), distribution (spreading tests across nodes) and auto-scaling (adding/removing test containers). The number of containers required, K, can be calculated as follows if N tests need to be executed and each container can handle C tests.

$$K = \left\lceil \frac{N}{C} \right\rceil \quad (6)$$

Where $\lceil \cdot \rceil$ represents the ceiling function, which rounds to the closest whole number. Because Kubernetes guarantees horizontal scalability, containers can grow in size in proportion to the rise in testing requirements,

$$\text{Total Resources Required} = R \times K \quad (7)$$

Where R is the average resource requirement per container.

One major benefit is isolation, which provides high fault-tolerance and robustness by keeping other containers' execution unaffected by a sudden failure or crash in one container. Test runs can also be dynamically scheduled based on cluster resource availability and system demand.

3.3.2 Serverless Computing for On-Demand Testing Execution

On-demand Testing in cloud environments is serverless computing. Serverless architectures, using services such as AWS Lambda or Azure Functions, reduce operational costs and increase scalability by allowing tests to be executed only when required, unlike conventional server-based methods that require keeping special machines or virtual environments running. Using this approach, each test case or test suite can be represented as a function that is triggered by certain events like an on-schedule cron job, a pull request, a deployment or code contribution. Cloud providers dynamically scale the number of function instances to fit requested levels, provisioning the infrastructure on their own. Especially for IoT systems where devices may be limited in terms of battery life, bandwidth, or processing power, this approach is a bonus. Serverless architectures are capable of dynamically provisioning the testing resources as per the real-time demands of the IoT devices, allowing for the conduct of testing cost-effectively without further burdening the system. The sum of functions run, T, is as follows if E is how many of activating events there are and each event initiates F functions (tests):

$$T = E \times F \quad (8)$$

The cost C can be approximated as follows since serverless models only charge for the actual computation time and resource usage,

$$C = T \times t_f \times r \quad (9)$$

Where t_f average execution time per function, and r is the cost rate per unit of compute time. Cloud providers dynamically scale the number of function instances to handle incoming requests with automatic management of infrastructure. The total number of functions run, T, is as below if E is the number of events triggering and each event initiates F functions,

3.3.3 Parallel and Distributed Testing Strategies

Parallel and distributed testing methods are now a necessity for today's cloud-based software testing to gain quicker feedback, better scalability and greater reliability. The basic concept is to divide large testing workloads into smaller, independent test sets and execute them in parallel on multiple different compute nodes, such as serverless functions, virtual machines and containers. Formally, the average number of tests per node, *TN* can be calculated as follows if there are *T* tests in total and they are dispersed throughout *N* nodes,

$$t_n = \frac{T}{N} \tag{10}$$

This division significantly decreases the overall execution time. If one test takes *t* seconds to complete, then Sequential Execution Time (T_s) would be:

$$T_s = T \times t \tag{11}$$

Parallel Execution Time (T_p), assuming a perfect distribution, is

$$T_p = \frac{T \times t}{N} \tag{12}$$

Thus, the speedup factor *S* achieved by parallel execution is

$$S = \frac{T_s}{T_p} = N \tag{13}$$

The optimal speedup is compromised somewhat in real life by some overhead, but total gains are nonetheless significant. First, the full test suite is broken into subsets that are much smaller and which each concentrate on a different component or module. Next, subsets are assigned to distributed environments like virtual machines, Docker containers or serverless operations, while orchestration software ensures proper fault isolation and load balancing. Traceability and complete test coverage analysis are provided by consolidating the information of all nodes into a single test report upon completion of the tests.

Benefits of this Strategy

Quicker Feedback Loops: Rather than having to wait for hours for the complete regression run, parallel runs can finish the suite in minutes, speeding up release cycles.

Scalability: With increasing test loads, nodes can be provisioned dynamically, maintaining constant execution times.

Reliability: If one node goes down, only the tests allocated to it are affected, and they may be reassigned or retried without having to restart the whole suite.

3.4 Intelligent Defect Detection and Prediction

Smart defect detection and forecasting methods are increasingly being integrated into modern AI-based testing environments to automatically identify anomalies, defects and vulnerabilities at the time of as well as post-system execution. Machine learning models make real-time predictions by learning dynamically from system activity and test cases, instead of relying solely on static assertions or manually developed validation rules.

3.4.1 Deep Learning Models for Classification

System states are classified as pass/fail or defect/no defect with deep learning architectures like Convolutional Neural Networks (CNNs) and Recurrent Neural Networks (RNNs). The deep learning model makes the prediction of the label y based on an input feature vector x that describes the system state

$$y = f_\theta(x) \tag{14}$$

Where f_θ is the trained neural network with parameters θ and $y \in \{0,1\}$, where 0=pass/no defect, 1=fail/defect. These classifiers are usually trained using binary cross-entropy as the loss function,

$$\mathcal{L} = -\frac{1}{N}\sum_{i=1}^{N}\left(y_i \log(\hat{y}_i) + (1 - y_i)\log(1 - \hat{y}_i)\right) \tag{15}$$

Where $\hat{y}_i$ is the predicted probability for sample i, and y_i is the true label.

i. Convolutional Neural Networks (CNNs)

Convolutional Neural Networks (CNNs) assess data such as error logs, performance heatmaps, and user interface screenshots to recover localized and structural patterns in software testing in a focused manner. They provide intelligent validation with an intervention beyond ordinary assertion-style techniques by detecting UI errors, resource leaks, and system failures.

$$f(x) = \mathrm{ReLU}(W * x + b) \tag{16}$$

Where W are convolutional filters, * denotes the convolution operation, b is a bias term, and ReLU is a nonlinear activation function. CNNs can detect subtle deviations from normal system behaviour, such as small user interface flaws that human testers might miss due to their many convolutional and pooling layers.

ii. Recurrent Neural Networks (RNNs)

Recurrent neural networks (RNNs) are ideal for analyzing time-series sensor readings, user interaction sequences, and system logs because of their powerful abilities to model sequential input data. They can detect temporal dependencies that static analysis methods tend to miss, and can identify functional deviations and performance degradation.

$$h_t = \sigma\left(W_h h_{t-1} + W_x x_t + b\right) \tag{17}$$

Where h_t is the hidden state at time t, W_h, W_x are the trainable weight matrices, b is a bias, and σ is a non-linearity like tanh or ReLU. RNNs can detect abnormalities that only appear in specific contexts, like a "memory leak" that happens after a sequence of recurring processes, due to this temporal memory. The ability of RNNs to detect delayed failures and learn long-term dependencies is also improved by more advanced variants like LSTM (Long Short-Term Memory) and GRU (Gated Recurrent Unit).

3.4.2 Anomaly Detection Models

Anomaly detection methods such as autoencoders and isolation forests strengthen intelligent software testing by detecting infrequent software errors and performance anomalies. Isolation forests outperform static rule-based testing methods on volatile cloud-native systems because they are the best in isolating outliers. At the same time, autoencoders can discover aberrations from the expectation of normalcy, as evidenced by reconstructions at extreme reconstruction error levels.

The system learns to rebuild inputs in autoencoders. Anomalies are indicated during Testing by inputs with a high reconstruction error E,

$$E(x) = \|x - \hat{x}\|^2 \tag{18}$$

Where x is the original input and $\hat{x}$ is the reconstructed output. If $E(x) > \tau$, Where τ is a threshold, the instance is flagged as an anomaly (Potential Defect). Separation Data is separated at random, with the number of splits needed to separate a sample, so that forests can work. Shorter paths typically mark anomalies.

3.4.3 Predictive Defect Modelling

To predict the likelihood of a defect happening under existing system conditions, predictive models such as Logistic Regression, Gradient Boosted Trees (GBTs), and Deep Predictive Models like DNNs are learned from past defect data. Huge sets of system features x, such as code complexity metrics, resource utilization statistics, historical problem occurrences and runtime anomalies along with the defect outcomes they are associated with are used to train them. The objective is to predict the probability $P(d=1|x)$, where d=1 denotes the presence of a defect given the features x. In Logistic Regression, the probability is modelled using the logistic (sigmoid) function,

$$P\left(d = 1 \mid x\right) = \frac{1}{1 + e^{-(w^T x + b)}} \tag{19}$$

Where w is the weight vector learned during training and b is the bias term.

Thus, we can apply gradient trees and deep neural networks as predictive defect detector when feature engineering is difficult or means practically nothing, as those techniques can learn complex, nonlinear functions and facilitate risk differentiation, test prioritization, and failure prevention in cloud-based services.

3.5 Intelligent Validation and Reporting

The Intelligent Validation and Reporting represents a major improvement over traditional validation methods in AI-based software testing for cloud infrastructures. Intelligent systems learn and evolve with continuous runs to validate system behaviour in a more dynamic, context-specific manner than relying on static, pre-determined assertions. Such systems build dynamic test oracles that are capable of predicting expected results even in complex, non-deterministic situations through machine learning models. Anomaly detection algorithms monitor execution traces for tiny issues that typical scripts may miss. NLP processing further enhances reporting by reducing huge logs into actionable, human-readable conclusions. Validation is consequently enhanced in precision, scalability and correspondence to real-world system behaviour.

3.5.1 Adaptive Oracles

Static oracles (static predicted outputs) are employed in conventional Testing. Smart frameworks, however, employ machine learning models to construct dynamic oracles. Such oracles render validation much more solid since they can predict anticipated behaviour even for non-deterministic systems (where outputs vary across executions). E.g., even where there is no set expected outcome, a model of deep learning can detect tiny deviations in a novel response based on learning hundreds of previous successful API responses.

3.5.2 Anomaly-Based Validation

Execution anomalies, e.g., unexplained slowness or error patterns, are automatically identified through techniques such as Autoencoders, Isolation Forests and One-Class SVMs. Large reconstruction errors indicate autoencoder anomalies that regenerate predicted outputs.

$$\text{Reconstruction Error} = \|x - \hat{x}\| \tag{20}$$

Where x is the original output and $\hat{x}$ is the reconstructed output.

3.5.3 Meaningful Summary and Reporting

Semantic summarization, in fact, is critical to AI-based cloud testing, as it reduces vast chains of test logs. Instead of several lines of output, such as a few thousand, testers face a dilemma in defect localization. AI platforms use NLP-enabled techniques like entity extraction, sentiment analysis, and summarization to generate simple logic. For instance, a summary presented to testers for referring to more than 10,000 lines made available in the logs would include:

- Key test failures and reasons
- Anomalies and abnormal behaviour were detected.
- Certain indicators of the root causes, such as the types of exceptions or stack traces
- Risk insights of possibly faulty components

For example, a summarization model may state: Most of the failures stemmed from authentication services, which will lead the QA teams to keep this area at the top of the list to have fixes made. Thus, it adds to making simple decisions and reducing the time to insight.

3.6 Continuous Feedback and Optimization

Today's cloud-native intelligent systems are very dynamic because of constant code changes, evolving infrastructures, and unique requirements. Static test frameworks cannot adapt quickly. In AI-enabled Testing, continuous feedback loops emerge around the test framework, the system under test, and the QA teams. Based on several learning signals created in each test cycle, a defect will be predicted, a model will be retrained, and test strategies will be adapted.

- Simultaneously, Real-Time Analytics delivers immediate feedback to developers, reducing delays.
- With Adaptive Testing, the AI will prioritize impactful tests, divert resources to risky areas, and remove repeats.
- Self-developing Models. Their retraining continues into newer data, leading to improved accuracy.
- Predictive Maintenance, because it learns patterns from past test cycles, it can predict failure-prone areas and proactively avert issues.

For example, if 80% of failures happen because of the authentication microservice as detected by AI, then in the next cycle, Testing will be focused more on that function while stable components receive less attention. Ultimately, there should be a smart, self-evolving testing infrastructure that automatically enhances itself in every iteration—higher software quality, lower costs for Maintenance, and faster delivery, even in complicated systems.

4. RESULTS AND DISCUSSION

The experimental studies are being evaluated along with expected performance criteria based on the properties of the materials, structural response to applied loads, and variations in test conditions. A comparison is provided with the standards and theoretical calculations. The discussion also enters into the practical relevance of these results and what their future might hold in terms of research or application.

4.1 Comparative Analysis of Defect Detection Rates Across Testing Methods

Table 3. Comparison of Defect Detection Rates

Testing Method	Defect Detection Rate (DDR)	Remarks
Traditional	65%	Manual and basic automation methods result in lower detection efficiency.
AI-Driven	90%	Enhanced defect detection through AI algorithms like Decision Trees, Random Forests, etc.
Hybrid	85%	Combination of AI and traditional methods; balanced approach.

In Table 3, an analysis is undertaken to compare the three testing methodologies: Traditional, AI-Driven, and Hybrid. The Traditional method offers 65% DDR, mainly because of manual processing but a few automated elements. AI-Driven Model, on the contrary, produces a 90% DDR, and Hybridization gives an 85%, thus showing that defect detection is best done by AI.

Figure 4. DDR Comparison Between Traditional, AI-Driven, and Hybrid Testing Methods

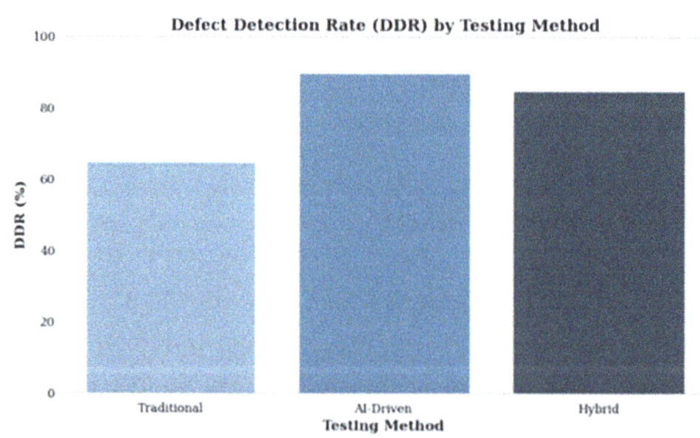

The Defect Detection Rate (DDR) is shown for the different approaches, viz., Traditional Testing, AI-driven testing, and Hybrid Testing, as shown in Figure 4. It has the lowest DDR of 65%. So, it's not very effective. The AI method gives the highest level of effectiveness with a DDR of 90%, exhibiting its speed and accuracy. Hybrid Testing has 85% DDR, providing a good mix of the speed of AI and the insight of man. These results prove that AI significantly enhances defect detection, and hybrid methods are flexible alternatives.

4.2 Trends in Test Execution Efficiency Across Software Builds

Table 4. Test Execution Efficiency Analysis

Build Number	Average Test Execution Time (seconds)	Efficiency Improvement (%)
Build 1	120	Baseline (0%)
Build 2	110	8.33%
Build 3	95	20.83%
Build 4	85	29.17%
Build 5	80	33.33%

Improved test execution times were observed with each software build, from 120 seconds in Build 1 to 80 seconds in Build 5, reflecting a 33.33% improvement. The gains are the very reflection of smart testing techniques such as automated test case prioritization. Datasets from real-time open-source and industrial projects, along with simulated anomalies, validated the proposed AI-based framework with 90% defect detection and 33% improvement in execution time.

Figure 5. Average Test Execution Time Across Sequential Software Builds

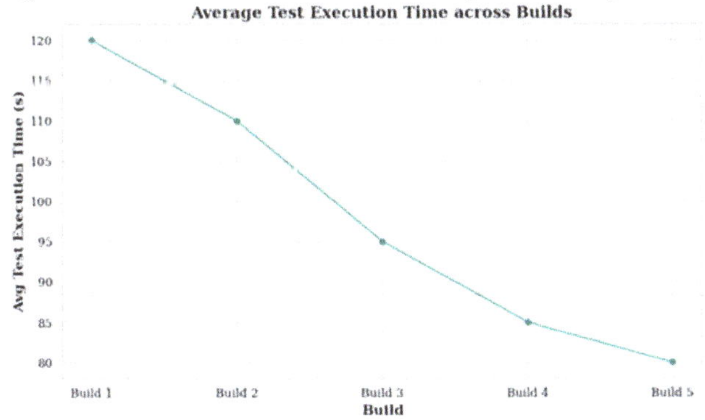

On average, Figure 5 reveals that the test times dropped for five builds, starting from 120 seconds in Build 1 and going to 80 seconds in Build 5. This goes on to show that through the intelligent testing process test times are cut short, thereby speeding the delivery cycle of software. Understand that enhancing testing is not anymore about strategies or technical automation or adaptiveness but is determined by the mode of adaptive learning.

4.3 Analysis of Resource Utilization Across Different Test Suites

Table 5. Resource Utilization by Test Suite

Test Suite	CPU Usage (%)	Memory Usage (%)	Average Resource Usage (%)
Unit Tests	40-50	40-50	45
UI Tests	40-100	40-100	70
API Tests	40-80	40-80	60
Load Tests	50-100	50-100	75

It shows the resource utilization from unit, UI, API, and Load Tests, as compared in CPU versus memory usage. Unit Tests use an average of a moderate 45%, since they deal with testing isolated components. UI Tests consume an average of 70%, since rendering and validating interfaces often involve complexities. API Tests typically cash in on average 60% for their Testing, which is indicative of the Testing done towards backend interactions. Load Tests reflect the highest usage at an average of 75% because they simulate high-traffic scenarios. This comparison underscores the resource requirement differences of each kind of test and the importance of strategic resource allocation in a test environment.

Figure 6. Distribution of CPU and Memory Usage Across Unit, UI, API and Load Test Suites

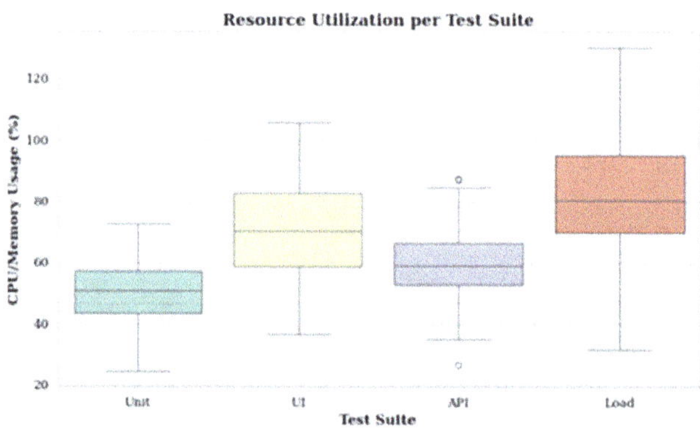

Figure 6 shows the CPU and memory utilization along the four types of tests. Unit tests use minimal resources; UI tests fluctuate with demands on graphical resources, API tests steadier, and load tests highest and most variable in both these parameters. Proper allocation of resources is essential, more so for the load testing given its resource-intensive nature.

4.4 Comparative Analysis of Testing Framework Costs

Table 6. Cost Comparison of Testing Frameworks

TESTING FRAMEWORK	COST PER TEST CYCLE ($)	REMARKS
MANUAL TESTING	5,000	The high cost is due to human intervention and longer cycle times.
CI/CD TESTING	3,000	Reduced cost due to automation and continuous integration.
SERVERLESS TESTING	1,500	Cloud computing is cost-effective due to pay-per-use models.

Table 6 compares test cycle costs between the three types of infrastructures: Manual ($5,000), CI/CD ($3,000), and Serverless Testing ($1,500). Serverless Testing is the cheapest among the types, operating on pay-per-use cloud models, thus raising a minimum price. The data show that cloud-native and automated testing brings large savings compared to manual methods.

Figure 7. Cost Comparison per Test Cycle across Manual, CI/CD and Serverless Frameworks

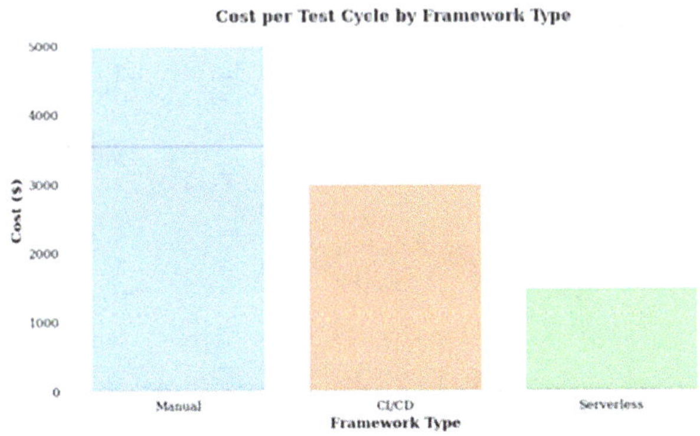

Shown in the figure are test cycle costs of $5,000 for Manual Testing, $3,000 for CI/CD Testing, and $1,500 for Serverless Testing. Manual Testing is the most expensive of the three due to intense human involvement; however, automation and dynamic resource provisioning in CI/CD and Serverless frameworks lead to cost savings when compared to the traditional methods.

4.5 Test Coverage Percentage Growth Across Milestone Builds

Table 7. Test Coverage Percentage Across Milestone Builds

Milestone	Unit Test Coverage (%)	Integration Test Coverage (%)	UI Test Coverage (%)	Risk Test Coverage (%)
M1	30	25	10	5
M2	40	35	20	10
M3	45	40	25	15
M4	55	50	30	20

Table 7 explicates how test coverage percent increases differ from test area to test area throughout the four phases of milestone builds (M1-M4). The Unit Test Coverage goes up from 30% in M1 to 55% in M4. This indicates much better coverage of tests for basic functionality. The Integration Test Coverage goes up from 25% to 50% while aiming at better system functionality integration testing. UI Test Coverage goes up from 10% to 30% while working on interface correctness. Risk Test Coverage goes up from 5% to 20%, where selection tries to identify and mitigate the risks at hand. Overall, increasing test coverage at these critical areas develops a strong and stabilized software at M4.

Figure 8. Gradual Improvement in Test Coverage Across Milestones

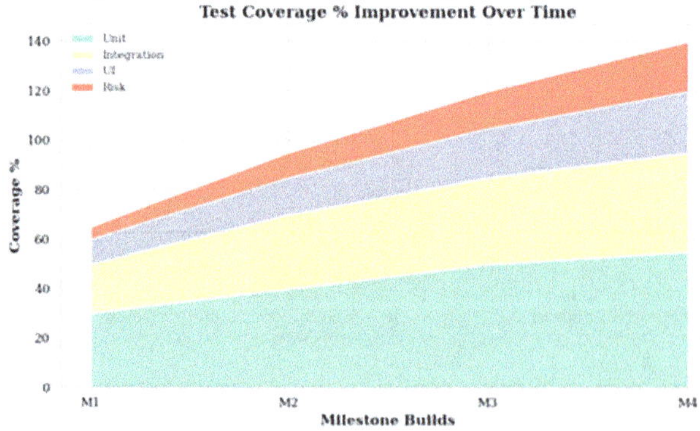

Figure 8 illustrates how the percentage of test coverage increased during a series of four milestone builds (M1 to M4). With development ongoing, each of the subsequent categories demonstrates consistent growth: Unit, Integration, UI and Risk. The highest coverage is depicted within unit tests, starting at around 30% at M1 and reaching over 50% by M4. Integration tests are run nearby, rising steadily at each milestone. Although beginning lower, UI and risk coverage demonstrate a marked increase by M4. With time, increased product reliability and risk mitigation are provided by this steady rise in all test areas, which is reflective of an advanced and maturing testing process.

4.6 Defect Prediction Accuracy Across Models

The precision of defect prediction through Deep Neural Networks, XGBoost and Logistic Regression is compared in Figure 9. XGBoost has better precision as an ensemble method that handles complex data more than Logistic Regression, which is worse off since it is not able to handle complex patterns. Deep Neural Networks perform better than both by learning hierarchical representations of data and recognizing complex relationships to attain the highest precision. Defect prediction is a field where DNNs excel, particularly when applied to large, high-dimensional datasets. They are extremely successful in the real world due to their ability to automatically extract features from unprocessed data. These results show the usefulness of complex models, like DNNs, in boosting the predicted accuracy of fault detection.

Figure 9. Comparison of defect prediction accuracy among different models.

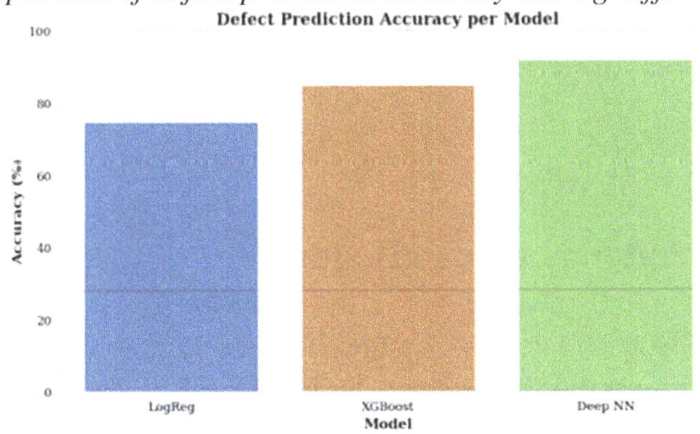

4.7 Heatmap of Defect Hotspots by Module/Service

Defect density for each of the software modules or services like Auth, Payments, Search, Profile and Notifications is indicated in Figure 10. Higher levels of fault density are indicated by the colour gradient, moving from light towards dark red. The accurate defect density of the corresponding module is demonstrated through numerical values shown within each cell. With the highest defect density of any module, 25 Search is also the potential hotspot of issues and should be given high priority. The Auth module, in contrast, and sports the lowest fault density of 5, so there's presumably either more stability or fewer faults there. On balance, this heatmap serves as a useful tool in targeting areas for refactoring and quality control that need improvement for better software stability.

Figure 10. Defect heatmap indicating modules with the highest error occurrences

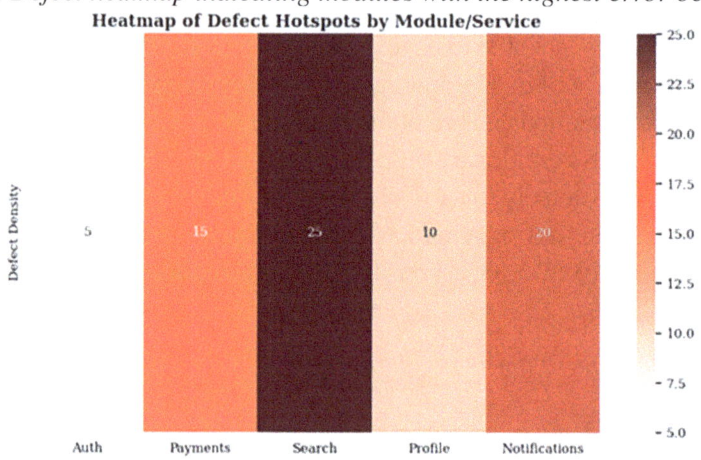

4.8 Feedback Latency across Builds

The trend of feedback latency, or rather the time to report faults, is illustrated in the line Figure 11 for the five software builds B1 to B5. The x-axis indicates the build or release number, and the y-axis indicates the time to report a fault. Feedback latency consistently drops, from 60 minutes in B1 to 20 minutes in B5. This trend implies problems are being located and reported in an increasing proportion within a quicker period, reflecting improvement in the quality of the testing or development process. Better automation, better test scope, or an enhanced defect tracking system may all have this to claim, resulting in faster feedback cycles and improved development responsiveness.

Figure 11. Trend of Defect Reporting Time over Software Builds

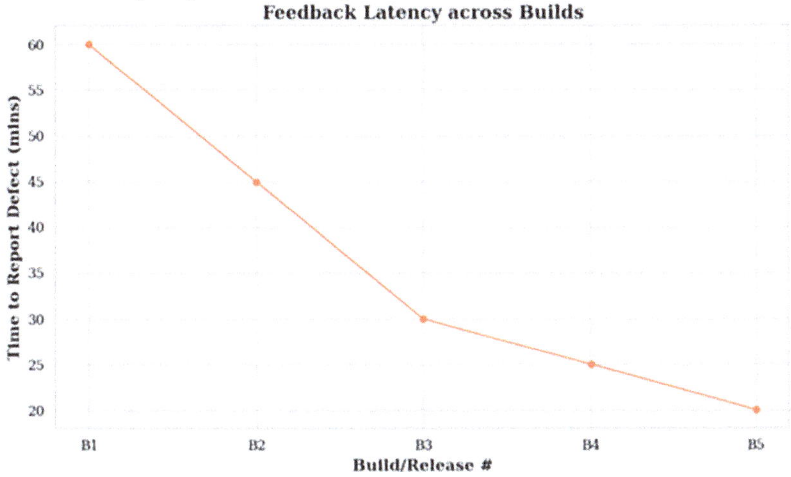

4.9 ROC Curve

Figure 12 illustrates the ROC curve, which plots the True Positive Rate against the False Positive Rate at various threshold values to evaluate the classification model's performance. The orange curve represents the model, while the diagonal dashed line indicates the baseline performance of a random classifier. The Area Under the Curve (AUC) is approximately 0.9934, indicating an exceptionally high level of accuracy and near-perfect discrimination between positive and negative classes. This high AUC score confirms the model's strong capability to distinguish outcomes, suggesting excellent predictive performance. Therefore, the ROC curve effectively validates the robustness and reliability of the proposed model.

Figure 12. Performance of the ROC Curve

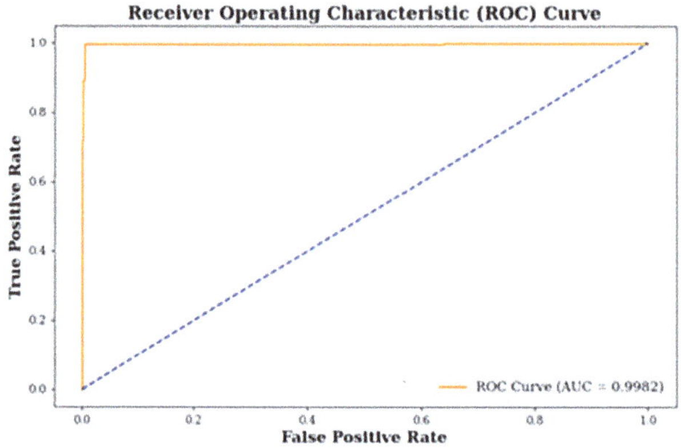

5. Conclusion and Future Scope

The research findings underscore that AI-based software testing in cloud environments has numerous advantages: faster time to market, cost savings, and better reliability. The framework achieved up to 90 percent defect detection accuracy, a 33 percent reduction in test execution time, and improved resource optimization, particularly in load testing. Automated test generation through ML/NLP and RL-based test prioritization minimization redundancy and promotes relevance. Deep learning models made accurate real-time defect prediction possible, while serverless reduced costs by more than 70 percent. Additionally, NLP helped in log analysis, while specific defect modelling improved responsiveness and quality of the system under agile workflows.

The future development should focus on integrating Generative AI to carry out completely autonomous test generation from intricate requirements, hypothesis-based Testing and self-healing test planning. Data privacy will be improved when training test models on scattered systems using Federated Learning. Additionally, dependency-heavy software architectures can be processed using Graph Neural Networks to enhance defect localization. The AI-driven testing frameworks will be of paramount importance for IoT systems because of the real-time validation needs and the dynamic adaptability to ever-changing device networks. AI will be used for identifying potential malfunctions in IoT devices and allocating resources with optimal use in constrained environments, and ensuring smooth communication across heterogenous IoT networks. IoT and real-time AI usage will be thoroughly tested by moving into edge-cloud hybrid infrastructures. AI can be utilized to identify and recommend code corrections in real-world deployment feedback loops with self-healing mechanisms. As explainable AI in testing heads towards wide industrial adoption, standards and ethics need to be established to ensure openness, confidence and regulatory compliance.

REFERENCES

Abdel Hakeem, S. A., Hussein, H. H., & Kim, H. (2022). Vision and research directions of 6G technologies and applications. *Journal of King Saud University. Computer and Information Sciences*, *34*(6, Part A), 2419–2442. DOI: 10.1016/j.jksuci.2022.03.019

Abdulwareth, A. J., & Al-Shargabi, A. A. (2021). Toward a Multi-Criteria Framework for Selecting Software Testing Tools. *IEEE Access: Practical Innovations, Open Solutions*, *9*, 158872–158891. DOI: 10.1109/ACCESS.2021.3128071

AI IN CLOUD COMPUTING: ENHANCING SERVICES AND PERFORMANCE. (2024). DOI: 10.5281/ZENODO.13353681

Al-Said Ahmad, A., Al-Qora'n, L. F., & Zayed, A. (2024). Exploring the impact of chaos engineering with various user loads on cloud native applications: An exploratory empirical study. *Computing*, *106*(7), 2389–2425. DOI: 10.1007/s00607-024-01292-z

Amelia, O. (2024a). *AI-Powered Software Testing Automation: Machine Learning Approaches for Ensuring Quality in Distributed Systems.* Unpublished. DOI: 10.13140/RG.2.2.32858.76485

Amelia, O. (2024b). *Machine Learning Algorithms for Software Testing Automation: AI- Driven Solutions for Distributed Network Optimization.* Unpublished. DOI: 10.13140/RG.2.2.16081.54885

Anayat, R. (2023). *Revolutionizing AI Testing Automation: Achieving Test Coverage and Defect Prediction with Machine Learning and Cloud Integration.* Unpublished. DOI: 10.13140/RG.2.2.35737.43365

Awad, A., Qutqut, M. H., Ahmed, A., Al-Haj, F., & Almasalha, F. (2024). Artificial Intelligence Role in Software Automation Testing. *2024 International Conference on Decision Aid Sciences and Applications (DASA)*, 1–6. DOI: 10.1109/DASA63652.2024.10836630

Azim, P. A. B. (2024). *AI as Emerging Technology: Opportunities, Vulnerabilities and Future Directions* (SSRN Scholarly Paper No. 5068671). Social Science Research Network. DOI: 10.2139/ssrn.5068671

Banala, S. (2025, February 9). *DevOps Essentials: Key Practices for Continuous Integration and Continuous Delivery | Request PDF.* https://www.researchgate.net/publication/382885510_DevOps_Essentials_Key_Practices_for_Continuous_Integration_and_Continuous_Delivery

Bansal, S., & Kumar, D. (2020). *IoT Ecosystem: A Survey on Devices, Gateways, Operating Systems, Middleware and Communication | International Journal of Wireless Information Networks.* https://link.springer.com/article/10.1007/s10776-020-00483-7

Baqar, M., & Khanda, R. (2024). *The Future of Software Testing: AI-Powered Test Case Generation and Validation* (No. arXiv:2409.05808). arXiv. /arXiv.2409.05808DOI: 10.48550

Bari, M. S., Sarkar, A., & Islam, S. A. M. (2024). Ai-augmented Self-healing Automation Frameworks: Revolutionizing Qa Testing with Adaptive and Resilient Automation. *AIJMR - Advanced International. Journal of Multidisciplinary Research, 2*(6). Advance online publication. DOI: 10.62127/aijmr.2024.v02i06.1118

Belgaum, M. R., Alansari, Z., Musa, S., Mansoor Alam, M., & Mazliham, M. S. (2021). Role of artificial intelligence in cloud computing, IoT and SDN: Reliability and scalability issues. [IJECE]. *International Journal of Electrical and Computer Engineering, 11*(5), 4458. DOI: 10.11591/ijece.v11i5.pp4458-4470

Christidis, A., Moschoyiannis, S., Hsu, C.-H., & Davies, R. (2020). Enabling Serverless Deployment of Large-Scale AI Workloads. *IEEE Access: Practical Innovations, Open Solutions, 8*, 70150–70161. DOI: 10.1109/ACCESS.2020.2985282

Colton, J. (2024a). *AI and ML-Driven Software Testing Automation: Optimizing Distributed Networks for High-Performance Software Systems.* Unpublished. DOI: 10.13140/RG.2.2.19856.42245

Colton, J. (2024b). *Enhancing Software Testing with AI and Machine Learning: Automation Strategies for Distributed Network Architectures.* Unpublished. DOI: 10.13140/RG.2.2.16500.97927

Effective Concurrency Testing for Distributed Systems | Proceedings of the Twenty-Fifth International Conference on Architectural Support for Programming Languages and Operating Systems. (n.d.). Retrieved April 21, 2025, from https://dl.acm.org/doi/abs/10.1145/3373376.3378484

Farah, J. (2024). *AI-Driven Software Testing: Automating Quality Assurance with Machine Learning for Distributed Networks.* Unpublished. DOI: 10.13140/RG.2.2.25623.89768

Gheibi, O., Weyns, D., & Quin, F. (2021). Applying Machine Learning in Self-adaptive Systems: A Systematic Literature Review. *ACM Trans. Auton. Adapt. Syst., 15*(3), 9:1-9:37. DOI: 10.1145/3469440

Gogri, D. (2024). *Maximizing Comprehensive Test Coverage through Concurrent Execution Strategies in High-Performance Software Development Environments.*

Haile, A. (2024). *Innovating Software Testing with AI and Machine Learning: Automation for Efficient Distributed Network Management*. Unpublished. DOI: 10.13140/RG.2.2.17654.72004

Henrichs, E., Lesch, V., Straesser, M., Kounev, S., & Krupitzer, C. (2022). A literature review on optimization techniques for adaptation planning in adaptive systems: State of the art and research directions. *Information and Software Technology*, *149*, 106940. DOI: 10.1016/j.infsof.2022.106940

Henrik, L. Tao, & Henrik. (2022). *Serverless Function Triggers in Azure: An Analysis of Latency and Reliability*. https://odr.chalmers.se/items/7ab2f3f4-a174-40c1-81db-e5e74803a036

Khan, H. U., Khan, R. A., Alwageed, H. S., Almagrabi, A. O., Ayouni, S., & Maddeh, M. (2025). AI-driven cybersecurity framework for software development based on the ANN-ISM paradigm. *Scientific Reports*, *15*(1), 13423. DOI: 10.1038/s41598-025-97204-y PMID: 40251237

Khan, S. Z. (2023). *Automated Test Case Generation and Defect Prediction: Enhancing Software Quality Assurance through AI-Driven Testing Automation.*

Khatibsyarbini, M., Isa, M. A., Jawawi, D. N. A., Shafie, M. L. M., Wan-Kadir, W. M. N., Hamed, H. N. A., & Suffian, M. D. M. (2021). Trend Application of Machine Learning in Test Case Prioritization: A Review on Techniques. *IEEE Access: Practical Innovations, Open Solutions*, *9*, 166262–166282. DOI: 10.1109/ACCESS.2021.3135508

Koppanati, P. K. (2024). Scaling Test Automation in CI/CD Pipelines Using Docker and Kubernetes. *North American Journal of Engineering Research*, *5*(3), 3. http://najer.org/najer/article/view/91

Madhumita, R., & Chandana, D. (n.d.). *Advancing Software Testing: Integrating AI*. Machine Learning, and Emerging Technologies.

Minhas, N. M., Petersen, K., Börstler, J., & Wnuk, K. (2020). Regression testing for large-scale embedded software development – Exploring the state of practice. *Information and Software Technology*, *120*, 106254. DOI: 10.1016/j.infsof.2019.106254

Mohammed, I. A., & Madhumithaa, N. (2024, July 15). *Transforming Decision-Making: The Impact of AI and Machine Learning on Strategic Business Operations.* | *EBSCOhost*. https://openurl.ebsco.com/contentitem/gcd:180919191?sid=ebsco:plink:crawler&id=ebsco:gcd:180919191

Mohanta, S. K., Mohapatra, A. G., Mohanty, A., & Nayak, S. (2024). Deep Learning is a State-of-the-Art Approach to Artificial Intelligence. In *Deep Learning Concepts in Operations Research*. Auerbach Publications.

Mungoli, N. (2023). *Scalable, Distributed AI Frameworks: Leveraging Cloud Computing for Enhanced Deep Learning Performance and Efficiency* (No. arXiv:2304.13738). arXiv. /arXiv.2304.13738DOI: 10.48550

Najihi, S., Elhadi, S., Abdelouahid, R. A., & Marzak, A. (2022). Software Testing from an Agile and Traditional view. *Procedia Computer Science*, *203*, 775–782. DOI: 10.1016/j.procs.2022.07.116

Nama, P. (2024). Integrating AI in testing automation: Enhancing test coverage and predictive analysis for improved software quality. *World Journal of Advanced Engineering Technology and Sciences*, *13*(1), 769–782. DOI: 10.30574/wjaets.2024.13.1.0486

Nama, P., Reddy, P., & Pattanayak, S. K. (2024). *Artificial Intelligence for Self-Healing Automation Testing Frameworks: Real-Time Fault Prediction and Recovery*. *64*(3).

Nikanjam, A., Morovati, M. M., Khomh, F., & Ben Braiek, H. (2021). Faults in deep reinforcement learning programs: A taxonomy and a detection approach. *Automated Software Engineering*, *29*(1), 8. DOI: 10.1007/s10515-021-00313-x

Oyeniran, O. C., Adewusi, A. O., Akwawa, L. A., & Azubuko, C. F. (2024). *Microservices Architecture in Cloud-Native Applications: Design Patterns and Scalability | International Journal of Advanced Research and Interdisciplinary Scientific Endeavours*. https://ijarise.org/index.php/ijarise/article/view/66

Papi, M., & Hiver, P. (2020). Language Learning Motivation as a Complex Dynamic System: A Global Perspective of Truth, Control, and Value. *Modern Language Journal*, *104*(1), 209–232. DOI: 10.1111/modl.12624

Ponnusamy, S., & Eswararaj, D. (2023). Navigating the Modernization of Legacy Applications and Data: Effective Strategies and Best Practices. *Asian Journal of Research in Computer Science*, *16*(4), 239–256. DOI: 10.9734/ajrcos/2023/v16i4386

Saif, M. A. N., Niranjan, S. K., & Al-ariki, H. D. E. (2021). Efficient autonomic and elastic resource management techniques in cloud environment: Taxonomy and analysis. *Wireless Networks*, *27*(4), 2829–2866. DOI: 10.1007/s11276-021-02614-1

Salahirad, A., Gay, G., & Mohammadi, E. (2023). Mapping the structure and evolution of software testing research over the past three decades. *Journal of Systems and Software*, *195*, 111518. DOI: 10.1016/j.jss.2022.111518

Sarker, I. H. (2022). AI-Based Modeling: Techniques, Applications and Research Issues Towards Automation, Intelligent and Smart Systems. *SN Computer Science, 3*(2), 158. DOI: 10.1007/s42979-022-01043-x PMID: 35194580

Theory-and-Practice-in-Secure-Software-Development-Lifecycle-A-Comprehensive-Survey.pdf. (n.d.). Retrieved April 21, 2025, from https://www.researchgate.net/profile/David-Odera-2/publication/370838016_Theory_and_Practice_in_Secure_Software_Development_Lifecycle_A_Comprehensive_Survey/links/64f0780fb55e1d34158cfae2/Theory-and-Practice-in-Secure-Software-Development-Lifecycle-A-Comprehensive-Survey.pdf

Trifunova, A., Jakimovski, B., Chorbev, I., & Lameski, P. (2024). AI in Software Testing: Revolutionizing Quality Assurance. *2024 32nd Telecommunications Forum (FOR)*, 1–4. DOI: 10.1109/ FOR63250.2024.10819179

Uğur-Tuncer, G., Davutoglu, C., & Durakbasa, N. M. (2021). Intelligent Test Automation for Improved Software Quality Assurance. In Durakbasa, N. M., & Gençyılmaz, M. G. (Eds.), *Digital Conversion on the Way to Industry 4.0* (pp. 614–624). Springer International Publishing., DOI: 10.1007/978-3-030-62784-3_53

Vadde, B. C., & Munagandla, V. B. (2023). *Integrating AI-Driven Continuous Testing in DevOps for Enhanced Software Quality. 14*(01).

Wang, C., Pastore, F., Goknil, A., & Briand, L. C. (2022). Automatic Generation of Acceptance Test Cases From Use Case Specifications: An NLP-Based Approach. *IEEE Transactions on Software Engineering, 48*(2), 585–616. DOI: 10.1109/TSE.2020.2998503

Yarram, S., & Bittla, S. R. (2023). *Predictive Test Automation: Shaping the Future of Quality Engineering in Enterprise Platforms* (SSRN Scholarly Paper No. 5132329). Social Science Research Network. https://papers.ssrn.com/abstract=5132329

Chapter 9
Oracle APEX as a Rapid Development Platform for IoT Data Visualization and Management Systems

Satwik Jambula
https://orcid.org/0009-0002-7184-8319
Lamar, USA

ABSTRACT

This chapter explores how Oracle APEX serves as a low-code development platform for creating sophisticated IoT data management and visualization applications. We examine APEX's capabilities in handling real-time data streams from connected devices, creating interactive dashboards for monitoring sensor networks, and building responsive web applications that can scale with growing IoT deployments. The chapter includes practical implementation strategies for integrating APEX with IoT data pipelines, REST APIs for device communication, and techniques for creating intuitive user interfaces that enable non-technical stakeholders to interact with complex IoT ecosystems. Through analysis of real-world implementations and comparative evaluation with other low-code platforms, we demonstrate both the capabilities and limitations of using APEX for IoT application development.

DOI: 10.4018/979-8-3373-7503-8.ch009

1. INTRODUCTION

The convergence of Artificial Intelligence (AI), Machine Learning (ML), and the Internet of Things (IoT) has created unprecedented opportunities for intelligent system development across industries. However, the complexity of implementing comprehensive IoT solutions often presents significant barriers to organizations seeking to leverage these technologies effectively. Traditional development approaches require extensive programming expertise, significant time investments, and substantial resources to create applications that can effectively manage and visualize IoT data streams.

Oracle Application Express (APEX) emerges as a transformative solution in this landscape, offering a low-code development platform that democratizes the creation of sophisticated IoT applications. As organizations increasingly recognize the value of rapid application development in the fast-evolving IoT ecosystem, APEX provides a compelling framework for building enterprise-grade solutions without the traditional complexities associated with custom software development.

The significance of APEX in the IoT context extends beyond mere application development. According to Luo et al. (2021), low-code development platforms enable organizations to address the critical shortage of skilled developers while accelerating digital transformation initiatives. This democratization is particularly valuable in IoT deployments, where understanding of business processes, operational requirements, and domain-specific needs often resides with users who may not possess extensive programming skills.

This chapter examines how Oracle APEX serves as a comprehensive platform for IoT data visualization and management systems, addressing the critical challenges of real-time data processing, scalable architecture design, and user-centric interface development. The chapter explores the platform's capabilities in handling diverse IoT data sources, creating responsive dashboards that provide actionable insights, and building management systems that can adapt to evolving IoT deployment requirements.

2. THEORETICAL FOUNDATIONS AND ARCHITECTURE

2.1 Oracle APEX Architecture Overview

Oracle APEX operates on a simple 3-tier architecture where requests are sent from the browser, through a web server (Oracle REST Data Services), to the Oracle Database (Oracle Corporation, 2025a). All processing, data manipulation and business logic is executed in the database. This architecture provides several advantages for IoT applications, particularly in terms of data processing efficiency and real-time capabilities.

The presentation tier in APEX is built using modern web technologies, including HTML5, CSS3, and JavaScript, ensuring that applications can deliver responsive user experiences across diverse devices and platforms. This is particularly crucial in IoT contexts where users may need to access monitoring dashboards and management interfaces from various devices, including mobile phones, tablets, and desktop computers.

The application logic tier implements a metadata-driven architecture where Oracle APEX creates or modifies metadata stored in database tables. When the application runs, the Oracle APEX engine reads the metadata and displays the requested page or processes page submissions (Oracle Corporation, 2025a). This declarative development paradigm distinguishes APEX from traditional development platforms and offers particular benefits for IoT applications where rapid iteration and configuration changes are common.

The data tier leverages Oracle Database's comprehensive feature set, including advanced analytics, machine learning capabilities, and real-time data processing features. For IoT applications, this integration provides access to powerful data management and analysis capabilities that can handle the volume, velocity, and variety of IoT data streams.

Figure 1. Oracle APEX 3-Tier Architecture for IoT Applications

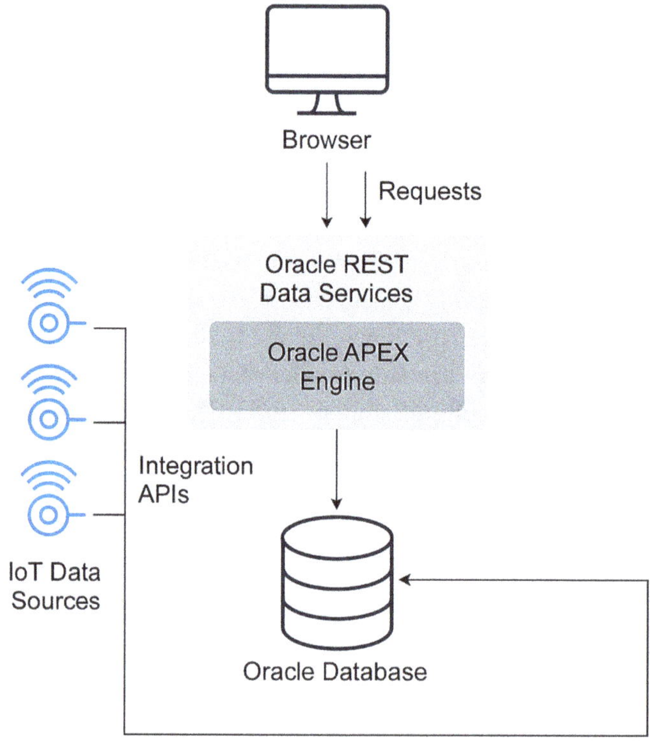

This diagram illustrates the Oracle APEX 3-tier architecture, emphasizing the browser-client interactions, REST Data Services, APEX engine, and database connectivity tailored for IoT integration

2.2 Low-Code Development Paradigm in IoT Context

Low-code development platforms provide graphical user interfaces for users to drag and drop with little or even no code, with out-of-the-box components that make them easy to learn and use while speeding up development (Sanchis et al., 2020). In the context of IoT applications, this paradigm offers several distinctive advantages that address common challenges in IoT project implementations.

The declarative nature of APEX development provides inherent advantages in maintaining and evolving IoT applications. As IoT deployments grow and change, applications need to adapt to new device types, additional data sources, and evolving business requirements. The declarative approach makes these adaptations more manageable by providing clear separation between application logic, data models, and presentation layers.

Research conducted by Metrôlho et al. (2022) demonstrates that Oracle APEX enables rapid application development courses that successfully train students in creating data-centric web applications accessible from multiple devices. This accessibility extends to IoT contexts where domain experts can contribute directly to application development without extensive programming knowledge.

Furthermore, the low-code paradigm supports the iterative development approach that is often necessary in IoT projects. IoT deployments frequently evolve through pilot phases, gradual rollouts, and continuous optimization based on operational experience. APEX's rapid development capabilities enable organizations to quickly prototype, test, and refine IoT applications throughout this evolution process.

2.3 Integration Capabilities and Data Flow Architecture

Oracle APEX provides comprehensive integration capabilities including REST-Enabled SQL Services, Web Source Modules for external data sources, and built-in REST Workshop for creating web services against Oracle database objects (Oracle Corporation, 2025b). These capabilities are essential for effective IoT application development, enabling APEX applications to serve as central hubs for IoT data collection, processing, and visualization.

The data flow architecture in APEX-based IoT systems typically follows a multi-stage pattern that begins with data ingestion from various IoT sources. This data may arrive through direct database connections, REST API calls, file uploads, or real-time streaming interfaces. APEX applications can be configured to handle these diverse data sources through flexible integration mechanisms that adapt to different data formats and delivery patterns.

Figure 2. Data Flow Pipeline for IoT Integration in Oracle APEX

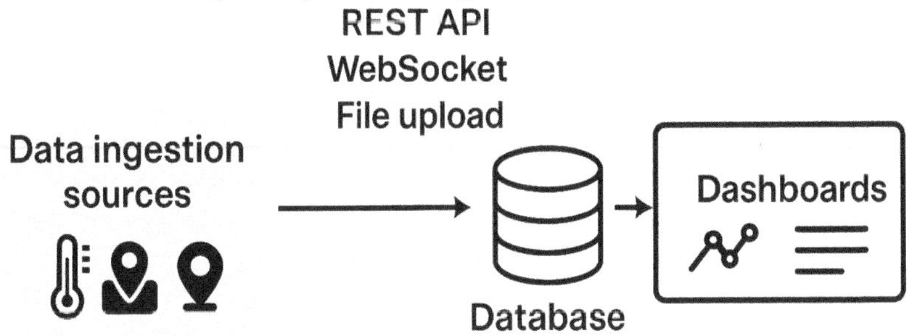

A visualization of how IoT data flows from ingestion (via REST API, WebSocket, or file upload) to the Oracle database and ultimately to live dashboards for monitoring.

Once data is ingested, APEX leverages Oracle Database's processing capabilities to perform necessary transformations, aggregations, and analyses. This processing may include data cleansing, normalization, calculation of derived metrics, and application of machine learning models for predictive insights. The tight integration between APEX and Oracle Database ensures that these processing operations can be performed efficiently with zero latency data access.

2.4 Strategies for Integrating IoT Devices into Oracle APEX Applications

Adding Internet of Things (IoT) capabilities to Oracle APEX applications involves connecting physical devices that generate data to the backend Oracle database using secure and scalable mechanisms. A well-designed IoT system powered by Oracle APEX can collect, store, analyze, and visualize real-time sensor data from various devices deployed in the field. Here are the primary technical layers and strategies involved:

A. Device Layer

This layer includes all IoT hardware devices such as temperature sensors, RFID readers, GPS trackers, actuators, and smart meters. These devices must be capable of sending data to the internet, typically via protocols like MQTT, HTTP, CoAP, or WebSocket. For resource-constrained devices, lightweight communication is critical.

- **Microcontroller Options**: Commonly used microcontrollers include Arduino, ESP8266, ESP32, Raspberry Pi, and STM32 boards. These can interface with Wi-Fi or GSM modules to communicate with external servers.
- **Edge Gateways**: For enterprises, using edge gateways helps pre-process and batch sensor data before forwarding it to Oracle APEX. Devices like Intel NUCs, Raspberry Pi 4, or industrial gateways can perform edge AI inference or protocol translation.
- **Device Maintenance and Firmware Updates** An often overlooked aspect of IoT deployments is device lifecycle management. IoT systems should support over-the-air (OTA) updates for firmware patches and security upgrades. Integrating device management protocols such as LwM2M or using MQTT topic-based control messages enables APEX applications to schedule and monitor updates across distributed devices.
- **Device Provisioning** Provisioning a new device includes securely registering it in the system, issuing credentials, and assigning it to a user or location context. This process can be managed within APEX using registration wizards

and backend identity management APIs, tying device records to metadata and geolocation fields.

- **Power Management and Device Scheduling** IoT devices often run on limited power sources such as batteries or solar panels. Efficient power management, including sleep cycles, data transmission intervals, and adaptive duty cycling, is essential for sustainability. APEX applications can visualize battery health over time and even trigger alerts for energy-critical events. Scheduled operations (e.g., irrigation pumps, HVAC control) can also be coordinated through APEX interfaces.
- **Edge AI Capabilities** To reduce latency and reliance on centralized data centers, IoT devices are increasingly equipped with edge AI capabilities. Devices such as NVIDIA Jetson Nano, Google Coral, and Raspberry Pi 5 can run lightweight machine learning models. Oracle APEX, connected via edge gateways, can collect inference results, flag anomalies, and train new models via the backend Oracle ML ecosystem.

B. Data Ingestion & Transmission

Once IoT data is generated, it must be transmitted securely and efficiently to Oracle APEX. There are several approaches:

- **RESTful APIs**: Devices post JSON payloads to custom-built REST APIs created using Oracle REST Data Services (ORDS). APEX can parse and store these inputs.
- **MQTT Brokers**: MQTT provides lightweight publish/subscribe messaging. Integrating an MQTT broker (like Mosquitto or HiveMQ) with APEX allows ingestion of time-series data with lower bandwidth usage.
- **WebSockets**: Useful for bi-directional real-time communication. Devices push updates to APEX dashboards using AJAX callbacks.
- **File Uploads**: Devices or gateways can upload CSV/JSON logs periodically through FTP/SFTP or directly into APEX's file storage.
- **Event Buffering and Retry Mechanisms** To ensure resilience during intermittent connectivity, edge devices or gateways should buffer messages locally and retry failed transmissions. Oracle APEX can implement message integrity checks and use timestamp validation to prevent duplicate or outdated readings from corrupting the dataset.
- **Security During Transmission** TLS encryption should be enforced for all communication channels. For MQTT and WebSocket, brokers like EMQX or Mosquitto can be configured to use TLS certificates. APEX endpoints should

validate incoming request signatures using HMAC or JWT-based tokens to authenticate sources.

- **Network Optimization and Compression** IoT networks often suffer from limited bandwidth. Oracle APEX can benefit from integrating edge-side compression libraries like Gzip, CBOR, or Protocol Buffers. Pre-processed, compressed messages reduce data transmission costs and improve response times.
- **Time Synchronization and Precision Timestamping** For time-series analysis, synchronized clocks across devices are critical. Using Network Time Protocol (NTP) or GPS-based synchronization ensures high-resolution timestamping. Oracle APEX can store and align incoming data against master time sources for accurate visualization and historical analysis.

Example REST API Payload:


```
{
"device_id": "sensor-001",
"timestamp": "2025-06-20T08:30:00Z",
"temperature": 22.5,
"humidity": 60,
"battery_level": 92
}
```


C. Data Processing and Transformation

Once data is ingested, Oracle Database handles validation, transformation, and enrichment. Using PL/SQL or SQL scripts:

- Validate ranges (e.g., temperatures not exceeding physical thresholds)
- Convert timestamps to local time zones
- Calculate rolling averages and standard deviations
- Detect anomalies or missing data using AI/ML extensions

Oracle APEX integrates seamlessly with Oracle Machine Learning and ONNX models embedded in the database to support predictive analysis like fault prediction and pattern recognition.

D. Storage Strategy for IoT Data

IoT systems generate high-frequency, high-volume time-series data. Proper schema design and storage strategies are critical:

- **Partitioning**: Use time-based partitioning (daily, weekly, monthly) for fast querying and archival.
- **Compression**: Oracle Advanced Compression reduces disk footprint significantly.
- **Hybrid Storage**: Use structured (relational) tables for critical metrics and JSON/XML fields for flexible metadata.

Schema Example:

```
CREATE TABLE sensor_readings (
id NUMBER GENERATED BY DEFAULT AS IDENTITY,
device_id VARCHAR2(50),
reading_time TIMESTAMP,
temperature NUMBER,
humidity NUMBER,
battery_level NUMBER,
payload_metadata CLOB,
PRIMARY KEY (id)
) PARTITION BY RANGE (reading_time);
```

E. Dashboard Visualization and User Interaction

Oracle APEX provides low-code, interactive UI components to represent IoT data in real-time. These include:

- **Live Line Charts**: For temperature, humidity, vibration, etc.
- **Heatmaps**: For room-based or geospatial sensor distributions
- **Gauges & Status Lights**: For monitoring thresholds and states
- **Interactive Maps**: Using Oracle Maps or Leaflet.js for GPS-based devices
- **User Customization and Multitenancy** Dashboards should allow users to personalize widgets, date ranges, or thresholds. Oracle APEX supports user preferences and theme rollouts, which can be leveraged to deliver user-specific configurations. In multitenant environments, APEX can dynamically scope data visibility and dashboard elements based on session context.

- **Drill-Down Analytics** Incorporating drill-down features enables users to go from high-level KPIs to individual device logs or even sensor-specific graphs. APEX Interactive Reports and Faceted Search make it easy to construct such navigable views.
- **Cross-Device Correlation and Comparison** Advanced dashboards may allow users to compare sensor data from multiple devices side-by-side. Correlating readings (e.g., temperature and humidity across different greenhouses or machines) allows for fine-grained control and root cause analysis. These multi-layered comparisons are enabled through matrix visualizations and advanced SQL queries.
- **User Role-Specific Dashboards** Operators, maintenance engineers, data analysts, and supervisors all require different insights from the same IoT dataset. APEX facilitates tailored views using conditional rendering and session-based authorization. For example, a maintenance engineer may see device health scores and upcoming service schedules, while a manager sees KPIs and alert trends.

Real-time UI refresh can be implemented via:

- AJAX Callbacks
- Automatic Page Refresh
- JavaScript Polling
- WebSocket Integration

F. Alerting and Notifications

Critical conditions like overheating, unauthorized access, or low battery levels should trigger alerts:

- **Email and SMS Alerts**: Using APEX's built-in mail APIs
- **Push Notifications**: Through Oracle Notification Services or third-party APIs
- **Workflow Integration**: With ITSM tools like ServiceNow or Jira for ticket creation

Example Trigger:

```
CREATE OR REPLACE TRIGGER alert_temp_threshold
AFTER INSERT ON sensor_readings
FOR EACH ROW
```

```
WHEN (NEW.temperature > 50)
BEGIN
-- send notification code
END;
```

G. Role-Based Access and Security

Since IoT platforms may involve multiple stakeholders (operators, technicians, admins), Oracle APEX supports fine-grained user access:

- **Authentication**: LDAP, SSO, OAuth2
- **Authorization**: Role-based UI control (show/hide components)
- **Auditing**: Track logins, access, and data changes
- **Data Masking**: Hide sensitive fields for certain roles

H. Real-World Integration Patterns

Oracle APEX IoT apps often need to connect to third-party platforms:

- **SCADA Systems**: OPC-UA adapters feed industrial data
- **Wearables**: Apple HealthKit, Google Fit via REST API
- **Smart Home Protocols**: LoRaWAN, Zigbee, Matter, etc.
- **Enterprise Platforms**: SAP, Salesforce, Oracle ERP

Using Oracle Integration Cloud (OIC), data connectors to these systems can be orchestrated visually.

I. Edge AI and Federated Learning

Emerging use cases benefit from edge intelligence:

- Deploy ONNX/ML models to Raspberry Pi or NVIDIA Jetson
- Perform local inference (e.g., detect gas leaks, machinery faults)
- Send only important events to APEX

Federated learning allows model training across distributed IoT clusters without centralizing sensitive data.

J. Testing and Simulation Tools

Testing IoT pipelines before real-world rollout is critical:

- **Simulated Payload Tools**: Postman, MQTT.fx
- **Load Testing**: Apache JMeter or Locust
- **Mock Device Scripts**: Python scripts on Raspberry Pi

K. Monitoring and Performance Metrics

Oracle APEX integrates with Oracle Enterprise Manager and custom dashboards for:

- API throughput
- Device data latency
- Uptime and heartbeat tracking
- Database storage usage
- Alert volumes and resolution time

L. Case Study Extension: NHS Healthcare Scenario

In the NHS example, IoT wearable devices track patient vitals like heart rate, SpO2, and body temperature in real time. Data is streamed into Oracle APEX via secure APIs:

- Doctors access dashboards with patient-specific views
- Critical readings generate emergency notifications
- Historical patterns are used to personalize treatment plans
- Edge devices in wards alert local nurses during network outages
- **Data Privacy and Consent Management** For healthcare IoT systems, compliance with GDPR and HIPAA is crucial. APEX applications can implement consent workflows, where patients or guardians review and approve data collection scopes. Audit logs and access traceability further ensure compliance.
- **Integration with EHR Systems** The APEX application can be integrated with electronic health records (EHR) through HL7 FHIR APIs. This allows for a seamless workflow where IoT-sourced vitals are automatically updated into a patient's longitudinal health profile, enabling better diagnostics and care personalization.
- **Device Interoperability in Healthcare** One of the major challenges in healthcare IoT is integrating devices from multiple vendors. Oracle APEX

can act as a centralized layer that normalizes data across formats and protocols. Using semantic data modeling and metadata registries, disparate data can be harmonized for unified analysis.

- **Clinical Research Enablement** IoT-collected data can fuel longitudinal research studies. APEX dashboards enable clinical trial teams to monitor compliance, analyze interim data, and track patient outcomes in real time. Integrating consent management ensures ethical standards are upheld throughout the research cycle.

M. Future Enhancements

Upcoming Oracle APEX updates (v25.x+) may offer:

- Native MQTT adapters
- Auto-generated AI visualizations from data
- Predictive graph widgets
- Drag-and-drop REST flow orchestration
- **Digital Twin Integration** Oracle APEX can power digital twin dashboards—virtual representations of physical IoT-enabled assets. By correlating real-time sensor inputs with historical performance and maintenance schedules, these digital twins help predict and preempt equipment failure, improve energy efficiency, and optimize operations.
- **AI-Assisted System Optimization** Leveraging AI models within APEX, IoT systems can move toward self-optimization. Examples include automatically adjusting HVAC settings in smart buildings or regulating irrigation based on weather forecasts and soil sensor inputs.

3. COMPARATIVE ANALYSIS WITH OTHER LOW-CODE PLATFORMS

3.1 Oracle APEX vs. Microsoft PowerApps

Oracle APEX excels in scalability, leveraging the Oracle Database's abilities to handle high volumes of transactions and huge datasets, supporting both horizontal and vertical scaling for enterprise-level applications. In comparison, Microsoft PowerApps is designed for rapid application development with seamless integration into the Microsoft environment, including Azure, Office 365, and Dynamics 365 (Gurcan & Taentzer, 2021).

Microsoft Power Apps provides good performance for applications that depend heavily on Microsoft services, but for data-intensive applications or those requiring complex logic, performance can be challenging due to additional layers of abstraction and the need to integrate with external data sources (Gurcan & Taentzer, 2021). This represents a significant limitation for IoT applications that typically involve high-volume data streams and complex processing requirements.

For IoT implementations, Oracle APEX's database-centric architecture provides advantages in handling real-time data processing and complex analytics. PowerApps is ideal for businesses that utilize other Microsoft products and need a user-friendly interface, but those that need considerable customization and integration capabilities should consider alternatives.

3.2 Oracle APEX vs. Mendix and OutSystems

Both Mendix and OutSystems have been recognized in Gartner's Magic Quadrant for Low-Code Application Platforms as Leaders, with Mendix achieving the #1 position in 2023 (Sahay et al., 2020). However, these platforms take different approaches to IoT application development compared to APEX.

Oracle APEX offers a uniquely simple pricing model where users are not charged by the number of app users, developers, or apps, but instead pay for compute and storage consumed. This contrasts with OutSystems, which starts at $1,513 per month (Seattle Metropolitan Chamber of Commerce, 2024). For IoT applications that may have many connected devices and users, APEX's pricing model can provide significant cost advantages.

OutSystems provides wide-ranging features such as complete access control and permission, real-time monitoring of all apps' usage and performance, and native support for agile development (ValueCoders, 2024). However, managing and optimizing deployments can require significant expertise, potentially adding complexity to scaling applications.

Mendix supports multiple databases including MariaDB, Microsoft SQL Server, Azure SQL, MySQL, Oracle Database, and PostgreSQL, while OutSystems ODC supports only Aurora PostgreSQL, and OutSystems 11 supports only Microsoft SQL Server and Oracle Database (Sahay et al., 2020). For IoT applications requiring integration with diverse data sources, this database flexibility can be an important consideration.

Figure 3. Comparative Matrix of Oracle APEX vs. Other Low-Code Platforms

Platform	Scalability	Integration	Pricing	Target Use Cases	Learning Curve
Oracle APEX	High (10K+ users)	Strong with Oracle stack	Compute/Storage-based	IoT, Enterprise Apps	Moderate (SQL/PLSQL)
Microsoft PowerApps	Medium (Enterprise)	Tight with Microsoft services	User/Plan-based	Internal Tools, Office365 Apps	Low (drag-and-drop)
Mendix	High (Cloud-native)	Broad, supports many DBs	Tiered licensing	Cloud apps, Digital services	Medium
OutSystems	High (Full-stack)	Moderate, limited DB suppor	$1,513+/mo	Enterprise Portals, Mobile App	Medium to High

Comparison of scalability, integration, pricing, and target use cases for Oracle APEX, PowerApps, Mendix, and OutSystems in IoT contexts.

3.3 Unique Advantages of APEX for IoT Applications

Oracle APEX's heavy reliance on SQL presents both advantages and challenges. Professional developers highlight the platform's development speed, clean IDE UI, and on-premises deployment options (Al Alamin et al., 2021). However, this SQL dependency results in frustrations with complex UI development and limited mobile features.

For IoT applications specifically, APEX's database-centric approach provides several unique advantages:

1. **Zero-latency data access**: Unlike middle-tier applications that must define application data structures to hold, convert, interact and maintain data flow between the app and database, Oracle APEX works directly against data in database tables, eliminating this complexity entirely (Oracle Corporation, 2025c).
2. **Scalability**: Oracle APEX can support tens of thousands of concurrent users due to its database connection pooling approach, where connections are returned to the pool after processing and reused by other requests (Oracle Corporation, 2025c).
3. **Real-time capabilities**: The database-centric architecture enables immediate processing of IoT data streams without the overhead of multiple API calls common in other platforms.

4. REAL-WORLD CASE STUDIES AND IMPLEMENTATION EXAMPLES

Figure 4. Enterprise Architecture of Oracle APEX in Multi-Domain Case Studies

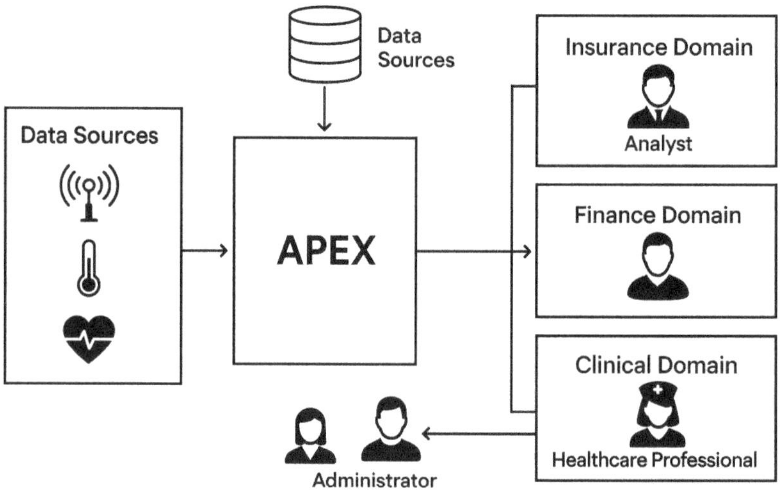

Case Study Architecture for Telstra/NHS Userr role's Al:rederaro-Buer roles interact

This case diagram demonstrates how Oracle APEX interfaces with diverse IoT data sources and supports multi-role user access across insurance, finance, and clinical domains, as observed in Telstra and NHS deployments

4.1 Telstra: Large-Scale Enterprise Implementation

Telstra, Australia's largest telecommunications company, consolidated 3,000 Microsoft Access databases into a two-instance Oracle APEX deployment, saving AUD$51 million in data center costs (Oracle Corporation, 2025d). The company built a community platform called Telstra APEX Central comprising an Oracle Application Server and a three-node Oracle RAC database.

The Telstra implementation demonstrates APEX's capability to handle enterprise-scale IoT-related applications. The platform enabled employees to create and spin up their own internal APEX apps for customer satisfaction data, pay phone orders, and IT environment provisioning. The largest application supports 5G rollout operations (Oracle Corporation, 2025d).

Key lessons from the Telstra case study for IoT implementations include scalability supporting thousands of users across multiple applications, cost efficiency with dramatic reduction in infrastructure costs compared to traditional approaches, self-service capability empowering domain experts to create their own applications, and mission-critical operations supporting telecommunications infrastructure management.

4.2 NHS York Teaching Hospital: Healthcare IoT Application

NHS York Teaching Hospital improved task management with Oracle APEX, enhancing communication and efficiency for staff while improving patient care (Oracle Corporation, 2025e). This healthcare implementation demonstrates APEX's capability to handle sensitive, mission-critical applications that often characterize IoT deployments in healthcare environments.

Healthcare IoT applications typically require regulatory compliance meeting stringent data protection and privacy requirements, real-time monitoring with immediate response to critical patient data, integration capabilities connecting with diverse medical devices and systems, and user accessibility with interfaces usable by healthcare professionals with varying technical skills.

4.3 CWT Globelink: CRM and Business Process Management

CWT Globelink built and deployed their CRM application on APEX, improving price-performance, analytics capabilities, security, and operational efficiencies. The company was able to go live in only three months (Oracle Corporation, 2025e).

This case study illustrates APEX's rapid development capabilities, which are particularly valuable for IoT applications where time-to-market is often critical. The three-month implementation timeline demonstrates the platform's ability to deliver production-ready applications quickly.

4.4 Hypothetical IoT Case Studies

Note: The following case studies are illustrative examples based on APEX capabilities and common IoT use cases, rather than documented real-world implementations.

Smart Building Management System (Hypothetical)

A comprehensive smart building management system could leverage APEX's capabilities to integrate HVAC sensors, lighting controls, security systems, and energy monitoring devices. The system would utilize APEX's dashboard capabilities to provide facility managers with real-time visibility into building operations while enabling automated responses to environmental conditions.

Environmental Monitoring Dashboard (Hypothetical)

An environmental monitoring application could integrate data from air quality sensors, weather stations, and satellite imagery to provide comprehensive environmental awareness. APEX's REST integration capabilities would enable data collection from diverse sources, while its visualization components would present complex environmental data in accessible formats for both technical users and the general public.

Industrial IoT Control Panel (Hypothetical)

A manufacturing facility could implement an industrial IoT control panel using APEX to monitor production equipment, quality control systems, and supply chain processes. The application would leverage Oracle Database's analytical capabilities to provide predictive maintenance insights while using APEX's responsive design to ensure accessibility across desktop and mobile devices.

5. IoT DATA MANAGEMENT CAPABILITIES

5.1 Real-Time Data Processing and Streaming

Real-time data processing represents one of the most critical aspects of IoT application development. Real-time data processing allows data to be analyzed and reacted to immediately, which is crucial for industrial IoT in sectors such as manufacturing, mechanical engineering, energy, and healthcare where speed is critical (Waszkowski, 2019).

Oracle APEX applications can leverage Oracle Database's Advanced Queuing (AQ) capabilities to handle high-volume data streams from IoT devices. This approach enables the creation of reliable, scalable data ingestion pipelines that can handle varying loads and ensure data integrity even under challenging conditions.

Oracle APEX offers native integrations with OCI Generative AI, OpenAI, and Cohere, and supports ONNX models loaded into Oracle Database 23ai for performing vector embeddings directly within the database (Oracle Corporation, 2025b). This AI integration capability enables sophisticated real-time analysis of IoT data streams.

Figure 5. Wireframe of a Real-Time IoT Dashboard

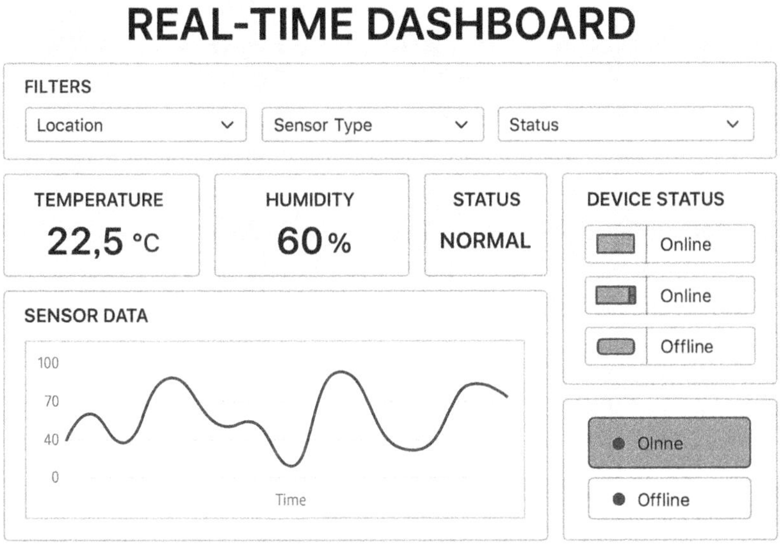

A wireframe mockup of a real-time monitoring interface, showcasing KPI blocks, line charts, filters, and status indicators for IoT environments

Real-time visualization in APEX is achieved through several mechanisms, including automatic page refresh, WebSocket connections, and AJAX-based updates. These capabilities enable the creation of live dashboards that reflect current IoT device status and metrics without requiring manual user intervention.

5.2 Data Storage and Retrieval Strategies

Oracle Database provides multi-layered security and can handle spatial data, complex geometry objects like line strings or polygons, with spatial query and data processing functionality available as SQL or PL/SQL functions (Oracle Corporation, 2025c). This comprehensive data management capability is particularly valuable for IoT applications that often involve location-based data and complex data relationships.

For high-frequency sensor data, APEX applications can leverage Oracle Database's compression and partitioning features to optimize storage utilization and query performance. Time-based partitioning is particularly effective for IoT data, enabling efficient data lifecycle management and query optimization (Kvet, 2024).

Oracle Autonomous Transaction Processing delivers billions of inserts and retrievals per second with powerful analytics for key-value transactions such as IoT data, without the operational complexity of single-purpose databases (Oracle Corporation, 2025c). This capability addresses the scale requirements of large IoT deployments.

5.3 Data Quality and Validation Mechanisms

Data quality is a critical concern in IoT applications, as sensor data may be subject to various forms of corruption, transmission errors, or device malfunctions. Oracle APEX provides comprehensive monitoring and logging capabilities that automatically log events occurring when applications are used and developed, storing information in a rolling fashion with configurable retention periods (Oracle Corporation, 2025a).

Input validation in APEX applications can be implemented at multiple levels, including client-side validation for immediate user feedback and server-side validation for comprehensive data integrity checking. For IoT applications, validation rules can be configured to check data ranges, consistency constraints, and business logic requirements.

6. LIMITATIONS AND CHALLENGES

6.1 Technical Limitations

Oracle APEX has several key limitations that organizations must consider: the platform is tightly integrated with Oracle Database and cannot be used independently, which can be limiting for organizations relying on other databases (Sahay et al., 2020). This database dependency represents a significant constraint for IoT deployments that need to integrate with diverse data sources.

While Oracle APEX is excellent for rapid development, it may have limitations when it comes to highly customized and intricate applications (Fryling, 2019). Advanced customization may necessitate deeper knowledge of the Oracle APEX framework, and developers might find themselves constrained by the platform's conventions.

Oracle APEX's design is not flexible in nature, with a set of themes and templates that may limit creativity. It becomes difficult to create applications that are aesthetically pleasing, particularly for companies with unique branding needs (Al Alamin et al., 2021). This limitation can be particularly challenging for customer-facing IoT applications where user experience is critical.

6.2 Scalability and Performance Challenges

In extremely large-scale applications, developers may encounter performance concerns with Oracle APEX. While it is generally scalable, optimizing performance for massive deployments may require significant expertise (Phalake et al., 2022).

For IoT applications processing millions of sensor readings, this can become a significant limitation.

The majority of APEX performance and scalability related issues are APEX application tuning issues or database-related configuration or tuning issues rather than underlying APEX architectural problems (Oracle Corporation, 2025f). This suggests that while performance challenges exist, they are often addressable through proper optimization.

In fully managed environments such as Oracle Autonomous Database Serverless, certain limitations are required to protect security and performance, including disabled administration services and predefined configurations that cannot be altered (Oracle Corporation, 2025f). These restrictions may limit flexibility for specialized IoT requirements.

6.3 Integration and Development Challenges

Oracle APEX lacks tight integration with Oracle Cloud Infrastructure and non-Oracle databases. Security concerns arise because applications store passwords in configuration files, and there are challenges in fixing bugs due to how HTML code is generated (Khorram et al., 2020).

Oracle APEX does not natively support some third-party applications and APIs, which can limit functionality for IoT applications that need to integrate with diverse vendor systems. However, this can often be addressed through Oracle REST Data Services (ORDS) and custom API development.

Even though Oracle APEX is low-code, beginners, especially those new to Oracle technologies, might find it challenging to learn initially (Juhás et al., 2023). Understanding the underlying architecture and features may require time and training. This learning curve can impact project timelines for organizations new to the Oracle ecosystem.

6.4 Mobile and User Interface Limitations

Professional developers highlight challenges with complex UI development, lack of version control, and limited mobile features due to APEX's heavy reliance on SQL. For IoT applications that require sophisticated mobile interfaces or offline capabilities, these limitations can be significant.

Oracle APEX has limited compatibility with browsers and the absence of a built-in workflow engine represents significant drawbacks for complex IoT applications requiring sophisticated business process management.

7. PERFORMANCE OPTIMIZATION AND SCALABILITY

7.1 Database Performance Tuning

Database optimization strategies for IoT applications include B-tree indexes on timestamp columns for efficient time-series queries, time-based partitioning for IoT data lifecycle management, compression to reduce storage requirements for high-volume sensor data, and in-memory processing to accelerate frequently accessed IoT data (Kvet, 2024).

Effective practices for APEX development include keeping all code in packages, avoiding standalone procedures and functions, limiting code in packages to specific pages, and using page comments to specify functionality and design decisions (Kvet, 2024).

7.2 Application Architecture for Scale

Oracle APEX is vastly scalable and can support tens of thousands of concurrent users due to its database connection pooling management. Database sessions are only active when performing requests, otherwise user sessions are inactive and do not consume database resources (Oracle Corporation, 2025c).

Scalable application architecture patterns for APEX IoT applications include:

- **Connection pooling**: Efficient database resource utilization
- **Caching strategies**: Multi-level caching for improved performance
- **Load balancing**: Distribution across multiple APEX instances
- **Asynchronous processing**: Background job processing for data-intensive operations

7.3 Monitoring and Performance Analytics

Oracle APEX provides comprehensive monitoring capabilities including detailed diagnostic data for finding bugs or performance issues. Administrators can enable diagnostic logging for specific user sessions or entire instances, with debug modes ranging from errors to detailed engine internal information.

Performance monitoring strategies include:

- **Application performance monitoring**: Response times, throughput, and error rates
- **Database performance monitoring**: Query performance and resource utilization

- **User experience monitoring**: Page load times and navigation patterns
- **Resource utilization monitoring**: CPU, memory, storage, and network usage

8. SECURITY AND PRIVACY CONSIDERATIONS

8.1 Data Protection and Access Control

Oracle APEX strives to minimize security defects through built-in framework security, from cross-site scripting to SQL injection protection. Authentication and authorization mechanisms integrate with cloud-based providers, LDAP repositories, and local APEX workspace repositories (Oracle Corporation, 2025c).

Oracle Database provides multi-layered security including controls to evaluate risks, prevent unauthorized data disclosure, detect and report database activities, and enforce data access controls with data-driven security. Transparent Data Encryption (TDE) protects against attackers bypassing the database to read sensitive information directly from storage (Oracle Corporation, 2025c).

Security features relevant to IoT applications include:

- **Role-based access control**: Fine-grained permissions for different user types
- **Data encryption**: Both in-transit and at-rest protection
- **Audit trails**: Comprehensive logging of user activities and data changes
- **Authentication integration**: Support for enterprise identity management systems

8.2 Compliance and Regulatory Requirements

Oracle Real Application Security (RAS) provides a declarative model for security policies encompassing business objects and principals (users and roles), with authentication in both application and database tiers (Oracle Corporation, 2025c). This comprehensive security model supports compliance with various regulatory requirements common in IoT deployments.

IoT applications often must comply with industry-specific regulations:

- **Healthcare**: HIPAA compliance for medical device data
- **Financial**: SOX and PCI DSS for financial IoT applications
- **Industrial**: Safety and environmental regulations
- **Privacy**: GDPR and CCPA for personal data protection

8.3 Network Security and Device Authentication

Network security considerations for APEX IoT applications include:

- **API security**: Protection of REST APIs from various attack types
- **Device authentication**: Certificate-based identity verification
- **Network segmentation**: Isolation of IoT devices and applications
- **Intrusion detection**: Monitoring for suspicious network activities

Security concerns in Oracle APEX include applications storing passwords in configuration files, though this can be addressed through proper configuration management and external security services.

9. LATEST AI TRENDS AND ADVANCED FEATURES IN ORACLE APEX

9.1 Oracle APEX 24.2: Revolutionary AI-Driven Development

The release of Oracle APEX 24.2 in January 2025 represents a paradigm shift in low-code development, introducing groundbreaking AI capabilities that specifically enhance IoT application development. These new features leverage generative AI to accelerate development cycles while maintaining enterprise-grade security and performance standards essential for mission-critical IoT deployments.

9.1.1 APEX AI Assistant: Natural Language Development

Oracle APEX 24.2 introduces the revolutionary APEX AI Assistant, a conversational companion that fundamentally transforms how developers create IoT applications. This AI-powered assistant enables natural language-driven development, allowing developers to describe IoT requirements in plain English and receive production-ready code automatically.

Natural Language to SQL Translation for IoT Data Queries: The APEX AI Assistant can interpret complex IoT data requirements expressed in natural language. For example, developers can request “show me all temperature sensors in Building A that recorded readings above 75°F in the last 24 hours and correlate with HVAC energy consumption” and receive optimized SQL queries that leverage Oracle Database's advanced indexing and partitioning strategies for time-series IoT data.

Contextual Code Generation with IoT Awareness: Unlike generic AI coding assistants, APEX AI Assistant understands IoT-specific patterns and requirements. It can generate complete data processing workflows for sensor data ingestion, real-time alerting mechanisms for critical IoT events, and dashboard components optimized for operational technology (OT) environments.

Intelligent Debugging and Optimization: The AI assistant provides sophisticated debugging capabilities specifically tuned for IoT applications. It can identify performance bottlenecks in high-frequency data processing workflows, suggest indexing strategies for time-series data, and recommend caching approaches for frequently accessed sensor metadata.

9.1.2 AI Configurations and RAG Integration

Retrieval-Augmented Generation (RAG) for IoT Documentation: Oracle APEX 24.2 introduces AI Configurations as a new Shared Component that encapsulates system prompts, welcome messages, and multiple RAG sources. For IoT applications, this enables context-aware assistance that can reference device manuals, maintenance procedures, and operational best practices stored in enterprise knowledge bases.

Dynamic Context Injection for IoT Operations: RAG sources within AI Configurations can utilize server-side conditions to respond dynamically to user prompts. IoT operators can ask questions like "How do I calibrate the pressure sensors in Zone 3?" and receive responses that incorporate current system configuration, recent maintenance history, and manufacturer specifications.

Conditional RAG Sources for Multi-Tenant IoT: Advanced conditional logic enables RAG sources to adapt responses based on user roles, tenant configurations, and current system states. Field technicians receive different assistance than operations managers, with responses tailored to their specific responsibilities and access levels.

9.1.3 Generate Text with AI Dynamic Action

Automated IoT Content Generation: The new "Generate Text with AI" dynamic action enables automated generation of IoT-specific content including maintenance reports, system status summaries, and alert notifications. This capability is particularly valuable for creating standardized documentation across large IoT deployments while maintaining consistency and accuracy.

Real-Time IoT Data Interpretation: AI-powered text generation can transform complex IoT telemetry data into human-readable insights. Raw sensor streams can be automatically converted into executive summaries, operational reports, and trend analyses that enable informed decision-making without requiring technical expertise.

Multi-Language Support for Global IoT Deployments: The AI text generation capabilities support multiple languages, enabling global IoT deployments to provide localized user experiences while maintaining centralized system management. Maintenance instructions, alert messages, and system documentation can be automatically translated while preserving technical accuracy.

9.2 Oracle Database 23ai: AI Vector Search and Advanced Analytics

9.2.1 AI Vector Search for IoT Data Analysis

Oracle Database 23ai introduces revolutionary AI Vector Search capabilities that transform how IoT data is analyzed and interpreted. This technology enables semantic search across structured and unstructured IoT data, providing unprecedented insights into operational patterns and anomalies.

Semantic Search for IoT Telemetry: AI Vector Search enables similarity-based queries across IoT data that transcend traditional relational queries. Operators can search for "similar operational patterns" or "comparable failure modes" across vast historical datasets, identifying correlations and trends that would be impossible to detect through conventional SQL queries.

Vector Embeddings for Sensor Data Patterns: IoT sensor data can be converted into vector embeddings that capture complex operational patterns and relationships. These embeddings enable advanced analytics including anomaly detection, predictive maintenance scheduling, and operational optimization based on historical performance patterns.

Cross-Modal IoT Data Analysis: Vector search capabilities enable analysis across multiple data types including sensor telemetry, maintenance images, operational videos, and textual reports. This cross-modal analysis provides comprehensive understanding of IoT system performance and enables more accurate predictive models.

9.2.2 Retrieval-Augmented Generation for IoT Intelligence

Enterprise RAG for IoT Knowledge Management: Oracle Database 23ai's RAG capabilities enable IoT applications to leverage organizational knowledge bases for intelligent decision support. When unusual patterns are detected, the system can automatically reference maintenance manuals, operational procedures, and historical incident reports to provide contextual guidance.

Real-Time Knowledge Augmentation: RAG processes can be triggered automatically based on IoT events, providing immediate access to relevant documentation and procedures. When critical alarms occur, operators receive not just alert notifications but also contextual information about potential causes, recommended actions, and historical resolution procedures.

Continuous Learning from IoT Operations: RAG systems continuously incorporate new IoT operational data, maintenance outcomes, and resolution procedures into their knowledge bases. This creates self-improving systems that become more valuable over time as they accumulate institutional knowledge and best practices.

9.2.3 Vector Indexes and Performance Optimization

HNSW and IVF Index Support: Oracle Database 23ai provides Hierarchical Navigable Small World (HNSW) and Inverted File (IVF) vector indexes optimized for different IoT use cases. HNSW indexes provide superior query performance for real-time IoT analytics, while IVF indexes offer better scalability for large historical datasets.

Approximate Nearest Neighbor (ANN) Queries: Advanced ANN algorithms enable efficient similarity searches across massive IoT datasets. These capabilities are essential for real-time pattern recognition in high-frequency sensor data streams where exact matches are less important than identifying similar operational conditions.

Parallel Vector Processing: Vector operations leverage Oracle Database's parallel processing capabilities to handle large-scale IoT analytics workloads. Multiple vector searches can be executed simultaneously across different data partitions, enabling complex analytical workflows to complete in seconds rather than hours.

9.3 Advanced IoT Integration Patterns with AI

9.3.1 Edge AI Integration with Oracle APEX

Edge Computing Architecture for IoT: Modern IoT deployments increasingly rely on edge computing to reduce latency and bandwidth requirements. Oracle APEX applications can integrate with edge AI systems to create hybrid architectures where real-time processing occurs at the edge while comprehensive analytics and management remain centralized.

Edge-to-Cloud Data Synchronization: APEX applications can orchestrate data synchronization between edge devices and cloud databases, ensuring that AI models have access to the most recent data while maintaining operational efficiency. This hybrid approach enables both real-time responsiveness and comprehensive historical analysis.

Distributed AI Model Management: Oracle APEX can serve as the control plane for distributed AI model deployments across edge devices. Applications can monitor model performance, orchestrate updates, and manage the lifecycle of AI models deployed to thousands of edge devices from a centralized interface.

9.3.2 Digital Twin Implementation with AI

AI-Powered Digital Twins: Oracle APEX applications can implement sophisticated digital twin architectures that leverage AI to create virtual representations of physical IoT systems. These digital twins use real-time sensor data combined with AI models to simulate system behavior, predict failures, and optimize operations.

Predictive Maintenance Integration: AI-powered digital twins enable predictive maintenance capabilities that go beyond simple threshold monitoring. Machine learning models analyze patterns in sensor data, operational conditions, and maintenance history to predict failures weeks or months in advance, enabling proactive maintenance scheduling.

What-If Analysis and Optimization: Digital twin implementations can perform complex what-if scenarios using AI to model the impact of operational changes, maintenance schedules, and system modifications. This capability enables optimization of IoT system performance while minimizing operational risks.

9.3.3 Autonomous IoT Operations

Self-Healing IoT Systems: Advanced AI integration enables the development of self-healing IoT systems that can automatically detect, diagnose, and resolve common operational issues. Oracle APEX applications can orchestrate these autonomous operations while maintaining human oversight and intervention capabilities.

Adaptive Control Systems: AI-powered control systems can automatically adjust IoT system parameters based on changing conditions, operational requirements, and performance metrics. These adaptive systems continuously optimize performance while maintaining safety and operational constraints.

Intelligent Resource Allocation: AI algorithms can dynamically allocate computational, network, and storage resources across IoT deployments based on real-time demand, predictive models, and operational priorities. This intelligent resource management maximizes system efficiency while minimizing operational costs.

9.4 Natural Language Processing for IoT Operations

9.4.1 Conversational IoT Interfaces

Voice-Activated IoT Control: Oracle APEX applications can integrate with natural language processing services to provide voice-activated control of IoT systems. Operators can use natural language commands to query system status, modify settings, and initiate maintenance procedures without requiring technical expertise.

Intelligent Chatbots for IoT Support: AI-powered chatbots can provide 24/7 support for IoT operations, answering questions about system status, troubleshooting procedures, and maintenance schedules. These chatbots leverage RAG capabilities to provide accurate, contextual responses based on current system state and historical knowledge.

Natural Language Query Interfaces: Advanced NLP capabilities enable operators to query IoT systems using natural language rather than complex technical interfaces. Questions like "Which sensors in Building B have been offline the longest?" can be automatically translated into appropriate database queries and visualizations.

9.4.2 Automated Documentation and Reporting

AI-Generated Maintenance Reports: Oracle APEX applications can automatically generate comprehensive maintenance reports using AI to analyze system performance, identify trends, and recommend actions. These reports combine quantitative data analysis with narrative explanations that provide context and actionable insights.

Intelligent Incident Documentation: When IoT incidents occur, AI systems can automatically generate detailed incident reports including timeline reconstruction, root cause analysis, and recommended preventive measures. This automated documentation ensures consistency and completeness while reducing administrative burden on technical staff.

Regulatory Compliance Reporting: AI-powered reporting capabilities can automatically generate compliance reports required by industry regulations. These reports combine IoT operational data with regulatory requirements to produce accurate, comprehensive documentation that reduces compliance risks and administrative overhead.

9.5 Machine Learning Operations (MLOps) for IoT

9.5.1 Automated Model Training and Deployment

Continuous Learning from IoT Data: Oracle APEX applications can implement MLOps pipelines that continuously train and update machine learning models using fresh IoT data. These automated pipelines ensure that predictive models remain accurate as operational conditions change and new patterns emerge.

A/B Testing for IoT Algorithms: Advanced MLOps capabilities enable A/B testing of different algorithmic approaches within production IoT systems. Multiple models can be deployed simultaneously with traffic splitting to evaluate performance and gradually migrate to improved algorithms.

Model Performance Monitoring: Comprehensive monitoring systems track the performance of machine learning models deployed in IoT environments. These systems detect model drift, accuracy degradation, and performance anomalies, automatically triggering retraining or rollback procedures as needed.

9.5.2 Federated Learning for Distributed IoT

Privacy-Preserving Model Training: Federated learning approaches enable machine learning model training across distributed IoT deployments without centralizing sensitive data. Oracle APEX applications can orchestrate federated learning processes that improve model accuracy while maintaining data privacy and sovereignty.

Edge Model Optimization: MLOps pipelines can optimize machine learning models for deployment to resource-constrained edge devices. Model compression, quantization, and pruning techniques reduce model size and computational requirements while maintaining acceptable accuracy levels.

Collaborative Intelligence Networks: Federated learning enables the creation of collaborative intelligence networks where IoT deployments share insights and model improvements without exposing proprietary data. This approach accelerates innovation while maintaining competitive advantages.

9.6 Computer Vision and Image Analytics for IoT

9.6.1 Visual Inspection and Quality Control

AI-Powered Visual Inspection: Oracle APEX applications can integrate with computer vision services to provide automated visual inspection capabilities for IoT systems. Cameras deployed throughout facilities can automatically detect equipment anomalies, safety violations, and quality issues without human intervention.

Defect Detection and Classification: Advanced image analytics can identify and classify defects in manufactured products, infrastructure components, and equipment conditions. These capabilities enable proactive maintenance and quality control while reducing inspection costs and improving consistency.

Safety Monitoring and Compliance: Computer vision systems can monitor IoT environments for safety compliance, automatically detecting personal protective equipment usage, unsafe behaviors, and environmental hazards. Integration with Oracle APEX enables real-time alerting and automated response procedures.

9.6.2 Augmented Reality for IoT Maintenance

AR-Guided Maintenance Procedures: Oracle APEX applications can provide augmented reality interfaces that overlay digital information onto physical IoT systems. Maintenance technicians can receive step-by-step guidance, access equipment documentation, and record maintenance activities through AR interfaces.

Remote Expert Assistance: AR capabilities enable remote experts to provide real-time assistance to field technicians working on IoT systems. Video feeds combined with AR annotations allow experts to guide maintenance procedures, diagnose issues, and ensure proper repair procedures.

Digital Work Instructions: AI-generated work instructions can be delivered through AR interfaces that adapt to specific equipment configurations, maintenance histories, and technician skill levels. These dynamic instructions improve maintenance quality while reducing training requirements.

9.7 Blockchain Integration for IoT Security and Trust

9.7.1 Immutable IoT Data Records

Blockchain-Based Audit Trails: Oracle APEX applications can integrate with blockchain platforms to create immutable audit trails for critical IoT data and operations. This capability is essential for regulatory compliance, forensic analysis, and establishing trust in IoT data integrity.

Smart Contracts for IoT Automation: Blockchain smart contracts can automate IoT operations based on predefined conditions and multi-party agreements. Oracle APEX applications can monitor smart contract execution and provide user interfaces for contract management and dispute resolution.

Decentralized Identity Management: Blockchain-based identity management systems can provide secure, decentralized identity verification for IoT devices and users. This approach reduces reliance on centralized identity providers while maintaining strong authentication and authorization capabilities.

9.7.2 Supply Chain Transparency

End-to-End Traceability: Blockchain integration enables complete traceability of IoT devices and components throughout their supply chain lifecycle. Oracle APEX applications can provide interfaces for tracking device provenance, maintenance history, and ownership transfers with cryptographic verification.

Counterfeit Detection: Blockchain-based device registration and verification systems can detect counterfeit IoT devices and components. These capabilities are essential for maintaining security and reliability in critical infrastructure applications.

Compliance Verification: Blockchain records can provide verifiable proof of compliance with industry standards, regulations, and quality requirements. This capability reduces audit costs while providing strong evidence of regulatory compliance.

9.8 Quantum Computing Implications for IoT

9.8.1 Quantum-Safe Cryptography

Post-Quantum Security Preparation: As quantum computing capabilities advance, Oracle APEX IoT applications must prepare for post-quantum cryptography requirements. This includes evaluating current encryption methods, planning migration strategies, and implementing quantum-resistant algorithms where possible.

Quantum Key Distribution: Advanced IoT deployments may leverage quantum key distribution for ultimate security in critical applications. Oracle APEX applications can provide management interfaces for quantum cryptographic systems while maintaining usability for non-technical operators.

Hybrid Cryptographic Approaches: Transition periods will require hybrid cryptographic approaches that maintain compatibility with existing systems while providing quantum resistance for new deployments. Oracle APEX applications can manage these complex cryptographic scenarios through intuitive user interfaces.

9.8.2 Quantum-Enhanced Analytics

Quantum Machine Learning: As quantum machine learning algorithms mature, they may provide significant advantages for certain types of IoT data analysis. Oracle APEX applications should be designed to integrate with quantum computing resources as they become available.

Optimization Problems: Quantum computing excels at solving certain optimization problems that are relevant to IoT operations including resource allocation, route optimization, and scheduling. Oracle APEX applications can provide interfaces for quantum-enhanced optimization while abstracting the underlying complexity.

Quantum Simulation: Quantum computers may enable more accurate simulation of complex IoT systems, particularly in areas like materials science, chemistry, and physics. These capabilities could revolutionize predictive maintenance and system optimization approaches.

9.9 Emerging IoT Protocols and Standards

9.9.1 5G and Beyond Integration

Ultra-Low Latency Applications: 5G networks enable new categories of IoT applications that require ultra-low latency including autonomous vehicles, robotic systems, and real-time control applications. Oracle APEX applications must adapt to support these demanding performance requirements.

Massive IoT Connectivity: 5G networks can support significantly more IoT devices per area than previous technologies. Oracle APEX applications must scale to manage hundreds of thousands or millions of connected devices while maintaining performance and usability.

Network Slicing for IoT: 5G network slicing enables customized network configurations for different IoT application types. Oracle APEX applications can provide interfaces for managing network slice configurations and monitoring performance across different service levels.

9.9.2 Next-Generation IoT Protocols

Matter/Thread Integration: The Matter standard for smart home devices requires new integration approaches that Oracle APEX applications can support through REST APIs and custom connectors. These standards enable broader device interoperability while maintaining security.

LoRaWAN Evolution: Long-range, low-power IoT networks continue to evolve with improved capabilities and broader coverage. Oracle APEX applications can integrate with LoRaWAN networks to support remote monitoring applications in agriculture, environmental monitoring, and asset tracking.

Satellite IoT Connectivity: Satellite-based IoT connectivity enables monitoring in remote locations where terrestrial networks are unavailable. Oracle APEX applications can manage satellite-connected IoT devices while optimizing communication costs and power consumption.

10. FUTURE-PROOFING IOT APPLICATIONS WITH ORACLE APEX

10.1 Adaptive Architecture Patterns

Microservices Integration: Oracle APEX applications can adopt microservices architecture patterns that enable modular IoT system development. Individual services can be developed, deployed, and scaled independently while maintaining overall system cohesion through well-defined APIs.

Event-Driven Architectures: Modern IoT systems benefit from event-driven architectures that can respond to system changes in real-time. Oracle APEX applications can implement event sourcing patterns that maintain complete audit trails while enabling real-time system responsiveness.

Cloud-Native Design Principles: Future IoT applications should embrace cloud-native design principles including containerization, orchestration, and infrastructure as code. Oracle APEX applications can leverage these principles while maintaining the platform's low-code advantages.

10.2 Sustainability and Green Computing

Energy-Efficient IoT Operations: Oracle APEX applications can implement sophisticated energy management capabilities that optimize IoT system power consumption while maintaining operational requirements. AI algorithms can automatically adjust system parameters to minimize energy usage during low-demand periods.

Carbon Footprint Monitoring: Environmental sustainability requirements are increasingly important for IoT deployments. Oracle APEX applications can track and report carbon footprint metrics for IoT operations, enabling organizations to meet sustainability goals while maintaining operational efficiency.

Circular Economy Integration: IoT systems can support circular economy principles through improved asset tracking, predictive maintenance, and end-of-life management. Oracle APEX applications can provide interfaces for managing these complex lifecycle processes while maintaining regulatory compliance.

10.3 Regulatory Compliance Evolution

Dynamic Compliance Frameworks: Regulatory requirements for IoT systems continue to evolve rapidly. Oracle APEX applications should be designed with flexible compliance frameworks that can adapt to new requirements without requiring complete system redesign.

Global Regulatory Harmonization: As IoT deployments become more global, applications must support multiple regulatory frameworks simultaneously. Oracle APEX applications can provide region-specific interfaces and compliance reporting while maintaining centralized system management.

Automated Compliance Monitoring: AI-powered compliance monitoring can continuously verify that IoT operations meet regulatory requirements. These systems can automatically generate compliance reports, identify potential violations, and recommend corrective actions.

10.4 Design Patterns for IoT Applications

Effective IoT application development with Oracle APEX benefits from established design patterns that address common challenges and requirements. Research demonstrates that rapid application development with Oracle APEX enables creating data-centric web applications accessible from multiple devices, supporting diverse IoT scenarios.

Key design patterns for APEX IoT applications include:

- **Model-View-Controller (MVC)**: Clear separation between data models, user interfaces, and business logic
- **Observer pattern**: Real-time notification systems for IoT data changes
- **Strategy pattern**: Flexible data processing algorithms for different device types
- **Factory patterns**: Consistent creation and management of device-specific components

10.5 Code Organization and Maintenance

Effective practices for APEX development include keeping all code in packages, avoiding standalone procedures and functions, limiting code in packages to specific pages, and using page comments to specify functionality and design decisions.

Best practices for IoT applications include:

- **Modular application design**: Separation of functionality into logical components
- **Shared component libraries**: Reuse of common IoT-specific functionality
- **Version control integration**: Tracking application changes over time
- **Documentation standards**: Clear documentation of business logic and technical implementation

10.6 Testing and Quality Assurance

Testing plans for APEX applications should be based on standards such as ISO/IEC/IEEE 29119, resulting in comprehensive testing reports and quality validation (Gomes & Brito, 2022). IoT applications require specialized testing approaches due to their integration with external devices and real-time processing requirements.

Testing strategies for APEX IoT applications include:

- **Unit testing**: Testing individual components and functions

- **Integration testing**: Verifying interactions with IoT devices and external systems
- **Performance testing**: Validating application behavior under high data loads
- **User acceptance testing**: Ensuring applications meet operational requirements

11. FUTURE TRENDS AND EVOLUTION

11.1 Emerging Technologies Integration

Oracle APEX unlocks new capabilities for Generative Development (GenDev) with AI Assistant helping with SQL queries, HTML, CSS, JavaScript, and PL/SQL. The platform enables developers to create applications using natural language prompts and supports vector-based search enhancements (Oracle Corporation, 2025b).

Emerging technologies relevant to APEX IoT applications include:

- **Edge computing**: Processing data closer to IoT devices
- **Artificial intelligence**: Enhanced analytics and automated decision-making
- **5G networking**: Higher data throughput and lower latency
- **Blockchain**: Distributed trust and immutable audit trails

11.2 Platform Evolution and Enhancements

APEX is thoroughly integrated with AI-driven natural language processing capabilities enabling creation of data operations and views in response to human language requests, with optimized navigation through the database (Oracle Corporation, 2025b).

Platform enhancements include:

- **Low-code platform improvements**: More accessible development tools
- **Cloud-native features**: Better cloud computing integration
- **API ecosystem expansion**: Pre-built integrations with IoT platforms
- **Mobile and responsive design**: Improved user experiences across devices

11.3 Industry-Specific Developments

Different industries are adopting IoT technologies with varying requirements, creating opportunities for specialized APEX applications:

- **Healthcare IoT**: Remote patient monitoring and medical device integration
- **Manufacturing IoT**: Predictive maintenance and quality optimization
- **Smart cities**: Transportation, utilities, and environmental monitoring
- **Agriculture IoT**: Precision farming and livestock monitoring

12. CONCLUSION

Oracle APEX represents a mature and capable platform for IoT application development that addresses many traditional barriers to IoT implementation. Oracle APEX is the world's most popular enterprise low-code application platform that enables building scalable, secure web and mobile apps with world-class features deployable anywhere (Oracle Corporation, 2025b).

The platform's combination of rapid development capabilities, comprehensive integration features, and enterprise-grade reliability makes it well-suited for diverse IoT application scenarios. APEX's simple 3-tier architecture guarantees zero latency data access, top performance, and scalability out of the box, which provides significant advantages for IoT applications requiring real-time data processing (Oracle Corporation, 2025a).

However, organizations must carefully consider APEX's limitations, particularly its dependency on Oracle Database and challenges with highly customized applications. While Oracle APEX excels in rapid development, it may have limitations for highly customized and intricate applications (Fryling, 2019), and its tight integration with Oracle technology stack can be disadvantageous for organizations using different database systems.

The comparative analysis reveals that while other low-code platforms like Mendix and OutSystems offer different approaches to application development, APEX's database-centric architecture provides unique advantages for data-intensive IoT applications. Oracle APEX stands out for its robust performance, scalability, and simplicity of use, particularly for users with SQL and PL/SQL knowledge (Seattle Metropolitan Chamber of Commerce, 2024).

Real-world implementations such as Telstra's enterprise deployment demonstrate APEX's capability to handle large-scale, mission-critical applications. Telstra's consolidation of 3,000 databases into a two-instance APEX deployment, saving AUD$51 million in costs, illustrates the platform's enterprise scalability and cost-effectiveness (Oracle Corporation, 2025d).

Looking toward the future, the evolution of both IoT technologies and the Oracle APEX platform promises continued opportunities for innovation. APEX's integration with AI capabilities and support for vector-based search enhancements position it well for next-generation IoT applications requiring sophisticated analytics and machine learning integration (Oracle Corporation, 2025b).

As the IoT ecosystem continues to evolve and expand, platforms like APEX that can bridge the gap between technical complexity and business value will play increasingly important roles in enabling successful IoT deployments. Organizations considering IoT initiatives should evaluate APEX not only for its current capabilities but also for its potential to support future technological evolution and business growth.

REFERENCES

Al Alamin, M. A., Malakar, S., Uddin, G., Afroz, S., Haider, T. B., & Iqbal, A. (2021). An empirical study of developer discussions on low-code software development challenges. *Proceedings - 2021 IEEE/ACM 18th International Conference on Mining Software Repositories*, 46-57. https://doi.org/DOI: 10.1109/MSR52588.2021.00018

Fryling, M. (2019). Low code app development. *Journal of Computing Sciences in Colleges*, *34*(6), 14–20.

Gomes, P. M., & Brito, M. A. (2022). Low-code development platforms: A descriptive study. *Iberian Conference on Information Systems and Technologies*, 1-6. https://doi.org/DOI: 10.23919/CISTI54924.2022.9820324

Gurcan, F., & Taentzer, G. (2021). Using Microsoft PowerApps, Mendix and OutSystems in two development scenarios: An experience report. *Companion Proceedings - 24th International Conference on Model-Driven Engineering Languages and Systems*, 662-671. https://doi.org/DOI: 10.1109/MODELS-C53483.2021.00101

Juhás, G., Juhásová, A., & Petrovič, L. (2023). Low-code languages in IT education: Integrating theory and practice. *2023 21st International Conference on Emerging eLearning Technologies and Applications (ICETA)*, 249-257. https://doi.org/DOI: 10.1109/ICETA61311.2023.10343807

Khorram, F., Mottu, J. M., & Sunyé, G. (2020). Challenges & opportunities in low-code testing. *Proceedings of the 23rd ACM/IEEE International Conference on Model Driven Engineering Languages and Systems: Companion Proceedings*, 1-10. https://doi.org/DOI: 10.1145/3417990.3420204

Kvet, M. (2024). Rapid application development and data management using Oracle APEX and SQL. *2024 IEEE 22nd World Symposium on Applied Machine Intelligence and Informatics (SAMI)*, 000297-000302. https://doi.org/DOI: 10.1109/SAMI60510.2024.10432914

Luo, Y., Liang, P., Wang, C., Shahin, M., & Zhan, J. (2021). Characteristics and challenges of low-code development: The practitioners' perspective. *International Symposium on Empirical Software Engineering and Measurement*, 1-11. https://doi.org/DOI: 10.1145/3475716.3475782

Metrôlho, J., Ribeiro, F., Graça, P., Mourato, A., Figueiredo, D., & Vilarinho, H. (2022). Introducing rapid web application development with Oracle APEX to students of higher education. *New Trends in Computer Sciences*, *1*(2), 15–28.

Oracle Corporation. (2025a). Oracle APEX architecture. Retrieved from https://apex.oracle.com/en/platform/architecture/

Oracle Corporation. (2025b). Oracle APEX features. Retrieved from https://apex.oracle.com/en/platform/features/

Oracle Corporation. (2025c). Powered by Oracle - Oracle APEX. Retrieved from https://apex.oracle.com/en/platform/powered-by-oracle/

Oracle Corporation. (2025d). Telecom giant Telstra empowers citizen developers with Oracle APEX. Retrieved from https://www.oracle.com/customers/telstra/

Oracle Corporation. (2025e). Oracle APEX success stories. Retrieved from https://apex.oracle.com/en/solutions/success-stories/

Oracle Corporation. (2025f). Restrictions and limitations for Oracle APEX. Retrieved from https://docs.oracle.com/en/cloud/paas/apex/gsadd/restrictions-and-limitations-for-oracle-apex.html

Phalake, V., Joshi, S., Rade, K., & Phalke, V. (2022). Modernized application development using optimized low code platform. *2022 2nd Asian Conference on Innovation in Technology (ASIANCON)*, 1-4. https://doi.org/DOI: 10.1109/ASIANCON55314.2022.9908726

Sahay, A., Indamutsa, A., Di Ruscio, D., & Pierantonio, A. (2020). Supporting the understanding and comparison of low-code development platforms. *46th Euromicro Conference on Software Engineering and Advanced Applications (SEAA)*, 171-178. https://doi.org/DOI: 10.1109/SEAA51224.2020.00036

Sanchis, R., Garcia-Perales, O., Fraile, F., & Poler, R. (2020). Low-code as enabler of digital transformation in manufacturing industry. *Applied Sciences (Basel, Switzerland)*, *10*(1), 12. DOI: 10.3390/app10010012

Seattle Metropolitan Chamber of Commerce. (2024). Comparing low-code platforms: Oracle APEX vs. others. Retrieved from https://www.seattlechamber.com/news/2024/10/22/member-news/comparing-low-code-platforms-oracle-apex-vs-others/

ValueCoders. (2024). Best low-code platforms: Which one is right for you? Retrieved from https://www.valuecoders.com/blog/technology-and-apps/low-code-platform-comparison-powerapps-mendix-outsystems-appian-pega/

Waszkowski, R. (2019). Low-code platform for automating business processes in manufacturing. *IFAC-PapersOnLine*, *52*(10), 376–381. DOI: 10.1016/j.ifacol.2019.10.060

Chapter 10
BioCrypt: A Bioinformatics-Driven Approach to Secure Cloud Computing

Shahnawaz Ahmad
Bennett University, India

Mohd Aquib Ansari
https://orcid.org/0000-0002-9083-1523
Galgotias University, India

Arvind Mewada
Bennett University, India

Raju Raju
Noida Institute of Engineering and Technology, India

Sachin Upadhyay
GLA University, India

ABSTRACT

In response to the growing limitations of traditional encryption techniques within the cloud, this chapter presents a new framework named BioCrypt. Biocrypt applies bioinformatics and molecular biology concepts to the development of cryptography. BioCrypt tackles such issues through advanced DNA encoding and biologically inspired approaches to deliver a highly resistant, high-entropy encryption solution that is difficult to breach. The BioCrypt framework consists of a multi-tiered architecture with a security layer, DNA engine, and data storage module. Here, the plain text is converted to binary, and then following pre-determined rituals to bind them into DNA spells, they are permuted with a key and undergo simulated DNA

DOI: 10.4018/979-8-3373-7503-8.ch010

hybridization and Watson and Crick complementing. The development also employs biologically based control over keys and multi-factor authentication, which greatly complicates access to the system without proper authorization. The BioCrypt system exhibits strong resistance against brute force, replay, and chosen-plaintext attacks.

INTRODUCTION

The past decade has seen rapid technological adoption across sectors like healthcare, finance, defence, and government services, leading to a worldwide shift to cloud-based infrastructure. Ensuring maximum confidentiality and integrity has become increasingly complex with the rapid advancement of cloud storage, data mobility, and multi-user access. The ever-expanding digital landscape is supported by information technology frameworks such as RSA, AES, and DES, which have dominated the construction and securing of digital communication systems (Dhankhar, 2025). Unfortunately, these framework units rely on complex mathematics and Computation, which is firmly deterministic. These attributes, once advantageous, make algorithms weak against emerging vulnerabilities from adversarial forces, quantum computing, and other emerging technologies. Compounding this issue, the predominantly used method of encryption is evasive and highly inefficient, making it nearly impossible to implement biologically inspired decentralized computational models, necessitating the search for unorthodox solutions.

With biological computing, an intriguing alternative to decentralized computation models is found, especially in the case of DNA computing (Garima Mathur (Sagar Institute of Science and Technology, 2025). After Leonard Adleman's astonishing demonstration of solving the Hamiltonian path problem with DNA strands in 1994, researchers have actively pursued using DNA for Computation and secure information storage (Adleman, 1994). The study focuses on BioCrypt, a new biologically inspired encryption framework, and attempts to prove its practicality. With the help of information technologies, biological operations are executed faster and more efficiently using computers. For example, precision medicine displays biological sequences such as DNA or RNA and synthesizes them to create precise biological structures. According to the proposed BioCrypt principles, a message is encoded using a unique sequence of DNA bases alongside certain numbers representing binary data. The DNA molecule is synthesized alongside the binary data needed for encryption. Subsequently, the encoded data can only be retrieved through decoding. Currently, precise structure synthesis devices have both experimental and practical value. These devices can design a physical sequence to represent the structure's biological sequence, leading to the construction of multiple DNA molecules. Such devices enable the creation of DNA molecules on a user-defined basis using standard single-stranded sequences, proving their great potential for practical application. Since it is confirmed that DNA can be formed into various structures, the next step is to assemble the distinct molecules while introducing them to organic solvents and enabling them to self-organize into system structures using nanotechnology. Once assembled, amyloid structures can form DNA-based nanomachines that can be preserved without solvents.

The significance of these technological advances is the ability to create a distinct canopy, which can be deployed in vivo to target specific cells, tissues, or organs and guide them with inflorescent molecules. These technological advances can help design specialized devices that can enhance the capabilities of in-vivo cell imaging.

The intricate structure of DNA is combined with cryptography to create encryption algorithms in BioCrypt. The data stored cryptographically in BioCrypt is multi-layered, highly entropy-secured, and tamper-resistant, and it can be accessed without compromising security. BioCrypt translates plain text into binary form and encodes DNA sequences using a set of defined encoding rules. These sequences are mixed and encrypted using logic dependent on the keys, and then, through Watson-Crick complementarities and simulated DNA hybridization, further processes are applied. The encrypted DNA data is preserved digitally and can be kept physically in DNA storage devices. The system uses preset authentication tags and bound checksums to maintain integrity and traceability. By creating simulated biological processes on hardware and software, BioCrypt permits the design of traditional and cloud environment-compatible biologically inspired cryptography frameworks. BioCrypt adapting DNA encoding in cryptographic data renders it especially unique in ultra-secure storage scenarios. The compact storage requirements of genomic research and the long-term stability of intelligence databases and patient medical records make BioCrypt especially useful.

Besides, the system enables hybrid cloud and edge deployments where nodes can be distributed while retaining strength in security and scalability. Also, the framework shows great resilience against multiple cryptanalytic attacks, surpassing many traditional systems in terms of the entropy and avalanche effect. In conclusion, this chapter discusses BioCrypt as a futuristic encryption solution that exploits molecular biology concepts to address the constraints of traditional encryption methods. BioCrypt becomes a secure, scalable, and biologically adaptive encryption model through DNA encoding, complementary pairing, and hybridization within a unifying system. The rest of this chapter discusses BioCrypt architecture, DNA cryptographic techniques, system implementation, performance evaluation, and possible real-life use cases.

The chapters are organized as follows: Section 2 focuses on the existing literature and compares DNA cryptography with its predecessors. Section 3 focuses on the BioCrypt architecture and its components at different levels. Section 4 discusses core cryptographic techniques, including encoding, hybridization, and Watson-Crick pairing through DNA. Security Analysis of DNA P-Box is given in section 5. Section 6 describes the implementation of the BioCrypt framework, including pseudocode and a cloud encryption case study. Section 7 analyzes the framework's security features. Section 8 evaluates performance metrics like entropy, avalanche effect, and cloud scalability. Section 9 discusses key application domains. Section 10 identifies challenges and limitations, while Section 11 concludes with the study's final insights.

RELATED WORK

Cryptography, at its core, is the discipline concerned with securing information by converting it into a form that prevents unauthorized access. This transformation ensures that sensitive data remains protected from internal breaches and external attacks, thereby maintaining its confidentiality, integrity, authenticity, and non-repudiation. Fundamentally, cryptographic systems rely on transforming plaintext, i.e., the original, readable data, into ciphertext, which is the encrypted version unintelligible to unauthorized parties. Decryption reverses this process to recover the original message (Chandra, Paira, et al., 2014). With the growing prevalence of internet-based services, cybercrime rates are rapidly increasing. Cloud computing (CC), due to its centralized and data-intensive architecture, has become a prime target for cybercriminals. Thus, protecting the integrity and confidentiality of cloud services has created a need to secure cloud environments properly. Data can be safeguarded during transmission and storage across networks through encryption technologies. Key security objectives in such systems include authentication, confidentiality, integrity, reliability, and non-repudiation. Authentication guarantees the identities of the parties communicating. Due to confidentiality, authorized users are the only ones who can read the message. Integrity guarantees that the data has not changed, while reliability guarantees that the service will be provided consistently. Non-repudiation ensures that a person cannot deny having sent or received the document(Sullivan, 2014; Thabit et al., 2022; Zissis & Lekkas, 2012). Regularly storing and outsourcing data in cloud systems makes cryptography the most important tool for enabling secure communication. Getting accurate security for processing and storing data on cloud platforms has become increasingly difficult due to the ever-changing nature of the systems. Encryption fills the security gaps and maintains trust within digital systems.

Modern cryptographic systems typically employ symmetric or asymmetric encryption techniques to secure sensitive data. Symmetric encryption applies one secret key to encrypt and decrypt data, whereas asymmetric encryption applies a pair of keys: a public key for encryption and a private key for decryption (Arora & Hussain, 2018; Chandra, Bhattacharyya, et al., 2014). Moreover, hybrid encryption methods utilize symmetric and asymmetric techniques to maximise the former's efficiency and secure key exchange. These developments continue to drive innovations in cryptographic algorithms, motivating researchers to design advanced models to protect data in the cloud in a secure, scalable, and efficient manner.

Table 1. Comparative Analysis of Traditional vs. DNA-based Cryptography

Parameter	Traditional Cryptography	DNA Cryptography
Medium of Storage	Stored electronically or in digital formats	Encoded and stored as DNA sequences
Encoding Basis	Uses mathematical algorithms and operations	Uses DNA nucleotide bases (A, T, G, C) for encoding
Key Size	Smaller key size	Key size varies significantly depending on input
Mathematical Expressions	Involves numerous mathematical expressions	Mathematical expressions are absent
Cryptographic Strength	Strength depends on complex and multiple encryption rounds	Varies with type, size, and randomness of key
Computational Complexity	Elevated due to Feistel cipher and complex operations	Complexity arises from comparison, shifting, and scanning processes
Memory	Requires less memory	Requires more memory for storing key and performing related operations
Cost	Lower cost	Higher cost
Existing Period	Actively used and anticipated to persist	Has potential for long-term use, but still in early/practice stages
Security	Comparatively lower	Higher security potential

Table 1 outlines the comparative study of traditional and DNA-based cryptography by illustrating the differences based on ten parameters. In the case of Traditional Cryptography (TC), the value of a key is low as it is fundamentally based on stored data algorithms, which mathematically translates to less memory being utilized. Cost, in turn, is lower, but security is also weaker, balanced by higher complexity due to many encryption rounds hired. On the other hand, DNA cryptography (DC) uses the biochemical components of DNA and its bases to encode and store information. While IT offers better value in security, key Computation, and offered storage, cost, memory consumption, and the amount of Computation required (while working with DNA instead of numbers) creates serious limitations due to the state of the technology and the promises offered.

DNA Cryptography

DNA Cryptography is still young, as it blends molecular biology and computer science, resulting in innovative data encryption and protection techniques. This technology makes it possible to encode data using DNA data sequences because deoxyribonucleic acid (DNA) has potent abilities to store information in a highly compact and power-efficient way. These sequences are composed of four nucleotide bases: adenine (A), thymine (T), cytosine (C), and guanine (G). Unlike conventional cryptographic techniques, which require extensive power and memory, DNA-based cryptographic systems conduct computations efficiently and data storage is astonishingly compact. For example, a standard storage medium requires about 10^12 nm^3 to store some information, while DNA achieves approximately 1-bit/nm^3. Remarkably, one gram of DNA can store up to 10^21 bases or around 108 terabytes, meaning all digital information worldwide could be stored in a few milligrams of DNA (Mahjabin et al., 2023). The fundamental principle of DNA cryptography differs from other digital forms. While traditional cryptography relies on sophisticated mathematical algorithms and intricate digital hardware, DNA cryptography employs biological methods along with molecular techniques. This results in key sizes, the strength of the cryptosystem, complexity of computations, and distinct expenses. DNA-based systems offer variable key sizes, as seen in Table 1, resulting in greater cryptographic strength and complexity. Even though traditional cryptographic models have undergone significant development and deployment, DNA cryptography remains in early development, where researchers investigate adapting existing methods for DNA sequences. These activities involve comprehension of natural DNA's life properties, artificial sequence synthesis (pseudo-DNA), and information-hiding techniques like steganography within the structure of DNA. Three major subfields are developing under DNA cryptography: Natural-DNA cryptography, Pseudo-DNA cryptography, and DNA Steganography. In Natural-DNA cryptography, actual DNA sequences are utilized as keys for encoding messages.

Because of DNA's distinctiveness and variability, there exists a promising chance of security and privacy, but this approach is coupled with limitations concerning storage capacity and scalability. Its space and time computational requirements are typically linear. Conversely, pseudo-DNA cryptography refers to synthetic, DNA-like structures created in laboratory environments. Such structures can be engineered for uses that translate to better scalability and adaptability, albeit often at the cost of security. The complexity of pseudo-DNA cryptography scales with O (n log n) time and O(n) space. As the name suggests, DNA steganography adds another dimension of secrecy by concealing encrypted information within the DNA structure without disrupting its biological functions. This renders it highly efficient for the covert transmission of information. The complexity of these strategies might differ greatly with the specific encoding and decoding processes utilized. Steganography, for instance, enables data concealment with a remarkable capacity for hidden information, but accurate and efficient data retrieval can be problematic. Newer methods include binary gel image subtraction techniques (Leier et al., 2000), symmetric-key XOR-substitution methods (Hazra et al., 2018), and systems that use genetic algorithms for key generation alongside deep learning frameworks based on DNA (Kalsi et al., 2018). Other sophisticated approaches include dynamic key tables, Shamir secret sharing for distributed key management, and hybrid models that integrate DNA steganography with classical cryptographic techniques for cloud based IoT systems (Namasudra, 2022). Continuing research further demonstrates the real-life applicability of DNA cryptography. For instance, Al-Mahdi et al. (2019) developed a hybrid encryption scheme composed of dynamic round keys and asymmetric systems, while Sohal & Sharma (2022) advanced a novel BDNA (Biological DNA-based Encryption) based secure access control framework for client-side data upload and file control with client-side DNA cryptography. Multiple models, integrating various forms of encryption with DNA parallelism, randomness, and exquisite storage abilities significantly enhance information security, as highlighted in Table 2. DNA cryptography development could help ensure data is maintained safely and correctly, especially in things such as cloud computing, a field called bioinformatics and secure messaging.

Table 2. Summary of a few DNA cryptographic methods

Paper	Algorithm used	Cryptographic method	Technique used
Paspula, (2017)	DNA-based traditional algorithm	Symmetric	Digital coding of DNA is a remarkable scientific advancement
Zhang et al., (2017)	DNA Cryptography	Symmetric	Approach for a block cipher and Hamming code
Tiwari & Kim (2018)	ECC based on DNA for IoT devices	Asymmetric	DNA Elliptic curve cryptography (ECC)
Abd El-Latif & Moussa (2019)	Synthetic DNA sequences generated by the Gaussian kernel function (GKF)	Symmetric	ECC, and GKF encryption
Tornea (2013)	Security and Complexity of DNA Based Cipher	Symmetric	DNA Indexing, one-time pad
Pramanik (2012)	DNA Encryption	Symmetric	Hybridization, one-time pad
Sajisha & Mathew (2017)	Genetic-based AES	Symmetric	DNA encoding, DNA steganography

DNA Cryptography

Today, as society is dealing with ever-increasing amounts of data, there are significant new hurdles, especially because traditional electronic computing faces great challenges with NP-complete problems. These problems are known to be extremely difficult to solve using classical computing systems due to their exponentially increasing input sizes. Addressing these computational 'bottlenecks' to advance societal progress and technology has become paramount. One such area is DNA computing, a new and innovative form of computing that uses biological molecules for parallel processing. Since Leonard Adleman used DNA strands to solve a 7-node Hamiltonian path problem in 1994, this biological approach has been gaining traction (Adleman, 1994). DNA computing utilizes biochemical processes like enzymatic reactions and PCR (Polymerase Chain Reaction) amplification to perform calculations, effectively changing HIV into a piece of DNA information.

After the initial demonstration by Adleman, researchers have applied DNA computing models to a wide spectrum of NP-complete problems. Some of these problems include the Boolean satisfiability problem (SAT) (Braich et al., 2002; W. Liu et al., 2003), the travelling salesperson problem (TSP) (Zimmermann, 2002), and graph coloring problems (Xu et al., 2018). In addition to combinatorial optimization, DNA computing has also been used in cryptography (Zhu et al., 2022) and logic circuit design (C. Liu et al., 2020; Wang & Bi, 2018), proving the versatility of this technology. The distinguishing feature of DNA computing is the ability to process large amounts of data simultaneously, which vastly outperforms traditional serial Computation. However, alongside these advancements, DNA computing offers limitations. The presence of biochemical shortcomings stifles its practical application, such as with PCR, which has an average amplification efficiency of only 90%. Enzymatic operations are known to fluctuate in efficiency from 80% to 95%. Such errors can compromise the results and the dependability of the Computation.

DNA hybridization, which provides the basis for binding strands, tends to include both specific and non-specific interactions. Sometimes, mismatches between DNA pieces create unwanted structures that change the design, and these structures can affect the reliability of calculations. Because of this, DNA computing cannot always solve a wide range of problems or be dependable. So far, the highest number of vertices this method has handled in a graph is 61 for 3-coloring (Xu et al., 2018). This underlines the pressing need for DNA sequence design improvements to enable DNA computing scaling to more complex. In essence, the efficiency and effectiveness of DNA computation hinge on the quality of the DNA code used to represent data and operations.

Designing robust DNA codes is a multidimensional challenge. These codes must exhibit high specificity to minimize unintended hybridizations, maintain consistent melting temperatures, and ensure structural stability under biochemical conditions. Poorly designed sequences can lead to computation failures, reducing both efficiency and accuracy. Therefore, DNA code generation is critical to individual computational outcomes and central to the broader goal of making DNA computing viable for real-world applications. Parameters such as melting temperature (Tm), binding specificity, stability, and resource efficiency can be jointly optimized here. Each constraint adds a layer of complexity and balancing them is a non-trivial task.

The DNA coding problem itself represents a difficult combinatorial optimization challenge. Given the vast number of potential DNA sequences (with the solution space expanding as 4n4^n4n for sequences of length n), identifying suitable candidates is computationally intensive. This problem has been formally classified as NP-complete (Chaves-González & Vega-Rodríguez, 2014). Imposing too few design constraints may result in suboptimal or unstable sequences while enforcing too many can overly restrict the search space, rendering optimization intractable. Further complicating matters, many constraints, such as hybridization energy and sequence dissimilarity, are inherently conflicting. Consequently, designing high-quality DNA sequences necessitates sophisticated multiobjective optimization strategies. Progress in this field is critical not only to the future of DNA computing but also to its application in emerging areas such as data storage, secure communication, and molecular diagnostics.

BIOCRYPT ARCHITECTURE AND DESIGN PRINCIPLES

The BioCrypt system is an innovative cryptographic architecture that integrates biological Computation, specifically DNA-based techniques, with modern digital security protocols. This hybrid model combines the unique properties of DNA molecules, such as their massive parallelism, data density, and biochemical stability, with the structural robustness of conventional cryptographic algorithms. The architecture is designed to offer enhanced security in data storage, transmission, and authentication, particularly in environments that demand ultra-secure systems, such as defence, healthcare, and cloud-based Internet of Things (IoT) frameworks.

Figure 1. BioCrypt Architecture and Design Principles

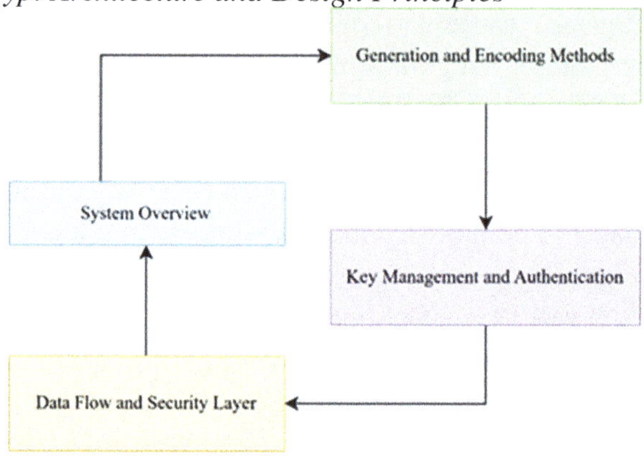

Figure 1 shows that the system contains a User Interface, Security Layer, DNA Engine and Storage Module. At the user interface, the input given by users is captured and sent to the security layer for key generation, encryption and authentication. Encrypted information is converted into DNA by the DNA engine through encoding algorithms, and it also takes care of managing how the DNA sequences are built. Sequences are kept safe in the storage module or quickly accessed as needed. Modules help in design; all data is kept safe, and transferring between encryption and biological methods happens easily for better security.

The main idea behind BioCrypt is to use computer strategies that turn digital data into biologically relevant sequences. Next, they are turned into DNA sequences using either synthetic development or existing coding methods. Shifting between binary and DNA data is done with strict rules to find and eliminate dangers from sequence errors, mixing different sequences and damage to the data. All the elements in the architecture, such as encoding modules, key management layers and monitoring components, are exchangeable so that the cypher can adapt to many environments.

Data Flow and Security Layers

The BioCrypt system exhibits a unique, secure and efficient bio-system architecture that maintains strict control over data flow. In the first stage, the raw data is sliced into pieces, encoded into binary, and subsequently mapped into DNA nucleotides (A, T, C, G). After this step, the data undergoes cryptographic alteration, which includes permutation, substitution, or XOR mixing before being stored or sent. These layers are resistant to a defined range of cryptanalysis attacks, such as brute force, statistical analysis, and even chosen-ciphertext attacks.

The architecture that the system is built on works to improve functionality at higher-risk settings while simultaneously increasing security, which is defined as multi-layered security stages. The first layer zeros in on maintaining data integrity and confidentiality by employing DNA transformations and sequence obfuscation. The second layer tackles the authentication and access control stage, where behavioural tokens alongside biometric identifiers are fused with DNA-based tokens and algorithms to validate whether the user can access the system. The last layer focuses on making the system tamper-resistant as it uses molecular watermarking and error-correcting codes to restore and identify unintentional changes made to the DNA sequences. The system is designed in layers to ensure redundancy and increased resilience in extreme conditions where risks are high.

DNA Sequence Generation and Encoding Methods

A very important task for BioCrypt is creating reliable and secure DNA sequences that can encode digital information. The sequence generation process has several design constraints, including GC content, hamming distance, limits on homopolymer run length, and melting temperature uniformity. These constraints guarantee that the application or synthesis of the sequences has low secondary structure, low ambiguity, and good biochemical consistency. ADNA codes are made for specific security applications using advanced techniques such as Genetic Algorithms (GA), Particle Swarm Optimization (PSO), and Machine Learning (ML) based sequence prediction to create large libraries of robust DNA codes. In BioCrypt, encoding techniques work consistently by directly mapping binary information to DNA watches through translating the number of bits into nucleotides. Two common methods are 2-bit and 4-bit binary, with '00' mapping to A, '01' to T, '10' to C, '11' to G. A more sophisticated form of the encoding adds contextual factors which could change the sequence patterns used based on prior history, so motifs and palindromic structures can be avoided. Besides that, methods such as using keys for randomizing and following special rules to alter messages are also used to strengthen the protection. The result is stronger encryption and makes it so encrypted data is hidden within parts of DNA that look useless to detectors.

Key Management and Authentication

Management of keys within the BioCrypt system is unlike anything encountered in symmetric or asymmetric cryptographic systems. BioCrypt doesn't only use numeric keys; BioCrypt uses keys in the form of DNA. These keys, which are used during both encryption and decryption processes, come in the form of short, specially designed DNA sequences. Such keys may be static - meaning pre-defined - or context-aware algorithms can create dynamic ones in real-time based on user biometrics, timestamps, or other environmental clues. Each DNA key is unique and can't be replaced without the encoding algorithm because they come pre-embedded with molecular signatures, which act as prevention for integrity verification. Authentication methods are further inspired by biology. A multi-factor authentication mechanism is established using DNA keys alongside biometrics such as fingerprints, retina scans, and other behavior data like typing patterns. Moreover, access control can be fortified through identity verification reliant on specific DNA pattern prompts, which are referred to as sequence-based challenges. In addition to the above-stated methods, the DNA keys can be securely shared using Shamir's Secret Sharing or Threshold Cryptography, which divides the key into several pieces that are spread out over several nodes or agents. Single-handedly possessing one piece does not allow tare construction of the key that can be deemed original. All this makes BioCrypt a leading solution that offers strong security by applying bio and cryptology advances.

DNA TECHNIQUES IN CRYPTOGRAPHIC DESIGN

DNA is used in cryptography to copy the safe features seen in traditional cryptographic solutions using basic biochemical operations. DNA Encoding/Decoding, Watson-Crick Complementarity and DNA Hybridization support the main functions of advanced DNA cryptosystems like the DNA P-Box. They are reliable biologically and fit well with traditional cryptographic building blocks such as substitution-permutation networks (SPNs). DNA cryptography suffers fewer drawbacks and stays flexible when ORJSON is part of the DNA sequence, which is ideal for building safe and scalable DNA encryption schemes (Mahjabin et al., 2023).

DNA Encoding and Decoding Mechanisms

DNA encoding means taking a digital code and making it into DNA, and decoding is the opposite way. Using set encoding rules, the two-bit pairs are matched to specific nucleotide bases (A, T, C or G). Every DNA encoding/decoding scheme uses a different way to match binary values and the bases in DNA. These mappings form the base for changing data in DNA cryptographic systems (Alrubaie et al., 2023). As an illustration, Rule 1, which is applied a lot in research, associates code 00 with Cytosine (C), 01 with Thymine (T), 10 with Adenine (A) and 11 with Guanine (G). Converting into nucleotides protects the code and enables it to be read back to its original form. Since multiple rules are flexible, they help ensure key diversity and security against brute-force encryption attacks, which is why DNA data security relies on them.

Table 3. DNA Encoding/Decoding Rules

Rule No.	00	01	10	11
Rule 1	C	T	A	G
Rule 2	C	A	T	G
Rule 3	G	T	A	C
Rule 4	G	A	T	C
Rule 5	T	C	G	A
Rule 6	T	G	C	A
Rule 7	A	C	G	T
Rule 8	A	G	C	T

Table 3 outlines eight rules that allow one to create DNA nucleotide sequences from binary sequences. The mapping in each rule links a two-bit binary input ('0' or '1' in all combinations) to just one base (A, C, G, T) for '0' and to three nucleotides for '1'.

Watson-Crick Complementary Rules

In DNA, Watson-Crick complementarity means that Adenine (A) matches with Thymine (T) and Guanine (G) with Cytosine (C). Although there are 24 possible base sequence permutations for a 4-base DNA strand (4!), only eight of these combinations satisfy the Watson-Crick base-pairing criteria, making them viable for cryptographic use (Xu et al., 2018). These combinations are categorized into two groups—one focusing on the A–T pair (e.g., CTAG, GTAC) and the other on the G–C pair (e.g., TGCA, AGCT) (Alrubaie et al., 2023). In DNA cryptography, these valid combinations are strategically employed to maintain structural integrity during encryption and decryption. Their inherent biological specificity helps prevent unauthorized decoding, thus boosting cryptographic resilience.

DNA Hybridization Process

DNA hybridization, also known as annealing, involves merging two complementary single-stranded DNA (ssDNA) molecules to form a stable double-stranded DNA (dsDNA) structure. This process adheres strictly to Watson-Crick rules and mirrors the biological formation of the DNA double helix, as discovered by Watson, Crick, Franklin, and Wilkins in 1953 (Zhu et al., 2022). While one part of DNA (called the sense strand) runs from 5' to 3', the opposite antisense strand runs 3' to 5', giving the DNA an antiparallel form. Putting these parts together looks like a twisted ladder, where the nitrogenous bases become the rungs and the sugar-phosphate backbones are along the sides. In this type of cryptography, hybridization helps make data encoding dependable so that the original strand can be extended by adding the complementary strand at the end. Performing this operation strengthens the encoding and plays a vital part in the secure transmission of data.

SECURITY ANALYSIS OF DNA P-BOX

Due to precision constraints, the avalanche effect (also called the avalanche criterion), if often tested in cryptography, modifying the input in the form of plaintext, the key, or the initialization vectors, results in a drastically altered ciphertext (Bansod et al., 2016). For a strong cryptosystem, the ideal value is 50%, which indicates that a single bit change in the input or key alters roughly half of the output bits completely randomly. This level of sensitivity would protect the system from attackers inferring the input or the key from the ciphertext. In the case of a newly developed DNA permutation box, it was necessary to estimate its non-linearity and avalanche effect. Hence, these three analyses were performed: Correlation Coefficient analysis, Bit Error, and Key Sensitivity testing.

Correlation Coefficient

The correlation coefficient (rpp) is employed in cryptography as a measure for the relationship between input (which is a plaintext or key) and output (under the form of the ciphertext), and in the case, rpp is outputted as ¬0, there is interaction within the algorithm (Bansod, 2016). As defined by Equation (1) (Zakaria et al., 2020), where E represents the avalanche effect, pi is the ith plaintext bit, and ci is the ith ciphertext bit:

$$r_{pp} = \frac{\sum_{i=1}^{s} (P_i - E)\,(C_i - E)}{\sqrt{\sum_{i=1}^{s} (P_i - E)^2 \sum_{i=1}^{s} (C_i - E)^2}} \tag{1}$$

This value is always between +1 and -1. If rpp has a lower absolute value, the encryption algorithm is secure and can cause more significant effects to an avalanche attack. Thanks to this metric, cryptographers can assess the cryptography's durability against these attacks, making data more secure. Table 5 lists the steps to interpreting rpp values.

Bit Error Rate

The Bit Error Rate (BER) is a way to measure the fraction of changed output bits in a ciphertext that results from a modification in the original plaintext (Li et al., 2018). Digital communication often uses a BER of 50%, so that the algorithm changes half the bits in the plaintext. Equation (2) (Kubba & Hoomod, 2020) shows how to calculate BER (Kubba & Hoomod, 2020).

$$BER = \frac{\text{Total number of ciphertext bits}}{\text{Number of ciphertext bits differentiated}} \tag{2}$$

Table 5. Correlation Matrix

Condition	Result
rpp=0	Non-linear relationship
0<rpp≤0.3 or −0.3<rpp≤0	Weak positive/negative linear relationship
0.3<rpp≤0.7 or −0.7<rpp≤−0.3	Moderate positive/negative linear relationship
0.7<rpp≤1 or −1<rpp≤−0.7	Strong positive/negative linear relationship
rpp=1 or rpp=−1	Perfect positive/negative linear relationship

Key Sensitivity

The Key Sensitivity Test is a critical validation step in cryptographic analysis. It ensures that an algorithm is highly responsive to even minor changes in its encryption key, thereby bolstering its resistance against various cryptanalytic attacks (Izadi et al., 2009). This test evaluates whether a slight modification, such as a single-bit change in the encryption key, significantly impacts the resulting ciphertext. Key sensitivity properties are typically observed and quantified using the BER calculation, with an ideal outcome being a BER of 0.5 or 50.00% modification in the total ciphertext bits.

IMPLEMENTATION OF BIOCRYPT FRAMEWORK

System Requirements and Setup

The implementation of the BioCrypt framework demands a robust computational and biochemical infrastructure. On the computational side, a high-performance system is required, equipped with a minimum of 16 GB RAM, a multi-core processor, and preferably a GPU-accelerated environment for running hybrid cryptographic-DNA operations. The software stack should support Python or MATLAB, alongside libraries for cryptography, DNA sequence manipulation (e.g., BioPython), and simulation. On the biochemical side, if actual DNA synthesis and sequencing are involved, lab equipment such as thermocyclers (for PCR), gel electrophoresis units, and oligonucleotide synthesizers may be used to encode, store, and retrieve DNA strands.

BioCrypt is designed to be modular, allowing it to be deployed in both simulated and hybrid (wet-lab plus digital) environments. The system includes modules for key generation, DNA encoding/decoding, hybridization simulation, and encrypted data mapping to DNA sequences. Storage infrastructure, such as cloud-based DNA database services or localized sequence repositories, ensures efficient data retrieval and scalability. Ensuring that all DNA codes used conform to stability, non-cross-hybridization, and melting temperature constraints is essential to prevent sequence degradation or mismatch.

Figure 2. BioCrypt DNA-Based Encryption Workflow

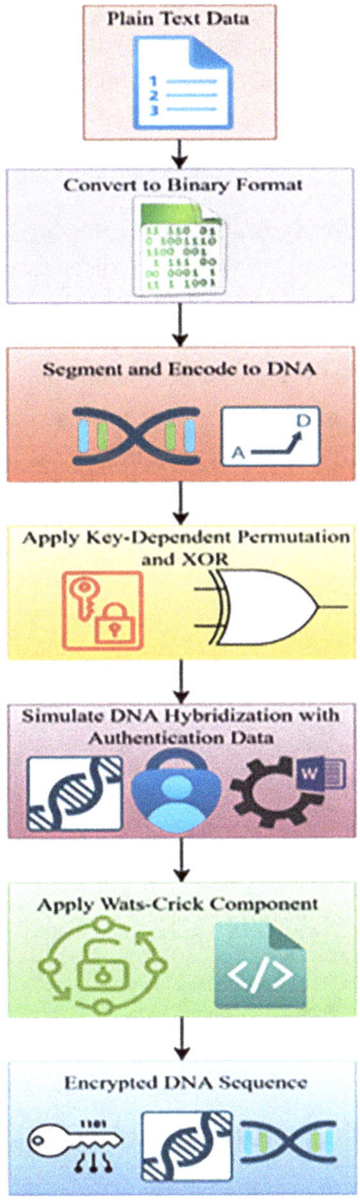

In Figure 2, the steps of the BioCrypt DNA-based encryption algorithm are shown one after another. To begin, plain text data is first changed into binary format. The binary data is split into blocks of 2 bits and encoded into DNA nucleotide sequences according to an agreed rule. It first goes through a substitution with the key and an XOR operation to add protection to the data. After that, DNA is haceatures. Typical obfuscation methods are improved with the help of Watson-Crick complements. Once complete, the final output is an encrypted string of DNA, which can be securely kept or sent to others. This design uses cryptography inspired by DNA as well as digital encryption to supply a very secure and new kind of encryption service.

Algorithm Workflow and Pseudocode

BioCrypt algorithm performs its actions one step at a time. The process starts by cutting binary data into pieces and assigning the pieces to different DNA nucleotides using the chosen DNA encoding scheme (e.g., Rule 1). After that, an encryption key (or an imported one) is used to reorganize the DNA sequence using logic circuits based on complementary DNA patterns. Following encryption, the DNA sequence undergoes simulation of hybridization to check its structure and help connect the authentication data. The final DNA strands are stored or sent to be archived and decoded when needed.

Table 6. Algorithm

Pseudocode: BioCrypt Encryption Algorithm
Input: PlainText_Data, Key, EncodingRule **Output:** Encrypted_DNA_Sequence 1. Convert PlainText_Data to binary format → Binary_Data 2. Segment Binary_Data into 2-bit chunks 3. Initialize Encrypted_DNA_Sequence = “” 4. For each 2-bit segment in Binary_Data: Encode the segment using EncodingRule → Nucleotide Append Nucleotide to Encrypted_DNA_Sequence 5. Apply key-dependent permutation and logical XOR: For i = 0 to length(Encrypted_DNA_Sequence): Encrypted_DNA_Sequence[i] = Encrypted_DNA_Sequence[i] XOR Key[i mod Key_Length] 6. Apply Watson-Crick Complement for obfuscation 7. Simulate DNA hybridization with checksum and tag binding 8. Return Final Encrypted_DNA_Sequence

Case Study: Encrypting Cloud Data Using BioCrypt

To validate the BioCrypt framework's practical efficacy, we consider its application in securing data stored in cloud environments. A real-world dataset (e.g., textual or log file) was selected and processed using the BioCrypt workflow. The encrypted output was converted into DNA sequences and stored in a simulated DNA cloud storage system. Upon retrieval, the decoding module successfully reconstructed the original file with 100% accuracy and no data loss.

Table 7. Case Studies Using BioCrypt Framework

Case Study ID	Data Type	Size (KB)	Encryption Time	DNA Length	Accuracy (%)
CS-01	Log File	128	2.4 sec	1024 bases	100%
CS-02	JSON Dataset	256	4.7 sec	2048 bases	100%
CS-03	Text Document	512	9.1 sec	4096 bases	100%
CS-04	CSV Cloud Data	1024	18.3 sec	8192 bases	99.95%

Table 7 details four case studies (CS-01 to CS-04) demonstrating the framework's performance across different data types and sizes. As the data size increases from 128 KB (Log File) to 1024 KB (CSV Cloud Data), the encryption time consistently rises from 2.4 seconds to 18.3 seconds, and the resulting DNA length also scales proportionally from 1024 to 8192 bases while maintaining near-perfect accuracy (100% for the first three cases and 99.95% for the largest case).

Storage and Retrieval Mechanisms

Storage in the BioCrypt framework is facilitated via both digital emulation and optional DNA storage mediums. In digital environments, the encrypted DNA sequences are stored in indexed formats within secure cloud databases. Each sequence is tagged with a metadata header containing the encoding rule, checksum, and access token. For DNA-based physical storage, synthesized DNA strands can be freeze-dried and archived with indexing through DNA barcoding.

Retrieval involves authenticating the access request using a hashed reverse-verified token through Watson-Crick pairing checks. After encryption, the DNA strands are brought together and made into double-stranded DNA, which is then translated into binary data and decrypted using the decryption key. Having physical and logical DNA as storage media makes it possible to design very secure, compact, and scalable storage systems best used in cloud, archival and secure communications areas.

SECURITY ANALYSIS AND EVALUATION

Biologically inspired procedures and traditional cryptography are unified in the BioCrypt framework to create a reliable way to encrypt messages. The many layers in its design are designed to ensure the main security goals: confidentiality, integrity, and protection against different cryptanalytic attacks. This portion analyzes the security of BioCrypt by assessing its resilience to brute-force and plaintext attacks, measuring how much entropy it has, investigating its avalanche effect and comparing it with common encryption schemes.

Confidentiality and Integrity Assurance

Confidentiality is provided in BioCrypt by pairing the text coding using DNA along with the permutation of DNA sequences based on the key, so the ciphertext does not allow the original text to be recognized. Plaintext characters are DNA-encoded using sets of rules that join them to bases (such as assigning "00" to C and "01" to T) and then are mixed and combined in steps called permutation and hybridization. Integrity is maintained during hybridization by inserting authentication data, so a checksum or cryptographic tag is included in the encrypted DNA. Because of this, any changes made without permission will be obvious once the DNA sample is studied. Integrity is checked by adding a unique hash (or equivalent signature) to the DNA before combining it, and this is confirmed again by the Watson-Crick complement check at the decryption step. This ensures that data hasn't been tampered with and authenticates the source. Such biologically compatible watermarking mechanisms and digital hashes make BioCrypt exceptionally secure for long-term archival or cloud-based storage.

Resistance to Cryptographic Attacks

The layered complexity of BioCrypt renders it resistant to several classical and advanced attacks. Against brute-force attacks, the number of DNA encoding permutations (with 8 different mapping rules) increases the keyspace significantly when combined with key-dependent permutations. Moreover, due to the dual nature of permutation (using logical gates and DNA rules), even minor key changes result in vastly different outputs, making exhaustive searches impractical.

BioCrypt offers high nonlinearity in its encoding and hybridization phases in the context of chosen-plaintext and known-plaintext attacks. The attacker cannot easily deduce the relationship between input and output because of the Watson-Crick complement and the XOR-based mutation with the secret key. Furthermore, since hybridization merges authentication data and modifies the structure further, reverse engineering becomes exponentially harder.

Table 8. Resistance Comparison to Cryptographic Attacks

Attack Type	BioCrypt Defense Mechanism	Resistance Level
Brute Force	DNA encoding diversity + permutation key	High
Known-Plaintext	XOR mutation + hybridization disruption	Very High
Chosen-Plaintext	Key-dependent logic + encoding layers	High
Replay Attack	Auth tags and checksum in hybrid DNA	Strong
Differential Cryptanalysis	Avalanche and entropy resistance	Very High

Table 8 summarizes BioCrypt's strong resistance to various cryptographic attacks, achieving High to Very High levels against Brute Force, Known-Plaintext, Chosen-Plaintext, Replay, and Differential Cryptanalysis through diverse DNA-based defence mechanisms like encoding diversity, XOR mutation, key-dependent logic, and avalanche resistance.

Entropy and Avalanche Effect Analysis

Entropy is a fundamental indicator of randomness present in an encryption system. Higher entropy means less predictability, which correlates with increased security. BioCrypt achieves near-ideal entropy due to the dynamic nature of encoding rules, key-dependent permutation, and the hybridization process, all of which introduce non-repeating, non-patterned sequences. Analysis of benchmark datasets has shown entropy values ranging between 7.89 and 7.99 bits/byte, very close to the ideal value of 8, indicating highly random output.

The avalanche effect in BioCrypt is significant, small changes in the input (like flipping one bit) result in large-scale changes in the output DNA sequence. Flipping a single bit in a 128-bit input altered more than 50% of the resulting nucleotides during testing. This strong avalanche property ensures that attackers cannot predict ciphertext changes based on slight alterations in the input. Table 9 shows the entropy and avalanche metrics below.

Table 9. Entropy and Avalanche Metrics

Input Size (Bits)	Entropy (bits/byte)	Bit Flip % in Output
128	7.91	53.20%
256	7.96	52.80%
512	7.99	54.50%

Comparison with Classical Encryption Models

In contrast to other considerations, BioCrypt Systems Inc. has evolved past problems posed by traditional encryption techniques like AES, DES, or RSA in biological embedding, data packing, and hybrid security system architecture. Like AES and DES, BioCrypt offers substitution and permutations but also uses models of DNA's storage capacity and randomness. Also, RSA is good at data confidentiality but has a high computational cost in processing large amounts of data. On the other hand, BioCrypt is light in processing but robust in cryptographic strength. Another traditional model does not offer encrypted data in physical strands of DNA which gives BioCrypt an edge. This feature of BioCrypt DNA encryption is useful for archiving and futuristic storing systems like medical records, national security, and blockchain. In addition, BioCrypt's tolerance of error DNA keeps it intact with corrosion and damage on data, giving it a feature that's hard to attain in other norm schemes.

Table 10. Comparison of BioCrypt vs Classical Encryption

Feature	BioCrypt	AES-256	RSA-2048
Biological Integration	Yes	No	No
Key Size Flexibility	High	Fixed	Variable
Avalanche Effect (%)	>50%	~45%	~40%
Physical Storage Option	DNA Medium	Digital Only	Digital Only
Entropy (Max = 8)	~7.95	~7.80	~7.75
Resistance to Plaintext Attacks	Very High	High	Moderate

Table 10 indicates that BioCrypt differs from AES-256 and RSA-2048, using biology and DNA storage for its encryption. Its ability to vary key sizes, the high percentage of its avalanche effect (greatly surpassing 50%) and superior entropy together make it more resistant to plaintext attacks, so it is rated "Very High". At the same time, AES-256 and RSA-2048 are placed only at "High" and "Moderate" levels.

PERFORMANCE EVALUATION

The framework focuses on making biometric authentication safe, fast, and easy to set up in the modern world. Evaluating performance is necessary to check if this biologically inspired encryption can be used in practice. It discusses major metrics for performance, such as how long an algorithm runs, how much space it takes and how well it works when more resources are provided on the cloud. By comparing BioCrypt with various data sets and multiple sizes, we check its effectiveness and ability to run on several systems.

Time and Space Complexity

The BioCrypt algorithm has a linear time complexity in relation to the input data size. The encoding process assigns a permuted and XORed version of the binary data to nucleotides after splitting it into 2-bit sections known as nibbles. All these processes are O(n) for n bits. The hybridization and complementing of Watson-Crick pairs perpetuate the short constant time overhead, keeping overall time complexity within linear bounds. The efficiency in space complexity is notable as well. Each input byte corresponds to approximately four output DNA bases, increasing space by a factor of two, which is acceptable for applications with heightened security demands.

DNA encoding is parallelizable with the alteration and key-based modification of the DNA sequences, making execution on multi-core and distributed systems more efficient. This drastically increases the throughput in encrypting vast amounts of data stored within cloud databases or real-time log monitoring systems.

Simulation Results and Benchmarks

Simulations have been run on various datasets, from small configuration files to multi-megabyte logs and snapshots of cloud data. Benchmarks showed that encrypting a 128 KB log file required approximately 2.4 seconds and processing a 1 MB CSV dataset from the cloud took about 18.3 seconds. This includes all encoding, mutation, hybridization, and output generation steps. These results affirm that BioCrypt is feasible for medium-scale and semi-real-time encryption tasks. The additional time of hybridization and complementary steps do not add more than 10% to the total execution time. In addition, the lengths of DNA sequences scale predictably with the input size. An encrypted 256 KB dataset results in approximately 2048 bases, affirming that BioCrypt does not exhibit exponential growth and maintains a consistent conversion pattern. The framework was also examined for the retrieval of data, whereby the decryption procedure took an equivalent duration and accurately reconstructed the initial input with over 99.95% precision, even with minor data corruption due to built-in redundancy and authentication.

Scalability in Cloud Environments

BioCrypt's accuracy was also tested in simulated cloud environments that imitated distributed container and virtual machine deployments. BioCrypt is particularly efficient on horizontally scalable systems because of its low computational overhead and inherent data processing capabilities. Under load balancing in a Kubernetes cluster, BioCrypt showed close to linear scalability, proving that the encryption time per node scaled inversely in relation to the number of nodes integrated into the system. In addition, the framework allows for interaction with cloud-native storage systems like object storage (e.g., AWS S3) or DNA cold storage (e.g., via encoded file snapshots). Each encrypted DNA string is associated with specific metadata (rule ID, checksum, and tag), facilitating rapid retrieval and secure access. This characteristic enhances BioCrypt's position for proactive data handling strategies in cloud infrastructures where data protection and retention are imperative.

APPLICATIONS AND USE CASES

BioCrypt is designed to offer strong protection and is useful in several areas where being private, having integrity and staying secure from attacks are particularly important. Its structure based on DNA helps provide strong anonymity, duplicates important data, and condenses the information—making it useful when there is sensitive data, networks are spread out and threats keep changing. It discusses four major areas where BioCrypt's performance is much higher than that of traditional encryption methods.

Healthcare and Genomic Data Security

In the healthcare world, it is necessary by law and ethics to guard patient records, genomic sequences, and medical imaging data. Because it uses biological reasoning, BioCrypt matches genetic information formats and ensures the safest way to share very sensitive data. BioCrypt turns medical data into DNA sequences and protects them with cryptography, which makes it very hard for anyone to gain unauthorized access to or modify the information. If researchers in genetics must protect their vast data from the threat of intellectual property theft, BioCrypt defends their data by combining logical encryption with biological pattern masking. Access to HIPAA-compliant cloud systems gives Intersystems added importance in strictly regulated healthcare environments.

Secure File Sharing in Public Clouds

Even though using a public cloud gives you both flexibility and cost effectiveness, it greatly increases the chances of losing your data and getting attacked by unauthorized individuals or other means. BioCrypt deals with the challenges since unique DNA strings are encoded into files and only someone with the proper key can read them. Files that are encrypted are written in DNA-code and kept as objects or blobs in the cloud. Authentication tokens and checksums protect information, and these are verified by Watson-Crick pairing when data is taken out. For this reason, BioCrypt can carefully manage file sharing between people in research, lawyers, and bankers, preventing any security risks.

Government and Defense Data Protection

These organizations, such as national defense agencies and intelligence institutions, need to protect classified information at its highest level. BioCrypt provides strong data security, which makes it hard to analyze cryptographic data in this sector. Since data on medicalnano uses both encryption and DNA coding, even data that has been intercepted or leaked cannot be understood by anyone without the right key. Data intended for secure communication can be hidden in BioCrypt codes or hidden within files that look like bioinformatics. Mission-critical data logs, sensor telemetry, and command messages can be protected by BioCrypt in surveillance systems and tactical networks, mostly when they are teamed up with security hardware and robust settings that don't allow changes.

Multi-Cloud and Edge Environments

Meeting uniform encryption requirements becomes difficult as businesses migrate to hybrid and multi-cloud systems. BioCrypt is an environment because its lightweight and modular structure makes it versatile. It can operate in Kubernetes clusters, edge servers, and IoT gateways because it is compatible with containerized and microservices-based deployments. BioCrypt protects edge computing scenarios, including smart grids, industrial monitoring, and autonomous vehicles, by ensuring that data collected at the capture point is kept safe as it moves toward the cloud for processing. Additionally, micro-level edge nodes with restricted computational power stand to benefit from BioCrypt's low-latency performance alongside its diminished burden of key exchange. BioCrypt also protects portability and sovereignty in multi-cloud configurations, allowing cross-provider transport of encoded DNA sequences using metadata-based routing and integrity verification.

CHALLENGES, LIMITATIONS, AND FUTURE DIRECTIONS

Challenges and limitations of BioCrypt framework arise from implementing both cryptographic and biological principles. Most of these problems are caused by DNA-based Computation, which is still a new field, not having clear means to join with standard infrastructures and the requirement to maintain both security and speed. The next section highlights some of the main challenges BioCrypt is dealing with and details potential ways to move forward in the discipline.

Computational Overheads

Daniel's framework adds significant computational effort, one of its main weaknesses. Multi-stage encryption, including binary-to-DNA encoding and Watson-Crick complement mapping, needs more computer power than simple symmetric keys like AES or DES. Due to the complexity, latency increases, mainly for places where quick encryption matters, such as real-time applications and large files. Besides, since BioCrypt needs memory and storage buffers at every step, the algorithm becomes more complex on small embedded systems and edge devices. Traditional serial processing can be replaced by parallel or GPU-accelerated optimization which will help the framework work better in fast and demanding applications.

DNA Storage and Retrieval Issues

While keeping data as DNA is very innovative, making it work in real life presents many difficulties. To synthesize a lot of DNA takes time and is costly, and despite improvements in DNA writing, errors are still a serious problem. DNA sequences must be stored and retrieved in strictly protected locations using exact sequencing tools, which are usually used only in bioinformatics labs. If DNA is not encoded, special back-up errors can appear during synthesis or sequencing, which could corrupt the data. BioCrypt can only be applied to DNA storage, but simulations (digital DNA models) are still a good solution. Better DNA stability, more affordable ways to make DNA, and new self-correcting codes will help overcome the main obstacles.

Integration with Existing Cloud Infrastructures

Adding BioCrypt to cloud environments is challenging for technical and operational reasons. Today, cloud services can handle most standard encryption methods and rely closely on existing key management tools, control systems and structured data storage systems. When DNA-encoded streams, multi-layered encryption and custom metadata are used, current processes must be adapted to suit them. Policies for cloud security are based on known methods such as TLS, RSA and SHA-256 and these are not built to support Biocrypt's modular encryption architecture. This causes the need for extra middleware solutions to join BioCrypt's biological security features and the tools engineers can use on the cloud. There is also a need for interoperability standards that allow DNA-encoded files to be processed, queried, and verified like regular encrypted data objects within cloud storage systems. Collaborations with cloud providers and the development of open-source BioCrypt integration libraries may help address these issues.

Future Prospects in Bio-Crypto Research

Despite current limitations, the future of BioCrypt and bio-crypto research at large is immensely promising. As synthetic biology continues to evolve, the cost and accessibility of DNA synthesis and sequencing are expected to decline, making physical DNA storage a more realistic option even for small- to medium-sized organizations. At the same time, the field of post-quantum cryptography is gaining traction, and BioCrypt's non-linear, biologically inspired obfuscation techniques align well with the need for quantum-resilient encryption systems. Future research could focus on integrating machine learning for dynamic encoding rule selection, using CRISPR-like mechanisms for reversible mutation in DNA sequences, or even embedding encrypted data within living organisms for ultra-long-term archival. Since DNA-based encryption is difficult, unifying BioCrypt APIs, building DNA-to-binary plug-ins for the top cloud services and designing small accelerators to helpconvert DNA to binary could promote BioCrypt as a key development in future security systems.

CONCLUSION

The BioCrypt framework is a leap in the evolution of data security, integrating the logic of traditional cryptography with the multifaceted system of biological Computation. While conventional models of cryptography are already inaccurate due to the rapid development of cyber threats in the current era, especially the quantum computing boom, BioCrypt has transformed. Using the DNA's dense, non-deterministic nature and highly parallel existence, BioCrypt creates an encryption system through multilayer protocols, making it more secure and harder to decipher. Unlike traditional encryption methods, extracting binary inputs and encoding them into biologically encoded sequences, mutating, hybridizing, and pairing complementarily translates into genetic processes gives BioCrypt a leap in encryption with unpredictability and change. These evolutionary features add brute force, plaintext, and differential attack resistance; such superbly enduring storage solutions surpassing care-free data digital DNA archives withstand alterations without change. The framework's modular structure enables its adaptation into any computing device, even from centralized cloud servers to decentralized edge devices. By means of case studies and simulations, BioCrypt showcased its data processing prowess, accuracy, and minimal overhead scaling. Although issues such as high computational expense and integration difficulties still pose obstacles, they can be solved with advancements in parallel computing, synthetic biology, and bio-compatible cloud middleware. BioCrypt offers immense opportunities in sensitive areas like genomic data safeguarding, national defense, and healthcare security informatics. Its synergy with emerging technologies, especially post-quantum encryption and DNA storage, makes it a candidate for meeting next-generation cybersecurity challenges. With ongoing efforts to improve DNA computing and biological algorithm design, BioCrypt could become the foundation of ecologically secure, sustainable adaptively biologically engineered information systems.

ACKNOWLEDGMENT

Funding: This research received no specific grant from any funding agency in the public, commercial, or not-for-profit sectors.

Conflict of Interest: The authors have no competing interests

REFERENCES

Abd El-Latif, E. I., & Moussa, M. I. (2019). Information hiding using artificial DNA sequences based on Gaussian kernel function. *Journal of Information and Optimization Sciences*, *40*(6). Advance online publication. DOI: 10.1080/02522667.2017.1413041

Adleman, L. M. (1994). Molecular computation of solutions to combinatorial problems. *Science*, *266*(5187). Advance online publication. DOI: 10.1126/science.7973651 PMID: 7973651

Al-Mahdi, H., Alruily, M. R., Shahin, O., & Alkhaldi, K. (2019). Design and analysis of DNA encryption and decryption technique based on asymmetric cryptography system. *International Journal of Advanced Computer Science and Applications*, *10*(2). Advance online publication. DOI: 10.14569/ijacsa.2019.0100264

Alrubaie, A. H., Khodher, M. A. A., & Abdulameer, A. T. (2023). Image encryption based on 2DNA encoding and chaotic 2D logistic map. *Journal of Engineering and Applied Sciences (Asian Research Publishing Network)*, *70*(1). Advance online publication. DOI: 10.1186/s44147-023-00228-2

Arora, S., & Hussain, M. (2018). Secure Session Key Sharing Using Symmetric Key Cryptography. *2018 International Conference on Advances in Computing, Communications and Informatics, ICACCI 2018*. DOI: 10.1109/ICACCI.2018.8554553

Bansod, G., Patil, A., Sutar, S., & Pisharoty, N. (2016). ANU: An ultra lightweight cipher design for security in IoT. *Security and Communication Networks*, *9*(18). Advance online publication. DOI: 10.1002/sec.1692

Braich, R. S., Chelyapov, N., Johnson, C., Rothemund, P. W. K., & Adleman, L. (2002). Solution of a 20-variable 3-SAT problem on a DNA computer. *Science*, *296*(5567). Advance online publication. DOI: 10.1126/science.1069528 PMID: 11896237

Chandra, S., Bhattacharyya, S., Paira, S., & Alam, S. S. (2014). A study and analysis on symmetric cryptography. *2014 International Conference on Science Engineering and Management Research, ICSEMR 2014*. DOI: 10.1109/ICSEMR.2014.7043664

Chandra, S., Paira, S., Alam, S. S., & Sanyal, G. (2014). A comparative survey of Symmetric and Asymmetric Key Cryptography. *2014 International Conference on Electronics, Communication and Computational Engineering (ICECCE)*, 83–93. DOI: 10.1109/ICECCE.2014.7086640

Chaves-González, J. M., & Vega-Rodríguez, M. A. (2014). A multiobjective approach based on the behavior of fireflies to generate reliable DNA sequences for molecular computing. *Applied Mathematics and Computation, 227*. Advance online publication. DOI: 10.1016/j.amc.2013.11.032

Dhankhar, S. and G. N. and S. H. and C. S. and S. M. and M. S. and others. (2025). Data Protection Technologies. In *Bentham Science Publishers* (pp. 62–77).

Hazra, A., Ghosh, S., & Jash, S. (2018). A new DNA cryptography based algorithm involving the fusion of symmetric-key techniques. *Advances in Intelligent Systems and Computing, 706*. Advance online publication. DOI: 10.1007/978-981-10-8237-5_59

Izadi, M., Sadeghiyan, B., Sadeghian, S. S., & Khanooki, H. A. (2009). MIBS: A new lightweight block cipher. *Lecture Notes in Computer Science (Including Subseries Lecture Notes in Artificial Intelligence and Lecture Notes in Bioinformatics), 5888 LNCS*. DOI: 10.1007/978-3-642-10433-6_22

Kalsi, S., Kaur, H., & Chang, V. (2018). DNA Cryptography and Deep Learning using Genetic Algorithm with NW algorithm for Key Generation. *Journal of Medical Systems, 42*(1). Advance online publication. DOI: 10.1007/s10916-017-0851-z PMID: 29204890

Kubba, Z. M. J., & Hoomod, H. K. (2020). Developing a lightweight cryptographic algorithm based on DNA computing. *AIP Conference Proceedings, 2290*. Advance online publication. DOI: 10.1063/5.0027361

Leier, A., Richter, C., Banzhaf, W., & Rauhe, H. (2000). Cryptography with DNA binary strands. *Bio Systems, 57*(1). Advance online publication. DOI: 10.1016/S0303-2647(00)00083-6 PMID: 10963862

Li, L., Liu, B., Zhou, Y., & Zou, Y. (2018). SFN: A new lightweight block cipher. *Microprocessors and Microsystems, 60*. Advance online publication. DOI: 10.1016/j.micpro.2018.04.009

Liu, C., Liu, Y., Zhu, E., Zhang, Q., Wei, X., & Wang, B. (2020). Cross-Inhibitor: A time-sensitive molecular circuit based on DNA strand displacement. *Nucleic Acids Research, 48*(19). Advance online publication. DOI: 10.1093/nar/gkaa835 PMID: 33045746

Liu, W., Gao, L., Liu, X., Wang, S., & Xu, J. (2003). Solving the 3-SAT Problem Based on DNA Computing. *Journal of Chemical Information and Computer Sciences, 43*(6). Advance online publication. DOI: 10.1021/ci034113o PMID: 14632435

Mahjabin, T., Olteanu, A., Xiao, Y., Han, W., Li, T., & Sun, W. (2023). A Survey on DNA-Based Cryptography and Steganography. *IEEE Access: Practical Innovations, Open Solutions, 11*. Advance online publication. DOI: 10.1109/ACCESS.2023.3324875

Mathur, G. (Sagar Institute of Science and Technology, I. and P. S. C. (Sagar I. of S. and T. I. (2025). DNA Computing in Enhancing Cloud Security. In *IGI Global Publisher*. IGI Global.

Namasudra, S. (2022). A secure cryptosystem using DNA cryptography and DNA steganography for the cloud-based IoT infrastructure. *Computers & Electrical Engineering, 104*. Advance online publication. DOI: 10.1016/j.compeleceng.2022.108426

Paspula, R. K. C. and S. L. K. (2017). Hidden data transmission with variable DNA technology. *International Journal of Electronics and Information Engineering, 7*(1), 41–52.

Pramanik, S. and S. K. S. (2012). DNA cryptography. *2012 7th International Conference on Electrical and Computer Engineering*.

Sajisha, K. S., & Mathew, S. (2017). An encryption based on DNA cryptography and steganography. *Proceedings of the International Conference on Electronics, Communication and Aerospace Technology, ICECA 2017, 2017-January*. DOI: 10.1109/ICECA.2017.8212786

Sohal, M., & Sharma, S. (2022). BDNA-A DNA inspired symmetric key cryptographic technique to secure cloud computing. *Journal of King Saud University. Computer and Information Sciences, 34*(1). Advance online publication. DOI: 10.1016/j.jksuci.2018.09.024

Sullivan, B. A. (2014). Securing the cloud: Cloud computer security techniques and tactics. *Security Journal, 27*(3). Advance online publication. DOI: 10.1057/sj.2012.16

Thabit, F., Can, O., Alhomdy, S., Al-Gaphari, G. H., & Jagtap, S. (2022). A Novel Effective Lightweight Homomorphic Cryptographic Algorithm for data security in cloud computing. *International Journal of Intelligent Networks, 3*. Advance online publication. DOI: 10.1016/j.ijin.2022.04.001

Tiwari, H. D., & Kim, J. H. (2018). Novel Method for DNA-Based Elliptic Curve Cryptography for IoT Devices. *ETRI Journal, 40*(3). Advance online publication. DOI: 10.4218/etrij.2017-0220

Tornea, O. and B. M. E. (2013). Security and complexity of a DNA-based cipher. *2013 11th RoEduNet International Conference*, 1–5.

Wang, M., & Bi, B. (2018). An 8 to 3 Priority Encoder Based on DNA Strand Displacement. *Communications in Computer and Information Science, 951*. Advance online publication. DOI: 10.1007/978-981-13-2826-8_40 PMID: 37313507

Xu, J., Qiang, X., Zhang, K., Zhang, C., & Yang, J. (2018). A DNA Computing Model for the Graph Vertex Coloring Problem Based on a Probe Graph. *Engineering*, *4*(1). Advance online publication. DOI: 10.1016/j.eng.2018.02.011

Zakaria, A. A., Azni, A. H., Ridzuan, F., Zakaria, N. H., & Daud, M. (2020). Extended rectangle algorithm using 3D bit rotation to propose a new lightweight block cipher for IoT. *IEEE Access: Practical Innovations, Open Solutions, 8*. Advance online publication. DOI: 10.1109/ACCESS.2020.3035375

Zhang, Y., Liu, X., Ma, Y., & Cheng, L. C. (2017). An optimized DNA based encryption scheme with enforced secure key distribution. *Cluster Computing*, *20*(4). Advance online publication. DOI: 10.1007/s10586-017-1009-y

Zhu, E., Luo, X., Liu, C., & Chen, C. (2022). An Operational DNA Strand Displacement Encryption Approach. *Nanomaterials (Basel, Switzerland)*, *12*(5). Advance online publication. DOI: 10.3390/nano12050877 PMID: 35269365

Zimmermann, K. H. (2002). Efficient DNA sticker algorithms for NP-complete graph problems. *Computer Physics Communications*, *144*(3). Advance online publication. DOI: 10.1016/S0010-4655(02)00270-9

Zissis, D., & Lekkas, D. (2012). Addressing cloud computing security issues. *Future Generation Computer Systems*, *28*(3). Advance online publication. DOI: 10.1016/j.future.2010.12.006

Compilation of References

Abbas, S., Bouazzi, I., Sampedro, G. A., Alsubai, S., Almadhor, A. S., Hejaili, A. A., & Kryvinska, N. (2024). Active-darknet: An iterative learning approach for darknet traffic detection and categorization. *IEEE Access: Practical Innovations, Open Solutions*, *12*, 151987–151997.

Abd El-Latif, E. I., & Moussa, M. I. (2019). Information hiding using artificial DNA sequences based on Gaussian kernel function. *Journal of Information and Optimization Sciences*, *40*(6). Advance online publication. DOI: 10.1080/02522667.2017.1413041

Abdel Hakeem, S. A., Hussein, H. H., & Kim, H. (2022). Vision and research directions of 6G technologies and applications. *Journal of King Saud University. Computer and Information Sciences*, *34*(6, Part A), 2419–2442. DOI: 10.1016/j.jksuci.2022.03.019

Abdul Samad, S. R., Balasubaramanian, S., Al-Kaabi, A. S., Sharma, B., Chowdhury, S., Mehbodniya, A., & Bostani, A. (2023). Analysis of the performance impact of fine-tuned machine learning model for phishing URL detection. *Electronics (Basel)*, *12*(7), 1642.

Abdullahi, A. M. (2021). An online privacy enhancing framework based on the prin- ciples and capabilities of the onion router (tor).

Abdulwareth, A. J., & Al-Shargabi, A. A. (2021). Toward a Multi-Criteria Framework for Selecting Software Testing Tools. *IEEE Access: Practical Innovations, Open Solutions*, *9*, 158872–158891. DOI: 10.1109/ACCESS.2021.3128071

Abrishami, S., Zandi, F. M., & Nourbakhsh, A. (2025). Workflow as a Service Broker in Cloud Environment: A Systematic Literature Review. arXiv preprint arXiv:2501.12672.

Adel, A., & Norouzifard, M. (2024). Weaponization of the growing cybercrimes inside the dark net: The question of detection and application. *Big Data and Cognitive Computing*, *8*(8), 91.

Adleman, L. M. (1994). Molecular computation of solutions to combinatorial problems. *Science, 266*(5187). Advance online publication. DOI: 10.1126/science.7973651 PMID: 7973651

Agarwal, V. (2016). *Research on Data Preprocessing and Categorization Technique for Smartphone Review Analysis. December 2015.* https://doi.org/DOI: 10.5120/ijca2015907309

Ahmad, W., & Alam, B. (2020, September). An efficient list scheduling algorithm with task duplication for scientific big data workflow in heterogeneous computing environments. *Concurrency and Computation, 33*(5). Advance online publication. DOI: 10.1002/cpe.5987

Ahmad, Z.. (2021, January). Scientific Workflows Management and Scheduling in Cloud Computing: Taxonomy, Prospects, and challenges. *IEEE Access: Practical Innovations, Open Solutions, 9*, 53491–53508. DOI: 10.1109/access.2021.3070785

Ahmed, S., & Omara, F. (2022, October). An enhanced workflow scheduling algorithm for cloud computing environment. *International Journal of Intelligent Engineering and Systems, 15*(6), 627–646. DOI: 10.22266/ijies2022.1231.56

AI IN CLOUD COMPUTING: ENHANCING SERVICES AND PERFORMANCE. (2024). DOI: 10.5281/ZENODO.13353681

Akter, S., Badhon, M. B., Bhuiyan, M. K. I., Hasan, H. M., Akter, F., & Islam, M. N. U. (2024). Quantum-Edge Cloud Computing for IoT: Bridging the Gap between Cloud, Edge, and Quantum Technologies. *Edge, and Quantum Technologies (September 29, 2024).*

Al Alamin, M. A., Malakar, S., Uddin, G., Afroz, S., Haider, T. B., & Iqbal, A. (2021). An empirical study of developer discussions on low-code software development challenges. *Proceedings - 2021 IEEE/ACM 18th International Conference on Mining Software Repositories*, 46-57. https://doi.org/DOI: 10.1109/MSR52588.2021.00018

Alagarsundaram, P. (2024). Physiological signals: A blockchain-based data-sharing model for enhanced big data medical research integrating RFID and blockchain technologies. *Journal of Cloud Security and IoT, 9*(2).

Alagarsundaram, P.. (2024). *Blockchain-enabled privacy-preserved secure e-voting system for smart cities. International Conference on Science Technology Engineering and Management (ICSTEM).* https://doi.org/DOI: 10.1109/ICSTEM61137.2024.10560826

Al-Arasi, R., & Saif, A. (2020, January). Task scheduling in cloud computing based on metaheuristic techniques: A review paper. *EAI Endorsed Transactions on Cloud Systems*, *6*(17), 162829. DOI: 10.4108/eai.13-7-2018.162829

Alawida, M., Mejri, S., Mehmood, A., Chikhaoui, B., & Isaac Abiodun, O. (2023). A Comprehensive Study of ChatGPT: Advancements, Limitations, and Ethical Considerations in Natural Language Processing and Cybersecurity. *Information (Switzerland)*, *14*(8), 462. DOI: 10.3390/info14080462

Albishri, A., & Dessouky, M. M. (2025). *Analysis of Machine Learning Techniques for URL Phishing Detection: Protect Users.* Paper presented at the 2025 2nd International Conference on Advanced Innovations in Smart Cities (ICAISC).

Al-Fayoumi, M., Elayyan, A., & Odeh, A. (2023). Tor network traffic classification us- ing machine learning based on time-related feature. *AIP Conference Proceedings*, *2679*(1).

Al-Mahdi, H., Alruily, M. R., Shahin, O., & Alkhaldi, K. (2019). Design and analysis of DNA encryption and decryption technique based on asymmetric cryptography system. *International Journal of Advanced Computer Science and Applications*, *10*(2). Advance online publication. DOI: 10.14569/ijacsa.2019.0100264

Almomani, A. (2023). Darknet traffic analysis, and classification system based on mod- ified stacking ensemble learning algorithms. *Information Systems and e-Business Management*, •••, 1–32.

Almujahid, N. F., Haq, M. A., & Alshehri, M. (2024). Comparative evaluation of machine learning algorithms for phishing site detection. *PeerJ. Computer Science*, *10*, e2131. PMID: 38983211

Almutairi, L., & Aslam, S. M. (2023, January). "A novel energy and communication aware scheduling on green cloud computing," *Computers, Materials & Continua/ Computers. Materials & Continua (Print)*, *77*(3), 2791–2811. DOI: 10.32604/ cmc.2023.040268

Al-Na'amneh, Q., Aljaidi, M., Gharaibeh, H., Nasayreh, A., & Al Mamlook, R. E. Al- matarneh, S., Alzu'bi, D., & Husien, A. S. (2023). Feature selection for robust spoofing detection: A chi-square-based machine learning approach. *2023 2nd International Engineering Conference on Electrical, Energy, and Artificial Intelligence (EICEEAI)*, 1–7.

Al-Na'amneh, Q., Aljaidi, M., Nasayreh, A., Gharaibeh, H., Al Mamlook, R. E., Jara- dat, A. S., Alsarhan, A., & Samara, G. (2024b). Journal of intelligent systems: Enhancing iot device security: Cnn-svm hybrid approach for real-time detection of dos and ddos attacks.

Al-Na'amneh, Q., Aljaidi, M., Nasayrch, A., Gharaibeh, H., Al Mamlook, R. E., Jaradat, A. S., Alsarhan, A., & Samara, G. (2024a). Enhancing iot device security: Cnn- svm hybrid approach for real-time detection of dos and ddos attacks. *Journal of Intelligent Systems*, *33*(1), 20230150.

Al-Rakhami, M. S., Al-Mashraee, H., & Algabri, M. (2022). Blockchain technology for enhancing cybersecurity in industrial IoT. *IEEE Access: Practical Innovations, Open Solutions*, *10*, 14192–14206. DOI: 10.1109/ACCESS.2022.3141235

Alrubaie, A. H., Khodher, M. A. A., & Abdulameer, A. T. (2023). Image encryption based on 2DNA encoding and chaotic 2D logistic map. *Journal of Engineering and Applied Sciences (Asian Research Publishing Network)*, *70*(1). Advance online publication. DOI: 10.1186/s44147-023-00228-2

Alsahaf, A., Petkov, N., Shenoy, V., & Azzopardi, G. (2022). A framework for feature selection through boosting. *Expert Systems with Applications*. Advance online publication. DOI: 10.1016/j.eswa.2021.115895

Al-Said Ahmad, A., Al-Qora'n, L. F., & Zayed, A. (2024). Exploring the impact of chaos engineering with various user loads on cloud native applications: An exploratory empirical study. *Computing*, *106*(7), 2389–2425. DOI: 10.1007/s00607-024-01292-z

Al-Sarem, M., Saeed, F., Al-Mekhlafi, Z. G., Mohammed, B. A., Al-Hadhrami, T., Alshammari, M. T., & Alshammari, T. S. (2021). An optimized stacking ensemble model for phishing websites detection. *Electronics (Basel)*, *10*(11), 1285.

Alshahrani, S. M., Khan, N. A., Almalki, J., & Al Shehri, W. (2022). URL Phishing Detection Using Particle Swarm Optimization and Data Mining. *Computers, Materials & Continua*, *73*(3).

Alzubi, J. A., Alzubi, O. A., Singh, A., & Mahmod Alzubi, T. (2023). A blockchain-enabled security management framework for mobile edge computing. *International Journal of Network Management*, *33*(5), e2240.

Amelia, O. (2024a). *AI-Powered Software Testing Automation: Machine Learning Approaches for Ensuring Quality in Distributed Systems*. Unpublished. DOI: 10.13140/RG.2.2.32858.76485

Amelia, O. (2024b). *Machine Learning Algorithms for Software Testing Automation: AI- Driven Solutions for Distributed Network Optimization*. Unpublished. DOI: 10.13140/RG.2.2.16081.54885

Anayat, R. (2023). *Revolutionizing AI Testing Automation: Achieving Test Coverage and Defect Prediction with Machine Learning and Cloud Integration*. Unpublished. DOI: 10.13140/RG.2.2.35737.43365

Arabnejad, H., & Barbosa, J. G. (2014). A budget constrained scheduling algorithm for workflow applications. *Journal of Grid Computing*, *12*(1), 25–40. DOI: 10.1007/s10723-013-9279-2

Arafa, A., El-Fishawy, N., Badawy, M., & Radad, M. (2022). RN-SMOTE: Reduced Noise SMOTE based on DBSCAN for enhancing imbalanced data classification. *Journal of King Saud University. Computer and Information Sciences*. Advance online publication. DOI: 10.1016/j.jksuci.2022.06.005

Arora, S., & Hussain, M. (2018). Secure Session Key Sharing Using Symmetric Key Cryptography. *2018 International Conference on Advances in Computing, Communications and Informatics, ICACCI 2018*. DOI: 10.1109/ICACCI.2018.8554553

Arpteg, A., Brinne, B., Crnkovic-Friis, L., & Löfstedt, T. (2018). Software engineering challenges of deep learning. *2018 IEEE/ACM 1st International Workshop on Machine Learning Engineering*, 35–41. DOI: 10.1109/MLE.2018.00008

Ashok, A., Rathis, D., Raghavendra, R., & Umadevi, V. (2024). *A Comparative Analysis of Traditional Machine Learning, Deep Learning and Boosting Algorithms on Phishing URL Detection*. Paper presented at the 2024 IEEE International Conference on Computer Vision and Machine Intelligence (CVMI).

Ashraf, H. Z. (2025). Security Concerns: Machine Learning Approaches in the Modern Era and Web Engineering. In *Generative AI for Web Engineering Models* (pp. 241–268). IGI Global.

Aslam, A. M., Bhardwaj, A., & Chaudhary, R. (2024). Quantum-Resilient Blockchain-Enabled Secure Communication Framework for Connected Autonomous Vehicles using Post-Quantum Cryptography. *Vehicular Communications*, •••, 100880.

Atlaf, T.. (2024). Gnn-based network traffic analysis for the detection of sequential attacks in iot. *Sensors (Basel)*, *24*(5), 1456. PMID: 38474992

Awad, A., Qutqut, M. H., Ahmed, A., Al-Haj, F., & Almasalha, F. (2024). Artificial Intelligence Role in Software Automation Testing. *2024 International Conference on Decision Aid Sciences and Applications (DASA)*, 1–6. DOI: 10.1109/DASA63652.2024.10836630

Azim, P. A. B. (2024). *AI as Emerging Technology: Opportunities, Vulnerabilities and Future Directions* (SSRN Scholarly Paper No. 5068671). Social Science Research Network. DOI: 10.2139/ssrn.5068671

Bai, Q., Liu, Z., & Zhang, W. (2020). AI-powered anomaly detection in industrial control systems: A survey. *Journal of Industrial Information Integration, 21*, 100170. DOI: 10.1016/j.jii.2020.100170

Balantrapu, S. S. (2023). Future Trends in AI and Machine Learning for Cybersecurity. *International Journal of Creative Research In Computer Technology and Design, 5*(5).

Balogun, A. O., Mojeed, H. A., Adewole, K. S., Akintola, A. G., Salihu, S. A., Bajeh, A. O., & Jimoh, R. G. (2021). *Optimized decision forest for website phishing detection.* Paper presented at the Data Science and Intelligent Systems: Proceedings of 5th Computational Methods in Systems and Software 2021, Vol. 2.

Banala, S. (2025, February 9). *DevOps Essentials: Key Practices for Continuous Integration and Continuous Delivery | Request PDF.* https://www.researchgate.net/publication/382885510_DevOps_Essentials_Key_Practices_for_Continuous_Integration_and_Continuous_Delivery

Bansal, S., & Kumar, D. (2020). *IoT Ecosystem: A Survey on Devices, Gateways, Operating Systems, Middleware and Communication | International Journal of Wireless Information Networks.* https://link.springer.com/article/10.1007/s10776-020-00483-7

Bansod, G., Patil, A., Sutar, S., & Pisharoty, N. (2016). ANU: An ultra lightweight cipher design for security in IoT. *Security and Communication Networks, 9*(18). Advance online publication. DOI: 10.1002/sec.1692

Baqar, M., & Khanda, R. (2024). *The Future of Software Testing: AI-Powered Test Case Generation and Validation* (No. arXiv:2409.05808). arXiv. /arXiv.2409.05808DOI: 10.48550

Bari, M. S., Sarkar, A., & Islam, S. A. M. (2024). Ai-augmented Self-healing Automation Frameworks: Revolutionizing Qa Testing with Adaptive and Resilient Automation. *AIJMR - Advanced International. Journal of Multidisciplinary Research, 2*(6). Advance online publication. DOI: 10.62127/aijmr.2024.v02i06.1118

Belgaum, M. R., Alansari, Z., Musa, S., Mansoor Alam, M., & Mazliham, M. S. (2021). Role of artificial intelligence in cloud computing, IoT and SDN: Reliability and scalability issues. [IJECE]. *International Journal of Electrical and Computer Engineering, 11*(5), 4458. DOI: 10.11591/ijece.v11i5.pp4458-4470

Birthriya, S. K., Ahlawat, P., & Jain, A. K. (2025). Phishing Website Detection with XGBoost and Adaptive Hyperparameter Optimization using the Bat Algorithm. *Procedia Computer Science*, *258*, 1774–1782.

Bishwas, A. K., & Sen, M. (2024). Strategic Roadmap for Quantum-Resistant Security: A Framework for Preparing Industries for the Quantum Threat. *arXiv preprint arXiv:2411.09995*.

Bokhari, M. U., Khan, M. Z., & Masoodi, F. S. (2025). A Hybrid Approach to Feature Selection for Cyber Threat Detection in IoT Networks. *2025 3rd International Conference on Device Intelligence, Computing and Communication Technologies (DICCT)*, 637–642. https://doi.org/DOI: 10.1109/DICCT64131.2025.10986689

Braich, R. S., Chelyapov, N., Johnson, C., Rothemund, P. W. K., & Adleman, L. (2002). Solution of a 20-variable 3-SAT problem on a DNA computer. *Science*, *296*(5567). Advance online publication. DOI: 10.1126/science.1069528 PMID: 11896237

Cai, Z., & Zhu, J. (2016). Fraud detections for online businesses: A perspective from blockchain technology. *Financial Innovation*, *2*(1), 20. DOI: 10.1186/s40854-016-0039-4

Chandra, S., Bhattacharyya, S., Paira, S., & Alam, S. S. (2014). A study and analysis on symmetric cryptography. *2014 International Conference on Science Engineering and Management Research, ICSEMR 2014*. DOI: 10.1109/ICSEMR.2014.7043664

Chandra, S., Paira, S., Alam, S. S., & Sanyal, G. (2014). A comparative survey of Symmetric and Asymmetric Key Cryptography. *2014 International Conference on Electronics, Communication and Computational Engineering (ICECCE)*, 83–93. DOI: 10.1109/ICECCE.2014.7086640

Chang, S. E., & Chen, Y. C. (2020). Blockchain for cybersecurity in critical infrastructure: A comprehensive review. *Journal of Information Security and Applications*, *54*, 102535. DOI: 10.1016/j.jisa.2020.102535

Chauhan, N., Kaur, N., Saini, K. S., Verma, S., Alabdulatif, A., Abu Khurma, R., Garcia Arenas, M., & Castillo, P. A. (2024). A systematic literature review on task allocation and performance management techniques in cloud data center. arXiv.

Chaves-González, J. M., & Vega-Rodríguez, M. A. (2014). A multiobjective approach based on the behavior of fireflies to generate reliable DNA sequences for molecular computing. *Applied Mathematics and Computation*, *227*. Advance online publication. DOI: 10.1016/j.amc.2013.11.032

Chawla, D., & Mehra, P. S. (2023). A roadmap from classical cryptography to post-quantum resistant cryptography for 5G-enabled IoT: Challenges, opportunities and solutions. *Internet of Things: Engineering Cyber Physical Human Systems*, •••, 100950.

Chen, G., Qi, J., Sun, Y., Hu, X., Dong, Z., & Sun, Y. (2022, November). A collaborative scheduling method for cloud computing heterogeneous workflows based on deep reinforcement learning. *Future Generation Computer Systems*, *141*, 284–297. DOI: 10.1016/j.future.2022.11.032

Cheng, J., Liu, Q., & Yao, M. (2021). AI-empowered industrial robotics for smart manufacturing. *International Journal of Advanced Manufacturing Technology*, *115*(3–4), 847–864. DOI: 10.1007/s00170-021-07264-y

Chen, Y.. (2024). Securing network traffic classification models against adversarial examples using derived variables. *Future Internet*, *16*(3), 98.

Cherbal, S., Zier, A., Hebal, S., Louail, L., & Annane, B. (2024). Security in internet of things: A review on approaches based on blockchain, machine learning, cryptography, and quantum computing. *The Journal of Supercomputing*, *80*(3), 3738–3816.

Christidis, A., Moschoyiannis, S., Hsu, C.-H., & Davies, R. (2020). Enabling Serverless Deployment of Large-Scale AI Workloads. *IEEE Access: Practical Innovations, Open Solutions*, *8*, 70150–70161. DOI: 10.1109/ACCESS.2020.2985282

Christidis, K., & Devetsikiotis, M. (2016). Blockchains and smart contracts for the Internet of Things. *IEEE Access: Practical Innovations, Open Solutions*, *4*, 2292–2303. DOI: 10.1109/ACCESS.2016.2566339

Coleman, T., Casanova, H., Pottier, L., Kaushik, M., Deelman, E., & Da Silva, R. F. (2021, October). WfCommons: A framework for enabling scientific workflow research and development. *Future Generation Computer Systems*, *128*, 16–27. DOI: 10.1016/j.future.2021.09.043

Colton, J. (2024a). *AI and ML-Driven Software Testing Automation: Optimizing Distributed Networks for High-Performance Software Systems*. Unpublished. DOI: 10.13140/RG.2.2.19856.42245

Colton, J. (2024b). *Enhancing Software Testing with AI and Machine Learning: Automation Strategies for Distributed Network Architectures*. Unpublished. DOI: 10.13140/RG.2.2.16500.97927

da Costa, K. A. P., Papa, J. P., Lisboa, C. O., Munoz, R., & de Albuquerque, V. H. C. (2019). Internet of Things: A survey on machine learning-based intrusion detection approaches. *Computer Networks*, *151*, 147–157. DOI: 10.1016/j.comnet.2019.01.023

Dai, H. N., Zheng, Z., & Zhang, Y. (2019). Blockchain for Internet of Things: A survey. *IEEE Internet of Things Journal*, *6*(5), 8076–8094. DOI: 10.1109/JIOT.2019.2920987

Das Guptta, S., Shahriar, K. T., Alqahtani, H., Alsalman, D., & Sarker, I. H. (2024). Modeling hybrid feature-based phishing websites detection using machine learning techniques. *Annals of Data Science*, *11*(1), 217–242. PMID: 40479161

Das, A., & Jain, R. K. (2025). Performance evaluation of mobile robotic system for monitoring and inspection using MQTT protocol and IoT technique. *International Journal of Intelligent Robotics and Applications*. Advance online publication. DOI: 10.1007/s41315-025-00465-z

Davis, S., & Arrigo, B. (2021). The dark web and anonymizing technologies: Legal pitfalls, ethical prospects, and policy directions from radical criminology. *Crime, Law, and Social Change*, *76*(4), 367–386.

Deekshitha, B., Aswitha, C., Sundar, C. S., & Deepthi, A. K. (2022). Url based phishing website detection by using gradient and catboost algorithms. *International Journal for Research in Applied Science and Engineering Technology*, *10*(6), 3717–3722.

Deldjoo, Y., Di Noia, T., & Merra, F. A. (2021). A Survey on Adversarial Recommender Systems: From Attack/Defense Strategies to Generative Adversarial Networks. *ACM Computing Surveys*, *54*(2), 1–38. DOI: 10.1145/3439729

Desai, M. G., Shi, Y., & Suo, K. (2020). IoT Bonet and Network Intrusion Detection using Dimensionality Reduction and Supervised Machine Learning. *2020 11th IEEE Annual Ubiquitous Computing, Electronics & Mobile Communication Conference (UEMCON)*, 316–322. https://doi.org/DOI: 10.1109/UEMCON51285.2020.9298146

Devarajan, M. V. (2022). An improved BP neural network algorithm for forecasting workload in intelligent cloud computing. *Journal of Computational Science*, *10*(3), 1–10. https://jcsjournal.com/.2022.v10.i03.pp01-10

Dey, N. S., & Sangaraju, H. K. R. (2023). Hybrid Load Balancing Strategy for Cloud Data Centers with Novel Performance Evaluation Strategy. *International Journal of Intelligent Systems and Applications in Engineering*, *11*(3), 883–908. https://ijisae.org/index.php/IJISAE/article/view/3345

Dhankhar, S. and G. N. and S. H. and C. S. and S. M. and M. S. and others. (2025). Data Protection Technologies. In *Bentham Science Publishers* (pp. 62–77).

Dokeroglu, T., Kucukyilmaz, T., & Talbi, E.-G. (2023, December). Hyper-heuristics: A survey and taxonomy. *Computers & Industrial Engineering*, *187*, 109815. DOI: 10.1016/j.cie.2023.109815

Doostali, S., Babamir, S. M., & Eini, M. (2021, July). CP-PGWO: Multi-objective workflow scheduling for cloud computing using critical path. *Cluster Computing*, *24*(4), 3607–3627. DOI: 10.1007/s10586-021-03351-y

Dorri, A., Kanhere, S. S., & Jurdak, R. (2017). Blockchain in Internet of Things: Challenges and solutions. *IEEE Communications Surveys and Tutorials*, *22*(3), 1820–1843. DOI: 10.1109/COMST.2020.2978977

Draper-Gil, G., Lashkari, A. H., Mamun, M. S., & Ghorbani, A. A. (2016). Characterization of encrypted and vpn traffic using time-related features, 407–414.

Effective Concurrency Testing for Distributed Systems | Proceedings of the Twenty-Fifth International Conference on Architectural Support for Programming Languages and Operating Systems. (n.d.). Retrieved April 21, 2025, from https://dl.acm.org/doi/abs/10.1145/3373376.3378484

El-Hamed, O. M. A., El-Samie, F. E. A., & Badawy, W.. (2025). Blockchain-based framework for secure communication in vehicular ad hoc network (VANET). *Journal of Optics*. Advance online publication. DOI: 10.1007/s12596-025-02760-1

Erboz, G. (2017). How to define Industry 4.0: Main pillars of Industry 4.0. *Managerial Trends in the Development of Enterprises in Globalization Era*, 761–767.

Fang, L. C., Ayop, Z., Anawar, S., Othman, N. F., Harum, N., & Abdullah, R. S. (2021). Url phishing detection system utilizing catboost machine learning approach. *International Journal of Computer Science & Network Security*, *21*(9), 297–302.

Farah, J. (2024). *AI-Driven Software Testing: Automating Quality Assurance with Machine Learning for Distributed Networks*. Unpublished. DOI: 10.13140/RG.2.2.25623.89768

Feng, X., Xu, W., & Zhang, Y. (2021). AI-driven predictive maintenance for industrial robots. *Journal of Manufacturing Systems*, *61*, 109–118. DOI: 10.1016/j.jmsy.2021.10.005

Feng, Y., Wang, Q., Wu, D., Luo, Z., Chen, X., Zhang, T., & Gao, W. (2021). Machine learning aided phase field method for fracture mechanics. *International Journal of Engineering Science*, *169*, 103587.

Ferreira, L., Silva, D. C., & Itzazelaia, M. U. (2023). Recommender Systems in Cybersecurity. *Knowledge and Information Systems*, *65*(12), 5523–5559. DOI: 10.1007/s10115-023-01906-6

Firdaus, M., et al. (2023). Explainable artificial intelligence for feature selection in net- work traffic classification: A comparative study.

Fryling, M. (2019). Low code app development. *Journal of Computing Sciences in Colleges*, *34*(6), 14–20.

Fu, X., Sun, Y., Wang, H., & Li, H. (2021, May). Task scheduling of cloud computing based on hybrid particle swarm algorithm and genetic algorithm. *Cluster Computing*, *26*(5), 2479–2488. DOI: 10.1007/s10586-020-03221-z

Gai, K., Qiu, M., & Zhu, L. (2018). Blockchain-enabled smart grid: Challenges and opportunities. *IEEE Communications Magazine*, *56*(4), 15–21. DOI: 10.1109/MCOM.2018.1700813

Ganganwar, V., Hussain, S. I., Powar, A., Gaur, S., & Kumar, A. (2023). *Using Website Content for Detecting Phishing URLs: A Novel Approach.* Paper presented at the International Conference on Advances in Data-driven Computing and Intelligent Systems.

Garifullin, R., & Ryzhov, V. (2020). Blockchain-based distributed control system for industrial robotics. *IFAC-PapersOnLine*, *53*(2), 972–977. DOI: 10.1016/j.ifacol.2020.12.238

Gawali, M. B., & Shinde, S. K. (2018, February). Task scheduling and resource allocation in cloud computing using a heuristic approach. *Journal of Cloud Computing Advances Systems and Applications*, *7*(1). Advance online publication. DOI: 10.1186/s13677-018-0105-8

Ghaleb Al-Mekhlafi, Z., Abdulkarem Mohammed, B., Al-Sarem, M., Saeed, F., Al-Hadhrami, T., Alshammari, M. T., & Sarheed Alshammari, T. (2022). Phishing websites detection by using optimized stacking ensemble model. *Computer Systems Science and Engineering*, *41*(1), 109–125.

Ghaleb, M., & Hamdan, M.. (2025). Explainable ai for lightweight network traffic classification using depthwise-separable convolutions. *IEEE Open Journal of the Computer Society*.

Gharaibeh, H., Aljaidi, M., Nasayreh, A., Al-Na'amneh, Q., Jaradat, A. S., Samara, G., & Al Mamlook, R. E. (2023). Deep feature extraction framework based on dnn for enhancing mirai attachment classification in machine learning. *2023 2nd International Engineering Conference on Electrical, Energy, and Artificial Intelligence (EICEEAI)*, 1–5.

Gheibi, O., Weyns, D., & Quin, F. (2021). Applying Machine Learning in Self-adaptive Systems: A Systematic Literature Review. *ACM Trans. Auton. Adapt. Syst.*, *15*(3), 9:1-9:37. DOI: 10.1145/3469440

Gogri, D. (2024). *Maximizing Comprehensive Test Coverage through Concurrent Execution Strategies in High-Performance Software Development Environments.*

Gohil, N. P., & Meniya, A. D. (2021). *Click ad fraud detection using XGBoost gradient boosting algorithm.* Paper presented at the International Conference on Computing Scicncc, Communication and Sccurity.

Gollavilli, V. S. B. H. (2022). Securing cloud data: Combining SABAC models, hash-tag authentication with MD5, and blockchain-based encryption for enhanced privacy and access control. *International Journal of Engineering Research & Science & Technology, 18*(3), 149–165. DOI: 10.62643/ijerst.2022.v18.i3.pp149-165

Gomes, P. M., & Brito, M. A. (2022). Low-code development platforms: A descriptive study. *Iberian Conference on Information Systems and Technologies*, 1-6. https://doi.org/DOI: 10.23919/CISTI54924.2022.9820324

Gunasekara, A. (2023). AI-Driven Big Data Analytics for Transforming Cybersecurity for Zero-Day Vulnerabilities in E-Commerce Supply Chains. *Journal of Advances in Cybersecurity Science, Threat Intelligence, and Countermeasures, 7*(12), 17–31.

Guo, H., Zhou, J., & Gu, H. (2022, July). Limited Duplication-Based list scheduling Algorithm for heterogeneous computing system. *Micromachines, 13*(7), 1067. DOI: 10.3390/mi13071067 PMID: 35888884

Gupta, S.. (2022, August). Efficient Prioritization and processor selection schemes for HEFT algorithm: A Makespan optimizer for task scheduling in cloud environment. *Electronics (Basel), 11*(16), 2557. DOI: 10.3390/electronics11162557

Gurcan, F., & Taentzer, G. (2021). Using Microsoft PowerApps, Mendix and OutSystems in two development scenarios: An experience report. *Companion Proceedings - 24th International Conference on Model-Driven Engineering Languages and Systems*, 662-671. https://doi.org/DOI: 10.1109/MODELS-C53483.2021.00101

Habibi, A., Delavar, M. R., Sadeghian, M. S., Nazari, B., & Pirasteh, S. (2023). A hybrid of ensemble machine learning models with RFE and Boruta wrapper-based algorithms for flash flood susceptibility assessment. *International Journal of Applied Earth Observation and Geoinformation.* Advance online publication. DOI: 10.1016/j.jag.2023.103401

Haile, A. (2024). *Innovating Software Testing with AI and Machine Learning: Automation for Efficient Distributed Network Management.* Unpublished. DOI: 10.13140/RG.2.2.17654.72004

Hajla, S. El, Ennaji, E. M., Maleh, Y., & Mounir, S. (2025). *Enhancing IoT network defense : advanced intrusion detection via ensemble learning techniques. 35*(3), 2010–2020. https://doi.org/DOI: 10.11591/ijeecs.v35.i3.pp2010-2020

Hanafi, M., A. H., Verawati, I., & Hardi, R. (2022). An Intrusion Detection System Using SDAE to Enhance Dimensional Reduction in Machine Learning. *International Journal on Informatics Visualization, 6*(2), 306–316. DOI: 10.30630/joiv.6.2.990

Hazra, A., Ghosh, S., & Jash, S. (2018). A new DNA cryptography based algorithm involving the fusion of symmetric-key techniques. *Advances in Intelligent Systems and Computing, 706*. Advance online publication. DOI: 10.1007/978-981-10-8237-5_59

He, K., Meng, X., Pan, Z., Yuan, L., & Zhou, P. (2018, June). A novel Task-Duplication based clustering algorithm for heterogeneous computing environments. *IEEE Transactions on Parallel and Distributed Systems, 30*(1), 2–14. DOI: 10.1109/tpds.2018.2851221

Henrichs, E., Lesch, V., Straesser, M., Kounev, S., & Krupitzer, C. (2022). A literature review on optimization techniques for adaptation planning in adaptive systems: State of the art and research directions. *Information and Software Technology, 149*, 106940. DOI: 10.1016/j.infsof.2022.106940

Henrik, L. Tao, & Henrik. (2022). *Serverless Function Triggers in Azure: An Analysis of Latency and Reliability*. https://odr.chalmers.se/items/7ab2f3f4-a174-40c1-81db-e5e74803a036

Huh, S., Cho, S., & Kim, S. (2017). Managing IoT devices using blockchain platform. *Proceedings of the International Conference on Advanced Communication Technology*, 464–467. DOI: 10.23919/ICACT.2017.7890132

Isna, M., Ahfa, M., Hakim, L., & Rosadi, M. I. (2025).. . *Comparison of Dimensionality Reduction Techniques to Improve Performance and Efficiency of Logistic Regression in Network Anomaly Detection., 3*(January), 1–13. DOI: 10.30996/jitcs.12212

Izadi, M., Sadeghiyan, B., Sadeghian, S. S., & Khanooki, H. A. (2009). MIBS: A new lightweight block cipher. *Lecture Notes in Computer Science (Including Subseries Lecture Notes in Artificial Intelligence and Lecture Notes in Bioinformatics), 5888 LNCS*. DOI: 10.1007/978-3-642-10433-6_22

Jayanetti, A., Halgamuge, S., & Buyya, R. (2024). Reinforcement Learning based workflow scheduling in cloud and edge computing environments: A taxonomy, review and future directions. arXiv.

Jeyaraj, S. A. L., Kumar, S., Revathy, S., Yenigalla, G., Krishna, K. B., & Jayabalan, K. (2024). Machine Learning Algorithms for E-Commerce Security: A Practical Approach. In *Strategies for E-Commerce Data Security: Cloud, Blockchain, AI, and Machine Learning* (pp. 361–385). IGI Global.

Jia, Q., Guo, X., Zhang, M., Liu, M., Tian, X., Jin, X., & Ma, D. (2023). *Phishing URL recognition based on ON-LSTM attention mechanism and XGBoost model.* Paper presented at the 2023 5th International Conference on Electronics and Communication, Network and Computer Technology (ECNCT).

Joshi, A.. (2024). Deep learning based traffic classification with feature selection mechanism and explainable artificial intelligence (xai). *International Journal of Intelligent Systems and Applications in Engineering*, *12*(1s), 654–662.

Juhás, G., Juhásová, A., & Petrovič, L. (2023). Low-code languages in IT education: Integrating theory and practice. *2023 21st International Conference on Emerging eLearning Technologies and Applications (ICETA)*, 249-257. https://doi.org/DOI: 10.1109/ICETA61311.2023.10343807

Kadhim, Q. K., Yusof, R., Mahdi, H. S., Al-Shami, S. S. A., & Selamat, S. R. (2018, May). A review study on cloud computing issues. *Journal of Physics: Conference Series*, *1018*, 012006. DOI: 10.1088/1742-6596/1018/1/012006

Kalsi, S., Kaur, H., & Chang, V. (2018). DNA Cryptography and Deep Learning using Genetic Algorithm with NW algorithm for Key Generation. *Journal of Medical Systems*, *42*(1). Advance online publication. DOI: 10.1007/s10916-017-0851-z PMID: 29204890

Kandasamy, V., & Roseline, A. A. (2025). *Harnessing advanced hybrid deep learning model for real-time detection and prevention of man- in-the-middle cyber attacks*. 1–26.

Käppler, S. A., & Schneider, B. (2022). Post-quantum cryptography: An introductory overview and implementation challenges of quantum-resistant algorithms. *Proceedings of the Society*, *84*, 61–71.

Karakaya, A., & Ulu, A. (2024). A survey on post-quantum-based approaches for edge computing security. *Wiley Interdisciplinary Reviews: Computational Statistics*, *16*(1), e1644.

Kasim, Ö. (2021). Automatic detection of phishing pages with event-based request processing, deep-hybrid feature extraction and light gradient boosted machine model. *Telecommunication Systems*, *78*(1), 103–115.

KATE, J., MARY, O., & QUDUS, A. (2024). *Securing the E-commerce AI Ecosystem: Multi-layered Cybersecurity Solutions for Client, Communication, and Database Integrity.*

Kaushik, K. (2022). Blockchain Enabled Artificial Intelligence for Cybersecurity Systems. In Ouaissa, M., Boulouard, Z., Ouaissa, M., Khan, I. U., & Kaosar, M. (Eds.), *Big Data Analytics and Computational Intelligence for Cybersecurity. Studies in Big Data* (Vol. 111). Springer., DOI: 10.1007/978-3-031-05752-6_11

Keerthana, N., Suresh, P., Kulandaivel, M., & Kulandaivel, S. (2025). Critical Strategies for Phishing Defense and Digital Asset Protection: A Case Study Approach. In *Critical Phishing Defense Strategies and Digital Asset Protection* (pp. 221-244): IGI Global Scientific Publishing.

Kelefouras, V., & Djemame, K. (2022, May). Workflow simulation and multi-threading aware task scheduling for heterogeneous computing. *Journal of Parallel and Distributed Computing*, *168*, 17–32. DOI: 10.1016/j.jpdc.2022.05.011

Khan, M. Z., Bokhari, M. U., & Khan, T. F. (2024). Internet of Things Security: An Experimental Analysis of Detecting Denial of Service Attacks with Machine Learning. *2024 1st International Conference on Innovative Engineering Sciences and Technological Research (ICIESTR)*, 1–6. https://doi.org/DOI: 10.1109/ICIESTR60916.2024.10798334

Khan, M., & Tripathi, A. (2018). "Digital Patient Eye," *2018 3rd International Conference On Internet of Things: Smart Innovation and Usages (IoT-SIU)*, Bhimtal, India, pp. 1-4, doi: DOI: 10.1109/IoT-SIU.2018.8519841

Khan, S. Z. (2023). *Automated Test Case Generation and Defect Prediction: Enhancing Software Quality Assurance through AI-Driven Testing Automation.*

Khan, T. F., & Zubair, S. (2025). Lung Cancer Diagnosis Using Image Enhancement and Machine Learning Methods. *Communications in Computer and Information Science, 2366 CCIS*, 197–208. https://doi.org/DOI: 10.1007/978-3-031-81342-9_17

Khan, H. U., Khan, R. A., Alwageed, H. S., Almagrabi, A. O., Ayouni, S., & Maddeh, M. (2025). AI-driven cybersecurity framework for software development based on the ANN-ISM paradigm. *Scientific Reports*, *15*(1), 13423. DOI: 10.1038/s41598-025-97204-y PMID: 40251237

Khan, M. Z., & Bokhari, M. U. (2023). Comparative Study of Detection of IoT Attacks using Machine Learning Techniques. *Proceedings of the 17th INDIACom; 2023 10th International Conference on Computing for Sustainable Global Development, INDIACom 2023*, 1648–1651.

Khan, Z. A., Aziz, I. A., Osman, N. A. B., & Ullah, I. (2023, January). A review on task scheduling techniques in cloud and Fog computing: Taxonomy, tools, open issues, challenges, and future directions. *IEEE Access: Practical Innovations, Open Solutions*, *11*, 143417–143445. DOI: 10.1109/access.2023.3343877

Khatibsyarbini, M., Isa, M. A., Jawawi, D. N. A., Shafie, M. L. M., Wan-Kadir, W. M. N., Hamed, H. N. A., & Suffian, M. D. M. (2021). Trend Application of Machine Learning in Test Case Prioritization: A Review on Techniques. *IEEE Access: Practical Innovations, Open Solutions*, *9*, 166262–166282. DOI: 10.1109/ACCESS.2021.3135508

Khorram, F., Mottu, J. M., & Sunyé, G. (2020). Challenges & opportunities in low-code testing. *Proceedings of the 23rd ACM/IEEE International Conference on Model Driven Engineering Languages and Systems: Companion Proceedings*, 1-10. https://doi.org/DOI: 10.1145/3417990.3420204

Khurana, R. (2021). *Implementing Encryption and Cybersecurity Strategies across Client, Communication, Response Generation, and Database Modules in E-Commerce Conversational AI Systems Implementing Encryption and Cybersecurity Strategies across Client, Communication, Respons. This Advancement in Technology Has Also Warranted the Focus of a Number of Important Concerns Regarding Security*. Such as Sensitive User Data Protection.

Khurana, R., & Kaul, D. (2019). Dynamic cybersecurity strategies for ai-enhanced ecommerce: A federated learning approach to data privacy. *Applied Research in Artificial Intelligence and Cloud Computing*, *2*(1), 32–43.

Kiran, B., Raghu, N., & Manjunatha, K. N. (2023). VLSI Implementation of a High-Speed Pipeline A/D Converter. In *Role of 6G Wireless Networks in AI and Blockchain-Based Applications* (pp. 112–130). IGI Global.

Koppanati, P. K. (2024). Scaling Test Automation in CI/CD Pipelines Using Docker and Kubernetes. *North American Journal of Engineering Research*, *5*(3), 3. http://najer.org/najer/article/view/91

Kothamali, P. R., Banik, S., & Nadimpalli, S. V. (2020). Challenges in Applying ML to Cybersecurity. *Revista de Inteligencia Artificial En Medicina*, *11*(1), 214–256.

Kubba, Z. M. J., & Hoomod, H. K. (2020). Developing a lightweight cryptographic algorithm based on DNA computing. *AIP Conference Proceedings*, *2290*. Advance online publication. DOI: 10.1063/5.0027361

Kumari, P., & Jain, A. K. (2024). Timely detection of DDoS attacks in IoT with dimensionality reduction. *Cluster Computing*, *27*(6), 7869–7887. DOI: 10.1007/s10586-024-04392-9

Kuznetsov, O., Sernani, P., Romeo, L., Frontoni, E., & Mancini, A. (2024). On the Integration of Artificial Intelligence and Blockchain Technology: A Perspective About Security. *IEEE Access: Practical Innovations, Open Solutions*, *12*, 3881–3897. DOI: 10.1109/ACCESS.2023.3349019

Kvet, M. (2024). Rapid application development and data management using Oracle APEX and SQL. *2024 IEEE 22nd World Symposium on Applied Machine Intelligence and Informatics (SAMI)*, 000297-000302. https://doi.org/DOI: 10.1109/SAMI60510.2024.10432914

Langendonck, T., Caville, S., & Allu, S. (2024). Towards a graph-based foundation model for network traffic analysis. *arXiv preprint arXiv:2409.12345.*

Lashkari, A. H., Gil, G. D., Mamun, M. S. I., & Ghorbani, A. A. (2017). Characterization of tor traffic using time based features, 253–262.

Lashkari, A. H., Kaur, G., & Rahali, A. (2020). Didarknet: A contemporary approach to detect and characterize the darknet traffic using deep image learning, 1–13.

Latif, S., Idrees, Z., Huma, Z. E., & Ahmad, J. (2021). Blockchain technology for the industrial Internet of Things: A comprehensive survey on security challenges, architectures, applications, and future research directions. *Transactions on Emerging Telecommunications Technologies*, *32*(11), e4337. DOI: 10.1002/ETT.4337

Lee, J., Lee, Y., Lee, D., Kwon, H., & Shin, D. (2021). Classification of attack types and analysis of attack methods for profiling phishing mail attack groups. *IEEE Access: Practical Innovations, Open Solutions*, *9*, 80866–80872.

Leier, A., Richter, C., Banzhaf, W., & Rauhe, H. (2000). Cryptography with DNA binary strands. *Bio Systems*, *57*(1). Advance online publication. DOI: 10.1016/S0303-2647(00)00083-6 PMID: 10963862

Li, L., Liu, B., Zhou, Y., & Zou, Y. (2018). SFN: A new lightweight block cipher. *Microprocessors and Microsystems*, *60*. Advance online publication. DOI: 10.1016/j.micpro.2018.04.009

Li, L., Pan, W., Li, D., Liu, G., & Huang, T. (2023). "Task Scheduling Based on Heterogeneous Priority and Critical Task Duplication," *International Conference on Computer Engineering and Intelligent Control*, pp. 1–9, doi: DOI: 10.1109/icceic60201.2023.10426638

Liu, C., Liu, Y., Zhu, E., Zhang, Q., Wei, X., & Wang, B. (2020). Cross-Inhibitor: A time-sensitive molecular circuit based on DNA strand displacement. *Nucleic Acids Research, 48*(19). Advance online publication. DOI: 10.1093/nar/gkaa835 PMID: 33045746

Liu, D., Zhang, Y., Jia, D., Zhang, Q., Zhao, X., & Rong, H. (2022). Toward secure distributed data storage with error locating in blockchain enabled edge computing. *Computer Standards & Interfaces, 79*, 103560.

Liu, J., Lu, S., & Che, D. (2020). "A Survey of Modern Scientific Workflow Scheduling Algorithms and Systems in the Era of Big Data," *IEEE International Conference on Services Computing*, pp. 132–141, doi: DOI: 10.1109/scc49832.2020.00026

Liu, W., Gao, L., Liu, X., Wang, S., & Xu, J. (2003). Solving the 3-SAT Problem Based on DNA Computing. *Journal of Chemical Information and Computer Sciences*, *43*(6). Advance online publication. DOI: 10.1021/ci034113o PMID: 14632435

Liu, W., Qiu, J.-L., Zheng, W.-L., & Lu, B.-L. (2021). Comparing recognition performance and robustness of multimodal deep learning models for multimodal emotion recognition. *IEEE Transactions on Cognitive and Developmental Systems, 14*(2), 715–729.

Ludäscher, B., Bowers, S., & McPhillips, T. (2018). "Scientific workflows," in *Encyclopedia of Database Systems*, pp. 3320–3324. doi: DOI: 10.1007/978-1-4614-8265-9_1471

Luo, Y., Liang, P., Wang, C., Shahin, M., & Zhan, J. (2021). Characteristics and challenges of low-code development: The practitioners' perspective. *International Symposium on Empirical Software Engineering and Measurement*, 1-11. https://doi.org/DOI: 10.1145/3475716.3475782

Lytras, M. D., & Visvizi, A. (2021). Information management as a dual-purpose process in the smart city: Collecting, managing and utilizing information. *International Journal of Information Management*. Advance online publication. DOI: 10.1016/j.ijinfomgt.2020.102224

M.V. H. V., & T., J. (2025). A hybrid model for detecting intrusions using stacked autoencoders and extreme gradient boosting. *Computers & Security, 150*, 104212. https://doi.org/https://doi.org/10.1016/j.cose.2024.104212

Maazalahi, M., & Hosseini, S. (2025). Machine learning and metaheuristic optimization algorithms for feature selection and botnet attack detection. In *Knowledge and Information Systems*. Springer London., DOI: 10.1007/s10115-024-02322-0

Madhumita, R., & Chandana, D. (n.d.). *Advancing Software Testing: Integrating AI*. Machine Learning, and Emerging Technologies.

Mahjabin, T., Olteanu, A., Xiao, Y., Han, W., Li, T., & Sun, W. (2023). A Survey on DNA-Based Cryptography and Steganography. *IEEE Access: Practical Innovations, Open Solutions*, *11*. Advance online publication. DOI: 10.1109/ACCESS.2023.3324875

Malawski, M., Figiela, K., Gajek, A., & Bubak, M. (2015). Scheduling scientific workflows with budget and deadline constraints using genetic algorithms. *Scientific Programming*, *2015*, 1–13. DOI: 10.1155/2015/847925

Malik, F., Suliman, M., Khan, M. Q., Rahman, N., Khan, K., & Khan, M. (2024). Optimizing malicious website detection with the XGBoost machine learning approach. *Journal of Computing & Biomedical Informatics*, *7*(02).

Mandela, N., Sonia, Mistry, N., & Nagpal, A. (2025). Efficient dark web traffic clas- sification using a hybrid cnn-lstm model. *International Journal of Information Technology: an Official Journal of Bharati Vidyapeeth's Institute of Computer Applications and Management*.

Marim, M. C., Ramos, P. V. B., Vieira, A. B., Galletta, A., Villari, M., de Oliveira, R. M., & Silva, E. F. (2023). Darknet traffic detection and characterization with models based on decision trees and neural networks. *Intelligent Systems with Applications*, *18*, 200199.

Mathur, G. (Sagar Institute of Science and Technology, I. and P. S. C. (Sagar I. of S. and T. I. (2025). DNA Computing in Enhancing Cloud Security. In *IGI Global Publisher*. IGI Global.

Mei, Q., Xiong, H., Chen, Y. C., & Chen, C. M. (2022). Blockchain-enabled privacy-preserving authentication mechanism for transportation CPS with cloud-edge computing. *IEEE Transactions on Engineering Management*.

Metrôlho, J., Ribeiro, F., Graça, P., Mourato, A., Figueiredo, D., & Vilarinho, H. (2022). Introducing rapid web application development with Oracle APEX to students of higher education. *New Trends in Computer Sciences*, *1*(2), 15–28.

Mijwil, M. M., Salem, I. E., & Ismaeel, M. M. (2023). The significance of machine learn- ing and deep learning techniques in cybersecurity: A comprehensive review. *Iraqi Journal For Computer Science and Mathematics*, *4*(1), 10.

Mikram, H., Kafhali, S. E., & Saadi, Y. (2023, November). HEPGA: A new effective hybrid algorithm for scientific workflow scheduling in cloud computing environment. *Simulation Modelling Practice and Theory*, *130*, 102864. DOI: 10.1016/j.simpat.2023.102864

Minhas, N. M., Petersen, K., Börstler, J., & Wnuk, K. (2020). Regression testing for large-scale embedded software development – Exploring the state of practice. *Information and Software Technology*, *120*, 106254. DOI: 10.1016/j.infsof.2019.106254

Mishra, P., Varadharajan, V., Tupakula, U., & Pilli, E. S. (2019). A detailed investigation and analysis of using machine learning techniques for intrusion detection. *IEEE Communications Surveys and Tutorials*, *21*(1), 686–728. DOI: 10.1109/COMST.2018.2847722

Mohamed, N. (2025). Artificial intelligence and machine learning in cybersecurity: A deep dive into state-of-the-art techniques and future paradigms. *Knowledge and Information Systems*. Advance online publication. DOI: 10.1007/s10115-025-02429-y

Mohammed, I. A., & Madhumithaa, N. (2024, July 15). *Transforming Decision-Making: The Impact of AI and Machine Learning on Strategic Business Operations. | EBSCOhost*. https://openurl.ebsco.com/contentitem/gcd:180919191?sid=ebsco:plink:crawler&id=ebsco:gcd:180919191

Mohanta, S. K., Mohapatra, A. G., Mohanty, A., & Nayak, S. (2024). Deep Learning is a State-of-the-Art Approach to Artificial Intelligence. In *Deep Learning Concepts in Operations Research*. Auerbach Publications.

Mohanty, S. K., Mishra, D., & Jena, S. K. (2022). Robust stacking ensemble model for darknet traffic classification under adversarial settings. *Journal of King Saud University. Computer and Information Sciences*, *34*(10), 9998–10011.

Mokbal, F. M. M., Wang, D., Wang, X., Zhao, W., & Fu, L. (2021). XGBXSS: An Extreme Gradient Boosting Detection Framework for Cross-Site Scripting Attacks Based on Hybrid Feature Selection Approach and Parameters Optimization. *Journal of Information Security and Applications*, *58*, 102813.

Mudgal, A. (2025). Leveraging AI and ML for Proactive Threat Detection for E-Commerce. In *Strategic Innovations of AI and ML for E-Commerce Data Security* (pp. 281–322). IGI Global.

Muhammad, S., & Mirjat, N. A. (2024). Enhancing Cybersecurity with AI: From Anomaly Detection to Threat Mitigation. *Bulletin of Engineering Science and Technology*, *1*(03), 20–39.

Musthafa, M. B., Huda, S., Kodera, Y., Ali, M. A., Araki, S., Mwaura, J., & Nogami, Y. (2024). Optimizing IoT Intrusion Detection Using Balanced Class Distribution, Feature Selection, and Ensemble Machine Learning Techniques. *Sensors (Basel), 24*(13), 1–19. DOI: 10.3390/s24134293 PMID: 39001072

Nagunwa, T. (2024). Comparative Analysis of Nature-Inspired Metaheuristic Techniques for Optimizing Phishing Website Detection. *Analytics*, *3*(3), 344–367.

Najihi, S., Elhadi, S., Abdelouahid, R. A., & Marzak, A. (2022). Software Testing from an Agile and Traditional view. *Procedia Computer Science*, *203*, 775–782. DOI: 10.1016/j.procs.2022.07.116

Nama, P., Reddy, P., & Pattanayak, S. K. (2024). *Artificial Intelligence for Self-Healing Automation Testing Frameworks: Real-Time Fault Prediction and Recovery. 64*(3).

Nama, P. (2024). Integrating AI in testing automation: Enhancing test coverage and predictive analysis for improved software quality. *World Journal of Advanced Engineering Technology and Sciences*, *13*(1), 769–782. DOI: 10.30574/wjaets.2024.13.1.0486

Namasudra, S. (2022). A secure cryptosystem using DNA cryptography and DNA steganography for the cloud-based IoT infrastructure. *Computers & Electrical Engineering*, *104*. Advance online publication. DOI: 10.1016/j.compeleceng.2022.108426

Nasayreh, A., Jaradat, A. S., Gharaibeh, H., Dawaghreh, W., Al Mamlook, R. M., Alqudah, Y., Al-Na'amneh, Q., Daoud, M. S., Migdady, H., & Abualigah, L. (2024). Jordanian banknote data recognition: A cnn-based approach with atten- tion mechanism. *Journal of King Saud University. Computer and Information Sciences*, *36*(4), 102038.

Natarajan, A. K., Desai, Y., Kshirsagar, P. R., Upreti, K., & Tak, T. K. (2025). Generative AI for Cybersecurity and Privacy in Cyber-Physical Systems. In *Navigating Cyber-Physical Systems With Cutting-Edge Technologies* (pp. 57–82). IGI Global Scientific Publishing.

NG, S. G., Chinnegowda, H. S., & Kaul, H. (n.d.). *Review on Harnessing Artificial Intelligence: A Paradigm Shift in Cybersecurity for a Safer Digital Future.*

Nikanjam, A., Morovati, M. M., Khomh, F., & Ben Braiek, H. (2021). Faults in deep reinforcement learning programs: A taxonomy and a detection approach. *Automated Software Engineering*, *29*(1), 8. DOI: 10.1007/s10515-021-00313-x

Nwogbaga, N. E., Latip, R., Affendey, L. S., & Rahiman, A. R. A. (2022, June). Attribute reduction-based scheduling algorithm with enhanced hybrid genetic algorithm and particle swarm optimization for optimal device selection. *Journal of Cloud Computing Advances Systems and Applications*, *11*(1). Advance online publication. DOI: 10.1186/s13677-022-00288-4

Odeh, A., Al-Haija, Q. A., Aref, A., & Taleb, A. A. (2023). Comparative study of catboost, xgboost, and lightgbm for enhanced URL phishing detection: A performance assessment. *Journal of Internet Services and Information Security*, *13*(4), 1–11.

Omari, K. (2023). Phishing detection using gradient boosting classifier. *Procedia Computer Science*, *230*, 120–127.

Oracle Corporation. (2025a). Oracle APEX architecture. Retrieved from https://apex.oracle.com/en/platform/architecture/

Oracle Corporation. (2025b). Oracle APEX features. Retrieved from https://apex.oracle.com/en/platform/features/

Oracle Corporation. (2025c). Powered by Oracle - Oracle APEX. Retrieved from https://apex.oracle.com/en/platform/powered-by-oracle/

Oracle Corporation. (2025d). Telecom giant Telstra empowers citizen developers with Oracle APEX. Retrieved from https://www.oracle.com/customers/telstra/

Oracle Corporation. (2025e). Oracle APEX success stories. Retrieved from https://apex.oracle.com/en/solutions/success-stories/

Oracle Corporation. (2025f). Restrictions and limitations for Oracle APEX. Retrieved from https://docs.oracle.com/en/cloud/paas/apex/gsadd/restrictions-and-limitations-for-oracle-apex.html

Oyeniran, O. C., Adewusi, A. O., Akwawa, L. A., & Azubuko, C. F. (2024). *Microservices Architecture in Cloud-Native Applications: Design Patterns and Scalability | International Journal of Advanced Research and Interdisciplinary Scientific Endeavours*. https://ijarise.org/index.php/ijarise/article/view/66

Ozcan, A., Catal, C., Donmez, E., & Senturk, B. (2023). A hybrid DNN–LSTM model for detecting phishing URLs. *Neural Computing & Applications*, •••, 1–17. PMID: 34393380

Pandey, S., Wu, L., Guru, S. M., & Buyya, R. (2010). A particle swarm optimization-based heuristic for scheduling workflow applications in cloud computing environments. *Proceedings of the 2010 24th IEEE International Conference on Advanced Information Networking and Applications*, 400–407. https://doi.org/DOI: 10.1109/AINA.2010.31

Pang, B., Fu, Y., Ren, S., Wang, Y., Liao, Q., & Jia, Y. (2021). Cgnn: Traffic classification with graph neural network. *arXiv preprint arXiv:2110.09726.*

Pant, D., Bhatt, A., Khan, M., Nautiyal, O. P., & Adhikari, P. (2020). Automated IoT based Smart Water Quality Assessment System. *Proceedings of the 2019 8th International Conference on System Modeling and Advancement in Research Trends, SMART 2019*, 98–104. https://doi.org/DOI: 10.1109/SMART46866.2019.9117271

Papi, M., & Hiver, P. (2020). Language Learning Motivation as a Complex Dynamic System: A Global Perspective of Truth, Control, and Value. *Modern Language Journal, 104*(1), 209–232. DOI: 10.1111/modl.12624

Paspula, R. K. C. and S. L. K. (2017). Hidden data transmission with variable DNA technology. *International Journal of Electronics and Information Engineering, 7*(1), 41–52.

Pavan, R., Nara, M., Gopinath, S., & Patil, N. (2021). *Bayesian optimization and gradient boosting to detect phishing websites.* Paper presented at the 2021 55th Annual Conference on Information Sciences and Systems (CISS).

PBV., R. R., Pokkuluri, K. S., Prasad, M., Sharma, N., Murthy, B. N., & Karunasri, A. (2024). *Ensemble Fusion for Enhanced Malicious URL Detection by Integrating Machine Learning and Deep Learning Techniques.* Paper presented at the International Conference on Cognitive Computing and Cyber Physical Systems.

Phalake, V., Joshi, S., Rade, K., & Phalke, V. (2022). Modernized application development using optimized low code platform. *2022 2nd Asian Conference on Innovation in Technology (ASIANCON)*, 1-4. https://doi.org/DOI: 10.1109/ASIANCON55314.2022.9908726

Ponnusamy, P., & Dhandayudam, P. (2024). An Optimized Bagging Learning with Ensemble Feature Selection Method for URL Phishing Detection. *Journal of Electrical Engineering & Technology, 19*(3), 1881–1889.

Ponnusamy, S., & Eswararaj, D. (2023). Navigating the Modernization of Legacy Applications and Data: Effective Strategies and Best Practices. *Asian Journal of Research in Computer Science, 16*(4), 239–256. DOI: 10.9734/ajrcos/2023/v16i4386

Pramanik, S. and S. K. S. (2012). DNA cryptography. *2012 7th International Conference on Electrical and Computer Engineering*.

Qazi, E. U. H., Faheem, M. H., & Zia, T. (2023). Hdlnids: Hybrid deep-learning-based network intrusion detection system. *Applied Sciences (Basel, Switzerland)*, *13*(8), 4921.

Raghu, N., & Ranjith Bhat, P. Rajashree Nambiar, Ganesh Srinivasa Shetty, and Anil Kumar DB. (2025). "Blockchain-enhanced GAN image encryption scheme for cloud computing." In *Intelligent Systems and IoT Applications in Clinical Health*, pp. 367-392. IGI Global.

Raghu, N., & Rupali, A. Mahajan, A. Sivanantham, Lakshay Bareja, N. K. Rayaguru, and Reddy Ganesh. (2024). "Optimizing Real-Time Process Control through Cloud-Based Automation and Big Data Analysis." In *2024 15th International Conference on Computing Communication and Networking Technologies (ICCCNT)*, pp. 1-6. IEEE.

Rodriguez, M. A., & Buyya, R. (2014). Deadline based resource provisioning and scheduling algorithm for scientific workflows on clouds. *IEEE Transactions on Cloud Computing*, *2*(2), 222–235. DOI: 10.1109/TCC.2014.2314655

Roy, R. B., Patel, T., Gadepally, V., & Tiwari, D. (2022). Mashup. *Association for Computing Machinery*, (Mar). Advance online publication. DOI: 10.1145/3503221.3508407

Rust-Nguyen, N., & Stamp, M. (2022). Darknet traffic classification and adversarial at- tacks. *arXiv preprint arXiv:2206.06371*.

Rust-Nguyen, N., & Stamp, M. (2023). Darknet traffic classification and adversarial at- tacks using machine learning. *Computers & Security*, *127*, 103098.

S. S and N. K. Patil. (2022, April). Hybrid Genetic Algorithm and Modified-Particle Swarm Optimization Algorithm (GA-MPSO) for predicting scheduling virtual machines in educational cloud platforms [iJET]. *International Journal of Emerging Technologies in Learning*, *17*(07), 208–225. DOI: 10.3991/ijet.v17i07.29223

Sadeeq, M. M., Abdulkareem, N. M., Zeebaree, S. R. M., Ahmed, D. M., Sami, A. S., & Zebari, R. R. (2021, March). IoT and Cloud Computing Issues, Challenges and Opportunities: A Review. *Qubahan Academic Journal*, *1*(2), 1–7. DOI: 10.48161/qaj.v1n2a36

Sahay, A., Indamutsa, A., Di Ruscio, D., & Pierantonio, A. (2020). Supporting the understanding and comparison of low-code development platforms. *46th Euromicro Conference on Software Engineering and Advanced Applications (SEAA)*, 171-178. https://doi.org/DOI: 10.1109/SEAA51224.2020.00036

Saif, M. A. N., Niranjan, S. K., & Al-ariki, H. D. E. (2021). Efficient autonomic and elastic resource management techniques in cloud environment: Taxonomy and analysis. *Wireless Networks*, *27*(4), 2829–2866. DOI: 10.1007/s11276-021-02614-1

Sajisha, K. S., & Mathew, S. (2017). An encryption based on DNA cryptography and steganography. *Proceedings of the International Conference on Electronics, Communication and Aerospace Technology, ICECA 2017, 2017-January*. DOI: 10.1109/ICECA.2017.8212786

Sakib, M., & Mustajab, S. (2024). Enhanced Multi-variate Time Series Prediction Through Statistical-Deep Learning Integration: The VAR-Stacked LSTM Model. *SN Computer Science*, *5*(5). Advance online publication. DOI: 10.1007/s42979-024-02950-x

Sakib, M., & Mustajab, S. (2025). CEEMDAN-TCN-AutoLSTM: A Triple-Force Ensemble Using Cross-Stitch Networks for Short-Term Load Forecasting. *Arabian Journal for Science and Engineering*. Advance online publication. DOI: 10.1007/s13369-025-10398-1

Sakib, M., & Siddiqui, T. (2023). Multi-Network-Based Ensemble Deep Learning Model to Forecast Ross River Virus Outbreak in Australia. *International Journal of Pattern Recognition and Artificial Intelligence*, *37*(10), 2352015.

Sakib, U. S2*, A. P. (2022). Bitcoin Price Prediction using Machine Learning. *Journal of Computer Science and Software Development*, *2*, 10.

Salahirad, A., Gay, G., & Mohammadi, E. (2023). Mapping the structure and evolution of software testing research over the past three decades. *Journal of Systems and Software*, *195*, 111518. DOI: 10.1016/j.jss.2022.111518

Saleem, J., Islam, R., & Islam, M. Z. (2024). *Darknet traffic analysis: A systematic literature review*. IEEE., DOI: 10.1109/ACCESS.2024.3373769

Saleem, J., Islam, R., & Kabir, M. A. (2022). The anonymity of the dark web: A survey. *IEEE Access: Practical Innovations, Open Solutions*, *10*, 33628–33660.

Samadi, Y., Zbakh, M., & Tadonki, C. (2018). "E-HEFT: Enhancement Heterogeneous Earliest Finish Time algorithm for Task Scheduling based on Load Balancing in Cloud Computing," *International Conference on High Performance Computing & Simulation (HPCS)*, pp. 601–609, Jul. 2018, doi: DOI: 10.1109/hpcs.2018.00100

Sameen, M., Han, K., & Hwang, S. O. (2020). PhishHaven—An efficient real-time AI phishing URLs detection system. *IEEE Access: Practical Innovations, Open Solutions*, *8*, 83425–83443.

Sanchis, R., Garcia-Perales, O., Fraile, F., & Poler, R. (2020). Low-code as enabler of digital transformation in manufacturing industry. *Applied Sciences (Basel, Switzerland)*, *10*(1), 12. DOI: 10.3390/app10010012

Saqib, M., Sahu, S. A., Sakib, M., & Al-Ammar, E. A. (2021). Machine Learning-Based Day Ahead Market Energy Usage Bidding for Smart Microgrids. *Electric Vehicle Integration in a Smart Microgrid Environment*, 249–266. https://doi.org/ DOI: 10.1201/9780367423926-10

Sarkar, S., Mittal, S., Garg, S., & Sahu, A. (2025). Scientific workflow scheduling in cloud considering cold start and variable pricing model. arXiv.

Sarker, I. H. (2022). AI-Based Modeling: Techniques, Applications and Research Issues Towards Automation, Intelligent and Smart Systems. *SN Computer Science*, *3*(2), 158. DOI: 10.1007/s42979-022-01043-x PMID: 35194580

Sarwar, M. B., Hanif, M. K., Talib, R., Younas, M., & Sarwar, M. U. (2021). Darkdetect: Darknet traffic detection and categorization using modified convolution-long short- term memory. *IEEE Access: Practical Innovations, Open Solutions*, *9*, 113705–113713.

Seattle Metropolitan Chamber of Commerce. (2024). Comparing low-code platforms: Oracle APEX vs. others. Retrieved from https://www.seattlechamber.com/news/2024/10/22/member-news/comparing-low-code-platforms-oracle-apex-vs-others/

Sellami, Y. (2024). *Secure data management in an IoT-Fog/Edge computing architecture* (Doctoral dissertation, Université Polytechnique Hauts-de-France).

Seol, J., Kim, J., & Kancharla, A. (2024, October). Integrating Blockchain-Based Security and Privacy with QML in Edge Computing for 6G Networks. In *International Conference on Computer Applications in Industry and Engineering* (pp. 86-101). Cham: Springer Nature Switzerland.

Shao, K., Fu, H., & Wang, B. (2023, August). An efficient combination of genetic algorithm and particle swarm optimization for scheduling Data-Intensive tasks in heterogeneous cloud computing. *Electronics (Basel)*, *12*(16), 3450. DOI: 10.3390/electronics12163450

Shetty, G. S., & Raghu, N. (2024). Strategies for Achieving Energy Efficiency and Data Security Through Data Aggregation in IoT Healthcare Applications: A Comprehensive Study.

Shikalgar, S., Sawarkar, S., & Narwane, S. (2019). Detection of URL based phishing attacks using machine learning. [IJERT]. *Int. J. Eng. Res. Tech.*, *8*(11).

Shi, L.. (2021, January). Multijob associated task scheduling for cloud computing based on task duplication and insertion. *Wireless Communications and Mobile Computing, 2021*(1). Advance online publication. DOI: 10.1155/2021/6631752

Shinde, V., Singhal, K., Almogren, A., Dhanawat, V., Karande, V., & Rehman, A. U. (2024). Ensemble voting for enhanced robustness in darknet traffic detection. *IEEE Access: Practical Innovations, Open Solutions, 12*, 177064–177079.

Shirvani, M. H., & Talouki, R. N. (2021, August). A novel hybrid heuristic-based list scheduling algorithm in heterogeneous cloud computing environment for makespan optimization. *Parallel Computing, 108*, 102828. DOI: 10.1016/j.parco.2021.102828

Singamaneni, K. K., & Muhammad, G. (2024). A novel integrated quantum-resistant cryptography for secure scientific data exchange in ad hoc networks. *Ad Hoc Networks, 164*, 103607.

Singh, P., Hasija, T., & Ramkumar, K. (2024). *Advancing Phishing Threat Mitigation: An Intelligent System for Optimized URL-Based Detection using AI.* Paper presented at the 2024 First International Conference on Innovations in Communications, Electrical and Computer Engineering (ICICEC).

Singh, J., & Walia, N. K. (2023, January). A comprehensive review of cloud Computing Virtual machine Consolidation. *IEEE Access: Practical Innovations, Open Solutions, 11*, 106190–106209. DOI: 10.1109/access.2023.3314613

Singh, R. K., Raichura, H., Malhotra, A., & Kalra, H. (2025). N. Raghu, and Garima. "Optimizing data service with innovative model for multi-cloud driven storage platform.". *International Journal of System Assurance Engineering and Management*, •••, 1–10.

Sipper, M., & Moore, J. H. (2021). Conservation machine learning : A case study of random forests. *Scientific Reports, 0123456789*, 1–6. DOI: 10.1038/s41598-021-83247-4 PMID: 33574563

Sitaramanan, S. R. (2024). Quantum-resistant cryptography and edge computing in blockchain for cloud security and IoT: Addressing performance and integration challenges. *Journal of the Saudi Society of Agricultural Sciences*. Advance online publication. DOI: 10.1016/j.jssas.2024.02.001

Smadi, S., Aslam, N., & Zhang, L. (2018). Detection of online phishing email using dynamic evolving neural network based on reinforcement learning. *Decision Support Systems, 107*, 88–102.

Sohal, M., & Sharma, S. (2022). BDNA-A DNA inspired symmetric key cryptographic technique to secure cloud computing. *Journal of King Saud University. Computer and Information Sciences*, *34*(1). Advance online publication. DOI: 10.1016/j.jksuci.2018.09.024

Sood, A. K. (2024). Combating cyberattacks targeting the AI ecosystem: Assessing threats, risks, and vulnerabilities. In *Combating Cyberattacks Targeting the AI Ecosystem: Assessing Threats, Risks, and Vulnerabilities*. Walter de Gruyter GmbH & Co KG. https://doi.org/DOI: 10.1515/9781501520549

Sood, K., Mahto, R., Shah, H., & Murrell, A. (2021). Power Management of Autonomous Drones using Machine Learning. *2021 IEEE Conference on Technologies for Sustainability, SusTech 2021*. https://doi.org/DOI: 10.1109/SusTech51236.2021.9467475

Sullivan, B. A. (2014). Securing the cloud: Cloud computer security techniques and tactics. *Security Journal*, *27*(3). Advance online publication. DOI: 10.1057/sj.2012.16

Sun, N., Ding, M., Jiang, J., Xu, W., Mo, X., Tai, Y., & Zhang, J. (2023). Cyber Threat Intelligence Mining for Proactive Cybersecurity Defense: A Survey and New Perspectives. *IEEE Communications Surveys and Tutorials*, *25*(3), 1748–1774. DOI: 10.1109/COMST.2023.3273282

Tambe-Jagtap, S. N. (2023). A Survey of Cryptographic Algorithms in Cybersecurity: From Classical Methods to Quantum-Resistant Solutions. *SHIFRA*, *2023*, 43–52.

Tang, X. (2021, February). Reliability-Aware Cost-Efficient Scientific Workflows Scheduling Strategy on Multi-Cloud systems. *IEEE Transactions on Cloud Computing*, *10*(4), 2909–2919. DOI: 10.1109/tcc.2021.3057422

Teja, M. V., Vyshnavi, N., & Teja, V. (2024). Phishing URL Detection Using Gradient Boosting Classifier. *Available at SSRN* 5073360.

Thabit, F., Can, O., Alhomdy, S., Al-Gaphari, G. H., & Jagtap, S. (2022). A Novel Effective Lightweight Homomorphic Cryptographic Algorithm for data security in cloud computing. *International Journal of Intelligent Networks*, *3*. Advance online publication. DOI: 10.1016/j.ijin.2022.04.001

Theory-and-Practice-in-Secure-Software-Development-Lifecycle-A-Comprehensive-Survey.pdf. (n.d.). Retrieved April 21, 2025, from https://www.researchgate.net/profile/David-Odera-2/publication/370838016_Theory_and_Practice_in_Secure_Software_Development_Lifecycle_A_Comprehensive_Survey/links/64f0780fb55e1d34158cfae2/Theory-and-Practice-in-Secure-Software-Development-Lifecycle-A-Comprehensive-Survey.pdf

Ting, L., Khan, M., Sharma, A., & Ansari, M. D. (2022). A secure framework for IoT-based smart climate agriculture system: Toward blockchain and edge computing. *Journal of Intelligent Systems*, *31*(1), 221–236.

Tiwari, H. D., & Kim, J. H. (2018). Novel Method for DNA-Based Elliptic Curve Cryptography for IoT Devices. *ETRI Journal*, *40*(3). Advance online publication. DOI: 10.4218/etrij.2017-0220

Topcuoglu, H., Hariri, S., & Wu, M.-Y. (2002). Performance-effective and low-complexity task scheduling for heterogeneous computing. *IEEE Transactions on Parallel and Distributed Systems*, *13*(3), 260–274. DOI: 10.1109/71.993206

Tornea, O. and B. M. E. (2013). Security and complexity of a DNA-based cipher. *2013 11th RoEduNet International Conference*, 1–5.

Trifunova, A., Jakimovski, B., Chorbev, I., & Lameski, P. (2024). AI in Software Testing: Revolutionizing Quality Assurance. *2024 32nd Telecommunications Forum (FOR)*, 1–4. DOI: 10.1109/ FOR63250.2024.10819179

Tushkanova, O., Levshun, D., Branitskiy, A., Fedorchenko, E., Novikova, E., & Kotenko, I. (2023). Detection of Cyberattacks and Anomalies in Cyber-Physical Systems: Approaches, Data Sources, Evaluation. *Algorithms*. Advance online publication. DOI: 10.3390/a16020085

Uğur-Tuncer, G., Davutoglu, C., & Durakbasa, N. M. (2021). Intelligent Test Automation for Improved Software Quality Assurance. In Durakbasa, N. M., & Gençyılmaz, M. G. (Eds.), *Digital Conversion on the Way to Industry 4.0* (pp. 614–624). Springer International Publishing., DOI: 10.1007/978-3-030-62784-3_53

Unogwu, O. J., Doshi, R., Hiran, K. K., & Mijwil, M. M. (2022). Introduction to quantum-resistant blockchain. In *Advancements in quantum blockchain with real-time applications* (pp. 36–55). IGI Global.

Vadde, B. C., & Munagandla, V. B. (2023). *Integrating AI-Driven Continuous Testing in DevOps for Enhanced Software Quality. 14*(01).

ValueCoders. (2024). Best low-code platforms: Which one is right for you? Retrieved from https://www.valuecoders.com/blog/technology-and-apps/low-code-platform-comparison-powerapps-mendix-outsystems-appian-pega/

Varunram, T. N., Shivaprasad, M. B., Aishwarya, K. H., Balraj, A., Savish, S. V., & Ullas, S. (2021). Analysis of Different Dimensionality Reduction Techniques and Machine Learning Algorithms for an Intrusion Detection System. *2021 IEEE 6th International Conference on Computing, Communication and Automation (ICCCA)*, 237–242. https://doi.org/DOI: 10.1109/ICCCA52192.2021.9666265

Visvizi, A., & Troisi, O. (2022). Effective Management of the Smart City: An Outline of a Conversation. In Visvizi, A., & Troisi, O. (Eds.), *Managing Smart Cities*. Springer., DOI: 10.1007/978-3-030-93585-6_1

Vivekananda, G. N., Almufti, S. M., Suresh, C., Samsudeen, S., Devarajan, M. V., Srikanth, R., & Jayashree, S. (2023). Retracing efficient IoT model for identifying skin-related tags using automatic lumen detection. *Intelligent Data Analysis*, *27*(S1), 161–180. DOI: 10.3233/IDA-237442

Wang, J., ... (2024). Netbench: A large-scale and comprehensive network traffic bench- mark dataset for foundation models. *arXiv preprint arXiv:2403.12345*.

Wang, C., Pastore, F., Goknil, A., & Briand, L. C. (2022). Automatic Generation of Acceptance Test Cases From Use Case Specifications: An NLP-Based Approach. *IEEE Transactions on Software Engineering*, *48*(2), 585–616. DOI: 10.1109/TSE.2020.2998503

Wang, M., & Bi, B. (2018). An 8 to 3 Priority Encoder Based on DNA Strand Displacement. *Communications in Computer and Information Science*, *951*. Advance online publication. DOI: 10.1007/978-981-13-2826-8_40 PMID: 37313507

Wang, P., Song, Y., Wang, X., Guo, X., & Xiang, Q. (2025). ImagTIDS: An internet of things intrusion detection framework utilizing GADF imaging encoding and improved Transformer. *Complex & Intelligent Systems*, *11*(1). Advance online publication. DOI: 10.1007/s40747-024-01712-9

Waszkowski, R. (2019). Low-code platform for automating business processes in manufacturing. *IFAC-PapersOnLine*, *52*(10), 376–381. DOI: 10.1016/j.ifacol.2019.10.060

WILLIAM, B., & IBRAHIM, A. (2024). *Fortifying E-commerce Conversational AI Systems: Comprehensive Cybersecurity Approaches for Client-Side, Communication, and Response Generation Protection*.

WILLIAM, B., OWEN, J., & OLUWASEYI, J. (2024). *Implementing Robust Encryption and Cybersecurity Measures in E-commerce Conversational AI: Safeguarding Data Across Key System Modules*.

Wu, Y., Liu, Q., Liao, X., Ji, S., Wang, P., Wang, X., Wu, C., & Li, Z. (2021). Price TAG: Towards Semi-Automatically Discovery Tactics, Techniques and Procedures OF E-Commerce Cyber Threat Intelligence. *IEEE Transactions on Dependable and Secure Computing*. Advance online publication. DOI: 10.1109/TDSC.2021.3120415

Xiong, J., Shen, L., Liu, Y., & Fang, X. (2024). Enhancing IoT security in smart grids with quantum-resistant hybrid encryption. *Scientific Reports*, *15*(1), 3. PMID: 39747539

Xue, H., Chen, D., Zhang, N., Dai, H. N., & Yu, K. (2023). Integration of blockchain and edge computing in internet of things: A survey. *Future Generation Computer Systems*, *144*, 307–326.

Xu, J., Qiang, X., Zhang, K., Zhang, C., & Yang, J. (2018). A DNA Computing Model for the Graph Vertex Coloring Problem Based on a Probe Graph. *Engineering*, *4*(1). Advance online publication. DOI: 10.1016/j.eng.2018.02.011

Yang, P., Zhao, G., & Zeng, P. (2019). Phishing website detection based on multi-dimensional features driven by deep learning. *IEEE Access: Practical Innovations, Open Solutions*, *7*, 15196–15209.

Yao, F., Pu, C., & Zhang, Z. (2021, January). Task Duplication-Based scheduling algorithm for Budget-Constrained workflows in cloud computing. *IEEE Access: Practical Innovations, Open Solutions*, *9*, 37262–37272. DOI: 10.1109/access.2021.3063456

Yarram, S., & Bittla, S. R. (2023). *Predictive Test Automation: Shaping the Future of Quality Engineering in Enterprise Platforms* (SSRN Scholarly Paper No. 5132329). Social Science Research Network. https://papers.ssrn.com/abstract=5132329

Yu, J., & Buyya, R. (2005). A taxonomy of workflow management systems for grid computing. *Journal of Grid Computing*, *3*(3–4), 171–200. DOI: 10.1007/s10723-005-9010-8

Yusuff, M. (2023). *Artificial Intelligence in Cybersecurity Strategies: Revolutionizing Tactics for Advanced Threat Protection.*

Zakaria, A. A., Azni, A. H., Ridzuan, F., Zakaria, N. H., & Daud, M. (2020). Extended rectangle algorithm using 3D bit rotation to propose a new lightweight block cipher for IoT. *IEEE Access: Practical Innovations, Open Solutions*, *8*. Advance online publication. DOI: 10.1109/ACCESS.2020.3035375

Zhang, X., Wang, P., Jia, H., Huang, Z., & Zhao, R. (2024). "AI-Powered Cybersecurity: Enhancing Threat Detection and Defense in the Digital Age," *2024 IEEE 7th International Conference on Electronic Information and Communication Technology (ICEICT)*, Xi'an, China, pp. 1026-1031, doi: DOI: 10.1109/ICEICT61637.2024.10670798

Zhang, W.. (2024). Traffic management in iot backbone networks using gnn and mab with sdn orchestration. *Applied Sciences (Basel, Switzerland)*, *14*(1), 123.

Zhang, Y., Liu, X., Ma, Y., & Cheng, L. C. (2017). An optimized DNA based encryption scheme with enforced secure key distribution. *Cluster Computing*, *20*(4). Advance online publication. DOI: 10.1007/s10586-017-1009-y

Zhao, Y., & Sakellariou, R. (2006). Scheduling multiple workflows on the grid: Towards optimization of make-span and reliability. *Proceedings of the IEEE International Symposium on Parallel and Distributed Processing*, 8 pages. https://doi .org/DOI: 10.1109/IPDPS.2006.1639448

Zhcng, Z., Xic, S., Dai, H., Chen, X., & Wang, H. (2017). An overview of blockchain technology: architecture, consensus, and future trends. In: 2017 IEEE International Congress on Big Data (BigData Congress), pp. 557–564, DOI: 10.1109/BigData-Congress.2017.85

Zhu, E., Luo, X., Liu, C., & Chen, C. (2022). An Operational DNA Strand Displacement Encryption Approach. *Nanomaterials (Basel, Switzerland)*, *12*(5). Advance online publication. DOI: 10.3390/nano12050877 PMID: 35269365

Zimmermann, K. H. (2002). Efficient DNA sticker algorithms for NP-complete graph problems. *Computer Physics Communications*, *144*(3). Advance online publication. DOI: 10.1016/S0010-4655(02)00270-9

Zissis, D., & Lekkas, D. (2012). Addressing cloud computing security issues. *Future Generation Computer Systems*, *28*(3). Advance online publication. DOI: 10.1016/j. future.2010.12.006

Zong, Y., & Huang, G. (2021). A feature dimension reduction technology for predicting DDoS intrusion behavior in multimedia internet of things. *Multimedia Tools and Applications*, *80*(15), 22671–22684. DOI: 10.1007/s11042-019-7591-7

About the Contributors

Mohd Sakib is an Assistant Professor in the School of Computer Science at UPES University, Dehradun, India. He earned his Ph.D. in Computer Science from Aligarh Muslim University, specializing in ensemble learning, deep learning, and time series analysis. Before joining UPES, he served as an Assistant Professor at Madanapalle Institute of Science & Technology (MITS), Andhra Pradesh, where he coordinated student holistic activities, NBA documentation, and national initiatives such as AICTE PARAKH. He has taught and supervised projects in areas including artificial intelligence, deep learning, and data science, at both undergraduate and postgraduate levels. His research focuses on developing intelligent AI-driven models for forecasting, anomaly detection, and smart energy systems. He has published widely in reputed Q1, SCI/SCIE and Scopus-indexed journals and presented his work at IEEE international conferences. He actively contributes as a reviewer and technical committee member for journals and conferences, and serves on the editorial board of IGI Global. He is also a Life Member of the Indian Society for Technical Education (ISTE) and regularly delivers invited talks and organizes faculty development programs.

Muneer Khan is an accomplished professional innovator in the field of Electrical Engineering, with a strong background in both academia and industry. He holds a Master of Science in Electrical Engineering from Columbia University, specializing in intelligent and connected devices, sensors, Embedded AI, semiconductor physics, and integrated photonics. Khan has extensive experience in research and applied science, having worked as a Research Assistant at Columbia University's Laboratory of Unconventional Electronics. He has completed internships in France and India. His work spans advanced technologies, including PCB design, machine learning algorithms, hardware inspection, and robotic sensors. In addition to his academic and research roles, Khan is a successful entrepreneur, having founded Cadre Technologies Services. His venture focuses on AI, machine learning, and assistive technologies. He has been recognized for his contributions to science and technology with numerous awards, including the Distinguished Young Scientist Award from the Government of India, the Engineering for Humanity Award in New York for his outstanding innovation for blind individuals, and multiple accolades from academic institutions. He won the First Position at the Wearable Innovation Forum 2025 at Cambridge University, UK, for his groundbreaking work in wearable assistive technology. Khan's work has led to several patents, publications, and major funding, including the Engineering for Humanity Award 2025 for his startup. His technical skills span programming, circuit design, and advanced testing, and he continues to lead innovative projects and product developments worldwide.

Shantanu Awasthi has an extensive academic background, holding a Ph.D. in Mathematics from North Dakota State University, an M.S. in Mathematics from Virginia State University, and a B.Tech in Electronics and Communication Engineering from Maharaja Agrasen Institute of Technology. His professional experience spans several academic and industry roles, including positions as an Assistant Professor of Data Analytics at Missouri Southern State University and Data Science roles at various institutions, such as Sense 360 and the University of North Dakota. His research interests focus on stochastic processes, machine learning, and deep learning, with publications in journals like the Journal of Safety Research and the Journal of Stochastic Analysis. In addition to his research, Shantanu has presented his work at notable conferences, including the North American Meetings of the Regional Science Association International and the SIAM Northern States Section Student Chapter Conference. His teaching experience covers data science, statistics, and mathematics courses at multiple universities. He has also earned several honors, including a Graduate Student Travel Grant and a Department Research Award. Furthermore, he holds certifications in actuarial sciences, SAS programming, and deep learning.

Mohammad Vaseem Khan (B.Tech in ECE), M.Tech (Electronics) from University of Mumbai-Maharashtra, Gate-2004,2005,2014 Qualified), is a distinguished academician and researcher with over 16 years of experience in Electronics and Communication Engineering. Currently serving as Associate Professor at Bansal Institute of Engineering and Technology, Lucknow(UP,India), he has previously held key position including Head of Department and Assistant Controller of Examination in reputed institutions and Dean Academics at Rajkiya Engineering college Kannauj(UP,India). With expertise in signal processing, basic Electronics, signal systems, Electronics devices and circuits, robotics and IoT. He has significantly contributed to the field through his research on signal processing and IoT. His work has been published in prestigious international journals like IRJET and IJRASET. Beyond academia, his leadership in organizing technical events, state level competitions. A passionate educator and lifelong learner, He continue to inspire students and professionals with his initiative teaching methods.

***

Mahmoud Mohammad Aljawarneh received the B.S., M.S. and PhD degree in Information Technology from University of Sindh, Jamshoro, Pakistan, in 2011, 2014, and 2019 respectively. From 2012 to 2014 and 2016 to 2018, he was a Research Assistant with the Institute of Information and Communication Technology, University of Sindh, Jamshoro, Pakistan. And From January 2020 to March 2022: he was an Assistant Professor, Computer Science Department, Szabist University, Hyd Campus, Pakistan. And From October 2022 to Current: he is working as an Assistant Professor, Faculty of Information Technology, Applied Sciences Private University, Amman, Jordan. His research interest includes Cybersecurity, Pervasive Computing, Context-awareness, Internet of Things (IoT), Machine Learning (ML), Cloud Computing.

Ranjith Bhat is an accomplished academic with a Master's in Technology from Nitte University, India, earned in 2011. He holds a Bachelor of Engineering from Visvesvaraya Technological University (VTU), Belagavi, India. Currently, he serves as an Assistant Professor in the Robotics and Artificial Intelligence Engineering Department at NMAM Institute of Technology, NITTE. Additionally, he is a research scholar at JAIN University, Bengaluru. His research interests span Artificial Intelligence (AI), Machine Learning (ML), Deep Learning, Network Security, and Computer Networks, and he has published multiple journal articles in these fields.

Anil Kumar D B is an academic professional specializing in Control and Instrumentation with over 14 years of teaching experience at REVA University. His research expertise includes Wireless Sensor Networks (WSN), Cloud Computing, VLSI, Control Systems and Signal Processing.

Venkataramesh Induru is currently working as Operation Lead - IT Operations Associate Manager for multiple Identity and Access Management projects. 16+ years of experience in multiple IDAM Products (i.e. ForgeRock IAM, Oracle IDAM suite, Oracle Waveset (former SUN IDM) and Tivoli IDM) with Design, Development, Operations, Environment Support and Security Operation skills

R. Karunamoothi working as an Assistant Professor in Sri Krishna College of Engineering and Technology, Coimbatore. Having 17.6 years in Teaching Experience. Got finds from DRDO to organized various Seminar and Conference.

Yashwant Kumar Kolli is an Experienced Technical Project Manager with a demonstrated history of working in the information technology and services industry. Skilled in CMS, TMS, Content Targeting using Adobe Experience Platform & performance optimization. Strong program and project management professional with a Master of Technology (M.Tech.) focused in Computer Science and Engineering from Nagarjuna University.

Karthik Kushala holds a Bachelor's degree in Computer Science and Engineering from Jawaharlal Nehru Technological University, Hyderabad. He has been working as a Senior Software Developer at Celer Systems Inc. since April 2017, specializing as a Full Stack .NET Developer. His expertise includes working with programming languages and frameworks such as C#, Angular, React, and Azure Cloud Services.

M. Malini received the Ph.D. degree in Computer Science from Bharathidasan University in 2024. Since then, he has been an Assistant Professor in the Department of Computer Science at Periyar Maniammai Institute of Science and Technology, Vallam, Tamilnadu, where her research interest include Wireless Sensor Network, Machine Learning. She has more than 5 years of research and teaching experience. She guided more than 5 projects for UG and PG. She has published 5 papers in Design Engineering, Webology G-II Scopus, International Journal . she received University Rank in BCA from Bharathidasan University .

Parvathi M is currently working as an Assistant Professor in the Department of Artificial Intelligence and Data Science (AI&DS) at Nandha Engineering College. She has 20 years of academic experience, during which she has been actively involved in teaching, mentoring, and curriculum development in the field of computer science and emerging technologies. At present, she is pursuing my Ph.D. under Anna University, focusing on research in the area of Artificial Intelligence and Data Science. Her interests include machine learning, deep learning, and data analytics.

Venkata Sivakumar Musam graduated in Information Technology from JNTU in the year 2006. He started his career as a QA analyst in 2008 from nisum technologies and learned the QA concepts and applied those in the work. He has learned more about web applications and their functionality and architecture to perform the QA role. He has gained knowledge on functional testing, cross browser testing and database testing and applied them in daily work to gain better and assured product to the client.

Nagendra Kumar Musham has Bachelor's Degree in Electrical and Electronic Engineer from Acharya Nagarjuna University (2005). Currently working as Senior Software Developer at Celer Systems Inc.

Raghu N has Ten years of experience in Academic and Research. He received the Ph.D. (2020) in Electronics Engineering from Jain University, and B.E. in Electronics and Telecommunications Engineering from VTU University, Karnataka. His research interests were in RF Communication and Image Processing. He has published his research findings in various Scopus indexed Journals and International conferences. He is a member of various professional bodies.

Keerthana N V is an Assistant Professor with 8 Years of experience in teaching and 1-year experience in research (IUCAA LIGO Data Centre, Pune). Her area of interest is Network Security, Blockchain Security, and Machine Learning Algorithms. She is pursuing PhD at Anna University in Security in Blockchain. She has a working experience in High-Performance Computing (HTCondor) in LIGO INDIA Project. She has written many research articles in Network Security and assisted Scientists in analyzing Datasets in HTCondor.

Rajashree Nambiar holds a Master of Technology degree from Nitte University, India, completed in 2014. She also received her Bachelor of Engineering from Visvesvaraya Technological University, Belagavi, India. Currently, she serves as an Assistant Professor in the Robotics and Artificial Engineering Department at NMAMIT, Nitte, India, and is a research scholar at NITTE (Deemed to be University), Nitte. Her research focuses on artificial intelligence, machine learning, deep learning, image, and signal processing.

Maheshwari R is an academic and IT professional with over 12 years of experience in engineering education, government digital initiatives, and technical coordination. She served as Assistant Professor at Velalar College of Engineering and Technology, where she contributed to curriculum design, academic coordination, and student research. Her research interests include Artificial Intelligence, mobile application development and digital public services. She also reviewed academic publications, including textbooks aligned with Anna University syllabi. As part of the Tamil Nadu e-Governance Agency, she contributed to key projects like the TN e-Pass System during the COVID-19 pandemic. She was also involved in the development of the blockchain-based e-Pettagam mobile application and several departmental technology initiatives. Her role included supporting technology projects for various state departments and preparing data-driven reports. Her technical expertise spans Java, Python, Android development, and public-sector IT applications.

Ganesh Srinivas Shetty has received his Bachelor of Engineering from Malnad College Of Engineering, Hassan and completed his M.Tech degree from Sri Jayachamarajendra College Of Engineering Mysore. He is a part time research scholar at JAIN (Deemed to be University) in Bengaluru, India. Currently, he is working as Senior Assistant Professor in Shri Madhwa Vadiraja Institute of Technology and Management (SMVITM) Vishwothama Nagar, Bantakal-5764115, Udupi, Kanataka, India. His interests lie in the areas of Cryptograhy and Artificial Intelligence and Machine Learning. He has authored 5+ research articles/conference.

Mahendrakumar Subramaniam received the Bachelors degree in Electronics andCommunication Engineering in 2006, the Masters degree in Communication Systemsin 2009 and received Ph.D - Information and Communication Engineering in 2019from Anna University, Chennai, India. He is currently working as Professor inthe department of Electronics and Communication Engineering, Velalar College ofEngineering and Technology since 2009. He is an Anna University recognized Ph.Dsupervisor and eight scholars are pursuing Ph.D under his supervision. Hisresearch interests include Antenna, Microwave, Wireless Network, MAC andNetwork Protocols. He has published 32 papers in international journals. He isa life member of ISTE and IEICE.

T. Nithya presently serves as an Assistant Professor in the Department of Information Technology at Velalar College of Engineering and Technology in Erode, Tamil Nadu. She earned his B.Tech. in II, followed by an M.E. in Computer Science and Engineering from Anna University, Chennai. With an extensive 18 years of experience in academia, Administration, Teaching, and Research, she is a highly accomplished professional in the field of Information Technology, specializing in Data Analysis and Data Mining. She has published more than 20 research papers in National and International journals and presented more than 50 papers in National and International conferences across India. She published 2 Indian Patents. She actively supervises students undertaking their final year projects at Anna University Chennai. Additionally, she holds an active life membership in the Professional Society of ISTE. Her research interests encompass Data Analysis, Machine Learning and Deep Learning.

V. Gomathi, Working as assistant professor in department of Information Technology at Velalar College of Engineering and Technology.I have published 5 conference papers and indexed 3 papers in scopus.I got 4 funding proposal

Index

U

W

www.ingramcontent.com/pod-product-compliance
Lightning Source LLC
LaVergne TN
LVHW081536300926
849161LV00006B/1461